Stéphane Grappelli

A Life In Jazz

© 2003 Paul Bulmer
This edition © 2008 Bobcat Books Limited,
part of The Music Sales Group

Order No. BOB10901R
ISBN: 978-1-84772-576-9

Exclusive Distributors:
Music Sales Limited,
14 - 15 Berners Street,
London W1T 3LJ, UK.

Music Sales Corporation,
257 Park Avenue South,
New York, NY 10010, USA.

Macmillan Distribution Services,
53 Park West Drive,
Derrimut, Vic 3030,
Australia.

To the Music Trade only:
Music Sales Limited,
8/9 Frith Street,
London W1D 3JB, UK.

Every effort has been made to trace the copyright holders of the
photographs in this book but one or two were unreachable.
We would be grateful if the photographers concerned would contact us.

Printed in the EU.

A catalogue record for this book is available from the British Library.

Visit Omnibus Press on the web at www.omnibuspress.com

Stéphane Grappelli

A Life In Jazz

BOBCAT BOOKS

For

Ruth, who gave me her books

Bill, who gave me rhythm

Jon and Carrie, who taught me love

Brendan, for constant inspiration and

Judy

without whom I'd never get anything done.

Contents

Acknowledgements

My sincerest of thanks are given to the following people and organisations who have given me so much help and time in making this book possible.

Ace Records, Charles Alexander (*Jazzwise*), Elizabeth Anionwu, Archives de l'Assistance Publique et Hôpitaux de Paris, Martin Allerton (*Mole Jazz*), Peter Anick (*Fiddler* magazine), Anthony Barnett, Alan Bates, Eileen Baxter, Don and Pauline Bishop for the *Alcantara* information, Robert Bridson for his album designs, British Newspaper Library, Christine Caine for apple pie and faith, Benny Carter for being patient, Ted Cherrett for *The Genius That Was Django*, Penny Chilton, Arantes Coelho Neto, Shalom Cohen 'for valour', Eileen Cohen, Concord Records, Conservatories de la Ville de Paris, Conservatoire National Superieur, Iain Cruickshank for *Django's Gypsies* and *The A-Z Of Django*, DA Music, Irving David, Jim Davis for inspiration, Jim Di Giovanni, John Duarte for services to music and good humour, EMI Classics, Roland H Flyge II, Pete Frame, Fremeaux & Associates, Matt Glasser, Ted Gottsegen, Chris Gower (Kingsland Colour Studio), Stephen Graham (*Jazzwise*), David Grisman, Clifford Hocking, Imperial War Museum, Ivor Mairants, Christine Jacquemart for opening doors, Lisa Jenkinson (BBC *Desert Island Discs*), John Jeremy for passing the baton (I will try to run true and straight!), Pete Johnson, Lesley Kelsall, Graham Langley (British Institute of Jazz Studies), Georg Lankester (Hot Club de France), Holland Foundation for many tapes and photos, Brendan McCormack (Mind Scaffolding Inc), Andy McKenzie, Mactwo, Marc Masselin, Carl B Margereson (Senior Lecturer in Adult Nursing, Thames Valley University), *Melody Maker* (IPC Media), Musée de Montmartre, Musée de Musique, Daniel Nevers for brilliant transcriptions and detective work, Mark Blair-Flyge Ostrian, Patrice Panassié, Pat Philips, Mike Piggott, RCA Victor, Babik Reinhardt for agreeing to talk, Malcolm Rowland for services to the Home Guard and of the precious discs, Steve Royall, Alyn Shipton, Andrew Simmons (National Sound Archive), my sisters Jean and Ruth for their love and putting up with the noise, Geoffrey Smith for his excellent book on Grappelli and his personal encouragment, Félix W Sportis, Yves Sportis (*Jazz Hot*) for so much personal help and also access to all the pre-war *Jazz Hot* archive, John Steadman (JSP Records), Marcel and Jean Stellman, George Shearing for that fantastic Shearing sound, Jon-Luc Ponty, Ettore Stratta, Maurice Summerfield for his excellent version of the Delaunay book *Django Reinhardt*, Tony Swain for editing and faith, James Taylor, Time Warner Books, Alan and Beryl Williams for believing, Bee and Walter Wyeth for book research, Sarah Young. A special thank you to David Greenaway and Dyanna Swindlehurst for so much encouragement and belief.

Author's Note

In his Paris home and the infamous cabaret Le Lapin Agile, Stéphane Grappelli told me his astonishing story. I discovered that, like so many of us, he was always in search of himself. To this end, he collected scraps of evidence. Clues.

In a dresser in his music room, he kept an oil painting and a lock of a lover's hair. These were all that remained of Gwendoline Turner, the woman he tragically lost in the London Blitz of 1940. He also kept a lock of his Italian father's hair and a letter from the gypsy guitarist Django Reinhardt.

There was a cartoon of Montmartre street urchins by Poulbot. A little book on the Paris district of Rochechouart. These areas he described as 'my Quartier'.

In his cellar at home he kept a set of cardboard shoeboxes full of hundreds of photographs – snaps and publicity stills. There was a portrait of Frank Sinatra signed, 'To Stéphane Grappelli, a great artist.' There were theatre hoardings, including music-hall posters and photographic exteriors – 'Carnegie Hall Sold Out', picturing some of his friends waving to the camera. There were also many rare photographs of the musical life of the '20s and '30s.

Stéphane kept a bank account, opened to help his father, but was saddened to find, after his death, that his father had left it uncashed.

There were other clues in the Rue Dunkerque flat: the portrait of Art Tatum over his piano; the Grappelli driving licence from 1953 – the year that Django Reinhardt died and when Grappelly again became Grappelli.

From 1953, the mythology of Django haunted Stéphane and his music-making. When I first met Stéphane in 1978, like so many others I made the error of mentioning Django – his eyes instantly went up to heaven (but only metaphorically; he was too polite to be rude). Legend is a difficult cross to bear. The Django myth is self-perpetuating even for people incapable of understanding Reinhardt's enigmatic music. So Stéphane would be quizzed frequently about Django, often by people who had never heard of Duke Ellington. He sent them away, telling them to come back when they knew the questions.

Unfortunately, the Django mythology clouded many people's understanding of Grappelli's genius. Stéphane knew this but was too pragmatic a man ever to complain. If people saw him in Django's reflection…well, at least they saw him; many of his musical friends had been completely ignored. Outside the closed jazz fraternity, few bothered to understand Coleman Hawkins, Ben Webster or Art Tatum. This is Stéphane's life, with and without Django.

Stéphane was a very private man, but here I've included the impressions of others to illustrate the character of the man. John Etheridge, who toured the world with him for five years, observed, 'He never got that close to any of us.' But John is a perceptive man and a powerful musician, his own man with his own music.

Martin Taylor expresses himself best through music – he's surely one of the world's greatest jazz guitarists. When he spoke of Stéphane, he eventually gave up on words and played 'Manoir de mes Rêves' – try to hear it if you can; it's an eloquent tribute. Above all, enjoy his musicianship; he and John Etheridge carry the lion's share of the Grappelli legacy.

Edward Baxter, Stéphane's UK agent, made my interviews with Stéphane happen, despite the lack of funding. He had vision.

Joseph Oldenhove, Stéphane's companion from 1981, is one of the most genuine people I have ever met in my life. He loved Stéphane and wanted his story to be told. He showed immense trust in me by giving me access to many of Stéphane's most treasured possessions, including his violins. Through these artefacts, and Joseph's trust, I came to feel tantalisingly close to Stéphane Grappelli. But not too close – he would never allow that. Instead, we must be content with whatever his bruised soul could stand to give.

Above all, listen to some of the 300-plus hours of the recorded music Stéphane left us. It's not jazz; it's 'a record'. Jazz essentially has to be experienced live – when it's gone, it's gone – but the recordings remain as a valuable clue. And the recordings exude a kind of life, a *joie de vivre*. If nothing else, try the Alan Clare album *Stardust*, which by some strange quirk of coincidence was recorded in Denham, the same English village as my Stéphane Grappelli DVD, *A Life In The Jazz Century*. That DVD contains a wealth of archive film, including Grappelli performances from every decade, from the 1920s to the 1990s, as well as the interviews that make up this book.

The Hot Club Quintet Of France toured as a music-hall act, and when you understand that, you realise how Stéphane never compromised. *The Michael Parkinson Show*, on which he duetted with Yehudi Menuhin; the Royal Command Performance; the Hilton Hotel – these were all ideal venues for a music-hall turn, and if that's what people wanted, he would deliver. But he understood jazz more than many a cool star or post-bop poseur. Just listen. It's all there.

I'm indebted to those who gave some of their lives to remembering Stéphane Grappelli, musician and chef d'orchestre, including Ed Baxter, Janet Baxter, Roger Baxter, Sidney Baxter, Julian Bream (CBE), Gary Burton, Judy Caine, Benny Carter, Regina Carter, Charles Chilton, Beryl Davis, Mario de Crescenzo, Diz Disley, John Etheridge, Christian Garrick, Coleridge Goode, Lord Lew Grade, David Grisman, Max Harris, Laurie Holloway, Nigel Kennedy, Michel Legrand, Lord Yehudi Menuhin, Michael Parkinson (CBE), Oscar Peterson, Pamela Reid, Ian Reid, Ric Sanders, Martin Taylor (OBE) and Bert Weedon (OBE). In turning Stéphane's story into a book, I'm indebted to Iain MacGregor for his trust and Alan Heal for his skilful editing. Above all, thanks to Joseph Oldenhove and Evelyne Tanasesco-Grappelli, without whom this book would have been impossible. I owe thanks to an extraordinary cross-section of people, all of whom understand or experienced something of this extraordinary man.

Stéphane Grappelli was a man of the Victorian era living in the 20th-century world of jumbo jets, the space race and race riots. To a large degree, he withdrew into himself. He poured himself into the music, all of it a worthy testament to genius, to be treasured and enjoyed. I hope this book gives some context to that outpouring of joy.

Paul Balmer
January 2003

1 Prelude

'Music is magic. It puts us in touch with the spirits of the past and also of the future.'

– Lord Yehudi Menuhin

Stéphane Grappelli made me smile. I wasn't alone. In Paris, Bombay or Singapore, seated on the grass at a youth festival or in the plush ruby velvet of Carnegie Hall, toes tapped, heads nodded. He was a little man, slightly comic, and exuded all the innocence of his childhood hero, Charlie Chaplin's little tramp. Always this old-fashioned gentleman could reach across the footlights and engage his audience.

Stéphane's violin bow excited electrons of air. Lacking the shackles of a spoken language, his rhythmic *joie de vivre* took his varied listeners on a shared emotional journey. Stéphane had lived and his joyful spirit, battered by tragedy, poverty and loss, sang in defiance. His audience, clad in saris and tuxedos, blue jeans and Royal satin, understood. His bow could weave an old black magic.

Some knew Stéphane's incredible story. A World War I street urchin, begging in true physical hunger, he possessed a gift for music that became his lifeline. His early fame buffered the miseries of the depression of the '30s, yet it was a success that was soon shrouded by World War II. He'd survived the London Blitz but had lost his first great love. His best friend, Django Reinhardt, had died prematurely at the age of 43.

Despite everything, Stéphane picked up the pieces and reinvented himself. His music exuded a survivor's spirit, and through his violin the world related. We all felt something.

Stéphane embraced his audience. He understood bebop and 'cool' jazz, he loved Miles Davis and Dizzy Gillespie, but he could no more turn his back on his audience than speak ill of his mother. His audience were his *raison d'être*, and he entertained in a tradition that reached back to New Orleans jazz originals like Preservation Hall's Willie Humphreys,* who believed, 'The music is supposed to be happy music, so you supposed to be happy giving it

*New Orleans clarinetist born Willie Humphry in 1900, a stalwart of Preservation Hall and devoted to the traditions and roots of real jazz.

y'understand? That's my way of thinking. You feel happy and you look happy, and you try to get the spirit, whatever you're doing, try to put out there with the public... That's how this music should be.'

Sometimes Stéphane's accompaniment would be the crafted piano of Laurie Holloway, sometimes a simple guitar. Other days saw the complex weave of Oscar Peterson's counterpoint, the daring fugue of bass maestro Niels Pedersen.

Whatever the harmonic bedrock, Stéphane bristled with invention. He once told me, 'The music we play is simple. It's the way we play it, comme ça!' Wherever the concert, the melodies that Stéphane took as a frame were the pop songs and dance tunes of an extraordinary century. He knew and worked alongside the men that were the source, such as George Gershwin, Cole Porter and Duke Ellington, whose melodic kernels were the thread on which he would weave the impossible. Jim Davis, first violinist with the BBC Midland Radio Orchestra, recalled, 'I once presented Stéphane with a notated transcription of one of his solos. Not only did he not recognise it, he couldn't read it!'

'When we played together,' said Yehudi Menuhin, 'he never repeated himself. I don't think he could.' While Fairport Convention's Ric Sanders recalled, 'His improvisation transcended the possible, reached beyond technique.'

There is much science in the alchemy of music. The technology of a violin still baffles acoustic physicists – 'so much sound, so little mass'. Such is the miracle of harmonics and resonance, the alchemy of Stradivarius and Gagliano.

The construction of melody, the science of scales and arpeggios – Stéphane knew all of this, but his art was to transcend all that in the construction of spontaneous melody. Perhaps when we are unmoved by music, it is when we feel the science. The genius of Grappelli was to take us through that sound barrier and to present a sound world that takes the listener closer to magic. For all these unconscious reasons, we gathered as his audience.

Backstage, Stéphane would draw from his fiddle case 'mon arme secrète' ('my secret weapon'), a flask of Chivas Regal. One swift dram and a salute to the Queen Mum – her photo in the lid of the case – and he was ready. At his 1970s peak, with the face of a child and the spirit of a teenager, this was a man who defied chronological time. He once told me, 'Age? There is no age! ...Why should I retire? I have my music and my friends. I'm happy making music with my friends and I get paid for it!'

I'd been one of Stéphane's audiences. Sometimes I'd share his art with millions via the magic of the television studio, and sometimes I was his sole listener. Whatever the circumstances, he played with the same intensity. As I began to research his life, I was sure his was a special talent, but as I listened I increasingly realised that this was genius.

There was nothing particularly new in the idea of a jazz violin. Will Marion Cook had played with the New York Syncopated Orchestra at Buckingham Palace in 1917, and even he was a latecomer – 'jazzy' fiddles had wailed in New Orleans in the 1870s, when Cook was a child. But Stéphane gave a face to the jazz fiddle, and everybody from Duke Ellington to Miles Davis acknowledged his artistry.

As Stéphane walked onto any stage, the applause would rise to a crescendo, cheers erupting spontaneously with no need for any artificial hype or publicist's spin. Everywhere there was real affection in his audiences' faces: grandmothers and their children, teenagers and pensioners. For 77 years, in every corner of the world, Stéphane took up his fiddle and charmed his audience.

2 Born In 1908

'I'm a bit of the north and a bit of the south. My mother was French and my father Italian.'

– Stéphane Grappelli

At 7am on a winter's morning, the candles still burned in ward Chappelle 19 as the attentive nuns shared a mother's joy on the birth of Stéphano Grappelli, son to Anna Emilie Hanocque and Ernesto Grappelli. Outside the Hôpital Laribroisière, on the busy Rue Ambroise, the air was filled with the groan of the wheelwright's art on pounded earth and unyielding cobbles. The cries of street sellers were lost in the wind, accompanied by the mechanical swirl of a buskers' *organ musette*.

Stephano's father, Ernesto, born 32 years earlier on 2 March 1876, had travelled to Paris at the age of 19 to seek a new start, hoping to pursue his ambition as writer and dilettante. Such an opportunity, he felt, wouldn't arrive in his birthplace, the remote Italian town of Nettuno, near Alatri. The latter was by then an historical backwater, lost on the road between Rome and Naples. In the past, the bastion walls had sheltered Saint Benedict at the Monastery of St Sebastian. In the medieval era, popes had visited and cardinals had been born there. Slowly, over 1,000 years, Alatri became a place of reflection and study, culminating with the founding of the 'fathers of the pious' schools in 1729.

The Grappelli family were prominent Alatri citizens, and indeed several became town mayors, such as Stephano's grandfather, who for a time was mayor of Nettuno. The graveyard of the Church of San Benedetto in Frosinone contains expensive carved marble monuments to the 'famyla de Grappellis', Joseph Grappelli and Bapta Grappelli, dating back to 1638. The Grappelli tower, a square two-storey stone lookout post, fated to survive into the 21st century. Once an impressive monument, by this time it was already in decline.

In 1895, Ernesto's father, Etienne, became implicated in a scandal involving the seduction of the local abbess. The social climate of a small town, the deeply felt Catholicism of rural Italy and the embarrassment for his mother, Madeline Colozzi, gave Ernesto the impetus to pursue his fortune elsewhere.

Many of Ernesto's youthful contemporaries had looked to the American Statue of Liberty for equality and fraternity. However, Ernesto lacked the funds for an Atlantic crossing. Even the steerage holds of the ships of the White Star Line were beyond the means of an aspiring writer. No doubt he had read of Paris, current capital of the cultural universe, already preparing to host the Great 1900 Exhibition. Surely the 'City of Light' held promise? The family *could* afford the price of a European crossing, and on his arrival in the French capital he found a little work as a freelance journalist and a teacher. However, Paris was expensive – the run-down artist's garrets of Montmartre, close to the Gare du Nord, had to suffice until better prospects arose.

While in Paris, Ernesto met Stéphane's mother, Anna Emilie Hanocque (born on 22 July 1871). Anna was also seeking more than her humble beginnings – in St Omer, Normandy. Her parents, Léon Eugene Benoit Hanocque and Louise Josephine Colombe, would no doubt disapprove of this handsome immigrant, but, to Anna, her dashing ambitious Italian, four years her junior, must have seemed a catch.

The happy couple visited a local photographer. As was the custom, they presumably hired Sunday-best clothes and gilded props, all part of a package. Faintly aristocratic poses were struck at the professional photographer's direction; again, it was expected. A photograph was a rare luxury and had to exude a lavish *décor*. Whatever the grimy reality, the photographer could be relied upon to weave a lasting spell of aspiration. Revealingly, Ernesto's shoes – presumably his own – are worn and losing their soles. For that first photograph, Anna already appears pregnant.

Stéphane's birthplace, the majestic architectural sweep of the Hôpital Laribroisière, also defies its appearance. Now a successful modern hospital, it was originally built in 1854 on the site of a convent. Its name celebrates its patron, Countess Laribroisière, who left her fortune to the city of Paris in order to provide care for the sick and poor. In 1908, the hospital was better known locally as 'the Versailles of misery'; as a last resort in the frequent cholera and typhoid epidemics, the grand façade became a beacon providing a much-needed service to the merging villages of Montmartre and Clingancourt.

The interior of the building in the early 20th century would have contained much of the starched nunnery of les Dames Augustines but little of the medical science of that still-new century. Only 50 years old, the hospital was already in dire need of repair – parts of the roof had already fallen on patients, and the acid fog generated by the coal-burning steam engines of the neighbouring Gare du Nord railway station had eaten into the masonry. The floors were frequented by diseased rats. Anna and Ernesto must have hurried to leave these dangerous wards with the young Stéphano. They returned to their cheap lodgings in nearby Rue Montholon.

As the Grappellis posed for a second photograph, now with their one-year-old son, crazy young men in flying bedsteads were taking to the air and defying God's law. Louis Blériot, a brave Frenchman, epitomised the spirit of the bold new century. In 1909, he launched himself at the grey cliffs of Dover, throwing all caution to the waves. He landed alive, bruised but triumphant, at a time when the British explorer Edward Shackleton returned from the South Pole, Commander Robert Peary, the black American Mathew Hensen planted an American flag at the North Pole and the suffragette Emily Pankhurst upset the British Government enough to be jailed. Stéphane was growing in a new century quick to celebrate the bold.

On 4 August 1909, in Portsmouth, Ohio, the Smiths, a musical family, had a son whom they named Hezekiah Leroy Gordan. Much later, he would become known on 52nd Street as 'Stuff' Smith, jazz violinist.

A year later, in January 1910, in Liverchies, Belgium, a gypsy performer by the name of Negros Reinhardt cancelled her nightly dance to give birth to a son, Jean Baptiste.

In October of the same year, also in Ohio, the Tatum family had a son. They called him Arthur, although he became known as Art. He was born blind.

In Paris, a conglomerate of villages was merging, their swelling boundaries blurred by the urban growth of the Industrial Revolution. For centuries, the southern slope of Montmartre as far as Rue Saint Lazare and the northern slope as far as Rue Marcadet had been cultivated mostly as vineyards. The Rue des Rosiers was lined with wooden shacks, barns and stables. The area attracted vagabonds and outlaws escaping the new *gendarmerie* of the city centre.

The hill of Montmartre, 'la Butte', was a natural site for windmills. There were once 30 big-sailed, stone-built giants, all searching for the direction of the hill's prevailing winds. The essayist Regnard saw them as a giant wind vane 'where 30 windmills, outstretched sails, teach me each day which wind blows the clouds'. Although many fulfilled their design function, driving the stones for grinding corn and crushing grapes, many escaped dereliction via a new role: as a home to the *bals musette*, the working-class music hall. The most famous were the two that make up the Moulin Gallette, dating from 1621. These cavernous towers and their outbuildings once rang to *bourrées* played on eerie cabrette bagpipes and the droning swirl of the hurdy-gurdy *vielle* of the folk musicians of the Auvergne.

The Paris of the second half of the 19th century was attracting rural peasants with a promise of work and glamour. Indeed, there were so many Auvergnats by 1867 that they even had their own newspaper. The air in these outlaw saloons became thick with the chink of cheap glass and the revelry of escape.

The outlaws remained in 1910, but the musette players had been introduced to the Italian style accordion by Guerino, a Neapolitan gypsy. Other gypsies camped at the Gare du Nord brought guitars and gradually replaced the vielle. The musicians knew it paid to be versatile and so learned the can-can, the java and the tango. In Didier Roussin's words, 'The Java...with it's simpler steps, close body contact and sexual overtones, came to symbolise the low-life aspect of the musette.' Meanwhile, the tango became so popular that many Italians pretended to be authentic Argentineans. Louis Aragon recalled, 'Large immodest women bend in the paleness of the tango, turning in the waltz...South Americans who are the colour of cigars. A carnival of hideous people, with physical defects, tragedies of the time, surrounds the fairy beings of this modern Eldorado.'

A contemporary photograph of the Moulin Gallette shows 100 revelling couples dancing gaily beneath lavish chandeliers heavy with candles, swimming through air alive with the smell of Pernod, sweating bodies and cheap perfume. The men wear suits and bowler hats, the ladies full-length skirts and bonnets. They pirouette around a model windmill as tall as the gilded ceiling. Other groups of men huddle at card tables with glasses of beer. These were the paying customers seeking a little solace in Montmartre's wild heyday. This mad village was also the haunt of artists, themselves outsiders from the respectable 'gay Parisiens' of La Belle Époque.

Claude Renoir lived at 12 Rue Cortot and painted La Moulin de la Gallette. He also found time to persuade the local pretty girls and their mothers to pose for him, sometimes even clothed. When he moved out, his place was taken by another painter, Maurice Utrillo, while the composer Erik Satie – one of 'les Six', a group of experimental musicians of the period – lived, appropriately enough, at neighbouring number six.

Rue de l'Abreuvoir had been home to Camille Pissaro, the oldest and most passionate champion of the Impressionist movement. Thirteen Rue Ravignon, a wooden shack, was known as 'le Bateau Lavoir' and became home to revolutionary art students Pablo Picasso and Georges Braque. Earlier, Vincent Van Gogh had painted the view from 55 Rue Lepic, the apartment he tempestuously shared with his brother Theo. Émile Zola, Claude Monet, Auguste Renoir, and Arthur Sisley all drank at La Nouvelle Athenes in the Place Clichy. It appears that turn-of-the-century Montmartre served as a magnet for creators in every medium.

Many artists of the time drew on music for inspiration and solace. The most infamous 'cabaret', Le Chat Noir on the Rue Cortot, echoed to the jaunty songs of flamboyant innovator Aristide Bruant, later immortalised in a poster by Toulouse Lautrec clad in a long black cape and matching fedora hat. Recordings survive of Bruant singing Le Chat's anthem, with all the pomp and circumstance of a ribald drinking song. The walls of his Chat Noir were decorated with a huge surreal fresco by Adolphe Willette depicting near-naked pre-pubescent sirens dancing with guitar-playing harlequins while a harlot rides a black cat across smoking chimneys, and a windmill's sails serve as a musical stave for wild crotchets and quivering quavers. The piano in the corner of Le Chat Noir sometimes flowed with the sensuous harmony of Satie and Debussy, often played by the composers themselves.

The cover of the November 1908 issue of *Musica* magazine depicted Yvette Guilbert, a Montmartre regular, 'Singer of the Chanson Français Contemporarie'. Her voice, on a surviving Edison cylinder recording, has all of the coquettish charm and her lyrics the knowing innuendo you would expect from a chanson entitled 'Madame Arthur'. Stéphano had not been born into an age of innocence.

The Moulin Rouge had opened in nearby Pigalle in 1889 and had rung to the shrieks of the dancers La Goulue and Nini Patte en l'Air. Their outrageous *quadrilles eccentric*, performed without the modesty of newly invented underwear, went on to become the can-can. The *Atlantic Daily News* reported from Le Taborin, 'The most curious of these night fête spectacles is the chariot parade, where pretty girls in the most varied of costumes, covered with flowers and verdure, disappear under a rain of bouquets and coloured ribbons... The scene is fairylike, while under the rays of light the dancers whirl and the incomparable orchestra...plays the most charming pieces.'

The 'court painter' Toulouse Lautrec had depicted La Goulue on many of his revolutionary and experimental posters. The dwarfed artist had died in

1901, but his art still kicked and leapt from posters for Le Taborin and the Moulin Rouge. The 20th-century flirtation with advertising as art had begun in Montmartre.

Surrounded by all this in their tiny apartment at the Square Montholon, the young Grappelli family came to terms with cold Paris winters and the frugal meals afforded by a freelance teacher, a foreigner, last in the queue for scarce work. Ernesto clung to his dreams, which were fuelled by meetings with the wild Paris set. A freelance magazine commission to write up the exploits of the eccentric American dancer Isadora Duncan took him to the outskirts of Paris at Melun.

Already infamous throughout America and Europe for her rapturous semi-naked dance and her tabloid-inspiring behaviour, Angela Isadora Duncan had been born in San Francisco in May 1877, as she put it, 'under the star of Aphrodite, the daughter of wind and wave and the winged flight of bird and bee'. She had discovered the sensual Paris during her visit to the 1900 Exposition, but had been disappointed in the Parisiens' approach to dance: 'It was all stupid, vanity, and vexation... They do not dance for love...they do not dance for the gods.' Nevertheless, she had danced to the piano of Maurice Ravel and mingled with Debussy, Verlaine, Man Ray and Colette. In 1912 she attended the Olympian ball at Versailles, where 'guests consumed more than 800 quarts of champagne. Isadora arrived as a woodland nymph, "Drunken with wine and with the splendour of the scene." She called for music and danced "a delirious improvisation"... Certain of the guests were moved to tears at so much beauty...rumours of orgies spread quickly through Paris.'*

Isadora now set out to inspire a new generation. In a Paris mansion, the sensuous wild child had established a school of dance, and bestowed upon herself the role of emancipator of Victorian youth. Children would no longer be seen and not heard – she would set them on a path of liberated spirits and self-expression. A generous donation from the heir to the Singer sewing-machine empire meant that Isadora's family of 'nymphs and shepherds' – 'the Isadorables', who arrived at Bellevue in April 1914 – could grow and flourish, while music for the dance came from visiting virtuosi and the orchestras of Paris and Cologne. Isadora's stylised bacchanalia was designed to inspire.

In her wild, untutored way, Isadora, the art-nouveau wild child, was exploring the principles of Swiss composer Emile Jacque Dalcroze,[†] who by

---

*Text taken from Isadora Duncan by Peter Kurth.

[†] The principles of the Dalcroze method emphasise the need for young children to explore music through the physicality of the engagement of large muscle groups. Isadora would later renounce Dalcroze's 'eurythmics' as being too formal, too military. He in turn complained about her lack of technique!

1910 was devising a method for what he called 'an education through and into music'. His was a studied response, while Isadora's was perhaps more instinctive, but at heart they both cared most about getting back to the roots of musical expression. They both explored the fundamental relationships between the stimulation of music and the urge to dance.

Although Ernesto Grappelli loved music, he knew little of either Dalcroze or Terpsichore, but he was impressed by Isadora's passion. His article has not survived, but the words of Lugne-Poe have: 'She seemed not to care what impressions she made in private or even in public. She wore an air of smiling shamelessness that suited her.' Cecile Sorel, meanwhile, reports, 'Isadora broke through the crowd in pursuit of some handsome guest, knelt and handed him flowers, saying, "Tonight, you are my god. I will dance for you."' Ernesto's chance meeting would have a profound repercussion on the life of his young son Stephano.

3 Art, Tragedy And War

'There were many times when I had to fight for a crust of bread. It was abominable.'

– Stephano Grappelli

Stephano lived with his parents at the western corner of the Square Montholon, laid out in 1863 by Alphand, the Paris Director of Public Places. Montholon is one of 24 miniature parks created under the second Empire and designed to offer a green refuge in a growing city. The park is named for Nicholas Montholon (1736–89), who was a local official. Restored to its original glory in 1971, it remains a haven away from the bustle and klaxons of nearby La Fayette. Glass globes that once provided gaslight have now been converted to Edison incandescence and sit on tall spikes of iron, and there are all the usual city-park props: slatted wooden benches, flower beds, twittering sparrows. It now resembles a typical 19th-century idyll.

The Grappellis had a room at number 28, on the corner of Rue Montholon. Old and run down, but affordable, the building was eventually demolished in the 1930s although other similar 19th-century buildings remain, seven stories tall with distinctive black ironwork surrounding each balcony, functional but lending a distinct Parisian character. The roofs are steep inclines dotted with artists' windows in attic garrets. Now many of the balconies are enhanced with red cascades of geraniums.

When I visited the park at the beginning of the 21st century, it was easy to imagine Stephano enjoying the play area with his mother almost a century earlier. A small boy fed the pigeons nervously, while another chased them – brave as a comic book cowboy. A shopping-laden mother watched her son in a giggle-filled game of hide and seek, all heads behind trees and tumbles on damp grass.

In 1911, the present traffic drone would have been a clatter of horseshoes and hard iron on cobbles. The perambulating lovers would have had parasols and crinolines, not Levis and leather. Perhaps the now-tall trees were not so shady, but pigeons' wings would still have flapped with the sound of dry paper, and there would have been the timeless shrieks of happy children.

I imagine that Anna Hanocque sat here in reflection in 1911, taking joy in her growing son like any mother. Stephano had been a late blessing – her first child, at the age of 37 – but she faced a terrible dilemma: she was fatally ill. Anna would soon have to surrender her brief happiness to the tumour already spreading in her womb. She must have agonised over Stephano's fate – Ernesto was a good father but not at all practical.

Every mother feels that her child will enrich the world – it's part of the maternal instinct, the same force that enables any mother to fight like a lioness to protect her young. I cannot but wonder if Anna had any suspicions of Stéphane's latent genius. The boy was precocious; with Ernesto's encouragement, already reading before he was four. Anna must have observed her son's curiosity, always full of questions, a child already saying 'Why not?' in a world intolerant of childish will. Did Stephano respond to sounds? Was his attention notably caught by a motor klaxon, his eyes studying the invisible, locked in a childish gaze? The huge low C of Sacre Coeur's new bell meant little to Anna – she knew Savoyarde, 'the biggest bell in the world', which had caused a stir as 28 horses and a hundred men dragged it to the summit of the Butte – but when the great bell rang, toning the vibrations of 19 tons of quivering bronze, did Stéphane perhaps pause in his play, locked by the rumble and waver, his eyes distant with a trance-like focus? When did those ears first learn to listen?

Anna must have been reluctant to return to the Hôpital Laribroisière. Its reputation was one of being 'a hospital for the poor', as only the poor would risk its shelter, while the doctors had a reputation for using their impoverished patients for scientific experimentation and performing unproven techniques. With little knowledge of contagion, many of its patients caught disease within the sheltering walls. The nuns, however, must have seemed sympathetic to Anna's plight when, on 9 November 1911, she admitted herself to their tender care.

Anna would never see Stephano again. On 6 December 1911, still in hospital, she married Ernesto. On 2 February the following year, in the pre-dawn darkness of 5:35am, she surrendered herself to her god.

Young death was common in the early 20th century, but tragedy was never more acute than the death from cancer of a new mother. On the cold steps of the Hôpital Laribroisière, Anna's demise left an inquisitive toddler of four and a father lost in grief. Ernesto had no supportive family in Paris and there was no going back to Nettuno.

Meanwhile, the Kaiser and generals of the newly united Germany were rattling sabres. Rumours of war and conquest filled the pages of *Le Figaro* and *Le Monde*. In 1911, Admiral Tirpitz added another 13 of the giant dreadnought battleships to an already swollen fleet. In the British Parliament, a debate raged: should the British feel threatened by the King's own nephew?

In Russia, Rasputin was casting a deadly spell over the despotic Czarina, a spell that would contribute to the downfall of a dynasty. In the village of Tomak, near Odessa, Isaac and Golda Winogradsky, like many middle-class Jewish parents, decided that a better future lay beyond the English channel. They took their sons, Louis and Boris, to start a new life in London's Brick Lane, in the East End. The young Louis Winogradsky became the anglicised Lew Grade.

Meanwhile, the French again saw their soil as Europe's battleground, and for all the protestations of the Republican Assembly, military strategists knew that their borders were indefensible; military tanks seen in experimental manoeuvres were not likely to be troubled by vineyard hedges.

In Paris towering from the peak of Montmartre, the Basilica of Sacre Coeur was at last complete, but in 1912 it remained unconsecrated. With newly cut marble glistening in the morning light, critics said that it resembled a wedding cake, but to the recently widowed Ernesto Grappelli, its sombre candlelit interior offered some solace and the opportunity to reflect.

'The Sacre' is Paris's most potent beacon. Eiffel's tower always disappoints – too slender, too blatantly phallic – while the Sacre has a quiet dignity, never diminished by its visiting throngs. Glimpsed through the narrow slots accorded by Montmartre's maze of *escaliers*, the daunting staircases lead you closer to the sacred heart. It is slightly unreal, a white wraith occasionally sugar-coated by sun on wet marble. Then, on rounding the corner into Rue du Cardinal Dubois, the lights come on. With a constantly shifting background of René Magritte's clouds on perfect blue, the three enormous domes loom with breathtaking grandeur. The Butte is already 100 metres above the level of the Seine, and the central bell tower ascends another 88. On ascending the emperor-sized staircase to the basilica's entrance, a panorama of all Paris lies below.

The vast interior is always cast in a reverential twilight. A thousand tiny candles focus flickering shadows on veiled heads. From the looming dome 55 metres above, shafts of sunlight backlight the airborne dust drifting in angel-thronged galleries. Above the altar, Christ, a giant clad in Romanesque white and gold, outstretches his arms in a global welcome. When his grieving father was drawn here in 1912, it must have all seemed a little daunting to the four-year-old Stephano, but the adult Stéphane would live most of his life in the benevolent shadow of Le Sacre.

The last 18 months could only have been a nightmare for Ernesto. Anna must have been everything to someone so isolated. He was essentially cut off from his family and now robbed of his lover, his young bride buried in her wedding dress, her only good gown, the expense of the funeral borrowed and promised against future fortune. The child was yet beyond understanding – what could a father say to a sad four year old? That his mother had 'gone with the angels', never to tell stories or dance again? It must have seemed impossible for Ernesto to return to his family, certainly not bearing a motherless child, which could have been interpreted by small-town gossips as a further scandal.

For nearly two years Ernesto and Stephano stayed at the Rue Montholon. Somehow the father combined the role of single parent with earning a precarious freelance living in an age before social welfare. There must have been many cold and hungry nights in that condemned, candlelit garret. Stephano did spend some time at well-meaning orphan houses, but he always ran away. If his father was travelling on assignment, he would rather make his own way.

Despite his artistic sensitivity, and at the age of 38 too old for active service, Ernesto eventually turned, as isolated men often do, to the army. This route must have seemed natural – to be an able-bodied man in France meant to join the national struggle. Ernesto was also an educated man – he had taught philosophy and Italian; he could translate Latin and Greek; his copperplate handwriting, on letters to Stephano, reveals a man of meticulous taste and fastidious detail. To such a man, informed by his journalistic contacts, war must have seemed inevitable, awaiting only the spark in the Balkans tinderbox that was the assassination of Archduke Ferdinand of Austria.

With the growing threat, a willing conscript could surely earn a better living in the military. Ernesto may also have felt that he had failed Anna as an artist. Was there perhaps a whiff of fatalism in this bereaved man, the same romantic notions that drove some of the trench-bound poets, perhaps finding a place with a vulnerable writer? Whatever the circumstances, the army would naturally have no provision for taking care of a four-year-old son.

In his desperation over Stephano, Ernesto made an inspired decision. He obviously remembered the visit to Melun and the article he'd written on Isadora Duncan's school for promising artistic children. Ernesto was a creative and impulsive man. He may have hoped that Isadora would recognise his plight, and perhaps had even thought of Isadora's school as an ideal place for Stephano on his previous visit.

The decision made, he still had to find the train fare to Melun, this time without a journalist's expense account. We can only imagine Ernesto walking, carrying and half dragging the young Stephano through streets festooned with newspaper placards warning of war. Would Isadora be open to such an impulsive and desperate man?

Miraculously, the dancer agreed to receive the distraught father. She understood personal loss, and indeed was still in mourning herself after her two young children, Dierdre and Patrick, had drowned in a macabre accident in April 1913. While in the care of their nanny, the children were being driven home when the car stalled at the riverbank. When the chauffeur hand-cranked the engine, the car careered into the cold waters of the Seine, killing all three. The tragedy had become a very public event with an elaborate funeral, the tiny coffins taken in procession across Paris to the cemetery of Père Lachaise.

Isadora, already seeking solace in a new pregnancy, was sympathetic to Ernesto, and perhaps Stephano showed some sensitivity and aptitude. This was to be Grappelli's first audition. 'I was accepted, to learn to dance!' he recalled.

Whatever the discourse, the young Stephano Grappelli had his first luck, apprenticed to an art-nouveau icon, apparently rich, certainly eccentric, and perhaps even a mother figure.

Initially, the sensitive Stephano was probably traumatised. To a child, Ernesto's action might have appeared to be the final desertion. He had lost his mother and now his father had apparently abandoned him to these strange, foreign-speaking adults. No doubt he soon had to come to terms with a group of similarly and probably equally strong willed contemporaries. Every child faces these dilemmas on a first day at school, but for most the parents return at tea time. Those first days and weeks would have marked the boy forever.

As an adult Stéphane particularly remembered disliking Isadora's taste in costume: 'We were asked to personify angels, which I was not. She dressed us in Greek costumes, with a wreath of flowers on our heads and a white peplum.' The scene is perfectly captured in the English director Ken Russell's 1966 documentary *The Biggest Dancer In The World*,* which brilliantly tells her tragic story. In one particular sequence, the school's young pupils circle the

* See the DVD *Stéphane Grappelli: A Life In The Jazz Century*.

great hall, all flowing lace and grandiloquent gestures. It's all art deco and romance but driven by a genuine passion.

Despite his reservations, the young Stephano had for the first of many times arrived at the perfect place at the perfect moment. This was an idyllic beginning for a child blessed with natural rhythm and perfect pitch. Mornings were spent in sunlit gardens with sylph-like children, mythic statuary and dew-decked flowers. The magic of a piano played by a visiting Russian genius. And maybe Isadora herself danced, resplendent in gossamer lace, hair flowing like mad reeds in a sky of painless blue. 'A dancer could hardly be more free from the grosser bonds of flesh and muscles and nerves, from all physical and material conditions that would bind her to the Earth,' wrote Henry Taylor Parker in the *Boston Evening Transcript*. 'Miss Duncan treads...as though it were the air; she moves through the air as though it were the finer ether; the impression, though the eyes do see, is that she is as incorporeal as the sylphs, as fairy-footed as the elves. Her dancing is as intangible, even as un-material, as fluid as are sound and light.'

Although no natural dancer, Stephano soon adapted and was rewarded with a key formative experience: 'Whilst I was there, Isadora booked an orchestra. It was the Orchestra Cologne, one of the greatest orchestras in the world. It was for an anniversary, in the park, and they were playing Debussy's *L'Après-Midi d'un Faune*. And despite I was only six, I can't describe the effect that had on me. Also in the park was some sculpture, a faun... I was dazzled. It was all there, the music, the setting, the beautiful blue sky. The music made me feel the faun. It was marvellous.' For the young Stephano the park's statue of a mythical faun, half man and half deer, became forever linked with that first musical memory.

Curiously, the grounds of Bellevue are a short walk from the Melun estate of the great sculptor August Rodin, a frequent visitor. On Saturdays, the children acted as models for him. In his 2001 book *Isadora Duncan*, Peter Kurth describes them 'running and dancing on the lawns and through the trees to such effect that Rodin was heard to say, "If only I had such models when I was young!"' Stéphane kept a picture of Isadora in his shoebox. In this portrait, Isadora was depicted as an art-nouveau goddess, barefoot in sackcloth, hands outstretched in supplication to the heavens.

In his late years, during private moments at his last home in the Rue Dunkerque, Stéphane would improvise at his piano, often in an Impressionist style that somehow combined Debussy's second book of *Préludes* with the syncopation of Art Tatum. In 1914, the former's *L'Après-Midi d'un Faun* was daring modern music, the harmonies built on modal strands by a composer proud to call himself 'le musicien Français'. His transparent structures and undulating rhythms were the complete antithesis of the solid tonal harmonies of the Classical first Viennese school of Mozart and Beethoven. Debussy's shimmering textures heralded a century lit by the electricity he'd witnessed at the Great Paris Exhibition of 1900. In his books of *Préludes* for piano, Debussy dreamt of the Exhibition's distant pagodas and reverberating Balinese gamelan.

In the year of Stéphane's birth, this futuristic composer had worked on the *Préludes*, a dazzling string quartet and a child's piano piece based on ragtime minstrelry. With this his *Golliwog's Cakewalk* of 1908, composed for his own young daughter, Debussy unknowingly created nursery 'jazz' for a future *musicien Français.*

As a journalist, Ernesto Grappelli was undoubtedly acutely aware of the artistic maelstrom into which he had come. He must have read of the artistic fireworks, driven to erotic fever pitch by Nijinsky's 'bestial' choreography for the first Paris performance of Debussy's *L'Après-Midi...* in 1912. This performance was staged by Diaghilev's *Ballets Russes*, the most inspired and revolutionary company in the history of Western ballet, and caused a Franco-Russian 'diplomatic incident'.

At this time, away from the spotlight in the quiet back alleys of Montmartre, Pablo Picasso had taken up Cézanne's challenge to the concepts of artistic perspective. In his wooden slum studio, the Bateau Lavoir, which he shared with Georges Braque, Picasso and Cézanne began together a new chapter in the history of Western art. The former's shocking masterpiece *Les Desmoiselles d'Avignon* of 1907 had drawn on Catalan sculpture, the African sculpture exhibited at the Trocadero Palace and the overt sexuality of his prostitute models.

Meanwhile, in the musical world, at the Théâtre des Champs-Elysées, against a backdrop by Nicholas Roerich, a riot broke out at the first performance of Stravinsky's *Le Sacre du Printemps*. The émigré Russian's music challenged every accepted rule of harmony and rhythm. In the same staging, Nijinsky challenged every rule of choreography.

Although Stephano was at this time an innocent child, his father's instinct about Paris had placed his son at the heart of a potent crucible. Isadora Duncan thrived on this artistic cauldron. She came to a Paris that was truly 'the current centre of the thinking universe'. Through her, Stephano had his first powerful engagement with the emotional potential of music.

World War I escalated. The conflict that many had predicted would be over by Christmas, turned into an unimaginable bloodbath. On the Western Front, 1,000 French soldiers died each day. Horse-mounted cavalry came to grim terms with a war fought with tanks and poison gas.

As Debussy died in despair to the sound of artillery booming across Paris, Isadora prepared for departure. The school was under political pressure because of its many German pupils and teachers. Bellevue had become a nightmare. Traumatised and weak after the death of her third baby at birth, she had little choice. In her words, she 'heard hammer taps closing the little box that was poor baby's only cradle. As I lay there, torn and helpless, a triple fountain of tears, milk and blood flowed from me, for in that death, it was as if the others had died again.' She handed over her dream location to les Dames de France for use as a military hospital: 'My temple of art was turned into a Calvary of martyrdom and, in the end, to a charnel house of bloody wounds and death.' Sending most of her pupils to England, she departed for Deauville, where the grand casino was also awash with the wounded. Then, in November, she departed for New York, her hair having turned white with shock.

With Isadora's leaving, Stephano's short idyll ended and, with his father engaged in the war, he became a helpless pawn. He was thrust into a Dickensian orphanage: 'Here my misery started. It was practically a jail.' Despite a supposed governmental responsibility for standards, Stephano slept on the floor, often going without food. 'There were many times when I had to fight for a crust of bread,' he recalled. 'It was abominable.'

The warders of the orphanage were disciplinarian bullies. Stephano, a sensitive child not yet aged seven, was traumatised and lonely. He wet his bed. The custodians paraded him and the soiled mattress before morning assembly. Demonstrating admirable resourcefulness Stephano again ran away, preferring a life on the streets, begging and foraging for scraps.

When I gently quizzed 87-year-old Stéphane on these war years, he dismissed the pain. If analysed by a modern psychiatrist, his stance on these years would be called denial. For Stéphane, I think it was more about dignity, survival and moving on. He had happier stories to tell. He was a motherless child in fear of losing his precious father to an imagined death amongst the distant thunder of battle. Around him the sorry, ragged flotsam of war drifted – mothers and children without hope, the enemy approaching the Gare du Nord. Somehow Stephano survived.

At this time, somewhere in the streets and courts of Montmartre, the child heard a busking violinist and stood there, watching his deft fingers caress a melody, punctuated by the muffled percussion of a few coins wrapped in newspaper, sailing down from a still-innocent sky.

The terrible war of 1914–18 cost the lives of over ten million young men. Of the eight million men that France had mobilised, there were six million casualties.

Meanwhile, a world away, in New York, Isadora Duncan took a studio at 311 Fourth Avenue, and at the nearby Bronx hospital of Mount Lebanon, on 22 April 1916, the Russo-Palestinian immigrants Moyshe and Marutha Menuhin had a son. They named him Yehudi.

4 A Way Forward

'Every place around here had a piano. Never in tune, mind you, but no matter; I could find the melody.'

– Stéphane Grappelli

Stéphane was a man of few words, choosing to speak through his music. If you insisted on words, he would consider your question and then deliver a short and often very succinct reply. In 1996, relaxed and sitting in his favourite Montmartre cabaret, Le Lapin Agile, he offered his reminiscences of pre-'20s Paris. He told me how, in his street days during the Great War, he had realised that a musician could always earn a few coins for bread: 'That was the best time for the musician, you know – no radio, no gramophone. If you want music, you must go to the musician! …When I saw a pianist constantly solicited for his services, I made up my mind: "I must learn that!"'

Before he possessed an instrument, Stéphane cheekily put upon the café and cabaret owners of Montmartre to practise on their pianos: 'Every place around here had a piano. Never in tune, mind you, but no matter; I could find the melody… As a matter of fact, it's around here that I heard my first live jazz in the last year of the war, "Hot Lips" played on a piano and saxophone.'

Le Lapin Agile is famous for being the haunt of writer Guillaume Apollinaire and can-can dancer Adele Decerf, the latter of whom was universally admired for her opulence and immortalised in verse:

> Adele!
> You're a beauty.
> I adore your big tits,
> Your roundness,
> Your blondness,
> And your titillating airs.

Appropriately for this ribald area, the first tune that Stephano mastered was

'The Can-Can' or, as Stéphane described it, 'the java of Mistinguett', naming it after one of the new dances emerging from this Parisian melting pot. Mistinguett,* a siren, starred as a singer at 'the Casino de Paris', her risqué art-nouveau posters by 'ZIG' rivalling those of the earlier Jane Avril. Whatever the source of Stephano's inspiration, the café proprietors of the city were happy with a child whose tiny stomach needed few francs to fill.

Stephano wasn't alone – the war had left many Parisian children to their own devices. The street urchins of Montmartre and its environs are well documented by the cartoonist Francisque Poulbot. Born in 1879, Poulbot spent his life documenting Montmartre and its people. His wit and satire were often used to defend Montmartre against the varied merits of unconsidered 'progress'. His urchin sketches show cheeky, resourceful boys arguing the street merits of Square Montholon, Stephano's old home, against those of Square St Pierre and playing soldiers with home-made wooden swords. In an early dose of hygiene propaganda, the boys can also be seen debating the virtues of lithium salts and other anti-nit products. Poulbot's cartoons were extensively published at the time in the magazines *Pele Mele* and *Le Petit Bleu*.

Whatever the hardship he found on the street, Stephano preferred that to the psychological torture of the orphanage. He was a free spirit, already imbued with the flame kindled by Isadora and her improvisations.

As 'the war to end wars' was finally concluded, the precise circumstances of Stephano's reunion with his father are unknown.[†] Ernesto may well have been proud of his son's resourcefulness, if shocked at his appearance. (He described himself as 'a malnourished waif, dressed in rags'.) The spirit of the occasion was no doubt triumphant and certainly ripe with gesture. A father who fought for France renamed his French-born son. The young Stephano was to be officially registered as Stéphane. On 28 July 1919, Stephano Grappelli became the Frenchman Stéphane Grappelli.

Stéphane showed initiative and musical talent and Ernesto determined he would be encouraged. Together, the two climbed to 'the gods' – the cheap seats – at Sunday concerts at Colonne, and together they enjoyed the music of Debussy and Ravel. Without his French mother Stéphane increasingly fell under the spell of Ernesto and his artistic dilettante ambition.

*Born in Enghien, France, on April 5, 1875, Jeanne Bourgeois aspired at an early age to be an entertainer. She assumed the stage name 'Mistinguett' and went on to become the toast of Paris, the most popular French entertainer of her time. Indeed, she was once the highest-paid female entertainer in the world. Stéphane referred to her as 'the queen of the night', while in Maurice Chevalier's words, 'She had a way of moving which was the pinnacle of grace, but she was more than loveliness alone; she *was* Paris, the symbol of gaiety and good humour and courage and heart.'

[†] In 1916, Ernesto remarried and considered moving to Strasbourg. Stephano disliked his stepmother.

With no training in music but with common-sense guile, Ernesto sought an instrument for Stéphane and a book of instruction. A fellow Italian who ran a shoemakers' shop in Montmartre was also a guitarist who busked in the flea markets at weekends and, prompted by Ernesto, he procured a discarded three-quarter-size violin that could be had for the pawn of an old suit.

Presented with the intriguing instrument Stéphane fumbled for a few days with its mysteries and then made a resourceful move: 'There were many musicians then in cafés, and I asked one to help me with tuning the violin, I think he was intrigued by this precocious child and he tuned it for me. Later my father gave me a tuning fork... [He] said, "If you want to make your way with music, you should read it," and he gave me a little book of *solfege*.'* Ernesto once more made the right decision in grounding Stéphane's musical future. Primed by Isadora's 'music and movement' and encouraged by his own fumbling at the keyboard, he acquired the perfect key to a musical improviser's future.

Stéphane described his first violin 'lessons': 'I go to the street and I watched the buskers. I watched where he put his hands. That was my first teacher.'

When Stéphane first put this concept to me, I took it with a pinch of salt – it seemed an unlikely way of acquiring a sound technique. However, the more I thought about it, the more the concept made sense. All music teachers demonstrate at the instrument, and all pupils follow. This is part of the most 'classical' of musical apprenticeships. In Europe, however, this experience is placed amongst the wider notions of reading music and practising scales and exercises. It's easy to forget that this isn't the norm for most of the world's musicians. On a global scale, most music is not written down, and musicians in most countries learn by apprenticeship. This is as true in the classical traditions of India and Japan as it is in the folk music of America and Europe. In this area, Stéphane and his later partner Django Reinhardt had remarkably similar early musical experiences.

My original scepticism at Stéphane's assertion was further confounded one recent spring day in Paris. Travelling by metro train on my way to visit a jazz club near Belleville, a group of buskers scrambled aboard my carriage. The accordionist and violinist played a musette waltz. In the rush-hour crush, I couldn't actually see the musicians, just a bow occasionally soaring between the heads of some anxious commuters. After a few moments, I realised there were in fact two violins being played in unison, one quieter and not so in tune.

*Solfeggio is used in French as a generic term for musical theory. However, more specifically, solfege is a tranposable system of musical scales. Today its value in music teaching is widely recognised, particularly in France. The sung 'sol-fa' scales move easily from key to key, as the ear is trained to recognise the musical intervals common to all.

As some passengers disembarked, I smiled as I realised that Stéphane's teaching tradition was alive and well – a small boy of about ten years of age gazed with rapt attention at his master's fingers, his bow mimicking the elder's every move.

Stéphane asserted his *auto-didacte* status right up to our final conversations in 1997. This concept, the pride of the self-taught, has a strong following in the early 20th-century European working class. The contemporary Spanish classical guitarist Andre Segovia also proudly declared himself *auto-didacte*.

This pride is particularly prevalent amongst migrants and their families. In fact, self-taught second languages and literatures are often absorbed more passionately by the committed immigrant than by the more blasé native. In Stéphane's case, this hard-won language was to be music.

Without doubt most of what is now perceived as 'the Grappelli sound' is unique and couldn't be taught because it simply didn't exist, certainly not within the hallowed walls of a musical conservatoire. However, in Stéphane's case, there is slightly more to the *auto-didacte* legend.

The records of the Paris Conservatoire National Superieur de Musique et Danse show a Stéphane Grappelli receiving a second *medaille de solfege* in 1923. In fact, the ever-resourceful Ernesto had arranged for Stéphane to sit in on some classes at the conservatoire with a neighbour, then 82-year-old Professor Paul Rougnon. Obviously impressed with the gifted child, the maestro offered Stéphane snippets of wisdom as they took the half-hour walk to his home in the Rue Martyrs each evening.

Throughout this period, Stéphane supported himself by busking: 'One day I was getting out of courtyard in the district and a man was waiting for me outside. He was an Italian playing guitar and singing. He used to sing Neapolitan songs in the courtyard and he said to me, "You know, you don't play too bad. Would you like to come in with me? I know some places in the evening, restaurants where we can make a little money, and if the weather is good we can play in the courtyard." I say yes and I go with him, and he knew a lot of good courtyards. He gave some tips to the concierge…and we make quite a good money, better than a professional playing in a restaurant. And during the time he was collecting the money, I was playing the Meditation of *Thaïs* by Massenet, and it was not very good but it was in tune and I knew that.'

This is a young Grappelli 'playing the popular classics by ear'. The Meditation from *Thaïs* remains a romantic favourite, one of those wonderful tunes everybody vaguely knows, even if the title eludes. Learning such tunes wasn't just good for business; the lyricism of the pieces would become the core of his ballad style.

The *solfege* technique helped the young Stéphane to recognise the intervals that make up these broad melodies. It's a system based primarily on ear training, without recourse to musical notation. Stéphane was acquiring the skills that would propel him on a particular course...

Another source of musical encouragement was the Montmartre-based Charpentier family. Gustave Charpentier, born in Dieuze in 1860, had been a pupil of Massenet and had achieved some success with his 1900 opera *Louise*. In 1902, Gustave founded his own Conservatoire Populaire, where working-class children could learn a little music and dance. Ernesto knew the family who lived around the corner, at 66 Boulevard de Rochechouart, and they gave Stéphane some encouragement and help. In fact, Stéphane remained in touch with the family into adulthood, particularly with the daughter, Louise Charpentier, who later became a distinguished harpist.

It's hard to imagine a world in the 1920s where musical concerts – rare enough in themselves – were also beyond the reach of most pockets. For an audience starved of music, with the many sources of music we now take for granted not yet available, the young Grappelli must have been a treat. Radio was still experimental and thought of principally as a maritime signalling device, while gramophones and wax cylinders were expensive high technology. Silent film or *cinématographe* was still a rare novelty requiring live musicians, and 'telephonic vision' seen in silent movies was a science-fiction fantasy. For most of the world, music appeared only for the price of a musician.

During this period, Stéphane skipped formal schooling and attended intermittently several Montmartre church schools, including one on Rue Milton. But with no mother most of his basic skills seem to have come from Ernesto, even though the latter was somewhat preoccupied in finding increasingly scarce employment.

Stéphane became streetwise from an early age. He called Le Lapin Agile cabaret in Rue des Salles 'the frisky bunny', no doubt after its famous symbol, a hand-painted poster of a leaping hare depicted escaping a boiling pan with a bottle of wine balanced precariously on his arm. He wears a red cummerbund and bowtie and leaps against a background of another of Montmartre's windmills.

Today, the cabaret remains active a picturesque cottage perched on the slopes of the Butte. During our visits there, the owner served Stéphane a traditional cherry brandy in a precious antique ceramic wine jug also modelled on the bunny. The interior has changed very little from Picasso's depiction, *Une Soirée Au Cabaret*. The tiny space resembles a front room, an original public house, with benches still lining the walls along with crude transom tables and scattered kitchen chairs. By night, an impassioned tenor might lead the gathered revellers in a familiar singsong, a 'chanson Française'. A coquettish girl might dance 'La Vie En Rose' to the accompaniment of her own musette accordion, or a guitarist might strum a racy ballad in the three-to-the-bar lilt of the java. A pianist might bash out a tango. Out of the gloom, a surreal wooden sculpture of the crucifixion remains on the wall where it inspired Picasso 80 years earlier.

From the mid-19th century to the early 20th Le Lapin remained the haunt of itinerant artists, their mistresses and harlots. Van Gogh, Apollinaire, Modigliani, Braque – they all paid for brandy there, and when the francs ran out a painting or poem was an acceptable alternative currency. As a result, until the 1990s, the Picassos on the walls were real. Unfortunately, a much-needed bout of recent repairs caused their sale for a king's ransom, but today fair copies sit in their place.

By day, Le Lapin Agile is dark. Tiny shuttered windows let out over Montmartre's last remaining vineyard. The atmosphere is a heady musk. The imagination easily takes a frisky leap to the days of *La Belle Époque*, when the silk-hatted gentry hurried past, perhaps on their way to the bright lights of Pigalle and the Moulin Rouge. This was the haunt of writers, wine-inspired philosophers and down-and-out artists full of dreams and fresh perspectives. 'One day my paintings will be exhibited in their own palace,' bragged the black-eyed Spaniard Pablo Picasso in 1907, and of course he was right.

Stéphane's most vivid memories, however, are of Francis Carco, 'standing on a table reciting poetry, and the then-student classic guitarist Alexandre Lagoya sleeping on the floor'. The cabaret's locale is the Butte of his youth, Montmartre's summit: 'All the top here was nothing, a desert.'

Contemporary paintings in the Musée de Montmartre show an open landscape of the quarries of Clingancourt, vineyards and ramshackle allotments: 'There were artists…living in the Bateau Lavoir. I fetched some clay for them in a little bag.' This clay, 'le porcelaine de Clingancourt', was the only surviving industry of Stéphane's Quartier. The clays and their associated quarries had once been a thriving business and, as with so many cities, the 19th-century industry attracted itinerant workers and immigrants. In Montmartre, the first wave of these were the agricultural workers of France's central Auvergne district, who brought with them their own songs. The musicians found work in ramshackle bars attached to coal merchant's yards, known as *cafés de charbon*.

In time, these evolved into the original open-air *bals musettes*, as seen in the paintings of Maurice Utrillo and others.

A later wave of immigration from 1870 onwards brought many Italians, who in turn brought their favourite instrument, the button accordion.* At first the foreigners were resented and ignored, even though many of these itinerants were talented musicians, including Charles Peguri, Albert Carrara and Guerino, a Neapolitan gypsy. Soon all of the rosettes for music at Le Bal Tabarin were awarded to Italians. Emile Milo Carrera went on to lead the band at Le Moulin Rouge and Chez Maxims, while young Avergnats like Jean Vaissade were brought up to adopt the more versatile Italian instrument, and indeed Vaissade preferred to be accompanied by gypsy guitarists. The first French accordion record was made by Peguri in 1913, who played a mandolinette, soon as integrated a part of Parisian café life as croissants and coffee.

In the early years of the 20th century, the young Stéphane Grappelli fetched materials from the quarries for these musicians and artists, many of whom, as struggling immigrants, favoured the area's cheap accommodation, including the Bateau Lavoir, Picasso's base of operations and a vestige of the old village. The original building was sadly destroyed by fire in 1970.

(In later life, Stéphane's own taste in painting ran to British watercolours and realist portraits of his hero, the pianist Art Tatum. It is of course in the nature of childhood to regard your immediate surroundings as the normal and entire universe, but whether he knew it or not at the time, his childhood home was alive with dangerous talent.)

Returning from adventures at Le Lapin Agile and Le Bateau Lavoir, Stéphane's new home with his father was a one-room flat at 59b Rue Rochechouart. This attic flat had one advantage: despite the infestations of cockroaches, which required frequent extermination, the tiny room was closest to the communal water tap. Sited on the landing, this rare luxury remains to this day, although it's now obscured by a jumble of discarded domestic junk, its services long replaced by more convenient plumbing. It's easy to imagine the young Grappelli fetching water for his father's shave and annoying the neighbours with impromptu improvisations on their newly acquired harmonium. It's unclear which chapel short of parishioners in this hedonistic village had resorted to pawning this instrument, but it's typical of Ernesto's encouragement that he acquired this musical instrument when money was still no doubt scarce. In another of Stéphane's recollections, in 1989, the keyboard at Rochechouart becomes a piano hired for 1F a day. Perhaps both were present at different times.

*The Italians adopted the accordion for song accompaniment after acquiring it from Vienna, where it was invented by Damien in 1829.

Whatever the keyboard arrangements, Stéphane's father soon settled back into a routine of freelance translating and occasional journalism. The work frequently took him away, leaving Stéphane once more to his own devices. The singer Beryl Davis once remarked that apparently Stéphane could do wonders with a tin of Spam luncheon meat, no doubt a legacy of these early years.

In the 1990s, Stéphane enjoyed looking at early photographs of Montmartre village, and I brought him a few that I'd collected from the local flea markets. It's striking to note the vast number of *bals musettes*, their slogans emblazoned on windmill towers and any vacant whitewashed wall. From within these establishments, Stéphane heard the last of the Auvergne bagpipes alongside the rise of the new accordions and the bawdy cabaret songs.

Originally, the *bals de familie* of the Auvergnats had been confined to Sundays, family affairs for an invited crowd, but, as the city grew and the toiling immigrants craved more opportunity to escape the daily grind, the bals were opened seven days a week. The area became the equivalent of New Orleans' Storyville, favoured by 'apaches',* dancing girls and pimps.

As a child, Stéphane must have been barred from these houses of ill repute, restricted to linger outside in the cart-wheeled mud and borrow tunes for courtyard busking, possibly competing for trade with the gypsy violinists camped at the Gare du Nord. There was certainly rich potential for a musical mix to inspire a talented ear: 'Immediately I knew a couple of tunes, I play in the street and make a little collection of money. But in those days, it was not so difficult as today – everybody was kind and generous. It was very amusing. Montmartre was marvellous. I don't say it is not now, but it changed. It changed like me.'

---

*In 1909, with partner Max Dearly, Mistinguett first performed the *valse Chaloupée* (Apache dance), an unusual routine in which the male throws and drags his female partner around the stage in a sort of domination-theme manner. In 1924, for her most applauded scene in the movie *Innocent Eyes*, Mistinguett portrayed a French maid sold by her callous father to a brutish Parisian Apache.

5 Silent Cinema And All That Jazz

'Mesdames et messieurs, ladies and gentlemen, this afternoon we present a dramatised account of the true-life adventures of Stéphane Grappelli, a 15-year-old cinematograph musician, as reconstructed from his own memoirs. Please, might we have a little hush in the stalls? Merci.'

EXTERIOR, DAY, THE ROCKY MOUNTAINS

The ominous locomotive leaned into the bend, its huge metal wheels inspiring the contraption-drummer to timpanic explosions. Chained to the track, the fair maiden quivered as a violin's tremolando cascaded around the cavernous cinematograph. Would anyone come to the rescue? Where was bold Dick now?

Cradling his precious violin, Stéphane still felt the suspense, even though this was today's third showing of this comic 'epic'. He had memorised all his violin parts, everything from a lover's rhapsody to his next cue. *Whooh whooh*, screeched his fiddle 'horn', echoing across the vast auditorium of Montmartre's Palais Rochechouart.

Learning to read music had been part of the deal for this job, and he would soon have his coveted Musicians' Union card. That white-and-pink-stamped scrap of board was the all-important key. Stéphane needed an opening in order to escape the cold winter streets, to remain in the cosy womb of the orchestra pit within the smoke-filled fug of the picture palace. 'I was accepted into the union in 1923, when I could read music,' he later recalled. 'I was 15. I stayed nearly two years.'

Stéphane enjoyed this cinematograph work; it was crazy and wild. Certainly he was given a guide of sorts, a sprawl of dots and squiggles – a sort of musical map – but he knew by now that, when he turned more to his own imagination and improvised a trill here, a glissando there, the audience responded with a shriek or a tear. More importantly, the *chef d'orchestre* caught his eye with a wink that said, 'Très bon. Encore!' The first violinist had a son who wasn't interested in the instrument and took Stéphane under his wing as a more willing apprentice. Stéphane was soon offered a permanent job.

Grappelli's luck was his *leitmotif*. Whenever life seemed to take a wrong turn, some *étranger providentiel* turned the next corner with a morsel. Isadora Duncan, the Neapolitan guitarist, his own father with that treasured violin – they all appeared in his bleakest hours. His cinema job had come along in a similar fashion.

The October of 1923 was a bitter one for Stéphane, now a precocious youth of 15. Streetwise and wary, he knew the survival tactics of the mean streets of Paris. As the wind lifted the dust at the corner of the Rue Dunkerque, he cursed the winter. Shutters tight clasped against the windmill fuel, nobody could hear his elegant trills and sweet vibrato. The cafés had closed their summer frontages and the grey courts lost their charm as the once-crimson geraniums wilted and petrified in the early frost. The Neapolitan guitarist Antonio, an old hand, had departed for the Riviera coast for the winter. Stéphane longed to see the sea, and nearly scrounged a wagon ride with Antonio's gypsy friends, but somehow he felt he owed it to his father to stay in Paris.

The summer had been good, with rich pickings from those mad artists and their sweet-smelling tarts. If a painting sold, everybody at Le Lapin Agile could sing again for a while – the Neapolitan knew the buttons to press to fuel a romance or to compel wine-inspired feet to a dance. 'We make a good living like that, you know,' Stéphane recalled. 'Better than a professional.'

Ernesto had come to rely on Stéphane's French sticks, wrapped in a scrap of newspaper or perhaps some overripe fruit, donated by a sentimental grocer on the Rue Lepic. Some days there was even a little spoilt wine from the little vineyard by Le Lapin.

But that had been back in the summer. Now, in the freezing winter court, an old lady gazed at him, looking shifty. She'd been watching Stéphane for too long from the gunmetal-grey shadows in the court stairwell. *Not another gypsy after my hat*, thought Stéphane. There wasn't much to take in the dusty cap, just a few sous he'd donated himself, the float that triggered the real offerings of those less poor than he. If it came to a chase, those gypsy sirens could shift. But he didn't care about the money; he worried about tripping over while carrying his lifeline – the precious fiddle. He stopped his melody mid-phrase, picked up the cap and offered the meagre sous to the woman. Often enough, he'd taken pity on a child poorer than himself or a lame beggar with no music to trade. The woman laughed: 'Don't stop. C'est bon. I love that tune.'

Here was a turnout, a music-lover daft enough to brave the cold.

'I've heard you before, in Rue Muller,' the old woman said. 'The winter wind too harsh around the Sacre?'

Stéphane recognised her now. Didn't she have a room at the Rue Rochechouart? 'Too cold,' he agreed. 'And no visitors, just poor priests. Prayers won't feed me.'

'Can you read music, too?' the woman asked with genuine interest.

'Of course,' lied Stéphane. He knew when to play to win. Perhaps this was another dancing master needing a cheap fiddle. He'd pick up any tune once somebody hummed it.

'My husband is sick and can't go to work. Will you substitute for him? He plays violin in the cinema at Boulevard Clichy.'

Stéphane could always return to the streets, but this new job in a grand palace of wonder was like a dream. But he also had his own dream, his one vague memory of his lost mother. They'd walked hand in hand once down a broad boulevard, and he'd felt proud and loved. Beside him, his mother had attracted the stares of gentlemen, scary in their tall silk hats and shiny boots. He'd thought her beautiful, an angel, like those in the church roof. Together they'd visited a temple of lights, the *cinématique*, a wonder of the new age where elephants danced and men could fly. That was all he had of his mother.

The silent cinema, of course, roared with music, one day accompanying cowboy lilts and lonesome trails, the next a sweeping romance of Valentino. And Stéphane learned every musical idiom. Each week he memorised the hastily scrawled themes, half reading them but mostly just listening, exploiting his remarkable natural ear. He then dreamt on the tunes, took liberties with the beat, milked every nuance of emotion from his fiddle, all the time lost in the wonder of those silver-shadowed images, comic and sad.

In the late afternoon, when the other players took a break, Stéphane preferred to stay in the warm: 'The show is three hours, 2:30 to 5:30 and 8:30 to 11:30. Between 5:30 and 8:30 there is just the piano, so sometimes I stayed for nine hours. They showed the news, a documentary, an intermission and then the big film.'

In the near-empty cinema, as only lovers canoodled in the back stalls, Stéphane deputised at the piano, a *casse-croûte* sandwich prepared by his father in one hand and his other caressing the ivories: 'The couples were at the back in a dark corner, so they don't care what I play.'

He loved the piano, a Bechstein. In its dark shiny, coal-black heart it could tremble like thunder or skip on the beat as a nymph danced. He didn't bother with music; the scant clientèle had more on their minds with their wandering hands. This was Stéphane's chance to experiment, to flow with the deft pictures sculpted on Hollywood and Vine. Stéphane the improviser dabbled in his emerging art.

'Tea For Two' – now there was a good tune. He wondered if they drank tea in ancient Arabia:* 'Rudolph Valentino – he was one of the greatest stars.'

With nobody taking any notice of his music, he decided to figure out the middle eight, regardless of the picture: 'It drive me crazy!'

Having been severely told off for his doodlings in the cinema, the precocious adolescent Stéphane probably thought that the chef d'orchestre had no sense of humour. For a young lad fresh from the street, Rudolph Valentino's Sheikh romancing his courtesan to 'Tea For Two' didn't seem too bad. He still hadn't cracked the middle eight, though.

Sent to cool his heels, Stéphane dodged the trams on the Rue Clichy and crossed over to Le Boudon, a grand café with stripped awnings all at sea. He and the sunshades boldly defied the ripping wind from the Butte. Too cold to sit outside, he lavished a hard-earned franc on a *café au lait* and a pastry. Three shows a day, two hours a show, a double-feature, a newsreel and an overture every time – Stéphane was learning his trade and getting paid for it. Life wasn't so bad.

Le Boudon had a machine that was bad news for musicians, however. Resplendent in polished walnut as tall as a wardrobe, the Multiphone was a wax-cylinder player. Le Boudon had belonged to Emile Pathé, and he and his brother Charles were so fascinated by the phonograph that the whole décor of their bar was built around mechanical music contraptions. The brothers had since moved on, and by this time were busy making a fortune with the cinematograph, but the machines remained.

Stéphane glared with youthful swagger at this ludicrous machine. So this scientific miracle was to replace real musicians? Perhaps if he gave it a kick it would make him feel better. With his foot poised, Stéphane glanced at the selection of tunes on offer from this prototype jukebox. There was 'Tea For Two'! 'So I had to hear that. It drove me mad. I have to hear that every day… But I make a mistake – it was not "Tea For Two"; it was "Stumblin'"' coming [out of the machine], and I was amazed so I ask the man, "What is it?" But he

---

*The silent epic *The Sheikh*, filmed in 1921. Stéphane couldn't remember whether he worked on this film or 1922's *Blood And Sand*. Both are possible for 1923, when he acquired his CGT union card. He certainly remembered playing for *Monsieur Beaucaire*. Set in the time of Louis XV, this film required a little Mozart, which stretched Stéphane's reading ability.

didn't know. But at least he gave me the name – it was Louis Mitchell and his band with "Stumblin'"."

By pressing the wrong button on the Multiphone (the term *jukebox* had yet to be coined), Stéphane had literally stumbled into the jazz age. His life was changed forever.

'And thank you, ladies and gentleman, for your indulgence. That ends our dramatised account. It was based wholly on Stéphane's own reminiscence.'

FIN

As Stéphane learned his trade, a musical revolution had hit Paris. Black African culture was familiar in Montmartre, with imported clothes and artefacts arriving with French colonials from Senegal and Morocco. Some Africans settled in the cheap flats and garrets next to Stéphane's attic in Rochechouart. The Africans were peace-loving traders seeking a quiet living and an honest franc. These *negri* were accepted by the French, a tolerant and free-thinking people, especially in this artists' menage of Montmartre. The Africans brought sun-dashed colour and lively rhythm to the French patois they'd learned at home.

But nothing had prepared Paris for *le tumulte noir*. This phenomena began during World War I, when America dispatched its 'Harlem Regiment' – the all-black 369th infantry – to march through Paris, ready to tackle the might of the German Empire. Originally 'the 15th Regiment of Colored Infantry', the company had been established in 1913 in a strictly segregated US Army. Volunteers rushed to join at temporary barracks in a disused dance hall on New York's 132nd Street. The 15th wished to be accepted as part of the 'Rainbow Division', but in the prejudicial climate of America they were told, 'Black is not a colour of the rainbow.' They were dispatched from Hoboken on 12 December 1917, although the High Command thought that blacks lacked the ability to fight and they were assigned to labouring. In France, they were attached to the French 161st Division and, finding no colour barrier, were at last assigned to combat. They became known as the Harlem Hellfighters, and were eventually awarded the Croix de Guerre for 'impressive conduct in battle'.

Straight from Harlem, the regiment brought with them their own band, and when backs were turned their military marches took a ragtime step. Under the baton of the jazz pioneer James Reese Europe, and with the swinging drums of Louis Mitchell, Paris greeted the liberators with flags and smiles. Fantastic contemporary newsreel footage shows the soldiers 'hoofing it' in ragged time, their eyes aglow with European adventure. The musicians were astonished to find the French addressing them as fellow human beings – this was a long way from the attitudes of the folks back home, who condemned jazz and negroes to the ghetto politics of Harlem.

In 1917, the jazz of the 369th Regiment was a noisy newborn. In *Sunburst Of The Soul* (Preservation Hall), written with William Carter, the great musicologist Alan Lomax described it thus: '[Jazz] was a magical fusion of many very big traditions: the tradition of concert music in Europe, the greatest of the African traditions, and the tremendous inventions of all the American frontiers and England, the blues, spirituals – all fused so that a new kind of music emerged.' Fused and conceived in the rich gumbo of New Orleans, the squalling infant had danced into mainstream America with the closing of Storyville, the racy red-light district that had been its mother and midwife. Out-of-work jazzmen took their screaming protégé to New York and Chicago while white Southern churchmen quickly condemned jazz as 'jungle music'. Its antecedent, the blues, was even worse – 'the Devils anthem', according to the racist lynch mob the Ku Klux Klan.

In Paris, though, the proud black soldiers danced openly in public with white French girls, and for some GIs this must have seemed like heaven. To French youths, jazz was *très joli*, *très chic*, *très moderne*, 'hot'. Something was stirring in smoky basements, and it wasn't a hurdy-gurdy.

Under the Treaty of Versailles and an uneasy peace, the 369th returned to America in February 1919 with 171 medals for bravery. Taking Uncle Sam's dime, many of the musicians returned with reinforcements under the maximum steam the White Star Line could muster. Jazz was really valued in Europe. At home it was ten cents a dime, regarded as bordello music by white America, whereas in Paris it was rare, exotic and, above all, new.

Hearing reports of available work and racial tolerance, Sidney Bechet, one of jazz's true innovators, arrived in Paris in 1919 with Will Marion Cook's Southern Syncopated Orchestra. Born in 1897 in New Orleans, Bechet enjoyed the French way of life and returned throughout his career. In 1919 he was a clarinetist, but he discovered the soprano saxophone on a trip to London and was the first to give it a jazz voice. Stéphane kept many photographs of their eventual meetings in jazz clubs in Paris's Latin Quarter.

Meanwhile, Louis Mitchell, one of the 369th Regiment's drummers, came back to France with Vernon and Irene Castle. By 1924, he had his own club, Mitchell's, in the Pigalle district of Montmartre. Observing the great showman at work, the artist Jean Cocteau described Mitchell as 'a barman of noises under a golden pergola laden with bells, triangles, boards and motorcycle horns. He mixed cocktails with them, putting in an occasional dash of cymbal, standing up, swaggering and smiling brilliantly.' This was Mitchell at his instrument, the still-being-invented 'contraption' drum kit, a jazz montage, the growing engine room of rhythm. The bass drum had come straight from a New Orleans marching band and was now being kicked with the American William Ludwig's new-fangled foot pedal. This now allowed the drummer to sit down, his hands freed for the military snare drum, which was fixed to a hand-made stand. But its heart and soul were liberated from a marching paradiddle, exchanged now for a riotous cakewalk. At the drumkit, jazz and vaudeville showmanship became brothers in arms.

Louis Mitchell's rival in the same rue was another tiny club, Le Grand Duc, soon graced by the legendary and equally flamboyant society magnet Bricktop, another queen of the night, whose drumkit was destined to be played by the British Prince of Wales. Bricktop had originally come to Paris as a singer. Born in 1894 in Alderson, West Virginia, as Ada Beatrice Queen Victoria Louise Virginia Smith, her mother – despite her blond hair – had been born a slave and her black father ran a whites-only barbershop. Ada grew up in a restaurant, and her striking red hair and matching temperament gave her the nickname that started a legend. Bricktop had learned her trade in Chicago and New York, touring with black vaudeville companies. Then, in Paris, she found eventual fame as a vivacious hostess and club owner. In the words of John Steinbeck, 'When Brick sang "Embracable You", it took 20 years off a man's life.'

The real jazz fireworks had started with the riotous opening of La Revue Nègre, ironically at Théâtre des Champs-Elysées, the same venue that had launched Stravinsky's *Le Sacre du Printemps*. In the warm autumn of 1925, this all-black review, produced by Andre Devan, was heralded in Paris by the audacious and vivid eroticism of a series of posters designed by Paul Colin. The onstage band included the return of the now-astonishing Sidney Bechet, while centre-stage and performing her newly created *danse sauvage*, like an erotic doll possessed of voodoo, was a teenage Joséphine Baker, naked but for feathers and beads.

Joséphine was a last-minute deputy for the established blues singer Maud de Forrest, but her choice as star was perfect timing. She had paid her dues in

Harlem's chorus lines, shared a dressing room with Ethel Waters and was infamous for mimicking everybody's parts. From the rich genetic pool of St Louis, Josephine could claim a bloodline that included Spanish, African and Appalachee Native American. She had absorbed her musical roots from the New Orleans showboats that plied the Mississippi trade, while her mother danced a winning cakewalk and her father was the best vaudeville drummer south of the river.

At the age of 19, Joséphine also knew the power of her sensuality. Tempered by a comic line in eye-rolling and gurning, she could get away with almost anything. The sight of this semi-naked dancer, forbidden fruit – and indeed soon to appear in a skirt fashioned almost entirely of bananas – attracted a brisk custom and every customer got to hear a line in jazz straight from the Bayou swamp.

In 1923, as Stéphane listened in wonder to the Multiphone renderings of 'Stumblin'' and its partner, 'Everybody Step', he had an astonishing preview of things to come, and confessed, 'I was amazed!' When you listen now to these tracks, it's almost impossible to imagine their impact on a 15-year-old boy used to a polite waltz and a gentle two-step, but Stéphane had the instinct of the improviser and must have felt a kindred spirit in these syncopated rhythms. Nevertheless, the random polyphony of a New Orleans frontline must have been as strange to Stéphane as Stravinsky's *Le Sacre...* was to pre-war Paris. However, to an ear which knew how to listen, this was transforming magic: 'It changed my life.'

For years, Stéphane didn't know the origins of this mysterious music. There were no books on jazz – the first *Jazz Journal* was still a decade in the future. He just absorbed its charm delivered fully formed, a 'found object' from a strange, remote, mythical other world called America.

In that remote place, as distant as the stars, in the romantically named city of San Francisco, a ten-year-old Yehudi Menuhin astounded audiences in 1926 with his concerto performances at the huge Civic Auditorium. In the same year, in London's Royal Albert Hall, Lew Grade was crowned World Champion Charleston Dancer by competition judge Fred Astaire.

The 80rpm records that Stéphane encountered in that Paris Multiphone had been recorded in France as early as 1921. Amusingly, working across a language barrier, Stéphane long assumed that 'Jazz Kings' was Mitchell's surname.

Soon driven mad by Stéphane's enthusiasm, Ernesto acquired their own wind-up gramophone. The money from a regular job enabled his son to afford occasional purchases of the expensive jazz records now being issued in Paris by Odéon and Pathé-Marconi: 'I used to have a little machine. I wind it myself – I still have it. Bix Beiderbecke at the piano and Frank Trumbauer on C melody saxophone. I was 18 when I heard that, and I played it all day long. It drove me insane.'

Enchanted by his discovery, Stéphane experimented, syncopating French tunes and weaving counterpoints with his friend and pianist Stéphane Mougin: 'We added a little perfume of jazz.' Stéphane instinctively did this at the piano, believing that there was surely no place for his 'classical' fiddle in jazz. However, Mougin impressed Stéphane so much with his fledgling improvisations that he would join in. Mougin even found some paying work for Stéphane, as so many people who saw Joséphine Baker wanted dancing lessons and every dance teacher needed a musician. For Stéphane, it meant a return to solo piano: 'I found some little jobs. In fact, I deputised for a young girl who played the mandolin – tango, foxtrot, whatever. The way Mougin was playing, it would make me change the way I play, and that was the first time I improvised on a tune.'

Straight or improvised, these were difficult times for fiddle players in popular music. Bandleaders liked a fiddle or two in the band as a kind of mark of respectability – the fiddle spoke of 'orchestra' and 'maestro'. The violinist in tailcoat and stiff collar embodied a credibility that society hostesses liked to see fronting their podiums. The violin was supposed to play sweet refrains in ballads, and, if in the more raucous charleston, it disappeared in a swell of saxophones and trumpets, then that was too bad. Stéphane and his new friend, fellow violinist Michel Warlop, must have pondered the dilemma.

Warlop differed from Stéphane in that he had a full classical conservatoire training. Although Stéphane admired that technique, his friend was more taken with Stéphane's ease at improvisation. The pair even shared a home for a short while, in Stéphane's first escape from the parental hold, at Warlop's mother's house, at the bottom of Avenue Junot. They no doubt exchanged the benefits of their differing musical experiences. Warlop worked with embryonic jazz ensembles and would eventually join the music-hall band Gregor And The Gregorians, but could always find work in classical orchestras.

The violin's awkward role, together with his lack of classical finesse, pushed Stéphane further into his piano playing. He discovered via another friend, trumpet player Philip Brun, that there was plenty of work to be had playing for tea parties, christenings and dancing lessons, mostly in the posh 16th Arrondissement, around Eiffel's famous tower. There, during society dancing lessons, he would get into trouble with his syncopated improvisation instead of the *Strictly Ballroom* style required. This was hardly the jazz he dreamt of, and indeed this period is probably the first indicator of the lesson Stéphane had learned on the street: to take the job and 'put a little butter on my spinach'. He would never forget it.

Another experience that Stéphane benefited from in the 1920s was playing for a student orchestra. This was paid work, presumably again at society venues, and mostly came at weekends, clashing with his cinema work.

On the way to work one day, the teenage Grappelli saw Joséphine Baker engaged in an early publicity stunt worthy of her tabloid future, when she famously walked her pet leopard along the Champs-Elysées. Although only two years older than Stéphane, her take on the jazz age must have seemed as remote and mysterious to him as the bizarre language she spoke.

Throughout this period, Stéphane stayed with the cinema orchestra, occasionally sending in deputies when the more lucrative solo-piano engagements clashed. In 1925, however, he gave it up and took a summer job at the resort town of Wimereux, near Boulogne. This was a prophetic gig in that the band featured his violin, two guitars and a banjo. Stéphane would remember the freedom and dynamic that that afforded. His violin could soar above such a small ensemble. However, the summer's end saw Stéphane – never too proud – once more busking the streets of Montmartre.

On 21 May 1927, the American aviator Charles Lindbergh crossed the Atlantic single-handed in his tiny, single-engine plane, *Spirit Of St Louis*, landing at Le Bourget before an excited crowd of 100,000 people. Twentieth-century technology continued to shrink the world and bring distant continents ever closer.

Also in Paris, the ten-year-old Yehudi Menuhin performed Lalo's *Symphony Espagnole* and stayed on in the city for lessons with his new teacher, George Enescu. While he was there, Stéphane was fortunate enough to hear the young virtuoso, although in 1927 there were too many barriers keeping their worlds apart for him to suspect that they would ever meet.

For most musicians, Europe and America remained divided by the Atlantic, the limits of the Blue Riband Run – the race for the shortest Atlantic passenger crossing, the fatal race for prestige that had been a contributing factor in the sinking of the *Titanic*. This meant a minimum of five days at sea on an unforgiving ocean. Paris, however, was hungry for talent, and the strange stories of the racial tolerance and enthusiastic crowds to be found there soon brought every major jazz artist to the banks of the Seine. 'In 1928, I was engaged at the

Ambassador for the French orchestra,' recalled Stéphane. 'I remember I spent my evenings there after we played. Paul Whiteman used to start about 8:30, and I was sitting down next to the pianist Oscar Levant. I watched the way he played. I stayed there all evening, and that's were I meet Joe Venuti.'

The impact of that first meeting with Venuti and hearing his guitarist, Eddie Lang, cannot be overestimated. Joe was a jazz violinist in a tradition that stretched way back to the genre's origins. Stéphane had no idea that the violin had played such a role. For Stéphane, Joe opened a window of possibility. Stéphane had discovered jazz, heard records of Louis Armstrong and Frank Trumbauer, but Venuti played *his* instrument and was also a white Italian!

Most importantly, this was jazz on strings, a revolutionary concept for Stéphane and may other Europeans. Before his eyes, Venuti taught Stéphane every rudiment of string jazz. A violin could swing and syncopate, could swoop to a note in an expressive blues style. And, unlike on a piano, you could flatten notes and seek the daring flattened fifths and thirds. Indeed, Stéphane had heard Louis doing the same with his trumpet valves and mouthpiece, and Traumenbaur with his slide trombone. He was inspired.

The guitar of Eddie Lang was just as important. In their duo spot in Paul Whiteman's programme, the violin was perfectly complemented. Lang was a master, one of the first great jazz guitarists. For an anonymous Bing Crosby, appearing on the same bill, Lang became a favourite and sensitive accompanist. On record in chamber solos with the great blues guitarist Lonnie Johnson, he showed that he could stretch out and understand jazz's mangrove-strong roots in the Mississippi Delta.

That night at the Ambassador, as the Venuti-Lang duo played Louis Armstrong's current hit, 'Dinah', the lesson for Stéphane was both profound and simple. The greatest swing fiddler of the 20th century had found his destiny.

By a curious coincidence, Stéphane and Venuti had much in common, despite Joe being five years Stéphane's senior. Joe claimed to have been born on an Atlantic crossing, as his family left Italy for the promise of Ellis Island and the Statue of Liberty. This was the same wave of emigration that had brought Ernesto Grappelli to Paris. (There must have been a lot of frascati downed that night!) Stéphane managed to talk to Joe, exchanged a few words of Italian and even took him sightseeing. The 'Italians' shared a sense of humour, and Venuti's love of practical jokes particularly endeared him to Stéphane. In the late 1990s, at the mention of Venuti's name, Stéphane immediately went into impressions of mad sousaphone players and pranks they had played on cowboy entertainer Tom Mix's horse (they sent his horse onstage at the London Palladium with a full erection, prompted by the deft attentions of their violin bows).

Jokes aside, the Ambassador in 1928, part grand building and part enormous marquee tent, required an extension to accommodate the crowds drawn by exotic and far-flung attractions. It held further surprise. Amongst the tiara-wearing flappers and bejewelled maharajahs, the spotlight turned on a diminutive American. 'I remember one evening the master of ceremonies announce, "The composer of *Rhapsody In Blue* is in town. He's here and he's going to play it for us, the first time in France,' Stéphane recalled, 'so Oscar Levant had a part and Gershwin played the solo. At the end, Gershwin retired to the dressing room. It was a very small space, and when I saw him coming he was patting Oscar on the back. He say to me, "Hello." That's all. Very good. What a souvenir!'

Stéphane, still a young man of 20, stood in front of genius and marvelled at the creative audacity of this extraordinary musician from that still-faraway place. The glamour and style of these wild colonial heroes must have been overpowering; with their flamboyant suits and gangster hats, they were movie stars in colour, leaping from the silver screen and living and breathing in Stéphane's own Paris. Gershwin described his *Rhapsody In Blue* as 'a musical kaleidoscope of America, our pep, our blues, our metropolitan madness'. Our young man felt it all.

Stéphane particularly revelled in Gershwin's take on orchestrated jazz, especially as, for those early performances, Gershwin improvised the solo piano part, emphasising the link to its jazz inspiration. For the rest of his long career Stéphane explored the same links between the aural experience, the written score and the improvised chorus. From that day on, there was rarely a Grappelli performance without a George Gershwin tune. In Stéphane's later years, he would nearly always introduce 'my lucky number, my Gershwin medley, "Someone To Watch Over Me". Is there anyone out there?'

Stéphane also loved to tell his story of another chance encounter in 1920s Paris, this time with Paul Whiteman's vocalist: 'In that band there was something extraordinary, a trio called The Rhythm Boys, three fabulous singers. At the rehearsal, one of them asked me, "Hey, man. Do you know where I can get a chaser?" So I took him to a bistro nearby, and fortunately the barman there understood because there were a lot of Americans in town – it was a cognac and a little glass of beer. He drank it and we went back to the Ambassador. I was curious to know his name, and then I saw the sign: "Trio Bing Crosby And The Rhythm Boys".'

The 1930 film *King Of Jazz* includes a contemporary excerpt of the young Crosby singing 'Happy Feet' in his inimitable style, ten years before his eventual fame as the first pop-star crooner. Stéphane proudly told me that he and Bing were roughly the same age (in fact, Crosby was four years his senior).

When first struggling with the immensity of Stéphane's story I was most of all struck by the audacity of his early ambition: to play American music, jazz, the music of a crazy diasporic melting pot that he had never visited. Beyond that, to play it on a gentle acoustic violin. It's only when you consider the extraordinary revolution that was Paris during the Roaring '20s that it makes any sense at all. At the same time, Hemingway was writing audacious fiction in a garret overlooking Le Bateau Lavoir, the surrealists were exhibiting toilet basins and *pissoirs* as art and, in a small club on Pigalle, the Prince of Wales was sitting in on drums for the charleston band. In this climate surely anything was possible. In later life, Stéphane never questioned *why?* He always preferred *why not?*

As if all this were not enough, there were Armenian boxers and gypsy princes soaking up the same heady brew. The stage was set, the lights dimmed and in the spotlight glare the master of ceremonies was in full dress...

6 Grégor Et Ses Grégoriens

'I think it's better that, when you start to play, play strictly melody. Everybody should be politeness to the composer. Play what he composed!'
– *Stéphane Grappelli*

In 1928, on London's Frith Street, the Scottish inventor John Logie Baird demonstrated his invention, the Televisor, which reproduced moving colour pictures. He even sent images across the Atlantic. Everybody who visited Baird was very impressed, but nobody could find a use for a radio with pictures. Of course, nobody, least of all Stéphane, could have foreseen the huge impact of this invention. How could the Televisor possibly affect an entertainment world still dominated by music hall? How could anyone predict that a former *bals musette* would eventually become a television studio?

In Paris, Stéphane was working the Moulin de la Gallette, which was then in its third incarnation as a sound studio. On 3 May 1929, he recorded four titles for the Edison Bell Company with The Orlando Tango Orchestra. This was his recording debut, and he would later express severe reservations about Orlando's stylised tangos. Also using the studio that day was a saxophonist, Edmund Cohanier, and a mysterious Turk called Grégor. In fact, Stéphane didn't tell anyone about these records and, apart from a white-label test pressing of one title, 'Escuhame', they are long lost. Grappelli must have played well, however, as Grégor soon booked him for a summer season on the Cote d'Azur.

By this time, Stéphane had become busy around the Paris club, cabaret and dance circuit – although Gershwin and Venuti inspired his musical ambition, he still had to earn a living. He soon learned that the trick to survival in the fickle world of popular music was to stay versatile. Never forgetting his time hungry on the streets, Stéphane took gigs as a pianist, violinist and even alto saxophonist.

There is a photograph from this era of Stéphane appearing with his fiddle amongst Ray Ventura Et Ses Collégians, a combo with a four-sax frontline, including a rare bass saxophone. As far as we know, Stéphane never recorded with the Collégians, but their output included such music-hall ditties as 'Vive Les Bananes' (a possible allusion to Joséphine Baker's radical dress style) and 'Le Nez de Cleopatre'. Another photo sees him smiling and laddish, clutching an alto saxophone with The Jacque Zarou Orchestra at the Montmartre Monte Christo Club, on Rue Fromentin. (Stéphane once told me that he gave up on the sax because it was 'très difficile'.) Yet another gig sees the young Grappelli on accordion in a Pigalle nightclub.

The best-documented engagement for this era, however, involves a conducting boxer, a performing dog and a trumpet player in a tutu: 'When I was 20, Philip Brun was playing with a band called Grégor et ses Grégoriens. One day, the pianist was ill and he gave me the job, because in those days I continued to play the piano.' This is another example of the Grappelli luck, the encounters with *étrangers providentiels*; he seemed to have the unerring knack of putting himself in the right place at the right time; at that time, Philippe Brun was a veritable star, coveted across the channel by the great British bandleader Jack Hylton.

The fabulous promotional film *Un Opéra-Jazz*, directed by Roger Lion, has preserved for us this late-1920s *époque* of French vaudeville. This is amongst the first synchronised music film in the world. After an interminable but historically precious pre-credit sequence, the 20-piece band appear at last in full evening dress.

'Ladies and gentlemen, I present for you Grégor et ses Grégoriens!'

The announcer, in broken French, is Grégor himself, an Armenian boxing champion who broke one too many noses and retired from the ring. Born Krikor Kelekian in 1898 in Constantinople, he fled Turkey in 1915, narrowly escaping the Armenian massacre. After a time spent touring Europe as an eccentric dancer, billed with his partner as 'Loulou et Grégor' and famed for his comic valour, by the late 1920s he was an impresario, his varied empire including the pioneering magazine *La Revue du Jazz*, founded in 1929. He was then set to conquer the *cinématographe avec son*.

In the film, as the music starts, Grégor waves his arms in emphatic time. Reading not a note of music, he choreographs to the orchestra and shows promise as a traffic policeman. It's great theatre, and deserves a posthumous Oscar (Best Musical Director In An Unsupportive Role?). The band mascot, an indeterminate hound in a frilly ruff collar, sticks out a tongue and pants.

The Grégoriens themselves consisted of three violins, a sousaphone, three saxophones, two trombones, the trumpet of Pierre Allier,* a fiddle bass, a

---

*Allier had replaced Philippe Brun, who by this time had been poached for the English band of Jack Hylton. A furious Grégor wrote an open letter in *La Review du Jazz* to complain about losing his biggest star.

ukulele, a banjo, a tenor guitar, a piano and a home-made contraption – or 'traps' – drumkit. Whatever his musical merits, Grégor must have done a fine job to find paying work for such an extravagant line-up.

The core of the filmed musical comedy is a sort of carnival of Venice-style theme and variations. Each soloist takes the theme and camps it up with flair. When Stéphane's turn arrives, it appears that he's forsaken his role as second piano. He recalled the change: 'Grégor keep me, and later on…we'd been to a nightclub and Grégor said to me, "You were a violinist before?" I said, "Yes," and he said to me, "Why don't you play the violin?" So the violinist let me have his instrument and I play a tune or two and Grégor said, "Ah, that's what I want in the band!" He obliged me to play the violin, so I give it up, the piano, and I was quite pleased, because [it means] I don't need to work without a stop!' The pianist would, of course, have had to provide an unbroken harmonic support.

Stéphane told Geoffrey Smith that he hadn't at this point played violin seriously for three years, and indeed had virtually given up. In fact, he was even without an instrument; his friend Michel Warlop, also in the Grégor band, lent Stéphane a violin by Pierre Hel of Lille that was dated 1924. This violin was apparently a prize given to Michel at the Paris Conservatoire. That 'Warlop violin' would eventually enter French violin legend.* Grégor clearly recognised Stéphane's talent and actually bought him his own first real violin, a Tua, hand-made in Nice.

In *Un Opéra-Jazz*, Stéphane performs a parody harking back to the by then old-fashioned Auvergnat *bals musettes*. There are three violins fronting the band, with Stéphane taking centre position, looking a little sheepish. As the fiddlers stand for their respective solos, they don wide-brimmed peasant hats sporting tails at the back. The musical parody seems to emulate the medieval hurdy-gurdy-like vielle[†] of the Montmartre Auvergnats. The fiddles carry the rustic drone to extremes and the players dip and curtsey in their choreographed vaudeville turns.

As Stéphane returned to the bandstand, there were visible signs of relief that his ordeal was finally over. He was perhaps already wishing for something more musically dignified. Perhaps he thought of Yehudi Menuhin, in his recent concert, which involved no dogs or tutus and in which the American boy was seen already playing a Stradivarius. Stéphane may even have been dreaming of the unheard-of notion of a jazz concert. Who could blame him when Grégor's

---

*According to Daniel Nevers, the Warlop violin is heard on the 1933 track 'Fit As A Fiddle'.

†Part of the hurdy-gurdy family, a kind of automated fiddle, with mechanically produced melody and drone strings. The vielle is often depicted in medieval art and cathedral sculpture.

film's grand finale features two of the musicians donning tutus over their dinner jackets and dancing *à la* sugar-plum fairies?

A controversy over the showman-like approach demonstrated by Grégor – whose motto was 'innovate and please – flared in the Paris music scene. Geoffrey Smith describes him perfectly: 'He had the instincts of a rock star. Onstage, non-stop energy, flashy costumes, music stands bearing his distinctive profile, even a primitive light show. Offstage, the act continued. His clothes were a combination of the elegant and fantastic: a morning coat with striped trousers, polychrome vest, cane, derby and an ever-present monocle (of plain glass) or a turban, in which he sometimes conducted, adorned with a plume. He strolled the boulevards with a perfect pair of Afghan hounds.' Meanwhile, pianist Alain Romans remembers, 'Grégor would drive up each evening in a large open car, wearing spats, a top hat and white gloves. He then marched up to the waiting orchestra, preceded by a small boy with a trumpet who blew a fanfare and announced, "Grégor! Le roi du jazz."'

Hughes Panassié, one of the very first jazz critics and later an esteemed author, took particular exception to this early victory of style over content. He wrote to *La Revue du Jazz* in horror at what he saw as a wasted opportunity. Grégor had surrounded himself with the finest jazz musicians in Paris but insisted on dragging them through comic turns such as *Un Opéra-Jazz*, which is apparently based on a stage piece he saw called 'Ah, The Strawberries And The Raspberries'. Panassié attended the rehearsal for one of Grégor's most ambitious concerts at the music hall L'Empire, where the band were billed as 'Gregor And The Gregorians – The Best Jazz Orchestra In The World'. Such a billing would present high expectations, and Panassié seemed impressed:

'Many people were launched at L'Empire – Jack Hylton and many other jazz pseudo-orchestras made their Parisian debuts here. I helped with orchestra rehearsals – he was really good, because he recruited a large group of the best French musicians, notably Fisbach and Lisee on the alto saxophone, Mougin on piano, Grappelly [*sic*] on the violin.

'It was a superior group to that of Jack Hylton's, firstly because he had the best soloists and arrangements, next because he showed that jazz had a bigger importance. They certainly merited to supplant Jack Hylton in our country.

'The last rehearsals, three or four days before the big première, gave me the impression that the orchestra was going to be a success. Léon Vauchant, one of the greatest jazz musicians, who had played for nearly two years with Jack Hylton, came to strengthen the orchestra at the last minute. Vauchant is not only an admirable trombonist but he can still play almost every instrument, write first-class arrangements and can transform an orchestra instantaneously with his valued advice. His unexpected arrival was a real advantage. The orchestra really achieved a fine standard, and there was a commercial side skilfully combined to seduce the majority of the public.

'The first cloud appeared the day before the "première" during the last rehearsal, which took place in the presence of the owner of L'Empire, Monsieur Audiffred. Someone had the excellent idea of getting a number called "Speciality" under way, which consisted of a series of solos, "hot" or "straight", executed by the lead musicians of the orchestra. This number showed the quality of the soloists and had the advantage of focusing all attention of the public towards the star musician.

'I remember that Grappelly, for his part, took a beautiful violin chorus from "Stay Out Of The South". M Audiffred listened without saying a word. The first solos were mainly straight solos, but then there was a magnificent piano chorus from Mougin, played in a slow tempo M Audiffred interrupted the solo, shouting, "It is too long! It's boring. You must play quicker or remove that solo!"

'Mougin looked at me with a bitter smile, which I understood. "You see, you will never understand jazz like this!" He then doubled the tempo in a resigned way. We removed this solo, which was one of the best musical moments of the concert!'

On the night, an audience expecting great jazz were loudly disappointed: 'When the curtain went up on the Gregorians, the evening of the première, the musicians had in front of them enormous music stands, which is very unfortunate in a music hall like L'Empire – Jack Hylton had not committed this mistake. The music stands made up the French colours – another mistake!

'Distanced, the musicians felt ill at ease and behaved in the least spectacular way possible. Behind their large music stands, they had a gloomy anxious look about them, which inhibited their spirit throughout the performance.

'Unfortunately, when the "Speciality" part came, which is at the end of the performance, it was past midnight and...the atmosphere became turbulent. Next to me, a woman whistled and did not stop making an uproar. One or two sentimental solos brought back some calm, but Vauchant, usually at his ease, had to push aside the onlookers because he hadn't arrived at his vibraphone to accompany one of the solos.

'Grappelly's solo passed by practically unnoticed in the general racket and the "Specialities" were cut short with the show finishing quickly amidst a storm of applause and whistles.

'The uproar made by the public throughout this première made me suspicious…and I knew that Grégor was hated by a large number of musicians. Thus we lost the unique opportunity to show off the best French musicians to the Paris public throughout 15 days. I was sickened by such stupidity.'

The critics were scathing, the 19 May 1930 edition of *Paris-Midi* branding the show a collection of 'pale jazz tunes that have already been heard', while *Comédia* on 21 May accused, 'Grégor's jazz is a very mediocre imitation of that of Jack Hylton's'.

Despite these challenges, however, his sojourn in the Grégoriens was important for Stéphane. At the very least, he enjoyed regular paid work and the opportunity to travel. Alongside many internal French trips, including a residency at the Nice club Le Palais de la Méditerrannée, in 1930 Stéphane accompanied Grégor on a remarkable adventure.

Setting out on the British steamer MV *Alcantara*, the band and full entourage took a 17-day Atlantic crossing to South America. Virtually alone on the ship, the band rehearsed throughout the voyage. As a preparation for their South American debut, Grégor also organised an onboard concert, a charity benefit gig with half the proceeds going to the Royal South Hampshire Hospital and the other half to the Buenos Aires Seamen's Mission. The concert, given mid-Atlantic on 6 October 1930, featured a 15-piece version of the Grégorians with guest appearances from a 'Jacky'. It's unclear whether Jacky was the mascot (a dog), a guest singer or a musician in a tutu – some vaudeville remains a comic mystery.

It is known, however, that the band consisted of drums, four saxes, two trombones, two trumpets, three violins, sousaphone, banjo and piano. In the printed programme, 'Stéphane Grappelli' (note the Italian spelling) has two credits as violinist and arranger, while his friend Stéphane Mougin appears as pianist and arranger. Also billed are 'Louys and Silvia', 'eccentric dancers from the London Palladium'.*

The programme for the concert provides an interesting insight into the range of music that Stéphane was performing and arranging. The band started with a prelude and rag written by Stéphane Mougin. This 'Tiger Rag', billed as 'Hot Piece Dixieland' and 'Harlem Madness', indicates the early jazz influence. Contrast is provided by Chopin's third piano sonata and a Grieg violin sonata, played by Mougin and the violinist S Schmidt.

*Possibly contemporary rivals of Louis Wynogradsky, by now doing the rounds as Louis Grade, 'table dancer'.

Comedy comes in the form of 'Mickey Mouse', presumably a cartoon music caricature in the style of Walt Disney's 'Silly Symphonies' cartoon of 1928, while folk song comes in the form of 'Tu Sais', arranged by Mougin, and 'Danny Boy', performed on solo 'cello by the trombonist Leo Vauchant.

The pieces performed by the 'eccentric dancers' are 'the parson's dance' and 'the parade of the wooden sailors', while Jacky – 'in his stuff' – performs 'Baby'. The whole ended with Irving Berlin's 'Puttin' On The Ritz' in 'a burning hot arrangement' by Leo Vauchant. With a sense of place on a British ship, for the first of many occasions Stéphane got to play 'God Save The King'. At this time, he had no English beyond the 'hot jazz' and 'swing' titles of his favourite music and had yet to visit Britain. The ship's photograph shows an immaculate dinner-jacketed ensemble set to conquer the New World.

Arriving first in the Brazilian capital of Río de Janeiro, Stéphane witnessed the engineering work on the imposing statue of Christ by Paul Landowsky that was beginning to tower over the port. More importantly, Stéphane became one of the first Europeans to hear authentic samba. What an experience for a Montmartre village boy, to hear this exotic blend of African rhythm, Portuguese *fadista* and exotic Amazonian soul!

The journey then continued to Argentina by boat and sleeper train. In Buenos Aires, Stéphane witnessed the real tango as played at its source in the brothels of the red-light district. As early as 1910, the 'cleaned up' tango had became a European fashion, but Stéphane could always demonstrate the authentic lilt and sway of the real thing. In 1952, he remarked, 'I play every kind of tune and I like them all, even tangos. I used to hate them, but ever since I was in the Argentine...and heard them played well by local bands, I have come to like them.' In the 1930s, Carlos Gardel took authentic *tango canción* to Paris and revitalised a trend that took a hold at dancehalls such as Le Bajolo. Further enhanced by diverse contributions from artists ranging from Stravinsky to Astor Piazzolla, the tango is alive and well in the 21st century. Now groups such as Soledad provide a powerful sense of the passion that Stéphane must have experienced in 1930. Asked to play 'Jealousy' in the 1970s, he retorted, ' "Jealousy"? That's not a real tango.'

This South American experience had a profound effect on the Grappelli sound. Part of Stéphane's inimitable style is the art of what musicians call 'true' rubato. Like so many Latin musicians, Stéphane borrows time from one bar and then makes it up in the next. This isn't, of course, exclusive to Latin music, but few do it better. Also evident after this South American trip, his early recordings with Grégor demonstrate Stéphane's 'folkish' informality, the deceptively casual style, characteristic of so much samba and tango but completely absent from, say, the fiddlers of the Café de Paris. The predominant tea-dance style was still conservatoire, the 'respectable violinist'. According to Stéphane, Grégor soon saw his potential as a 'swing fiddler' and put the other two 'classical' violinists around him.

The return to Europe took Stéphane to Rome, and by this time the band featured the glamorous vocalist Damia, whose *pièce de résistance* was her rendition of 'La Violettera'. During one performance, annoyed by a complacent foreign audience jangling keys and reading papers, the enraged Damia showered them with bunches of violets. Thinking it part of the act, the master of ceremonies insisted on a repeat performance every night. The Romans were entranced by this French display of chic (or should that be cheek?).

Further engagements took Stéphane to Nice, St Tropez and Cannes, where he enjoyed the regal company of dukes and duchesses on their yachts. More interesting, though, were their gramophone collections; here, for the first time, Stéphane heard Cole Porter and Jerome Kern.

This was the beginning of two important love affairs for Stéphane: one with *The Great American Songbook*, which would provide the basis of his repertoire, and one with the balmy climate of Cannes. He may even have dreamt that one day he could live in that paradise, far from the cold streets of Paris.

Back on the bandstand, one number, 'I Want To Be Happy', required four saxophones, and so, always obliging, Stéphane learned the requisite two notes. He dressed his performance up with a comic back twitch of the legs, charleston style, and he was a hit. He was coming to enjoy a rare and early exposure to a shrinking 20th-century world and learning the value of playing to the crowd.

Indeed, people were starting to recognise Stéphane – and many of them were English or American. Inevitably, many English speakers unfamiliar with Italian would announce him as 'Grappell-eye'. This prompted Grégor to encourage Stéphane to utilise the Grappelly spelling of his name, which would stay with Stéphane for the next 23 years.

Another hurdle crossed in St Tropez was membership of La Société des Auteurs, Compositeurs et Éditeurs de Musique. Stéphane learned early that a musician can survive the lean periods only if he has some royalties to fall back on, and so he took a pen and put his six best ideas on manuscript, the Société showed vision and he was accepted.

Although Grégor certainly had his shortcomings, musically, he was a shrewd employer of popular talent and Stéphane found himself playing amongst an elite. On some dates, the saxophones were French jazz greats Andre Ekyan and Alix Combelle, a formidable pairing so good that, when they later recorded with American stars, many said that they couldn't always tell who was taking which solos. Networking with players like these led Stéphane to undertake more recording sessions, recording at least 38 tunes at the Ultraphone studio on the Avenue de la Grande-Armée. For many of these sessions he played piano, but 46 seconds into the surviving recording of 'Fit As A Fiddle' by Grégor and one of his all-star line-ups, an unmistakable voice rings out. From three-quarters of a century of crackle and swish emerges a fully formed jewel, Stéphane Grappelly, rhythmic and swinging and with that indefinable ingredient that sets musical genius apart – you immediately know who it is. Listening to his personal voice, it's clear that Stéphane was already improvising in a true jazz style.

Something very special happens when a musician cuts the strings that tie him to the musical ground. For the duration of his flight, he becomes a composer/musician breathing his existence into sound. For those brief moments, the listener and artist are joined by air in an intimate vibration. When it's good, minds meld.

'Fit As A Fiddle' marks the beginning of an extraordinary series of recordings. From this point on, Stéphane improvised into the microphone every year for the next 63 years. (Ironically, this first flight is a curious early fitness record – the flipside being 'Young And Healthy'.)

His Grégorian experience was good for Stéphane and it lasted off and on until the fateful year of 1933, when once more the ominous spectre of war hung over Europe. In Berlin, the Reichstag was burned and Hitler took power over a vengeful Germany. The great economic depression took its toll on the entertainment industry and the Grégoriens disbanded in December.

By this time Stéphane had grown into a seasoned professional musician. He read music, he could improvise on popular songs, he'd toured with a band, he'd performed his first recording sessions and he'd featured in a short film.* Grégor had even encouraged him to try his hand at musical arrangements. He was just 25 years old.

---

*According to Daniel Nevers, there is another film of Grégor in which Stéphane plays piano. This is part of the 1933 piece *Miquette Et Sa Mère*, directed by Henri Diamant-Berger, in which Grappelly accompanies singer Blanche Montel for the song 'Deconvenue'.

7 Django Reinhardt: Truth And Legend

'He was a giant of the jazz world, and all his fans know he was a gypsy, but many people don't realise what an enormous effect being a gypsy had on his music, which in fact transcended jazz. His behaviour was at times puzzling to non-gypsies. Every true genius behaves differently to the rest of us. But above all, my father was a gypsy.'

– Babik Reinhardt*

Less than a mile from the bohemians and visiting gentry of Montmartre, but living in an entirely different world, were the Romanies, the last great nomad tribes of Europe. In the 1880s, Vincent van Gogh painted the 'Manouche Roulotte' at the gates of Paris, although they had probably set up camp there hundreds of years before that. Doubtless that camp drew the same mixture of suspicion and intrigue that Romany camps still do. Van Gogh's painting is a rural idyll depicting a lush meadow on a summer's day, the gaily painted *roulotte* vans surrounded by happy children and contented horses. There were surely days like these, although considering the northern European climate there must have been many more days when the nomadic life of the 1920s was a real and practical nightmare.

Children do not choose their lifestyles, and the Romany are born on the road. The seasons and the rise and fall of the sun are their only unbreakable constants – everything else is subject to change. As the children grow in a shifting environment, where nothing, not even food and warmth, is a given, they surely absorb a unique perception of our shared world. As house dwellers, the descendants of Iron Age farmers who gave up the hunter-gather lifestyle thousands of years ago, most people are ill equipped to understand the nurturing mechanisms that protect the Romany spirit. Quiet introspection and unpredictability are the norm in a world without mechanical measures of time. The Romany perceive a different world, both physically and imaginatively.

In prehistory, all of the European nomadic clans had originally emerged from India, and the Manouche had reached Europe through Central Asia and

*Django's second son by his second wife, Naguine, in Ian Cruikshank's book *Django's Gypsies*.

the Middle East, veering north once through the Balkans.* The other main group, the Gitanes, had taken a southerly route through Spain. The Reinhardt family were of the Manouche tribe, their name taken from the Romany *manus* ('gypsy man') and a people with an oral history that recalls the area of Strasbourg. Some left for France with the German unification of 1870, others with the annexation of Alsace-Lorraine; the colossal new Germany was clearly no place for the disenfranchised Romany.

The Reinhardts and their relatives had travelled Europe and North Africa before reaching their camp at the Gare du Choisy. This no man's land at the point of the old medieval fortifications of Paris had become a series of gardeners' allotments, a place of weekend flea markets and random rubbish tips. From 1907, the French police had strict orders to photograph gypsies and send details of their movements to a central Paris registry.

Born in Liverchies, Belgium, on 23 January 1910, the boy Jean-Baptiste Reinhardt had shown an early flair for the banjo and guitar. Soon adopting the name Django, he became a fine gypsy fiddler, and from his recorded material it seems probable that his musical development began very early, perhaps when he was aged five or six. At that age, he would have been considered too young, his tender fingers too pliant, for the unforgiving steel of guitar strings. Stéphane told the UK music paper *Melody Maker*, 'One of his uncles was an expert on violins. Like Django, he was an illiterate man, but he used to be consulted by important dealers about the age and authenticity of valuable instruments.' Perhaps, as he watched his elder cousins with a child's hypnotised attention, Django was inquisitive enough to try the shorter, gentler gut strings of his uncle's violin, strumming it first as a ukulele, seeking confirmation of his instinct by testing the family faces for approval, weaving the open string notes into loops of rhythmic novelty. Recently, at the Samois Festival, I observed the unflinching bravado and almost blind confidence of very young Manouche players. Children as young as seven lunge at their guitars with a wild, unfettered panache. They are not all good musicians, but the confidence and fearlessness is astonishing and completely unknown in the dry world of academic music. Django's talent would have grown in a similar fertile climate.

In Paul Paviot's charming 1958 film *Django Reinhardt*, Django's son Babik is depicted engaged in the same wild exploration, improvising a motif on an adult guitar. He looks to his mother for comment. Caught 'accidentally' on film, this is a rare and wonderful example of the documentary quest for truth through observation. There is little recorded evidence of a child on the lonely

*See Jeremy Marre's television films entitled *Beats Of The Heart*, which carry two episodes covering the gypsy trail.

road to self-taught aurally based music learning. Stéphane and Django shared a common root in this mysterious experience.

Where their paths diverge is that Stéphane lived in an environment based on literacy. Ernesto Grappelli worked as a journalist and had given his son a book of *solfege*. He also encouraged Stéphane to read and write French, in his own highly cultured script. Through his walks with Professor Rougnon and his work in the cinema, Stéphane amalgamated ear training with the written tradition, a rich but self-confining resource, and his musical liberation came through his accidental discovery of jazz. He had to work harder than Django to be free, but like all great partnerships their difference was to be complementary.

Django's talent was always free from a written tradition. According to his friend and early biographer Charles Delaunay, Django had only one day at school in his life, and even that in the mobile school on wheels of Old Man Guillon, a formal, well-meaning teacher who visited gypsy fairs and tried to entice the Romany children to a world of literature. Django preferred to spend his afternoons in the company of street gangs and 'Apaches', sneaking into silent cinemas to watch the wild exploits of *The King Of The Indians*. Escaping the written discipline left Django's fertile imagination to grow wild, eccentric and unique. When marvelling at how he plays effortlessly across the barline, it's important to remember that he had never seen a barline in his life and was therefore free from that tyranny. When his musical pulse varies effectively from verse to chorus, it's because his is the pulse of a human heart, changing from minute to minute, not to a mechanical metronome. Django escaped the applied reason of musical literacy.

As the child grew up, Reinhardt's acknowledged father, Jean Vees, and his mother, La Laurence, recognised his musical talent. His mother – nicknamed 'Negros' for her classic raven-black hair and dark complexion – together with his brother, Joseph, encouraged contact with other musicians. Jean Vees himself worked in the noble tradition of the troubadour, a kind of musical clown, and played guitar and violin, but a catechism of music would be as strange to Django's parents as the concept of a shopping list.

A child learning music in this aural tradition faces unbelievable challenges in blissful innocence. Initially, Django would have observed other players, absorbing the aural and mechanical experience as a bewildering and magical alchemy. At this level of listening, all of the instruments in a group combine into one unfathomable but wonderful sound. The intriguing confections of wood and wire, skin and bone, weave spells of enchantment. Indeed, many of us live our whole lives in this state of naïve musical enjoyment. For a Stéphane or a Django, however, the focused and curious mind gradually manages to separate the individual voices, begins to understand their roles in the musical mix. For them, the bewildering, beguiling whole that is music for the casual listener starts to give up its secrets.

The next step is often the final stumble. Many children pick up a stringed instrument and never recover from the broken spell when, at their first tentative touch, the magic vanishes into thin air and all they get instead is a rude squeak or even a muted scuffle. At this critical point, we must assume that the young Django and Stéphane received some guidance or encouragement – after all, as string players, they first had to tune their instruments. Both geniuses used conventional tunings for their instruments, although Django's gypsy camp had no tuning forks or pianos as reference points and he probably turned to his father or brother for guidance. If a stringed instrument is nearly in tune, the gifted child can make a fine adjustment, hearing the slight discordance as a kind of subtle but physical pain and instinctively knowing how to resolve this. Gradually, they learn to make even the giant step to restringing an instrument from cold. At the advent of the 21st century, no super-computer has yet enough processing power to even contemplate this monumental task with any degree of listenable accuracy.

If Django or Stéphane were lucky, a friend would show them where to put their fingers to form a simple melody. This first step taken, the gifted soon realise that the notes of this tune can be used to form another. In a tutored academic environment, there would be talk of scales and the grammar of music. However, the ear-trained musician is here presented with the greatest challenge and the most potent freedom: with no learned professor to rap the errant knuckles, all notes, including those first shown, are available; there are no 'wrong' notes, no 'wrong' chords, no asymmetric rhythms. Indeed, any child with a modicum of talent struggles with the bewildering array of potential notes.

The genius, however, is fascinated by this new sound kaleidoscope. Indeed, like the visual toy, the musical genius plays with the crystalline aural landscape and until they have learned to understand it all, not in a scientific analytical way but swallowed whole. The most ironic experience for anyone trying to teach or even observe a musical natural is that they don't know how not to do what they do. This remains a profound and wonderful mystery.

Playing with that first three-quarter-sized fiddle or small guitar, a Django or a Stéphane wouldn't need to be told the power of an octave or the mesmerising quality of a minor second. They would immediately hear this, find a use for it and stretch its application. The mathematical 'rules' of music need not be explained; they hear them and break them, and that's when it becomes interesting for us as listeners.

In a 1944 edition of the French magazine *Sept Jours*, it was alleged that Django received his first guitar from his mother at the age of nine, and there are accounts of Django enchanting his listeners in that first year as a performer. Even at this age, then, Django knew how to charm an audience in the ramshackle Paris markets. The famous *bals musette* accordionist Guerino* is said to have taken him off the streets and given him some lessons and encouragement, an arrangement that lasted for six months, until Django escaped back to his gypsy encampment.

Meanwhile, a mile away in Montmartre, Stéphane was offered a job by a keen-eared busker after a few months of his own *auto-didacte* trial and error. In my own early days as a music teacher, I occasionally witnessed much lesser genius and found it both disarming and breathtaking. These talented children make up their own musical vocabulary, making the guitar throb in imitation of a horse's gallop, untroubled by the theoretical complexity of the rhythm, slapping violin strings on the fingerboard for comic and dramatic effect, innocently naïve of Italian terms like *pizzicato* and *spiccato*. Simply having creative fun…

From the very beginning of their musical careers, Django and Stéphane had this idiosyncratic and creative approach in common. Blessed with genius, they became inimitable, inventing their own styles and, because nobody will ever live in the same way, these styles are unrepeatable. Django, of course, was further set apart by his gypsy lifestyle, and he absorbed the art of living in the moment, drinking in full from today's promise – 'Yesterday an unwritten past; tomorrow we may be hungry.' It's a way of life far removed from the industrial world's need for systems and timetables.

Sensibly for his art Django neither understood nor cared for systems; for him the modern world was insane. Better just to sleep and play music. Stéphane remarked in 1954, 'He was very much a man of the present, living always on the spot. He was incapable of planning anything, even for the next day, because on the next day he would be in a different mood and feeling differently about what we had arranged to do.' For Django, a pocket watch would be nothing but an attractive ornament, a piece of amusing jewellery. In his young life, the only work that mattered was keeping horses alive and making something you could trade for food – tinkering, perhaps, or, even better,

*Django and Guerino would eventually record together in 1933. See 'Discography'.

crafting a tune. After all, what's time when you have no solid walls on which to hang a clock?

On 20 June 1928, at the age of 18, Django made his first recordings, for the Gramophone Company. Most amusing of the four sides recorded is the banjo accompaniment to a whistle or musical-saw solo on the track 'Griserie',* on which Django provides a very appropriate, even tasteful improvised obbligato, while on 'Parisette' his youthful enthusiasm gets the better of him and he overplays, his too-busy performing getting him pushed away from the microphone. Some of these early takes are pre-electric, and the white coated engineers are clearly doing battle with the problems of recording the percussive transient power of xylophones and banjos, guaranteed to make the cutting needle jump out of its groove.

Reinhardt is variously credited as 'Jiango Renard', 'Jeangot' and eventually as 'Django' on these recordings, and in his early discography Charles Delaunay identifies 16 records featuring Django released in 1928. On these 78rpm recordings, Django plays a supportive role to the singer Chaumel and accordionists Jean Vaissade and Maurice Alexander. There is even a trio featuring xylophonist Francesco Cariolato, with colourful castanets, for 'Amour de Gitane', on which the sound is clearly that of the comic vaudeville, and the musical saw probably fitted perfectly between the clown acts and bird impersonators. Even if Django was a virtuoso, these settings present little opportunity for that to become apparent.

Django was familiar to these *bals musette* players from his nocturnal adventures at Le Bal des Auvergnats. These disreputable, working-class music halls near the Porte de Clingancourt and the Porte d'Italie were the haunts of gamblers and prostitutes. However, they also featured the same musicians of the Auvergne tradition that Stéphane knew and imitated in Grégor's vaudeville parody. By now, however, the vielle and the cabrolette bagpipe had given way to the ubiquitous accordion, which was easier to play, loud and versatile.

A few years earlier, Django had won a prize for his performances amongst these seasoned traditional players. Although obviously talented, he was

---

*In 'Griserie', the musical saw may feature instead of a slide whistle. At this time, there were several virtuoso saw players operating in Paris, one of whom wrote a concerto. On playing the piece to modern-day saw exponent John 'The Professor' Percival, he was at first convinced that it was a saw and was then confused by two staccato notes very difficult to achieve on the instrument.

The saw/whistle debate remains a mysterious sore point. The whistle was, of course, very popular at the time. Even Louis Armstrong played one on his early Hot Five recordings, serving as a further reminder of the lack of division between jazz musician and entertainer – Louis played music halls. Meanwhile, Adrian Rollini, with Eddie Lang's Hot Five, played 'hot fountain pen'!

considered audacious to play the strange, foreign music he was picking up by eavesdropping in Pigalle, where he'd heard the likes of Billy Arnold's band playing at the Abbaye de Thélème. Already, he was experimenting with American jazz hits such as 'Dinah'.

In fact, Django is out of place in these late-1920s recordings. Indeed, he must have driven the other musicians mad. He is often pushing the beat, trying to swing in the new jazz style. This is particularly marked on 'The Sheikh Of Araby' and 'Au Pays de l'Hindoustan', released in the autumn of 1928. Almost everyone else on the recording plods along, mostly in the familiar *um-cha* rhythm of the comic quickstep. On 'Moi Aussi', the vocal whistler sounds like the typical '20s crooner, but Django is wildly experimental, providing a syncopated counterpoint, almost as if he'd been exposed to bluegrass music. But how was that possible in late-1920s Paris? Had he heard Paul Whiteman's rhythm section at the Ambassador? Clearly, 'Jiango' was already dreaming of New Orleans.

On these first recordings, Django plays an instrument credited as 'banjo', which is in fact a banjo-guitar given to him in 1922 by a man called Raclot, who occupied a neighbouring caravan. This odd instrument has a banjo shape and construction but a guitar's six strings and tuning. A guitarist can pick up a banjo-guitar and instantly play it, though the tone colour is instantly banjo-esque. The instrument's sound has a rapid decay, which lends itself to a percussive, driving attack. Django would never forget the power of a short phrase cutting across the prevailing rhythm, as demonstrated here.

At this time, the banjo was the more popular fretted instrument and many guitarists would claim to be banjoists, if that was what the customer wanted. Many photographs and recordings of late-1920s jazz bands feature one or even two banjos. Louis Armstrong's banjoist Johnny St Syr played a six-string hybrid just like Django's, although how Raclot acquired his in Paris during the 1920s is another mystery. In that city, the guitar had a place as a parlour instrument for ladies, an embryonic place in the visiting Gitanos' flamenco and as an accompaniment to Neapolitan ballads. But in 1928, the guitar's rise to becoming the most popular musical instrument ever was inconceivable; indeed, as late as 1933, when the pioneering English guitarist Bert Weedon began playing, people would stop him in the street and ask what his strange instrument was. Ironically, he said it was a bit like a banjo, an instrument they recognised.

Although a guitarist in technique, Django probably enjoyed the banjo-guitar's piercing mid-range loudness. At those early recording sessions for Ideal and the Gramophone Company at Cité Chaptal, the engineers and arrangers were taken aback at Django's projection, sometimes drowning his fellow musicians. Indeed, in his ensuing career Django favoured volume, opting for Maccaferri and Selmer guitars,* both designed by the Italian classical guitarist Mario Maccaferri. Mario's commission was to supply Selmer – one of the world's biggest manufacturers of musical instruments – with a loud instrument for the growing jazz market. The new jazz orchestras were dominated by Selmer's own brass instruments and saxophones, which could easily drown out the acoustic rhythm sections. Maccaferri responded by producing a guitar built to focus on the ear's sensitive mid-range, an instrument famous to this day for its strident tone. These large-bodied guitars, with their single cutaways enabling access to high-octave fretting, are ideal for acoustic-jazz soloing and have become a potent symbol of what we now know as 'gypsy jazz'.

Of course, Django would eventually adopt the electric guitar, which he would amplify to the point of distortion. Photographs of Django in the recording studio always show him edging closer to the microphone, with a soloist's urge to be heard. He seems to be an early developer of that prima-donna tendency of 'I'm not playing if I'm not the loudest and the complete focus of attention'. Every band has one. However, he was discriminating; if other players were his equal, he would give them space and even enhance their solos.

It's worth saying that, despite the scant evidence of the 1928 recordings,[†] Django was already receiving offers of work from distinguished foreign artists. The foremost British bandleader Jack Hylton is supposed to have been considering him for the guitar seat in his well-established band. Hylton's outfit, although dance-band tame rather than raucous jazz, was deservedly famed for its wonderful section ensemble, and on the basis of recorded evidence it was arguably superior to some American bands. With Ted Heath on trombone, Hylton also had a firm recording contract with an important record label. Even the American saxophone innovator Coleman Hawkins would eventually respond to Jack's call.

Tempted or not, Django was already an enigma; even when he was billed to perform, Hylton would expectantly turn up at the venue and consistently discover a depping 'cousin'.

---

*In 1932, Django experimented briefly with a guitar by the Spanish maker Julian Gomez Ramirez. This unusual instrument is steel-strung and of an experimental shape (see 'Appendix'), originally built for Django's cousin Ferret, and can be seen in a photo from 1932 of La Boîte à Matelot's Orchestra Guerino. Ramirez was originally from Madrid, but his connection with the great Ramirez family of luthiers is in question.

[†] There are still some recordings unaccounted for in Django's early discography, notably 'Sur La Place d'Opéra'/'E Viva La Carmencita' (Henry 962, probably 1926), on which he accompanies the singer Chaumel.

★

By 1928, Django had taken a wife, the Parisienne Florine Mayer. Although both were only 18, this was not unusual in his Romany world. In the Manouche custom, they would have 'jumped the broomstick' as a gesture of their love, cutting their wrists and binding them to intermingle their blood. Bride and groom might also have sworn an oath 'to leave the other once love has ceased'. With no written tradition, common law was the only law. To finance his lifestyle and love of fine clothes, Django continued his work in the *bals musettes* and the tiny cellar clubs of Paris.

To raise extra cash, his child bride experimented with the traditional craft industry pursuits of the Romany. The newly invented celluloid, one of the fascinating new 'plastics', appealed to her. The material must have seemed perfect for the manufacture of attractive and saleable artificial flowers. How and where she acquired this modern and potentially lethal product is unclear, but, unable to read of the dangers of highly flammable materials, she set about hand-making dozens of semi-transparent blooms and selling them at the nearby cemetery.*

In legend, on the evening of 2 November 1928, returning late from an engagement at the Java club in Rue de Faubourg du Temple, Django found the caravan dark and filled with exotic flowers. Hearing a rustling within the surreal mound, he lit a candle to see if a visiting mouse was consuming their merchandise. The celluloid burst into flames.

The resulting conflagration was disastrous. The wooden caravan became an inferno. Trapped by smoke, robbed of oxygen and inhaling noxious fumes, Django was barely conscious as he narrowly escaped a hideous death, using a blanket to shield his face from the incendiary cocktail of wood and celluloid. His wife lost much of her hair in the blaze, but Django was in a more critical state. The full extent of his injuries was only realised after an emergency dash to the Hôpital Laribrosière, where the nuns found him extensively burned, predominantly on his left side, from knee to waist. He was admitted to the surgical Nelaton Ward. The surgeons, horrified by this early example of wounds from a high-temperature chemical blaze, discussed amputation of his left leg, but worst of all for the musician was the fact that his left hand, clutching the protective blanket, was horribly inflamed and twisted.

Django denounced his wife at the hospital, declaring himself unmarried. Florine was admitted to Gosselin, another surgical ward, where she remained until 16 November.

---

*An intriguing possibility is that the celluloid was actually scrap motion-film stock. The Manouche *Rosette* reports her family touring and taking silent film shows to remote villages at this time. Nitrate film stock is so highly inflammable that it's illegal in many countries.

The talk of amputation terrified the family. The Romany lifestyle relied on able-bodied men. There is little scope on the road for a cripple, and the world of the 1920s had no concept of special needs beyond the life of a beggar. In legend, and as told to Charles Delaunay, Django was physically abducted from the hospital by his clan and later admitted to a nursing home at Rue d'Alesia.

In fact, on 2 November, Django had already been in hospital for six days! The meticulously kept records of the Hôpital Laribroisière clearly indicate both patient admissions, Django and Florine consecutively, on 26 October. The only explanation for this is that the tragic fire occurred on that date, not 2 November. A note in the surgical records, underlined in red, denotes 'affaires judiciare' (suspicious circumstances), and the police were probably routinely involved, as might be expected in the case of a serious fire. Far from being smuggled out by his clan, however, Django remained in the care of the nuns until 22 November, his denounced wife leaving a week earlier. In a further complication, Django later told Stéphane that his own cigarette had caused the ignition of the celluloid.

Whatever the precise circumstances of the fire and Django's nursing, the physical incapacitation persisted for 18 months, costing Django's father-in-law a small fortune in medical attention. Despite that well-meant family intervention, the trauma no doubt contributed to the complete collapse of Django's common-law marriage, and the shock that the teenage guitarist suffered is hard to imagine. He would always thereafter have difficulty in moving around, and he would also be mentally inhibited by the terrible scars his body suffered – the wounded left hand was grotesque, and in photographs Django is often seen with it concealed in a pocket. His instinctive therapy was to immerse himself once more in music.

Again, there is the mystery of genius. The prospect of picking up the guitar again would elude any normal psyche, but in a process close to a miracle this unworldly youth set about reinventing the guitar's left-hand technique. In a two-year convalescence, Django constructed a new method for the instrument. His first and second fingers were largely undamaged, so he strengthened these to the point at which he achieved a tone and controlled vibrato unequalled before or since. Furthermore, he developed a speed and dexterity that earned him a reputation rivalled only by players of the much shorter scale violin.

With Django's new technique, 90 per cent of his effort was given to the phrasing of single-line melody, freeing him from the acoustic guitar's tendency to chordal accompaniment. Most conventional harmonic requirements, he decided, could be delegated to his brother and cousins. Instead, he employed chords on his guitar purely for dramatic effect. In a strange irony, it proved easier for Django's distorted and paralysed third and fourth fingers to play exotic jazz ninth chords than the more prosaic common triads of the *bals musette*.

The contortion of Django's hand lent itself to the relatively unexplored use of harmonic parallelism. Locking his semi-paralysed hand into one fixed shape on the fingerboard, he would move that shape up and down in legato cascades of kaleidoscopic harmony. This effect was further enhanced by the use of open strings in conjunction with stopped strings, a convention borrowed from the flamenco style of the Gitanos. At the time, this device was so seductive and new, breaking all the rules of conventional harmony, that he probably inspired Paris-based Brazilian composer Heitor Villa-Lobos* to write some of the greatest music ever written for classical guitar. Django would have failed a Grade 1 harmony exam, but instead he started a revolution. Every jazz guitarist in the future would assimilate this device.

Django tested his new technique by busking in the area around the Bal Tabarin, on the corner of Pigalle and Rue Victor Masse – the meeting place for musicians looking for work. Knowing the area and making his own luck, he was heard by Stéphane Grappelly's friend and fellow jazz enthusiast Stéphane Mougin. This led to an immediate engagement at Les Acacias, where at last Django got to play a kind of neo-jazz.

Was he prepared? Django had been fortunate during his convalescence in meeting the great French photographer Emile Savitry, a bohemian of Paris's other great artistic ghetto, Montparnasse. Through him, Django met painters and poets and was regaled with stories of the photographer's adventures in the South Seas and beyond. Most importantly, Savitry possessed a gramophone and an eclectic mix of recordings – discs of Maori choirs, Bach toccatas and fugues and, imperatively, the jazz of Louis Armstrong, which thrilled Django.

It's important to remember that, to Django, all this music was new and uncharted territory. All music came to him as pure unfettered sound. As an illiterate, he was unencumbered with the idiotic literary snobbery that divides music into apartheid ghettos; Django borrowed from everything, like a child given a free hand in a sweet shop.

By 1931, Django had risen from the proverbial ashes, his guitar spouting

---

*Reports of an encounter between Django and Villa-Lobos remain unconfirmed, but the evidence of the latter's guitar preludes and studies is very compelling. According to guitar expert Brendan McCormack, Django's 'Improvisation No 2' of 1938, particularly, exhibits shades of Villa-Lobos's 'Study No 7' of 1929, while the cadenza for the Brazilan's *Guitar Concerto* of 1951 has the flavour of Django's 'Improvisation No 1'. They may both, of course, have learned their parallelism from Debussy.

a new demonic fire that left both musicians and audience dazzled and bewildered. In that year's recordings with Lois Vola And His Orchestra du Lido da Toulon, it's possible to hear his struggle to swing against an orchestra with leaden feet. Having been exposed to Louis Armstrong and Duke Ellington, Django is clearly desperate to move on.

Of particular interest in the Vola recording is the violin of Jules Pouzalgues. Straight as a dye, this is the violin of the Victorian palm-court orchestra – you can almost hear the chef d'orchestre's threat: 'Syncopators will be prosecuted.' Django liked to work with acoustic stringed instruments that did not drown his guitar, but he had to find players sympathetic to his new jazz sensibilities. In the Paris of 1931, he must have doubted that such a person existed.

8 La Croix Du Sud

'Standing at the crossroads, tried to flag a ride.'

– Robert Johnson

In 1931, five years before the celebrated bluesman Robert Johnson recorded his famous anthem 'Crossroads', Stéphane Grappelly unwittingly came to a career junction of his own. Another of his *étrangers providentiel* sought him out on his tiny podium at the club La Croix du Sud at 3 Boulevard du Montparnasse: 'I was going from one place to another when I was playing at La Croix du Sud. I was engaged there by a good friend of mine, Alain Romans, the pianist. I was approached by a gentleman, dark, brown, dressed like a gangster. I was a little afraid. He said, "Monsieur Drappelli?"

'I said, "Oui."

'He said, "I would like to talk to you about music."

'I said, "Why not?"

'He told me he lived in one of those gypsy caravans and I said I was curious to see that, so we arranged a time – a Sunday, I think. I went and he was there with a lot of gypsy people.'

The present site of 'the Cross of the South' is a mass of undistinguished concrete. Nobody in this redeveloped urban wilderness had heard of a little cabaret club of 1931, yet this was once the meeting place of Jean Cocteau and Jacques Tati, as well as the eccentric painter Willem de Kooning, whom Stéphane recalls turning up barefoot in shorts. Jazz had flourished in this bohemian den from as early as 1918, when Alain Romans had been its first pianist. In the '20s, Stéphane recalled the Prince of Wales prophetically doing one of his drum solos on 'Putting All My Eggs In One Basket', when many thought he might make be better sticking to his day job.

This forgotten dive is the site of probably the most important event in European jazz, the meeting of Django Reinhardt and Stéphane Grappelly. For Stéphane, it was a major turning point: 'My life started when I met Django... Before him, I was a musician playing here, playing there, but I realised when

I was with Django, we can produce something not ordinary.' Venturing to the gates of Paris in 1931 at Reinhardt's invitation, Stéphane met Negros, Django's mother, and Naguine, his new wife. Stéphane was stunned by the casual vibrancy of the nomad lifestyle: 'After we had lunch, we played some music. Everybody bring some food, some drinks and all that, and afterwards I remember the weather was not so good, so I stayed and slept in one of those caravans. It was raining and it was very agreeable to sleep like that... We used to play all night, non-stop, in his *roulotte* and get a little bit drunk...playing for the sake of the music.'

Stéphane was 23 with all the ambition and zest of a young man who has seen a little of the big world and has a thirst for more. This crazy gypsy and his colourful entourage must have seemed shocking yet tantalising. Stéphane immediately recognised Django's potential as a musician, but he must have wondered how that could possibly square with the refined, dinner-jacketed world of the Ambassador club; even when he experimented with jazz at La Croix du Sud with Alain Romans and the rising saxophone star Andre Ekyan, they could – and occasionally did – fall back on the occasional tango. But the possibilities Django suggested were new and dangerous, and 1931 was a poor time for taking risks.

For Django's part, when you listen to the recordings of him playing the violin, you realise the respect he must have had for Stéphane. Django was a good fiddle player, gypsy in style, free and eloquent. 'Vous Et Moi',* recorded in Brussels in 1942, when Stéphane was out of reach, is one of only four recorded examples of his violin work, yet it is considered good enough to be included in a Disque d'Or compilation entitled *Violin Jazz*. Django told Stéphane at their first meeting 'that he once played the violin and liked violin music above all'.

Django's playing on this rare record is extraordinary. He first states the theme on his violin – the tone is assured, the intonation perfect and his audacious portamento slides perhaps in tribute to Stéphane. Despite his crippled fingers, he double-stops with confidence. He then picks up the theme on guitar, a jazz rhythm in double tempo, before closing with an *a tempo* return to the fiddle. There's no doubt concerning to whom the 'Vous Et Moi' refers.

This compilation album also features four tracks by 'Grappelly' and others by Sven Asmussen, Eddie South, Ray Nance, Stuff Smith, Joe Venuti, Michel Warlop and several others. In such distinguished violin company, Django is nevertheless amongst musical equals.

When he ventured to La Croix, looking for Stéphane, he had recognised

Violin Jazz (Fremaux & Associes, FA 052). See 'Discography'.

something special, somebody who had heard Joe Venuti, someone who understood the concept of swing. Django had already heard Venuti and Lang via the photographer Savitry, and he could hear possibilities in their music that he could use as his own. But the American duo had only just scratched the surface. With characteristic frankness, Django remarked to Stéphane, 'There is nothing to be learned from Lang.' Curiously, Eddie Lang was also another American-Italian, born Salvatore Masso in Philadelphia in October 1902. He was also an accomplished violinist and shared a schoolboy violin with Joe Venuti, his lifelong partner. For many musicians, his work marks the beginning of jazz guitar, and I'm sure that Django did learn something from him.

But Django clearly wasn't disappointed with what he'd heard of Stéphane. The many duo recordings they made together provide some sense of that historic Sunday when 'gypsy jazz', a whole new genre of music, was conceived.

In turn, Stéphane was clearly impressed by Django: 'He played the melody with just his first two fingers. That's why he had such a great sound, because they are the strongest. He was very strong anyway, and he somehow adapted his deformity so that he could do impossible things with those two fingers. He found his own way of playing chords, sometimes using his two crippled fingers as well, but only in a limited way – for example, adjacent to each other on the top two strings.' Despite the mutual admiration, however, that first jam session at the Port St Denis Romany camp was not a total or immediate success, the two musicians possibly feeling that their music was too revolutionary, a fascinating but dangerous hybrid.

There were many barriers to cross; other than simply playing, Stéphane and Django had no musical form of communication. Django couldn't read music, so even an elementary chord chart or notated melody was an unfathomable mystery. The pair could explore only those tunes that they both already knew or spend time teaching each other tunes. A jam session after lunch, surrounded by restless children, in a gypsy camp is not the ideal time to pursue the new musical idiom of 'jazz on strings'. It's doubtful whether either of them even talked in these terms; this was just an opportunity to kick around a few ideas. They probably resorted to familiar territory – perhaps a gypsy refrain from Django that Stéphane would assimilate and use as a source of improvisation.

The two men shared an admiration of Louis Armstrong, and Stéphane thought that he recalled playing a few choruses of 'Dinah', though he couldn't be sure. They were both familiar with Armstrong's hit of 1925, and certainly Stéphane had heard the Venuti/Lang version. Django had also acquired a copy of Armstrong's 1929 'Dallas Blues', which he'd found in a Paris flea market. There was evidently some common ground.

However, this was the first encounter of two great musicians, and when giants of this calibre come together they are prone to circle each other like rival tigers at a kill. Initially, they often try to compete, but this doesn't always result in great music – neither wants to give ground and play a supporting role; both are seeking dominance. The encounter between Django and Stéphane was a meeting of complementary equals, and it would have taken time and patience to establish an order of battle.

The pair parted with a vague notion of another jam the following week, but for some reason this didn't happen. Maybe Django, with his gentle philosophy, was caught up in his engrossing card games, or perhaps they both had engagements – a musician never turns down a paying gig.

Paris in 1931 was also suffering a terrible economic climate. At first, France had seemed to escape the effects of the Wall Street Crash of 1929, and the cultural capital of the world was still famed for its lavish parties. The fashion designer Jean Patou roofed over her garden, covered walls, ceilings and trees with silver foil and gave lion cubs to her guests as prizes. When General Motors closed, Renault had taken on most of its workforce and their competitors Citroën lit up Paris every night with 200,000 lightbulbs zigzagged around the Eiffel tower with 90 kilometres of wire – George Orwell's 'enormous snakes of fire'. But by 1931, the franc had lost four-fifths of its value and the War Minister, still reeling from France's losses from World War I, had spent seven billion on 150 miles of military defences, named for André Maginot. Unemployment had gone from 12,000 to 190,000 in one year as industrial production plummeted. Bankruptcy grew by 60 per cent and earnings halved.

An ocean away, in Winnipeg, Canada, on 27 May 1931, William Charles Disley was born. The family moved to Wales when he was four and eventually settled in Yorkshire, England. The young Disley soon developed a fascination for music.

In Paris, Stéphane and Django were having fortuitous meetings at recording sessions with potential musical collaborators. The Paris music scene in the early '30s was clearly a small circle – in June 1931 Louis Vola turned up playing the accordion on a session with Django on guitar. Vola was a versatile all-rounder who also played piano and drums, although most significantly he dabbled on the new jazz instrument: the bass viol. His reputation, however, was founded on his work with the famous music-hall band Ray Ventura Et Ses Collegians, rivals to Grégor.

The accordion was still the dominant force in French popular music in the 1930s, and a contemporary recording of Roger Chaput, playing banjo with his own orchestra, features Albert Carrara on the fox trot 'Je Ne Saurais Jamais Dire Ça'. Stéphane had met Chaput – who was one year his junior at Le Tabac, the musicians' networking spot – after the latter had left Montlucon to pursue a career on the Paris music scene. Stéphane chuckled as he remembered Roger's sense of humour and his amusing caricature sketches.

By this time, the depression was really biting – restaurants and clubs were closing and, according to one observer, even the pretty girls at Le Moulin Rouge were having to buy their own drinks. The musicians at Le Tabac started to look for richer pickings amongst the millionaires' playground of the Cote d'Azur.

In 1932, Louis Vola heard the Reinhardt brothers busking on a beach in Toulon and booked Django to play in his band at the Palm Beach Casino in Cannes. Mistrusting the devalued currency, the gypsy demanded payment in the form of jewellery for his mother. When Vola turned up at the venue, he discovered outside a line of gypsy caravans – the whole clan had turned up to hear their son. When money became even tighter, Louis and Django resorted to working as an accordion-and-guitar duo.

At around the same time, another young violinist, by the name of Yehudi Menuhin – already being revered as the new Paganini – was travelling from his home at Ville d'Avray, near Paris, crossing the English Channel to London for a recording session at the newly opened Gramophone Studios in Abbey Road, where Sir Edward Elgar conducted his violin concerto in its premier recording. This was soon considered to be one of the great recordings of the 20th century.

In March 1933, in the wholly different world of cabaret, Django was recording with yet another accordionist, the esteemed Guerino, as part of Son Orchestre Musette de la Boîte à Matelots. The outfit recorded a Neapolitan waltz. On these *musette* recordings, Django excels. Unlike his contemporaries, he is always in tune, and in his solos and introductions he already displays the precocious virtuosity of a caged tiger. In contrast, the anonymous violinist sounds very square, still clinging to the 19th century, with no notion of swing or a jazz syncopation.

A contemporary photograph shows Django with his Ramirez guitar surrounded by his fellow jolly Matelots. They are in the Matelots' club, aboard a fake barge emblazoned with the slogan 'A Girl In Every Port'. He is supported by the gypsy guitarist Pierre 'Barro' Ferret. Not much scope for jazz, perhaps, although by this time the Ferret dynasty of guitarists was developing a whole new hybrid of 'swing musette', blending jazz and musette. The guitar was replacing the banjo, providing a more subtle, lighter swing for the waltz. In fact, Django wrote some tunes in this style, but he was already looking for something much more audacious.

Also in March, Stéphane played violin and piano on a Grégor session with another bass-viol player and future quintet partner, Roger 'Toto' Grasset, recording such delights as 'Whispering' and 'Put On Your Grey Bonnet'. Then, in May, they reconvened for 'Music Hath Charms' and 'Daisy', while that December it was Stéphane's turn to take the hornpipe and tackle 'A Selection Of d'Air à Matelots' (parts 1 and 2)!

In January 1934, Grappelly (violin) and Reinhardt (guitar) featured on their first recorded outing together, with the bassist again being Roger Grasset. But this wasn't the groundbreaking session they dreamt of, simply more bread and butter for jobbing melody makers. On this recording, Django does contribute a bluesy, almost Lonnie Johnson-style* solo to 'The Day You Came Along', providing a smooth melody line that would have been impossible on the banjo, with its rapid percussive decay. However, the crooner Jean Sablon is the star vocalist here. The session even produced a minor hit, 'Prenez Garde Au Mechant Loup' ('Who's Afraid Of The Big Bad Wolf?'), for which Stéphane provides a melodic obbligato. A third, unreleased track, 'Pas Sur La Bouche', has Django frenetically overplaying behind an unremitting barrage of *oom-pah* brass. As often happens, musical history is not always synonymous with great music.

Ironically, or perhaps as intentional light relief, these comedy records emerged during a crisis. The economic situation had worsened, alongside a more general social dissatisfaction. At this time, French women still couldn't vote or get passports without their husbands' permission and a public phone call typically took three hours to connect. The police relied on torture and persecution as corrupt politicians carried on expensive *amitiés amoureuses* with *les célèbre horizontales*. The French Judiciary still carried the ultimate sanction of Madame Guillotine, complete with horse-drawn lanternlit tumbrils for the hapless accused. Students rioted in Paris and taxpayers took to the streets of Burgundy, Normandy and Languedoc.

The crisis came to a head on 4 February in the Place de la Concorde. Political argument in the Chamber of Deputies had resulted in physical violence and a

---

*It's possible that Django had by this time heard Eddie Lang working with Lonnie Johnson on their duet outings of 1928/9, as these may have found their way into Savitry's collection.

suspended sitting. The enormous amphitheatre of the Concorde, the setting for the guillotining of Louis XVI, was soon filled with a diverse mob of disaffected citizens, from communists to disillusioned war veterans. At dusk, stone-throwing was met with cavalry charges with bared sabres. The rioters responded with improvised javelins and the razor-slashing of horses' bellies. Soon a smoke-filled square rang with gunfire and the Marine Ministry was set ablaze. The violence spread and ultimately 2,000 people were injured, 15 fatally, in France's worst civil violence since 1871. The third Republic seemed doomed.

Fortuitously for Stéphane and his new friends, in times of crisis ordinary people seek solace in escapism, often in the form of music and dancing, wine and song, and for those who couldn't afford a band, the new-fangled gramophone would suffice. In February and March 1934, Stéphane and Django recorded amongst a gathering of fellow jazz aspirants including Alix Combelle on tenor sax, Andre Ekyan on clarinet and Roger 'Toto' Grasset on bass. Stéphane appeared on piano, and significantly the orchestra was billed as 'The Michel Warlop Orchestra'. But this was horn-based music with a vocal refrain, and the duo played a supporting role. The band also had a drummer – never a good sign when you're struggling with acoustic strings, and this was an age before sophisticated amplification levelled the dynamics of the musical platform. Only later in the 20th century would a successful blending of drums, violin and acoustic guitar become a possibility.

It's worth noting that there were many other violinists in the popular-music field in Paris at this time. The Michel Warlop Orchestra was fronted by Stéphane's friend and probable rival. Born in Douai, France, Warlop was Stéphane's junior by three years but had been heralded as a classically trained infant prodigy, with all the baggage that carried. His technique was good enough for Michel to record a classical record in 1934 as Waclaw Niemczyk,* accompanied by Leon Kartun.

Like Stéphane, Michel also played piano and violin for Grégor, and Warlop would always remain in awe of Stéphane's freedom and invention. In turn, Stéphane envied Michel's awesome technique. The latter's 1935 recording of 'Strange Harmony' is a blues accompanied by Django's 'cousins' Jean Matlo and Etienne Savanne Ferret. (Django was already flouting tradition by working occasionally with these Gitanes rather than Manouche gypsies. Django had set

*Foreign-sounding pseudonyms were commonplace and were thought to impart mystery and glamour. In Warlop's case, there was also grounds for separating 'respectable' work from 'hot jazz'. As late as 1946, the great classical guitarist Julian Bream, then aged 13, was almost launched as 'Yuri Leschenko'.

his heart on the new American music and just wanted to work with the best, whatever background they happened to be from.) This track is particularly helpful in trying to understand Django's choice in approaching Stéphane at La Croix. Although Warlop obviously understood the blues in theory, grasping its form and pentatonic base, he had clearly never lived it. His technique is impeccable, however – he could surely play Paganini. On 'Harmonique', a later track, he demonstrates a mastery of harmonics that Stéphane never even attempted.

Most telling, however, is 'Christmas Swing', a track with Django. Here, Warlop sounds like he's being auditioned, and given that Stéphane often told Django what he thought of his unpredictability, perhaps he felt he was. Michel plays his socks off, initially sounding thrilled by Django's invention and drive, although unfortunately the violin soon sounds rehearsed; there is little here to approach Stéphane's genuine spontaneity or wit. As Warlop plays more and more choruses, the invention runs out and the prepared licks are spent.

Most importantly, the listener becomes aware of the barlines, those ridiculous barriers that so many aspirant jazzers can never forget. When a musician is brought up reading music, it's almost impossible to forget that barlines are an artificial device imposed to help readability. In the real world, sound has no such restriction. Playing across the barlines, a pre-requisite of swing, comes easiest to those musicians who have never been subjected to notational mathematics. As Ellington famously put it, 'It don't mean a thing if it ain't got that swing.'

Interestingly, in the same year Django tried a duet session with the visiting American fiddler Eddie South. On 'Eddie's Blues' there is little room for Django. Reduced to a powerful rhythmic player, the Manouche wizard would have undoubtedly been uncomfortable spending any length of time sharing a spotlight with a natural bluesman like Eddie.

When Django discovered Stéphane, he found a perfect match for his abilities and talents. Paris now had all the ingredients for something new, but it needed a catalyst, a focus, to pull these diverse and eccentric characters together.

Until 1933, Stéphane was still providing violin duties for Grégor et ses Grégoriens, and increasingly his own distinctive style emerged. On returning to the recording of 'Fit As A Fiddle' and that startling first entry of Stéphane's violin, the accompaniment and the ensemble intro are a gentle plod – the band are a relic of the '20s. When Stéphane enters, though, what's instantly recognisable is the influence of the current Louis Armstrong – the newly emerged trumpet player, not the vintage cornetist. The ear is drawn to the syncopation and the phrasing, a true rubato, the give-and-take with time that is essential to swing. As Nigel Kennedy described Stéphane's playing in the 1990s, it was a case of 'pushing and pulling, stretching out like a vocalist – comes in really early, finishes really late'.

Somehow, at the age of 25, Stéphane had found his voice. Now with his access to a gramophone, he continued to explore the still-rare American recordings that were nevertheless slowly becoming more common in Paris.* Inevitably, these would have been a sporadic and mixed bag, and this is reflected in the often-bizarre repertoire that the French musicians of the time chose to record. As a pianist, Stéphane was enthralled by the improvised counterpoint and daring rhythmic playfulness of the early Fats Waller records he heard. Grégor recognised this same versatility in Stéphane's playing, which meant that he would keep swapping his violin stool with Michel Warlop.

Through Django, and probably through hearing other Hungarian rather than Manouche players, Stéphane was also influenced by the Romany fiddle – for instance, his use of exaggerated portamento, daring octave swoops and open harmonics. However, he absorbed influences – some gypsy, some Joe Venuti, some Heifetz, perhaps even some young Menuhin – and made them his own.

The best insight into Stéphane's absorption of the gypsy style is illustrated in the later feature film *King Of The Gypsies*. Playing David Grisman's music for the opening sequence, Stéphane consciously imitates the gypsy style, deliberately accenting things that today's listeners are so used to hearing within the unmistakable Grappelli voice. He does this for effect, and it works – Stéphane could summon his influences at will. Indeed, what is now called 'gypsy jazz' started with Stéphane and Django. Their collective and unique genius became the catalyst to the integration of these 'new' materials as they all converged at the troubled crossroads that was 1930s Paris.

---

*The importance of the gramophone to the spread of jazz cannot be overestimated, and not just that found outside America. Louis Armstrong's Hot Five played live in public on only two occasions, and both of these were promotional appearances for the record companies.

9 Le Jazz Hot

'He is hot from head to foot. He just cannot be anything but hot.'*
– Hughes Panassié

Le Hot Club de France had been created in 1932 at the suggestion of some jazz-crazed students. Initially, the enthusiasts had approached Hughes Panassié and Jacques Bureau, the already-established publishers of the magazine *Jazz Tango Dancing*. These hopefuls were not so much interested in a periodical as in establishing a society that could promote more jazz dances and concerts.

The publishers were devoted jazz enthusiasts and appointed a secretary, the student and amateur drummer Pierre Nourry. Panassié took on the role of President of the new society, which organised its first live event on 1 February 1933 with Garland Wilson and Freddy Johnson. Later in 1933, Nourry asked Django to headline a concert, although nothing came of this until February 1934, when Reinhardt depped at the last minute for three star trumpeters who didn't show up. The irony of that incident can only prompt an astonished *sacre bleu!* There was even a good write-up in *Jazz Tango Dancing*.

Emboldened by this early success, the organisation wanted a resident band to sustain interest in the new 'hot' jazz. To this end, pianist Freddy Johnson quickly put together an outfit known as The Harlemites, and this led to several inspired jam sessions with visiting black Americans. However, Freddy soon departed for America and Pierre Nourry began the search for a home-grown replacement. When the house *Tango* band were taking a break there were rumours of jazz jam sessions at Claridges, on the Champs-Elysées, and Nourry set out to locate the elusive guitarist Django Reinhardt, who was said to be involved.

*The term *hot* in relation to jazz was by 1932 in common parlance. It probably found popularity after being enshrined by Louis Armstrong with his 1920s Hot Fives, but it had been used in as early as 1886 in Theodore Metz's 'Hot Time In The Old Town Tonight' and in 1914 for 'Hot House Rag'. It discriminated 'hot' jazz from 'sweet' dance-band music. The first memory Stéphane has of live jazz is hearing 'Hot Lips' in the 1920s.

The French took to the term more than anyone else, and in 1935 *Jazz Hot* magazine carried an advertisement for a five-lesson correspondence course inviting readers to learn 'le hot' - results guaranteed at a moderate price.

1934 was to became a dramatic year for the fledgling Hot Club. Louis Armstrong, the uncrowned king of the hottest jazz, arrived in Paris and stayed for six months. Ostensibly on holiday, he nevertheless turned up everywhere that was blowing a tune, even re-recording 'St Louis Blues' with a pick-up band of French and Caribbean musicians. He reluctantly auditioned Django in his Hotel room but wasn't impressed. Django was reportedly in shock.

Hughes Panassié also caused a stir with the publication of his book *Le Jazz Hot*, the first work to treat jazz as serious music and, astonishingly, coming from France. The distinguished American record producer and promoter John Hammond wrote, '*Le Jazz Hot* is marvellous from start to finish. [Panassié's] taste is always of the best and the details and definitions in the book make it by far the most important single event that has ever befallen swing music. I know of hundreds of musicians who are just clamouring for this book [in the US].'

Panassié was born in southwest France in 1918 the son of an aristocratic French family who had made their wealth in Russia before the revolution. He died in 1974, but his son Patrice can now be found in Cyprus, where his family run a small business. Patrice recalled happy days at their château near Fontainebleau when his father regularly entertained jazz royalty: 'Louis Armstrong came to the château when I was just a small boy. He did incredible things musically with just the trumpet mouthpiece, and he always had the best room in the château. He gave me a silver dollar from his birthdate of 1901. Sidney Bechet gave me a signed engraved fountain pen.' On the subject of his father's early advocacy for jazz, Patrice explained, 'At the age of 14, in 1926, my father had contracted polio, which was in those days usually fatal. He survived but was physically weakened by the disease. His father bought him a saxophone as a form of therapy and he had lessons in Paris with Christian Wagner. The saxophone was his compensation for not being able to run. In 1929 he also had lessons with Milton Mezzrow – or, as he was known then, Mesirow [a Georgian born in Chicago in 1899]. This was his introduction to jazz.' Mezzrow had learned sax in jail in 1917, and by 1923 was a professional who couldn't work in France for lack of a foreign work permit. 'My father bought Milton's sax, a Martin, enabling the player to buy a professional Selmer. Later, when he came back to France, we travelled in Milton's Lincoln car, which was very flash for the time.'

Hughes Panassié's passion for jazz eventually led to him amassing a collection of 13,000 records, all carefully catalogued. His writings received a warm reception by the predominantly white jazz critics, but for some he leaned too heavily on the white musician's role in jazz. There may have been some connection between

Panassié's advocacy of Django and Armstrong's rejection of the guitarist. Although the controversy over the black-musicians-versus-white-musicians issue was less important in Paris, it was nevertheless present there. However, controversy works as publicity, and there is, of course, no such thing as bad publicity. In 1934, Paris became the undisputed jazz capital of Europe.

Another Frenchman, the drummer* and aspirant record producer Charles Delaunay, wanted to start a magazine in the hot capital to replace Grégor's defunct *La Revue du Jazz* and extend the jazz ambitions of *Jazz Tango Dancing*. However, that would have to wait for now, as he had seen potential in a young band. The idea was to combine the credibility of black American vocalist Bert Marshall with the emerging French stars of the Hôtel Claridges jam sessions. Delaunay made his first recording attempts in a Rue Albert studio in September 1934 with a band he dubbed Delaunay's Jazz.

The itinerant jam band comprised Django on guitar, Stéphane on fiddle, Lois Vola now on bass and the rhythm guitars of Roger Chaput and Joseph Reinhardt. This was a trial recording with no record contract signed and comprised 'I Saw Stars' and 'Confessin''. These quaint pop songs leave Marshall sounding as if he's just put down his megaphone. There is something there, but hot it is not. This simple demo does, however, contain all the ingredients for the creation of jazz history.

The genesis of The Hot Club Quintet, the most famous line-up in the history of European jazz, is a mixture of mythical legend, film fantasy and a soupçon of actual magic.

Hôtel Claridges on the Champs-Elysées was a good engagement in 1933. Stéphane had been booked there by Louis Vola for a tea dance with a 14-piece band. Louis Vola, born in 1902 in the Riviera town of La Seyne Sur Mer, was already a veteran of music-hall bands such as Ray Ventura's. With all his experience, he was able to work as a fixer, providing musicians with a range of venues and recordings.

The Claridges band had a front line of three saxophones, played by Alix Combelle, 'Coco' Kiehn and Max Blanc, supplemented by Alex Renard on trumpet and the two 'respectable' violins of Sylvio Schmidt and Stéphane, while an unusual rhythm section featured two pianos, played by Marcel Raymond and Pierre Dorsey, as well as the bass of Francis Luca and 'Lofty' Gaby Bart on trap-drum set. Django was also there on guitar, when he turned up. Otherwise, Roger Chaput or Joseph Reinhardt would substitute. Out front were Bert Marshall and Vola himself, who might wave a baton.

*Delaunay turns up as late as 1940 playing drums for Django on 'Panassié Stomp'. Django apparently fell about laughing at the writer's stickwork during the session.

The grand line-up alternated with a smaller unit specialising in the risqué tango, still all the rage amongst the Claridges smart set. Stéphane takes up the story as the main band takes a break and he attends to running repairs: 'Django was waiting for half an hour in an armchair – because he didn't like to move too much – smoking a cigarette. One day…I broke a string and I didn't want to repair that in front of everybody, so I went behind. When I start to tune up, Django took some chords. That's how we started.'

As Stéphane later pointed out to the guitarist John Etheridge, the tune 'Daphne' actually sprang from the violin's tuning notes, which Django took up as a theme. He expanded the story for Peter Anick in *Fiddler* magazine: 'When I was tuning up with the harmonics, I do the harmonics to see if the violin was in tune, and that was enough material to build something… Django used to improvise…but I was there to put it down when we found something…sometimes out of the blue. We got something we develop it, and then I write. We never prepared anything, because when you prepare something, it's not very good; it's not very natural. The difficulty, when you get an idea, is to remember, because it's like a bird – when you open its cage, he goes out and you don't see him. Improvisation is like that – the moment you want to write it down, it's already forgotten. Daphne was a friend of mine.'

In another version of the story, Stéphane told Charles Delaunay that the first tune was 'Dinah': 'Django used to get behind a screen… He'd retreat into a corner and leave the communication of his thoughts to his guitar. Sometimes he would pluck the strings as his fancy took him; at others he would lean on his instrument and stare thoughtfully into space, through an open window, with that melancholic look of his. I still didn't know him very well. Sometimes I'd sit down at his side to listen to him. One day, to amuse myself, I picked up my violin and started to play with him. He asked me to play a little riff that he'd just put together. The effect pleased both of us and we went on to play some more tunes. The next day, we waited impatiently for the intermission so that we could go and play backstage again. It was 'Dinah' we played, I can remember quite clearly. We went on and on! Maybe we played for half an hour or so. Roger Chaput, an artist if ever there was one, soon hastened to join us, followed by friend Vola – inquisitive as a caretaker – who had gone off to fetch his bass.' A single snapshot of this band with Bert Marshall still survives, taken, legend has it, during that backstage moment.

Stéphane's first account, has a charming echo in the film publicity 'short' *Le Jazz Hot*, made by the quintet a few years later.* After the film's outrageous

*Probably in April/May 1938, although a production company for the origination of this film has not been identified.

start, in which an American announcer (who must have sounded patronising to people even then) provides the facts of the 'jazz-hot revolution', an orchestra and modern grand piano chime in, possibly the Claridges band, playing Handel's famous 'Largo', 'daring not to change a single note of the composer's divine intention'.*

There then follows a set of musical impressions: Louis Armstrong, Jack Teagarden and Benny Goodman. Then they attempt to jazz up a tune, though rather unconvincingly.

Next we hear 'J'Attendrai', in its tea-dance version. Finally we see Django and Stéphane backstage and looking deeply cool, Django with his cigarette, lounging in an armchair, his feet resting on an art-deco wireless. Stéphane tentatively plays a snatch of 'J'Attendrai', Django takes a few of his famous parallel chords, and meanwhile the band – looking exactly like gangsters, with American trilbys and sharp suits – play poker in a waft of *film noir* smoke. The band act impressed, as far as musicians can be expected to act, and we cut to the chase.

This performance of 'J'Attendrai' is the first and only known synchronised-sound clip of Le Quintet du Hot Club de France, and they play in an inimitable and unmistakable style. For the first chorus, Stéphane – the 'posh' violinist – weaves a straight version of the tune dressed up here and there with a gypsy portamento, while the rhythm guitars and bass plod along. Django, freed from harmonic padding, doubles the beat tremolando, his guitar sounding like a mandolin on steroids. Stéphane bows out with a cheeky turnaround, a 'ragged time' parody.

Then Django enters gently, the seasoned soloist saving himself. His single-line variations dance across barlines he's never seen and so doesn't worry about. His second chorus ends with some impossible rhythmic extensions, which he wouldn't attempt to play if he'd seen them written down, while the third starts with a series of bluesy string bends, direct from the Mississippi Delta via the records of Lonnie Johnson. Django soon diverts to jazzy chromatics.

There follows an audacious two-finger run, impossible with four fingers, dreamt up by a man with only two. At this point, every time this clip is shown, any guitarists who happen to be watching gasp, having just witnessed the impossible. It always provokes an astonished smile.

Unfazed, Django carries on. For the next few phrases, he is again a minimalist, gently coaxing his guitar with the immense strength in his two unparalysed fingers. The strength is used musically, for tone and control. An effortless vibrato, whole-tone bends – every technical device is there to serve the music.

*Never mind the fact that Handel had never seen or heard a piano. It was still an experimental fortepiano in his lifetime.

Stéphane then picks up the theme, his bow dancing on the steady chop of the three-guitar rhythm, before Django offers a syncopated flourish of parallel chords and heralds a sudden end.

'Take a Vola, Mr Solo!' Django famously asked Vola on an earlier recorded session. As it happens, M Vola is absent – the bassist is Roger Grasset – so the film doesn't quite represent the first jam session. In fact, The Hot Club Quintet's line-up changed so often that even the indomitable band historian Pete Frame couldn't come up with an intelligible family tree.

As a complete synchronised record of the Quintet in action, this short film is all that survives. Of over 100 tracks recorded by Le Quintet du Hot Club, this is the only movie record. But it's a gem, and in 2002 it finally appeared on a DVD, digitally restored.* After spending nearly 70 years in a dusty Paris basement, this footage illustrates beautifully what man can do when he doesn't know he can't.

Back in 1934, the unique qualities of the fledgling band were an immediate live success. On 2 December, with the billing still heralding 'Djungo' and the band without a name, they took the École Normale by storm. In a curious development, nobody danced – they listened ! Chamber jazz had arrived, played by a delicate string quintet, and the band was rebooked for 16 February. It needed a name, though, and the idea of a house band for the Hot Club still appealed to the secretary, Pierre Nourry. Stéphane wasn't keen, but Django saw the potential. For its second gig, the band became Le Quintette du Hot Club de France.

The coveted record deal still eluded them, however. The playbacks of the Odéon Company demo with Bert Marshall had been an exciting revelation for Stéphane and Django. Grappelly dreamt of 'jazz on strings', and there it was. For him it worked: 'Hughes Panassié, head of the Hot Club, was trying to get us on record. He'd been everywhere. I remember one, Odéon, said they couldn't take us because it was too modern! What a stupidity!

'And then he went to another place, Pathé-Marconi. They too said they were not interested because they liked jazz with brass people. We were absolutely new, playing American music with strings.'

Delaunay persevered. 'Finally, he found an obscure little label called Ultraphone,' recalled Stéphane, 'and the director, Raoul Caldione, said, "I'll do that, but you embarrass me, because I don't know if I'll get my money back."

'So anyway, a contract was made and we were given 500 francs – 100

*See the Music on Earth DVD Stéphane Grappelli: A Life In The Jazz Century.

francs each. In those days, you can manage to live with just 100 francs a day. It was a very poor engagement, but in any case we manage to play four tunes: "Tiger Rag", "I Saw Stars", "Lady Be Good" and "Sweet Sue".'

In fact, 'Sweet Sue' wasn't recorded until March 1935, although 'Dinah' was part of that first session. For some reason, Stéphane forgot the most famous of their early recordings, possibly because it featured one of the most famous glitches in recorded history. At the end of a rousing take, everyone smiled with relief and Stéphane, in his enthusiasm, bumped the single microphone with his violin bow. There was a minor fracas, resolved when the wise Delaunay convinced the distraught engineers that, bump or not, that was the definitive take. They were pushed for time – Django had arrived half an hour late, and everything had to be recorded in the remaining precious hour.

On the 78rpm record label, the accepted track is credited to 'Djungo Reinhardt et le quintette du HOT CLUB DE FRANCE avec STEPHAN* GRAPELLY', recorded in December 1934 (catalogue number AP 1422). The band finally had a recording deal, even if it was a terrible one. Django received a royalty, but Stéphane never did, and he would never forget that contractual mistake. He disliked those early recordings, yet Django celebrated their completion by buying a new white hat, which was a real American Stetson. His eyes were already set on an Atlantic conquest.

As contracts were addressed, it wasn't just Django who had spelling problems. In fairness, there was no correct spelling of 'Django' until it became a written entity. Like his music, Django's name was an aural tradition, until he signed up for the British MCPS. Indeed, he had been rejected by La Société des Auteurs, Compositeurs et Éditeurs de Musique because he couldn't write his name. Django took this slight to his education hard – it was the catalyst that prompted him to persuade Stéphane to teach him to write. They started with his signature, and for weeks after this lesson Django signed everything, including, according to Stéphane, a few café tablecloths: 'There was not enough paper in the room to satisfy him. Everywhere I looked I saw 'D Reinhardt'. It was a relief because few things were ever more difficult than getting that man to sign his name... Afterwards he regularly asked in odd moments at the theatre how he should put certain sounds down on paper. Correct spelling did not worry him, but he was interested in being able to write phonetically. "Grappelly," he would say, "what does so-and-so mean? How would you write this down?"'

*A unique version of the spelling.

Stéphane's situation was different. Taunted for his foreign name, with its Italianate spelling, his father had acquiesced to adopt the Francophile version, Grappelly, although all of the family identity papers retain the Italian spelling. To the end of his life, if you gave Stéphane a copy of 'Dinah' to autograph, he would sign it 'Grappelly'.

Whatever the spellings, the record company were happy to pay Stéphane his 50 francs but were outraged at Django's demands and wrote to Pierre Nourry to say so as follows:

Société Ultrophone Française
46 rue de la Bienfaisance
Paris, 8ème.
December 26th 1934
Monsieur Pierre Nourry
15 rue du Conservatoire
Paris

Dear Sir,

I shall not attempt to conceal that I am somewhat taken aback by the exorbitant demands of the musicians in your quintet.

Perhaps you are unaware that the normal fee currently paid to first-class jazz soloists never exceeds 150 francs for each three-hour session at which six sides are generally made.

On that basis, the demands of the three supporting musicians far exceed the usual fees. Naturally, I am not speaking of Grappelly.

The most favourable conditions I can contemplate are as set out below:

For the three accompanists (two guitarists and a double-bassist), an outright payment of 30 francs per side.

For Grappelly, an outright payment of 50 francs per side.

For Reinhardt, a royalty of 5 per cent and 50 francs royalty advance on each side recorded.

In view of the probable commercial value of the suggested recordings, you will understand that I cannot commit my company to paying fees that mean there would be no profit even when five hundred records had been produced.

I rely on you to give your artists a more realistic idea of the fees they can expect to receive.

Yours faithfully,
Societe Ultraphone Française
Caldairou (signed)

'Dinah' was a hit, with even the critics praising its wit and elegance. The French found this string ensemble a chic refinement of a music that had arrived in the '20s with *le tumulte noir*. For many socialites, The Hot Club Quintet was the acceptable white face of jazz, especially for those outside the close-knit circle of enthusiasts. Delaunay put it like this in 1961: 'Up to then, this music had been considered "a cacophony", "a series of discords": it was reserved for negroes or, as it was said, "savages", and whites only made themselves ridiculous by showing interest in it; after all, only a handful of fanatics were concerned with it. With the arrival of the quintet and the reassuring presence of string instruments, jazz became a more delicate music, one that could be more easily assimilated by outsiders.'

These are key issues. Even today for some, the name Paul Whiteman smacks of a world unable to accept the concept of worthwhile art from a black source. Hughes Panassié, in his treatise *Le Jazz Hot*, lays great emphasis on an academic and analytical approach to understanding jazz. This was no doubt a search for 'respectability' and acceptance. He defines swing as 'a sort of rocking movement, the rhythm executed with complete ease and yet with power and which takes the form, without any harm to the rhythm of a slight dragging on each note'. The advertising for the book – '380 pages at 30 francs with numerous illustrations' – carries a noble review by the distinguished classical composer George Auric.

This rarefied consideration is, as ever, a long way from the sharp end where jobbing musicians are faced with entering a studio and making a recording that people are happy to pay for. What is it about a popular recording that makes it a hit when so many fail? Is it simply the power of the music itself, or is it more about timing? The truth lies somewhere in the synergy when the two coincide.

Paris, Ultraphone Studio, December 1934

As the shiny new needle settles on the 78rpm master, the white-coated engineer draws the swarf from the virgin groove and Delaunay waves the band to commence. They tentatively launch into 'Dinah'. The guitars almost fumble the introduction, but Django enters boldly, pulling the beat together. Within four bars, Django is skipping along with style. His phrasing is vocal, with a natural rubato. Next, he pushes the rhythm in staccato stabs, then pulls back in laid-back string bends. Audacious triplets descend to tremolando clashes of open and stopped strings in discordant semitones. He pulls from his magician's hat every trick he can find: more dazzling descending runs, a series of parallel chords phrased like brass stabs and then some repeated notes to bring in Stéphane.

Grappelly takes the soundstage in syncopated refinement. The 'posh' violin has acquired a cheeky jazz lilt. Django complements with an alto counter-melody and Stéphane responds, stretching out, growing more daring as Django interjects with more tremolando. Django then switches to mandolin-like repeated notes, introducing tension as the guitar clashes in the violin octave. *Les deux amis* are duelling counterpoint like two New Orleans cornetists at a gypsy feast.

A wave from the control room indicates that the wax platter is reaching its end, so with a sudden rallentando it's all over, the dying reverb with added percussion from Stéphane's errant bow.

The engineer clocks the recording at 2:35 on his railwayman's stopwatch. The wax disc could easily accommodate another 30 seconds! But like so many pop tunes, 'Dinah' benefits from its brevity. The listener's urge is to play it again, and thus is born the familiarity and growing popularity of a catchy refrain.

Stéphane related the session to Peter Anick: 'I remember there were two engineers there. They were dressed like doctors with the white coats… In those days there was no tape; it was the wax pancake, fetched from the fridge. We were obliged to make four tunes. They have eight matrices, two for each tune, so if you make a mistake, it's finished… Of course, if something wrong happens, a string breaks, then they put another pancake.'

On listening to The Hot Club Quintet's first hit, it doesn't sound particularly 'French'; these nomadic adventurers have shaken off the bustle of the *bals musette*. Nor is it the music of a Mississippi bordello, or the Harlem Apollo. It's a million miles from Joséphine Baker's 1926 comic operatic rendition of 'Dinah', all jaunty temple blocks and tra-la-la wordless refrain. Nor is it the polite 1928 version of Venuti and Lang, a version firmly rooted in the refined world of Paul Whitman's 'high society' and sounding stilted in comparison. The Quintet's 'Dinah' is something new, with its own voice. In fact, it stands up well next to Louis Armstrong's Paris stab at 'St Louis Blues', from the same year, and is instrumentally superior. What sets Louis's platter apart is his vocal – next to that sensuous growl, the gentle Quintet are still a little refined.

But what's heard on the Quintet's recording is the invention of European jazz. The gypsy brothers and Stéphane, 'the wayfaring stranger', have adopted a Delta orphan, a musical echo that strayed far from Storyville into the Apache territory of Montmartre. The charm of the new sound, and the secret of its success, is the perfect match to the place and the time. Seventeen years after James Reese Europe marched his Harlem Regiment into Paris, jazz had found a residency. As Parisiens listened to the Quintet's 'Dinah' in candlelit restaurants with good company over *un petit vin de table*, for a short moment they were filled with *joie de vivre*. As Stéphane would say, why not?

10 The Perfect Antidote

'If anybody asked me which European soloist came nearest to the greatest hot musicians, I think I would reply Stéphane Grappelly. He has given me some of the greatest musical thrills of my life.'

– Hughes Panassié, 1935

The precarious world of 1934 needed some joy. The harsh realities of life in a century that had already seen millions die in a war that still made little sense had created a thirst for escapism. In the Roaring '20s, liberated flappers had danced the charleston in a new and fragile peace. Now the '30s had developed its own brand of *laissez-faire* decadence.

France faced particular challenges as 250,000 French were now unemployed. Drowning their sorrows, they had one bar for every 81 individuals, and in an average year each citizen consumed over 200 litres of wine. The bars offered other consolations – Paris was infamous for it's 25,000 prostitutes. Four million people – ten per cent of the population – suffered syphilis.

Throughout Europe, political order was crumbling. Many of the nations created by the new and coldly political map that emerged from the war settlements were confused and angry. In Germany, the crippling reparations negotiated in Versailles in 1918, coupled with the French insistence on the complete humiliation of the German people, had fuelled the rise of Adolf Hitler's fascism. In Munich, the Night of the Long Knives saw Hitler dispose of his remaining political opponents, clearing the way for his SS bully-boy tyranny. In Rome, Mussolini turned the football World Cup into a propaganda opportunity, then desecrated Venice with a reception for Hitler. Even in moderate urbane London, Oswald Mosley held a fascist rally at Olympia.

Americans, meanwhile, were briefly distracted from the disastrous dustbowl-creating agriculture of the Midwest by the final ambush of romanticised outlaws Bonnie and Clyde. And in mysterious still-medieval China, unknown peasant Mao Tse-Tung began his Long March at the head of his Communist column.

As the economic Depression took a firm hold on Paris, the workers again took to the streets. The CGT, the Communist-dominated trade union of which Stéphane was indirectly a member, marched with placards demanding jobs. Even distinguished classical musicians were busking in Stéphane's old haunts.

Although short of money, the escape-seeking public would fill the cinemas three times a day, every day of the week. This was the boom time for the great Hollywood musicals. MGM and Warner Bros couldn't churn out their brand of escapism fast enough. As society crumbled, the dream merchants invented ever more elaborate worlds, peopled with sirens in satin and silk. But even Hollywood felt the financial downturn, and in 1933 Warner Bros had cut salaries across the board by 50 per cent. However, the move to synchronised-sound talkies in 1927 meant that the popularity of the movies provided no consolation for laid-off cinema musicians.

The same live-for-today spirit that filled the cinemas took the wealthier set to the clubs and dance halls of Pigalle. For a while, at least, business was still hot for Bricktop's club and lavish restaurants like Maxim's. The wonderful contemporary photographs taken by the Transylvanian Gyula Halasz brilliantly illustrate the privileged enjoying society's frenzy.

Like Stéphane, Halasz had also changed his name. Arriving in 1924 from Brasso, Romania, he adopted the name Brassai in recognition of his origins. His stark luminescent black-and-white prints were first published in 1932 as *Paris de Nuit* and depicted a Paris of deep contrasts: while the smart set with old money flaunted their wealth, all silver cigarette holders and outrageous peacock clothes, Brassai's knowing pictures of Montmartre's brothels and *bals musettes* illustrate the French society's deep divisions, the new century's neon lighting etching electric fireworks on the shots taken by his heavy Voigtlander camera. A telling Brassai print from 1932 shows the exterior of Pigalle's American Bar and, across the wet gaslit street, the incandescent invitation to Bricktop's.

Bricktop, the singer turned hostess, had come a long way since teaching the Prince of Wales to dance the black bottom. In 1926, she opened her own club, and by 1930 she was a legend immortalised forever in the lyric of Cole Porter's 'Miss Otis Regrets'. Her new *boîte*, Bricktop's, had taken over behind the grand art-nouveau façade of the ancient Monico club in 1931, and 'the queen of the night' inserted her own regal photograph above the door. Inside, where Pissaro, Gaugin and Manet had once sat, a grand ceiling centrepiece resembled a flying saucer, the stage glittered with Lurex drapery, and the champagne flowed. The Devil could wait another night for the souls of Europe's ribald dukes and every black musician in Paris.

Against the trend, hostess Bricktop held to strict rules, refusing to admit any unescorted women – which closed the doors to Montmartre's prostitutes – and all diners were expected to attend in full evening dress. Gradually, however, even this glittering palace began to feel the pinch. Business took a boost only when the drum-kit playing Prince of Wales brought Wallis Simpson to dine.

One champagne-fuelled evening in 1934, Stéphane received an excited telephone call: 'Bricktop called to say Louis Armstrong was in her club. It was five in the morning, but she insisted that Django bring his guitar. Naturally, Django and I set off at once, and for the only time in my life I heard Louis sing, accompanied only by Django's guitar. There was no talk about what key or the tune; Louis began and Django followed. It was a revelation.' This exciting night was probably the catalyst to the Quintet's eventual bookings, not at the Monico but across the road at Bricktop's restaurant.

No doubt Stéphane was increasingly aware of his gypsy partner's talent. Django might be difficult and unpredictable, but clearly he could hold his own with the greatest jazz stars in the world. Stéphane, of course, also wanted to pursue jazz, and together they were a unique team. Stéphane was two years Django's senior, and except for spats over star billings Django usually deferred to him, in accordance with the Romany tradition of respect for clan elders.

Amongst Django's own family, Joseph Reinhardt, younger by two years, was expected to carry his older brother's guitar, as well as a supply of strings and plectrums for the acknowledged maestro. Joseph seems to have been suppressed by his brother, never playing solos with the Quintet, despite his recorded facility to do so.

The other Quintet guitarists seemed to come and go according to availability and Django's quixotic mood. Whoever they were, they were only allowed to play rhythm. Stéphane and Django also differed over the need for two rhythm guitarists, Django insisting that he needed two guitar accompanists, as Stéphane had two behind his solos, and Stéphane thinking that this was more 'a family matter' – jobs for the boys, perhaps? The early second guitars include the non-gypsy Roger Chaput and Pierre 'Baro' Ferret, both born shortly after Stéphane in 1909. They shared musical roots in the *bals musette* and from working with many star Italian accordionists.

Despite the superficial glamour, the life of a musician is essentially antisocial. They work nights and hours and locations change daily and at short notice.

They travel widely, both nationally and internationally, usually without their families. Relationships suffer.

With only his father as family, however, Stéphane was a footloose bachelor, and his own personal photographs of the time provide a glimpse of the life he enjoyed. Now he would be referred to as a pop star. He is seen in clubs in the company of glamorous American celebrities including the musicians Louis Armstrong, Coleman Hawkins and Benny Carter, and the Hollywood screenwriter Daniel Taradash.

Stéphane is also seen in intimate company with a succession of extremely glamorous women, amongst them the Norwegian singer Carola Merrilo and several other anonymous admirers. In 1934, this handsome young man at the front of the band also attracted the attention of a young French girl by the name of Sylvia Caro. They had a brief affair, and on 13 May 1935 Sylvia had a daughter, whom they named Evelyne. Stéphane immediately acknowledged his parental responsibility, though he continued his travels as a musician. However, on returning to Paris one night, Stéphane discovered that Sylvia and Evelyne had disappeared. When he finally rediscovered his daughter, she had been left with her maternal grandmother. He was excluded access to his daughter for years, and indeed they never had any real time together until Evelyne was 11 years old.

Django, on the other hand, carried his clan with him, including his second wife, his cousin Sophie Ziegler, better known as La Guine or Naguine, a reference to her rosy cheeks. Django had known Naguine as a 14-year-old girl and had dated her at the same time as he dated his first wife. The pair were reunited when Django left the nursing home following the disastrous caravan fire. While working in Montmartre, the couple set up a makeshift home in a hotel room, next to the Bateau Lavoir on the Place Émile Goudeau. To the proprietors' dismay, they shared the space with a pet monkey.

Within France, the Quintet's bass players and guitarists were recruited on an *ad hoc* basis, but usually with the faithful Joseph as dependable second. These were the days before the tour bus, and transport arrangements were ramshackle – it wasn't unusual for a band to take the public tram. (My own father, Bill Balmer, often loaded his trap drum kit, fully assembled on wheels, onto the open plate on the back of a Liverpool tram, while in the 1930s guitarist Bert Weedon used a baby's pram as a trolley, wheeling it to gigs. By comparison, Stéphane's violin was an easy load!) The guitars in the *Le Jazz Hot* film clip look well travelled, even battered. It's almost as if, when not driving a rhythm, they service as doorstops and cricket bats. Unfortunately, this is an era before the snapshot was common and there are very few candid shots of the band on tour.

In Paris, the Quintet members found work at Stage B on the Boulevard du Montparnasse, where they would alternate with other musicians, including Arthur Briggs on trumpet and Alix Combelle on sax, players who would in 1935 record with the Quintet. They also met the great American great jazz saxophonist Coleman Hawkins. Stéphane excitedly recounts a marathon jam sessions with 'the Hawk': 'He would improvise for an hour and a half on "Sweet Sue". We played from ten until four in the morning for 90 francs, but we had a whale of a time.'

Paris engagements as The Hot Club Quintet were rare and not always well received. A concert from the Théâtre des Champs-Elysées on 5 February 1934 was a particularly discouraging flop, while another provincial concert for the Nancy Hot Club ended in a financial loss for the organisers. A Paris gig left the American agent Irving Mills completely nonplussed, and unfortunately he said so in the important trade journal *Melody Maker*. It seems it was the band's stage conduct, rather than the music, which led to his published remark: 'It is not enough to be an artist. One must be a gentleman too.' The Reinhardt cousins had apparently laughed onstage during the vocalist Jean Tranchant's spot. Mills had been considering booking the Quintet to appear in America and had stayed on in Paris especially to hear them. It's intriguing to speculate what New York might have made of this particular early example of taking coals to Newcastle. It's hard to imagine a Depression-hit America taking very kindly to French jazz. Even in the 21st century, Europe remains a suspicious musical territory for many Americans.

As it transpired, the Quintet's first regular engagement came at the Grand Écart on the Rue Fromentin, a cabaret newly renamed Nuits Bleues, where they were billed as 'Djuongo Reinhardt, Stéphane Grappelly and their Virtuosos'. Celebrity guests included the great American alto saxophonist Benny Carter, but the run was dogged by Django's intermittent attendance – the guitarist preferred to stay in bed. Stéphane eased the situation by playing piano in the intervals, but this merely put more pressure on himself.

Fortunately, help was at hand. In March 1935, Hughes Panassié and Charles Delaunay at last founded the magazine *Jazz Hot*, dubbing it a 'Revue Internationale de la Musique' and the 'Organe Officiel du Hot Club de France'. In that first issue, they set out their mission: 'Up to the present day, no review, paper or periodical has been exclusively consecrated to jazz music. This lacuna has to be filled up, and that is why *Jazz Hot* has been founded... Our aim is to propagate and to make known under its real aspect jazz music, which is so far greatly ignored and misunderstood.' They demonstrated the seriousness of their intent with the recruitment of a roster of 21 foreign correspondents including Mugsy Spanier in the United States, Joost van Praag in Holland, Michael Andrico in Romania and Stanley F Dance in the UK. They wanted Louis Armstrong as 'honorary president', a role he accepted officially two years later and which he retained for life.

The first historic issue, priced at just three francs, has a 'Letter From America' by John Hammond: 'I'm sure that it will be a better magazine even than *Jazz Tango*, which always had to devote valuable space to unimportant musical matters such as the tango.'

Panassié himself contributed a critique on Coleman Hawkins and George Hilaire wrote a piece on Panassié in which he praised Panassié's recent book, *Le Jazz Hot*, in the spirit of the time: 'The great value of Hughes' work resides in the utter loyalty the author has shown in his properly scientifical spirit of investigation, in his instinctive application of Descartes's methods.' However, he has little time for 'those snobs who boosted jazz in 1924 at the Boeuf sur le Toit and...let it down immediately afterwards, or...those modern composers who will not admit the flowing musical composition of jazz because it goes against all the habits and customs of comfortable bourgeois harmony.' Fighting talk indeed, although it gives a flavour of the passion of the time for jazz in Paris. It's also the beginning, for good or ill, of the intellectualisation of jazz.

That first issue carried a full page photograph of 'Le Quintette à Cordes du Hot Club de France', showing Stéphane smiling with the same Odéon band that included Bert Marshall, although, in an early feat of trick printing, Bert has been painted out. There is also a full page advertisement by Ultraphone for 'DJANGO REINHARDT et le Quintette du Hot Club de France avec Stéphane GRAPPELLY', offering four 78s: 'Dinah'/'Lady Be Good', 'Tiger Rag'/'I Saw Stars (instrumental)' and two other records offering vocals, this time by the singing British drummer Jerry Mengo.

The Quintet records are reviewed separately, and favourably. On 'Dinah', Grappelly's solo 'is without doubt one of the three or four most beautiful solos on the "hot" violin ever recorded. He is a French musician in the same class as the great American soloists.' Meanwhile, a quintet concert that took place on 16 February is declared 'a veritable triumph with... splendid interpretations and…better than their records'. So for Stéphane, things were at last looking up. Similar praise was in fact meted out for Django, but on balance more was given for Grappelly.

Live onstage, a guest spot with the greatest tenor saxophonist of the day, Coleman Hawkins, on 23 February 1935 at the Salle Pleyel was also a success. For *Jazz Hot*, Madeleine Gautier reported, 'The String Quintet of the Hot Club of France were a true revelation, each item received with an enormous ovation… Stéphane is extraordinarily "hot" in all his phrases. Many hot fans protested because someone said that Stéphane was a better musician than Venuti. Better is an understatement; Stéphane is a far better musician than Venuti… Almost all [Venuti's] records are full of fast endless passages, bits of sentimental melodies, fragments of Italian songs – it is horribly stale. I know nothing more boring, more monotonous than the famous 'Stringing The Blues', and they want me to lower Stéphane to a comparison with Venuti! …In Django and Stéphane we have two hot musicians as extraordinary as the best American players. For the rhythm section, Roger Chaput, Joseph Reinhardt and Vola are as good as the soloists. This Quintet is certainly the hottest orchestra of European musicians ever.'

The early comparison to Venuti is interesting, but the rest of that evening's bill also warrants some attention. The Hawk had performed with a hastily assembled local band including Joseph Reinhardt, and although the band were clearly under-rehearsed, Hawkins impressed with his solos, particularly on 'After You've Gone'. Stéphane and Django then made another appearance, backing Arthur Briggs' trumpet. Gautier reported, 'This light, varied accompaniment helped him admirably, allowing him not to strain as he would have been obliged to do to dominate an orchestra… Another big attraction of the evening was the dancer Freddy Taylor, one of the most astonishing I have ever seen… Freddy sang as he danced and Michel Warlop composed for him a beautiful orchestral arrangement.'

The *Melody Maker* reported that there was a happy crowd of 1,200 at the Salle Pleyel, while *Jazz Tango* had it that there was a sell-out at 1,700. Whatever, *Jazz Hot* was certainly swelling the interest in this new and exotic escape from the very real blues of the 1930s.

The success led to a recording session with the Hawk on 2 March. Credited as 'The Michel Warlop Orchestra', Django played guitar with Stéphane on piano in their classic recording of Hoagy Carmichael's 'Stardust'. Here, sadly, beyond a sensitive introduction, Stéphane is confined to a backseat. However, he was certainly listening, absorbing the Hawk's rhythmic and inventive approach to phrasing, as it would re-appear in many of Stéphane's own later violin solos. Coleman Hawkins was the first exponent of the great modern school of jazz tenor saxophone, and no doubt in these concerts, jam sessions and recordings Stéphane was revelling in this opportunity to study his hero.

For 'Blue Moon', 'Avalon' and 'What A Difference A Day Made', the trio were joined by Andre Ekyan and Alix Combelle on saxophones and Pierre Allier on trumpet, as well as the future Quintet bass player Eugène d'Hellemmes* and other regular Paris sessioners.

The Hawk was four years Stéphane's senior. Born in St Joseph, Missouri, by 1923 he was already causing a storm in Fletcher Henderson's band, and by the time he reached England and France in 1935 he was an acknowledged original. He stayed in Europe for five eventful years, refining his distinctive rhapsodic style and a big fat 'modern' sound. Improvising around chords, 'playing the changes', rather than working from a purely melodic base, Hawkins was laying the groundwork for the bebop players of the '40s. The saxophonist might have inspired Stéphane to be freer with time, prompting the pushing and pulling across the beat that's so prominent in his later work. Stéphane and Django were there at the birth of a whole new school, and thanks to Delaunay, they were missing no lessons.

In their own right, the Quintet were enjoying their success on record, and by July this was being acknowledged from as far away as Chicago by the 'hot' correspondent Helen Oakley: '"Dinah" and "Lady Be Good" were really magnificent and have been greatly admired over here. Their work ranks with the best of the Americans. Personally I prefer Grappelly to any fiddle player I have ever heard. I hope they gain their proper recognition in France.'

In France, Hughes Panassié was particularly impressed by Stéphane, even comparing him on the well-known track 'Ultrafox' to Louis Armstrong. For the B-side, 'Ton Doux Sourice', he remarked, 'Grappelly's first chorus on this sentimental number is really out of this world. Stéphane is unbelievably majestic... Even when he plays straight the most vulgar tune he is hot. He cannot be anything else but hot. I must point out Grappelly's wonderful tone on this disc. More than one classical violinist would envy it... The two choruses by Grappelly in "Sweet Sue"...these choruses are amongst the hottest violin solos ever recorded.'

But the Quintet were still tied exclusively to their poor deal with Ultraphone,

*Born in 1909 in the north of France, Eugène d'Hellemmes was originally involved with the *musette* scene. He later accompanied Jean Sablon and Charles Trenet and worked with many visiting American jazz stars. In 1941 he left with Ray Ventura for Brazil, where he remained until his death, in 1963.

negotiated at a time when any deal was a good deal. Now that the tide had changed, however, the solution was to record clandestinely at the Polydor studio in Paris's 13th Arrondissement under the pseudonym Stéphane Grappelly And His Hot Four. This line-up has the two leaders with Joseph Reinhardt and the Gitan Pierre Ferret on guitars and either Vola or Tony Rovira on bass. They recorded eight titles in this incarnation in September and October of 1935, including their wonderful version of 'St Louis Blues', although Django was never happy with the assumed name.

The sixth issue of *Jazz Hot* appeared in November 1935 and carried a full-page feature on Stéphane. Alongside a proud portrait of Grappelly 'in full dinner dress', the article by Helen Oakley and Hughes Panassié declared, 'Stéphane Grappelly is one of the best hot musicians. Maybe he is the first man to play fiddle in jazz the way it should be played, as a fiddle, not pushing it into a jazz medium but making a place for it. His fiddle is not forceful or barrelhouse or crude; Venuti attempts to attack with the fiddle – he makes it aggressive he stomps with it. This man just sings... Grappelly has a real genius for melodic invention.'

It's very strange now, looking back at that 1935 review and seeing Grappelly described as a genius. It seems quite obvious today, given the abundant supporting evidence, but in those days he was only one year into his featured soloist career, with only four records generally available. Panassié shows incredible foresight.

Despite this success, however, Stéphane was still doing support work on some rather bad pop records. In September 1935, he and Django found themselves back at Ultraphone accompanying Nane Cholot, a comic singer with a line in Chinese impressions. This thanks to a kind of first-call arrangement that Ultraphone had with the Quintet members that committed them to provide this service. Another session has Stéphane back on piano for the Paul Robeson soundalike Bruce Boyce. As money was still tight, the work, though a long way from jazz, was probably welcome.

With their reputation growing, The Quintet were now ready to broaden their horizons throughout Europe. Success came quickly and unexpectedly in January 1936 in Barcelona, where the Quintet members had been hastily summoned together to accompany the brilliant Benny Carter. Stéphane had been working in Monte Carlo, but he leapt at the opportunity. The occasion was such a success that the number of performances was doubled to cope with demand. 'We had a magnificent reception,' said Stéphane. 'After each concert, hats rained onto the stage like a bullfight. It was wonderful.' However, the promoters absconded with all the profits, and all the Quintet could take away was a review from *La Publicicad* describing them as 'one of the best groups in Europe.* It must have been tempting at this stage to give up their original Quintet concept, as much of their live success seemed to come in the presence of their American heroes. Stéphane remembered the takings swindle for 50 years and was always reluctant to return to Barcelona.

By this time broadcasting was growing in popularity, and in fact television signals were being broadcast from the Eiffel tower, which had at last found a practical use as a radio mast. Less than 200 television sets existed in France, but radio was heard by thousands. These audiences sought an escape from the unremitting economic situation through light entertainment.

In February, Stéphane and Django were once again invited to accompany the singer Jean Tranchant, for the radio programme *Micro de la Redoute*, but this time without the cousins, who had giggled their way through their previous encounter. Seizing the opportunity to reach a new audience, on a recording of this broadcast Stéphane plays a tasteful obbligato to Tranchant's vocal and piano on 'Les Baisers Prisioniers'. Django, however, overplays like crazy, throwing in all his brilliant armoury: lightning-fast single-string runs and trademark chordal flourishes. He may well have been bored, as he was in the *bals musette* bands of 1928, or perhaps expressing his annoyance at the exclusion of his family.

Four tunes survive from this historic occasion, but again, as with 1934s 'Who's Afraid Of The Big Bad Wolf?', it's not really a musical event, although 'Le Piano Méchanique' is very funny, in a sort of comedy-pianist style, almost a 1936 French equivalent of comedian Les Dawson.

The growth of broadcasting was presenting new opportunities for musicians. Despite the worst economic depression in history, or perhaps encouraged by the need for more light entertainment, programming became ever more ambitious. In Britain in 1936, the first high-definition television service was inaugurated by the BBC (tellingly, one of it's first endeavours was the outside broadcast of a football match between Arsenal and Everton), and one of the first musical contributions was Paul Robeson singing 'Old Man River'. In France – where a television set cost a prohibitive 7,427 francs – the equivalent show featured 'J'Attendrai'.

---

*In as early as 1936, *Swing* magazine compared Stéphane to Yehudi Menuhin: 'After the first few bars, the cold rigid atmosphere is dispelled and the contact is made between executants and listeners, that contact which is the secret of the really outstanding musicians of a Szigeti , a Menuhin of the Kreisler of old as of an Armstrong or a Hawkins... Grappelly is swing incarnate.'

The Depression continued. The breadline riots that had become a regular sight in the world's cities even came to the cinema via the humour of Charlie Chaplin's 1936 film *Modern Times*, which also worked as an effective satire on the wasted resources of the Depression. The music for the film included the poignant 'Smile, Though Your Heart Is Breaking', which became an anthem for an era, and the film quickly appeared in a French version.

In Paris, the Quintet's fan and supporter Bricktop was more interested in the Depression's impact on live entertainment: 'The Depression brought the people of Montmartre closer together than they had ever been before. The entertainers, most of whom lived there, got to know the French better and we found out more about one another than we'd ever learned in the days when we'd lived it up as if there was no tomorrow. There was a surprising lack of bitterness. The most common sentence wasn't "I wish things were the way they used to be"; no, it was "Have you got any money?" We all shared what we had and looked out for one another.'

On 28 April 1937, Stéphane and Django were reunited with bass player Eugène d'Hellemmes as part of Coleman Hawkins And His All-Star Band. That day, the trio took part in one of the most celebrated recordings of the era, a recording that would launch the world's first dedicated jazz record label: Charles Delaunay and Hughes Panassié's Swing label. Stéphane's memory is vivid: 'Every American artist visiting Paris did a record with Swing, and I remember I was accompanying them – Django on guitar and myself, with drums and bass. One of the sessions included "Honeysuckle Rose". For that session, Delaunay engaged two Frenchmen, Andre Ekyan and Alix Combielle, and two Americans, Coleman Hawkins and Benny Carter. I remember that in less than ten minutes, for the four voices, two tenor and two alto saxophones, Benny Carter arranged "Honeysuckle Rose"!' At this time, 'Honeysuckle Rose' was a new song – the composer, Stéphane's hero Fats Waller, has only just recorded it himself. Stéphane can clearly be heard enjoying himself in his supporting role on piano, and together he and Django recorded three other now-legendary tracks, all in one hour-and-a-half-long session!

But all of this is still somehow reflected glory. Again Stéphane and Django must have been wondered whether there was anyone out there interested in them for their own sakes. In fact, Swing Records' second issue did feature the Quintet, on 'The Charleston',* which had actually been recorded before the All-Stars record, released on 21 April. But with a new company to launch, Delaunay and Panassié clearly saw the American stars as their best proposition.

*With Louis Vola, Baro Ferret and a mysterious guitarist Marcel Bianchi.

The daring new label Swing was founded on the principle of recording only the finest jazz in Europe. Delaunay had struck a unique deal with Pathé-Marconi, as Panassié recalled: 'The agreement…was a very favourable one. We had complete freedom in the choice of bands and musicians and in the supervision of the music we wanted them to record. They in turn handled the actual recording, pressing and distribution.'

Clearly, in the three short years they had been in business, Panassié and Delaunay had generated a huge amount of trust and respect in this whole new area of hot jazz, and Swing was an immediate success, both commercially and artistically. It was certainly bucking the financial trend, and Stéphane and Django were in the right place at the right time.

As the global financial situation worsened, Bricktop reluctantly closed her beloved Monico club. Across the road, the French-German family of Madame and Monsieur Fricka, who had come to Paris from the Alsace region, wisely took Bricktop as a hostess. Bricktop, with all her connections, agreed to book the entertainment. Although she was keen to book the now 'Hot' Quintet, friends warned Bricktop about the group's frail structure. Django particularly had a reputation: 'If he doesn't like the colour of your dress, he'll walk out. If he doesn't like the way a client is looking at him, he'll also walk out!'*

Regardless, Ada went ahead with her plans. Django eventually took to addressing Bricktop affectionately as 'minou', meaning 'cat', and Bricktop called the youthful faced Stéphane 'my baby'. Stéphane was touched to find that Bricktop had also lost her mother at the age of four, and they became close and conciliatory friends. With Django, he composed her a tune, 'Bricktop', which the Quintet officially recorded in November 1937.

Stéphane certainly enjoyed the unique atmosphere Bricktop created: 'Here the aristocracy acted like the bourgeois – instead of the bourgeois pretending to be aristocracy,' he observed. Nevertheless, though, the musicians were still staff, 'obliged to come in through the service entrance, taking care not to touch the carpets and concealing themselves carefully behind the potted plants'.

Stéphane was particularly pleased to meet the great songwriter Cole Porter, a Bricktop regular from way back. Grappelly was amused to discover they had a song title in common, both having composed entirely separate melodies called 'In The Still Of The Night'. One night, Stéphane also heard an early rendition of 'I've Got You Under My Skin' performed by the composer. Thereafter, the violinist insisted that the American Mabel Mercer, another regular at Bricktop's, sing it every night to his piano accompaniment. He continued to work long

*Delaunay

stints, playing piano while the Quintet took a break. 'Sometimes Bricktop paid and sometimes she was bankrupt, but it was good to work there,' he recalled.

The High Society restaurant attracted talent scouts from around Europe. If an artist was good, he or she could be found wherever you could find Bricktop. These regular gigs at Frickas gave the Quintet star billing on the door frontage as 'Django Rheinhardt and Stéphane Grappelly with their Hot Club Orchestra'.

Meanwhile, June 1937 marked a significant turning point in French political life. On the fourth of the month, under Léon Blum, the socialist Popular Front came to power, ending the worst of the social unrest. Within days, the worst strikes were over and pay rises of up to 12 per cent had been awarded, while more revolutionary still were concessions on paid holidays and collective bargaining. The union leader Leon Jouhaux remarked, 'For the first time in history, an entire class has won improved conditions.'

The excitement is clearly audible in recordings of the crowd at Pigalle's Big Apple, where the host was again the redoubtable Bricktop. The distinguished clientèle at this establishment sometimes included President Roosevelt's son, as well as the English composer Constant Lambert. More importantly, the venue was the setting for an extraordinary and surviving transatlantic broadcast; on 13 June, the Quintet were booked to broadcast live to the United States.

The prestige of such a high-profile show had Stéphane and Django on edge, and the situation was compounded by the inevitable time difference. For the show to be broadcast at a sensible time in America, the Quintet had to go on air at dawn in Paris. As the announcer hooked the musicians to the airwaves, he asked in a distinctly American accent, 'Have you cats had half enough yet? Well, last year some interesting recordings from France found their way to America and the Swing fans here discovered a distinctly European contribution to swing, a string combination that swung in a style that was off the beaten track of hot music. The combination was The Hot Club Of France Quintet, with Stéphane Grappelly on violin and the sensational guitarist Django Reinhardt. They've been heard in America only on record, and *The Swing Club* thought it would be swell to bring them in direct from Paris, so here we go to France, by short-wave radio, where it's almost 20 minutes to six in the morning. We have a treat. Swing it, Paris!'

Then, in Paris, another American takes over, 'First "Djangology", a composition of Stéphane Grappelly.'

After a short pause, Django starts to play, despite being deprived of his credit. Django then has his revenge by taking virtually every chorus. As 'Djangology' ends, the announcer paints the scene: 'As the rising sun filters through the streets of Montmartre, The Hot Club Quintet give you "Limehouse Blues".' As the Quintet give a rousing version of 'Limehouse…', there's a real sense of the noisy, excited crowd at Bricktops – the all-string adventurers are really having to dig into their instruments to make themselves heard. This is probably the norm, though, and they all seem unflustered as they finish, with Django egging Stéphane on with some dramatic flourishes.

'Next we hear "Break-up", a composition of Stéphane Grappelly and Django Reinhardt.'

This is, of course, 'Bricktop', but at least this time the announcer pronounces Django's name correctly. The Quintet, perhaps thrown by the wrong title, get off to a shaky start and are soon interrupted by a voiceover: 'From the Bricktop cabaret in Montmartre, Paris, this is Ed Morrow speaking and saying, "Swing it, America!" Thank you, Stéphane Grappelly and The Hot Club Of France!'

It could have been worse – he might have announced 'Stéphane Grappelly And His Hot Four'. Either way, Django was never happy unless he was top of the bill, and a sulk no doubt ensued.

Of course, the Quintet was always more a loose collective than a permanent band. Even for this important show, they had Gusti Malha on guitar in lieu of Roger Chaput (who was probably busy with his own orchestra) and all of the members had other musical commitments. Vola as a bandleader and Stéphane and Django were still freelancing with at least four other outfits. This situation wasn't unusual at the time.

However, every band, even one as loose as the Quintet, has an internal dynamic with many complex and intertwining components. The audience sees five musicians working in apparent harmony, all marching to the beat of the same invisible drum, but away from the bandstand the reality is very different. Offstage, Stéphane was an easygoing but refined violinist. He could never forget his childhood misery on the streets and was always happy to be working, whereas Django displayed a contempt for work even when he was broke. 'We had no work and I was offered a private party engagement by a rich industrialist,' reported Stéphane, 'so I accepted immediately. I found Django in his little Montmartre room. He went there when he couldn't be bothered going back to his caravan. So I told him about the job, but he said he preferred to stay in bed. As I left him, Naguine asked me for five francs to buy some sugar! He had not a penny in the house, yet he turns down a substantial sum of money.'

With the fire incident Django had also suffered an immense trauma, his survival in part driven by immense ambition and ego. By this time, the guitarist had seen a host of American stars including Louis Armstrong and Duke Ellington, and his sights were set on conquering America and, by definition, the jazz world. He had bigger fish to fry, but he clearly wanted America to come to him.

Louis Vola meanwhile was just a jobbing musician who still played accordion when not engaged as a double-bass player. Django had his own views on bass players, and Stéphane obligingly tried to deliver: 'First, I must say we enjoyed playing together, but he was very difficult with other musicians. I don't think he liked people who played badly. I remember he was always getting annoyed with the bass players, and I was often obliged to find one at the last minute. He would do nothing – all the difficult jobs he left to me.

'Fortunately, when we were in Paris, playing in Montmartre, it was easy for me to find players who went to the Tabac to look for appointments. I could find one at very short notice, which often happened because the one who came the day before didn't want to come back because Django was so rude. He was very difficult with bass players. So I told him, "If you like a bass player, you must pay him." He was so mean – he didn't want to pay them and couldn't find good players. I don't want to be rude, because if I had a friend in my life, it was him.

'He played cards, and every time he was playing billiards, despite the fact he was a great player, he always lost because he wanted to play with people who were better than him. So sometimes he was penniless, and it embarrassed me to find the money to help him.'

Vola contributed an interesting insight into the volatile relationship between these two talented young men: 'There was much jealousy between them. Grappelly, when he played in a cabaret, would take five, six, ten choruses and…sometimes Django would get so mad he'd drop his guitar and go across the street for a drink, and then I'd have to go and fetch him back.'

This jealousy would have been fanned by the readers' poll of *Jazz Hot* magazine, published in August. Although Django did well, polling third place behind Albert Casey and Eddie Condon in the guitar category, Stéphane was polled first amongst the violinists above Joe Venuti, Eddie South, Michel Warlop and Stuff Smith. These early magazines make interesting reading as there is a consistent pattern of Grappelly being rated and praised far more than Django.

Charles Delaunay, meanwhile, seemed to be always on the lookout for new ways to present the Quintet, especially with visiting and more instantly credible

Americans. At one point in 1937, the esteemed jazz violinist Eddie South, 'the black angel of the violin', turned up in Paris to play at the American pavilion of the Universal Exposition. Born in Louisiana, Missouri, in 1904, Eddie had trained as a classical violinist at the Chicago Conservatory and in Paris with Firmin Touche, but had turned to jazz when the prospects for a black-American musician reaching Carnegie Hall had seemed bleak.

In September 1937, Delaunay put him together in the studio with Stéphane, Django and Michel Warlop. On 'Eddie's Blues', featuring just Eddie and Django, the southern and Chicago feel is immediately apparent, second nature to Eddie but never really comfortable ground for Stéphane. Eddie had breathed in the Bayou air and knew about life in Chicago's tenement blocks. Then, in Django's arrangement of Gershwin's 'Lady Be Good', the three violinists play in sweet ensemble, but there is little room for Stéphane to shine. Stéphane surely picked up a few tricks, though, particularly Eddie's audacious octave swoops.

In November, Delaunay proposed that Stéphane and Eddie should get together again as an experiment, this time to play the Bach concerto for two violins in a syncopated and partly improvised interpretation. Hughes Panassié probably had a part to play here; according to his son Patrice, 'he considered Bach the precursor of jazz'.

Stéphane was initially opposed to the idea: 'There is plenty of classical music and plenty of jazz music. Why put them together? I hadn't studied Bach at this time, and Django couldn't read the piano part. In fact, none of the guitarists could read and Vola was more at home with java than Bach. Eddie South had more of a classical training than me.'

The recording went ahead, however, although Panassié, on listening to the recordings, thought that the musicians sounded far too inhibited and insisted on another session two days later. This time the fiddlers warmed up with 'Fiddle Blues' and, according to Stéphane, Panassié 'whipped away the music' to encourage more spontaneity.

Stéphane confessed that he was never happy with this record, although the second take does have some jazz about it and is a lot more successful. That first take has a strange echo into the far distant future, with television coming of age and classical virtuosi daring to take gambles in front of millions of viewers. Who could have imagined any of that in November 1937?

The record did enjoy some novelty success, however, and ironically Stéphane, Eddie and Django had laid the foundation for a French 'jazz Bach' movement. This would later flourish in the '50s and '60s under the guidance of innovators like Jacques Loussier with his Jazz Bach Trio and Ward Swingle with his acclaimed Swingle Singers. But that jazz Bach required a lot of careful arranging.

Stéphane did study and come to admire Bach, and much later, in the '80s, he harboured a secret ambition to record a Bach triple concerto. As well as playing the violin, he wanted to overdub the viola and harpsichord parts himself, and indeed he got as far as searching for a viola before his ambition was thwarted by a loss of movement in his right hand, forcing him to give up the keyboard. As a joke, he sometimes duetted Bach during the 1980s at the Rue Dunkerque with his neighbour, who was a keen harpsichordist. They did this without leaving their respective apartments, the walls being thin enough to allow a spontaneous jam session.

In October 1937, the Quintet enjoyed some success in Holland and Belgium, and on the tenth of that month, in the Hague, they were presented as part of a Dutch amateur band contest. The event attracted some media attention and was probably the reason for one of those rare events when the Quintet came to be filmed in action. Sadly, like much newsreel footage of the time, it was filmed with no sound, and many attempts have since been made to restore some appropriate audio to the one-minute fragment. What survives is a tantalising glimpse of one of the greatest bands of the century in full flow. In the clip,* Stéphane is first seen alone, suave and poised in black tuxedo and bowtie. Then Django appears, rapt in his rhythmic accompaniment, while the frontal shot shows the whole Quintet, all dependent on one huge microphone, so big it nearly obscures Joseph's head. The band are clearly having a good time, swaying to the infectious beat. Django nods his head, lost in the music, pushing Vola and his guitar-playing brothers to a trance-like synergy. Even without sound, it's clear that this was an exciting performance. Post-sync'd to an appropriate soundtrack, it's all that survives of the band onstage. Watching this tantalising glimpse, you know you're witnessing a little dangerous magic.

Despite that enthusiastic Dutch reception, however, according to Charles Delaunay the band returned to Paris penniless.

After this, Britain seemed to be the next challenge and offered a better prospect – after all, the spoken language of jazz was American and, by default, English. The Quintet had made themselves heard in Britain already via a few records, and also in May that year BBC Radio arranged a link-up to a Paris studio. A very poor recording exists of this historic broadcast.

The Quintet were announced in the clipped English of the time: 'The Quintet was founded by its present leader, Django Reinhardt...and they have

*Seen on the Music on Earth DVD *Stéphane Grappelli: A Life In The Jazz Century*.

become renowned for their brilliant playing and the originality of their arrangements, and now we are taking you over to Paris to hear them playing from the studio.' The band then launch into 'Pennies From Heaven', 'Exactly Like You' and 'In The Still Of The Night', on which Django plays some wonderful stuff, sadly only just discernible above the mush of the only remaining acetate discs. The Quintet then finishes with 'Fat', which turns out to be an early version of 'Minor Swing', and this time it's Stéphane's turn to shine. It may have been this broadcast that drew the Quintet to the attention of the Collins & Grade Vaudeville Exchange.

Back in 1937, Bricktop had had to take a job in somebody else's establishment, the depression was growing ever worse and the Quintet was still more an inspired idea than a touring reality. Then, one night at Bricktop's, an Englishman asked after the Quintet's 'businessman', and Django pointed the distinguished cigar-smoking stranger to Stéphane...

11 Lew's Vaudeville Contract

'Something I learned from Maurice Chevalier: You must start well and
end well. In the middle, who knows?'

– Stéphane Grappelli

'When we were in Bricktop's in 1937,' remembered Stéphane, 'some people
were writing to us in English. In those days I didn't read English and I was with
Django, who was too lazy to answer. One night we had a visit From Lew Grade,
and Django referred him to me.'

After pursuing a successful career as an 'eccentric dancer' – billed in music
hall as 'the man with the musical feet' – Lew Grade had turned impresario.
The former Louis Winogradsky obviously inherited his father's flair for the
kaztatzke and other acrobatic Cossack steps. In 1924 he took the £25 first
prize at the Ilford Hippodrome and the title of Charleston Champion of London.
At this point, he made his first name change to the more stage-friendly Louis
Grad. Then, in 1926, he became the world-champion charleston dancer. The
prize this time was a four-week professional engagement as a dancer at London's
Piccadilly Hotel for the princely fee of £200.

To keep earning, Louis developed an original gimmick: he danced frantically
in silk shirt and trousers on the top of an insubstantial oval card table. He
successfully toured Britain as a novelty act and in 1930 found his name in lights
outside the great Paris music halls Le Moulin Rouge and Le Bal Tabarin.

In 1934, Louis' knees collapsed, along with the charleston craze, and at
the age of 27 he set himself up as a manager for the harmonica player Louis
Almaer, an arrangement which led to support work with the established Joe
Collins agency.

By 1937, Lew had returned to Paris seeking acts for the growing agency.
According to the man himself, 'I was in Paris, and I'd heard about Le Quintet
du Hot Club de France. I thought, "Well, I might as well go in and have a look
at them," and I was absolutely amazed when I heard this quintet, Stéphane
Grappelly and Django Reinhardt, who were the leaders of the Quintet. When

I heard Stéphane play, it was revelation to me; I'd heard about a very famous jazz violinist called Joe Venuti, but to me Stéphane was remarkable. I just couldn't believe it. And Django Reinhardt, of course, absolutely shocked me because there was no doubt in my mind that he was the best guitarist in the world – and he was; he was phenomenal. And together they were a most remarkable team.

'So I thought, "Well, I'll have a go and try to book them in England." I spoke to them, became very friendly with them and said, "Look, I'm going to try to bring you to England. Will you come?" They were delighted.'

Of course, such an important foreign tour required a signed contract from the Quintet's leaders, but obtaining this wasn't easy as, despite French-speaking contractual assistance from Parisian agents the Marouani brothers, Django could still neither read nor write. Stéphane tried to save Django embarrassment by a clever charade, which backfired: 'I said to Django, "Listen, Django," because he couldn't read; Django was illiterate, "I will show you the paper, and when I'm reading, if I said OK, remember: OK. I'll give you the paper and you say OK. Bon?" He said OK.

'The day after Lew Grade came and he showed me the paper and everything was correct, "OK." And I gave it to Django, like it was arranged, and suddenly Django said, "I don't like that." Everybody jumped and "that" was "travel paid first-class return". I said, "Look, shut up, you idiot."'

A nervous Lew returned to England, full of hope for his first major signing: 'I came back to England and I booked them at the Ardwick Empire in Manchester and said they had to be headliners. I'd never booked a headliner before – I just booked acts – and I was very nervous about it, and so were the management. I went for the opening night, of course – in fact, I went for the night beforehand and watched them rehearse. I arranged that they could have rehearsals on the Sunday, and they were a sensation, an absolute sensation. They'd never heard anything like it.'

The Manchester engagement (probably at the Ardwick Hippodrome rather than the Empire) was recalled for me by a 90-year-old Lord Grade at seven o'clock one morning in 1996. Brandishing one of his legendary nine-inch cigars, he stalwartly refused even to consider that this video-taped interview be conducted without his trademark Havana. Political correctness and no-smoking lobbies meant little to this giant theatrical Cossack: 'No cigar, no Lew Grade.' As a concession, though, the cigar remained unlit. 'I booked them at the London Palladium [billed below Tex Ritter and his performing horse] and every theatre in England.'

Lew did eventually put them on the British variety circuit in 1939, but not before a rightly famous jazz debut.

In Britain, especially amongst musicians, the Quintet's reputation had preceded them. In as early as 14 September 1935, the *Melody Maker*, under the headline 'Swing On Strings', had hailed them as 'a small orchestra which makes a big effort to get away from the stereotypes...a singular combination... The star men in the orchestra are Stéphane Grappelly and Django Reinhardt...'

The American influence in Paris meant that the Quintet's string bass or bass viol – a fairly recently takeover from the sousaphone – was the accepted instrument for the bottom harmony and rhythmic drive. In London, however, the instrument was still a novelty in a jazz-solo context, and the paper seemed unconvinced, stating, 'Whether the string bass ought to be used as a solo instrument is a debatable point. The rhythm section works like one man...a proof that the intuition of the various members must be highly developed. Let us hope they can be brought together for an early visit to England.'

In the same issue, the great jazz record producer John Hammond reviewed the augmented Quintet's recordings of 'Avalon' and 'Smoke Rings'. Under the headline 'Venuti's Rival: Remarkable Hot Fiddling By Stéphane Grappelly,' Hammond continues, 'Venuti undisputed king of rhythmic fiddlers for ten years is being challenged for supremacy... [Grappelly's] fiddle-playing [is] altogether astonishing for a European... It is Grappelly who is the real star of the band. His fiddle-playing has a bite and vitality which places it in a class of its own, for there is little copying, for once, of Venuti's tricks and clichés.

'His tone has a vibrancy that reminds one more of the golden days of Eddie South. Grappelly's phrasing is always near perfection and his technique more than ample. Hughes Parnassié is right when he places him amongst the finest swing fiddlers anywhere... Reinhardt would be magnificent but single-string guitar pyrotechnics are bound to become fatiguing in the long run... Grappelly is really magnificent.' We begin to see why Stéphane might feel at home in this land of astute musical criticism. It's worth noting that Hammond was well qualified to make the comparisons with Venuti, having supervised his Columbia recordings of 1934.

The first Quintet visit to England was highly anticipated. The 1 January 1938 edition of the *Melody Maker* advertised a 'big party from France coming to town for Grappelly-Reinhardt *Melody Maker* concert. All 3/6-penny tickets sold out.' Four weeks before 30 January, the scheduled date of the concert, even the five-shilling tickets in the dress circle were sold out. The best seats in the house cost 7/6 (a little over $1). The Quintet concert was selling tickets faster than any previous concert by Duke Ellington, Louis Armstrong or Benny Carter.

The Cambridge Theatre is a relatively small intimate theatre and the *Melody Maker* writer recognised this as being a perfect for acoustic guitar and violin solos. In 1938, onstage amplification was still a very primitive art; two carbon microphones, a valve amplifier and a couple of over-worked cardboard coned speakers were the best that could be expected.*

The concert was a sell-out and was attended by non other than Hot Club secretary Pierre Nourry. The band, comprising Stéphane, Django, Eugenne Vees,† Roger Chaput and Louis Vola, opened the first half and were introduced in grand style by master of ceremonies Chappie d'Amato.

Charles Chilton, the legendary BBC *Goon Show* producer, was one of a lucky audience of 1,200 musical aficionados: 'When they came on, the response was riotous. They played all their records… Usually, if there was a black player in the band, they screamed for him to do a solo. (Quite often this might be an innocent West Indian who had never even seen America.) In this case, however, it wasn't Stéphane or Django they screamed for; it was the bass player, Vola, because in those days the string bass was relatively new. English bandleaders Henry Hall and Bill Cotton had sousaphones and banjos. The bass was a novelty, so the audience screamed for this man to solo a few choruses and applauded the roof off… It was a wonderful afternoon, a tremendous success.'

Mathison Brooks, also there for *Melody Maker*, described the event: 'Salvoes of applause crashed over their deserving heads as they lined up in front of the tabs, grinning delightedly at their overwhelming success. If they missed, during their playing, the familiar calls of the French "cats" and the wild clapping after every solo passage such as they get at home, they will now realise that the rapt attention paid to every note by their British audience was nonetheless flattering and, in its way, even more complimentary.'

Both witnesses remark on the Quintet's odd stage manner. Charles Chilton reports, 'When the curtains opened, the Quintet were already there, Django sitting in the middle, a guitar either side, bass behind. Now I think the guitarists must have been his brothers, because they looked like him, and they sat there with their guitars parallel with the ground, not as they should be, pointing up at 45 degrees, and they sat there like they held rifles, playing chords – *chump,*

---

*Truvoice receive thanks in the concert programme for 'the careful amplification', which according to Charles Chilton was first class.

†Vees worked with the Quintet off and on since Django and Joseph fell out in the new year of 1937. Joseph was allegedly fed up with his lot and also Django's no-show for a recent Zurich engagement. Vees was a cousin of Django's, born in Algeria in 1915. He died in Bagnolet in 1977.

chump, chump – all the time absolutely together, both rhythm guitarists playing exactly the same thing. They looked bored to death! And Django would shout at them in French, "Another chorus!" or something. The bass player looked very happy because he was an individual, but the others were automatons. Of course, Django himself was a sensation and [there was a great] contrast when Stéphane came forward with an entirely different sound. He played the fiddle like he was making love to it.'

Mathison meanwhile, remarked, 'Grappelly, standing, works to the mic with great skill and experience. Unobtrusively, he moves to the flank when he is tacet, a polished, good-looking, grave-faced sort of fellow who plays like an angel.'

Sidney and Janet Baxter, meanwhile, were also in the crowded auditorium: 'It was so exciting you lost track of time... "Night And Day", "Daphne", "Sweet Georgia Brown" and "Mystery Pacific"... They went absolutely crazy on "Mystery Pacific". I don't know how they got those train effects.'

'Mystery Pacific' was a Quintet favourite of the time, based on Ellington's 'Daybreak Express' and similar train-named tunes. At last the band had a use for the three guitars, strumming themselves into an ever-accelerating frenzy, with Django the steady anchor as the boiler set to burst. 'Most of the time Django was totally impassive,' Sidney Baxter continues. 'He seemed to play as if no one else other than the Quintet was in the room. It wasn't as if he was unfriendly – he seemed a warm person – but he was just completely absorbed in his music... He seemed totally relaxed and he hardly looked up from his guitar. But sometimes, when he played something really special, he would look up at the audience and give a twinkling half-smile as if to say, "What do you think of *that?*"'

The Quintet also took audience requests: 'It was fantastic – they could play whatever people asked. Django would look across to Stéphane, perhaps say a couple of words, then off they would go. They made it look so easy... There was a fantastic rapport between Django and Stéphane Grappelly. They seemed to know exactly what each other was going to do, there was never any hesitation about anything.'

Unobserved by all was a little incident recalled by Stéphane: 'The first time we went to England, we were playing near Cambridge Circus. It was packed. We were on the stage, behind the curtain, and the master of ceremonies, in full dress, announced, "Ladies and gentlemen, Stéphane Grappelly, Django Reinhardt and The Hot Club de France." And I was there – before the band, behind the curtain with my violin – and nothing happened. Django didn't start, because his name was not the first! So, in any case, me, I'm an old trouper you know? I don't care, I start alone. But one minute later, Django started – it was OK. Then once more I told him, "Django, don't do that again, because I don't need you to work, you know? If anything goes bad, I can still return to the courtyard. Be careful." But that was Django Reinhardt – what can you do? Sometimes I enjoyed so much to play with him when he was on good form. *C'est la vie*. It was difficult.'

Another fan in that enraptured audience was the 19-year-old blind accordionist George Shearing. 'They were entirely new,' he recalled. 'No brass, no piano, no drums, but they swung, and the English public really appreciated it.' George had in fact joined the audience from backstage before performing way down the bill as part of Claude Bampton's Blind Orchestra.

It's interesting to note that the *Melody Maker* thought the Quintet perhaps too good to dance to, stating, 'Who wants to dance to music as good as that? Who wants to dance to Ellington?' This is not a revelation, but it does mark a change in the perception of jazz, the beginnings of a division between the dance-band orchestra – literally engaged for dancing – and the emerging notion of chamber jazz, music to listen to while seated comfortably in a Sunday-afternoon concert. This harks to the future and the serious-music notions of any number of artists from Thelonious Monk to The Modern Jazz Quartet.

Baxter states, 'As the concert went on, the audience got more and more excited. There was a group of French people at the back, probably Nourry and friends from the French Hot Club, and they were going absolutely crazy, screaming, shouting and stamping their feet… We were all standing up and shouting and cheering at the end of each tune… The audience would not let them go… They played several encores. It is a night I will never forget. I suppose now, when I look back, it was a night of real history.'

Triumphant and with the energy of young men, the very next day, Monday 31 January, at London's Upper Thames Street Studios, the Quintet recorded eight 78rpm sides, including their virtual anthems 'Honeysuckle Rose' and 'Sweet Georgia Brown'. On Cole Porter's 'Night And Day', Stéphane demonstrates all the taste and poetry of phrasing that would make him justly famous, and his articulation inspires Django to give his melodic best. The sessions are also famous for Django's comic speech in 'My Sweet': 'Would M Vola like to take a solo?', while on 'Take One', in a slip of the foreign tongue, he asks 'Would M Solo like to take a Vola?'

The Quintet had arrived, *Stompin' At Decca* for the princely sum of £65 a session.

While in England, Stéphane and Django offered Decca some novelties in the shape of solo records. Django revived the ever-popular 'J'Attendrai' with Stéphane at the piano, while for his outing Stéphane chose 'It Had To Be You' and his own 'Nocturne', both with just Django. As he often did, Stéphane doubled on piano so Django could avoid playing completely solo, something that the guitarist was never comfortable with, having worked so hard on developing such a strong single-line technique.

In April 1938, they pair kept the English connection alive by broadcasting on short-wave programme from Paris with English announcements, in which they played the Quintet standards 'Djangology' and 'Daphne'.

It must have been an anti-climax to return to a still-depressed Paris, where Stéphane was now renting a small apartment in Montmartre's Rue du Faubourg. Fortunately, the new Swing label did give Stéphane and Django the opportunity to increase their recording experience. They also met the American harmonica player Larry Adler, playing at the Alhambra music hall. Adler had been born in Baltimore in 1914, and by the 1930s he had established his humble instrument as a solo feature with both Duke Ellington and George Gershwin. The Quintet were impressed enough to record with him in May. With Roger Grasset again on bass, they committed to shellac versions of 'Body And Soul', 'Lover Come Back To Me', 'My Melancholy Baby' and the inevitable 'I Got Rhythm'. Larry comes over as a novelty vaudeville virtuoso, and on 'I Got Rhythm' Stéphane contributes one of his most spirited early piano performances. The musicians were billed on the 78rpm record as 'D'Orchestre Swing'. The world's first jazz record label raised its profile once more.

Other than these recordings, things were still a little flat. Stéphane realised perhaps that it was easier to be a prophet in a foreign land and soon departed for Scandinavia. A semi-formal publicity photograph of Stéphane and Django survives from this tour and Stéphane kept it in his shoebox collection. It pictures the duo outside a theatre, Django dressed remarkably fashionably in a bomber jacket fit for a film star, both he and Stéphane with cool cigarettes at jaunty angles. The pair are proudly standing beneath a very modern-looking theatre hoarding proclaiming the 'Franska Hotkvintett'. Next to a poster of black minstrels, harking back to Paul Colin and La Revue Nègre, the entrance to the theatre carries a montage of publicity stills for forthcoming attractions. Alongside glamorous vamps and acrobatic daredevils is the most famous Hot Club Quintet photograph of all: the Collins & Grade Vaudeville Exchange image of the Quintet onstage in white tuxedos. This was a variety venue and clearly a new and lucrative platform for the versatile Hot Club Quintet.

Back in Paris, near Pigalle, down a little passage off the Rue Chaptal was a tiny office and studio. Surrounded by trees in a shady garden, this was to be the new headquarters of Le Hot Club du France. The studio's grand opening had as its guest Duke Ellington, while live music came from the Quintet. Hopes were high that the Duke, suitably impressed, would propose an American tour. Pictures were taken, but the Duke, though obviously charmed, had enough problems at that time in keeping his own band together. He even subsidised his orchestra's pay from songwriting royalties. Small bands were the future, but you couldn't expect the Duke to be too enthusiastic.

In June, Stéphane found himself in a full-page portrait on the cover of *Jazz Hot*. This publicity shot, taken for Swing, shows him looking very young for 30, with heavily Brylcreemed hair and a very earnest Hollywood-star expression. The same issue carries banner headlines for 'La Grande Nuit de Jazz: A Manifestation Without Precedent In The Annals Of French Jazz', staged once more at the famous Moulin de la Galette. The event was important enough to prompt an enterprising Jacques Bureau to make a recording, not an easy task in 1938, when tape-recording was still a research project and portable disc equipment weighed several tons. The historic building, which still stands, was a principle venue for the early Hot Club, and it's fascinating again to hear the band playing there, in a live situation. They sound as if they're playing for hot dancing, Stéphane and Django again digging in to emphasise the rhythmic quality of 'Daphne', 'Limehouse Blues' and 'Swing Guitars'. This is a less restrained Quintet, very confident and enjoying the enthusiastic response from the clearly packed windmill. Stéphane is particularly loose and swinging, living up to the recent accolades from Panassié and others. A surviving poster advertises the string band at the top of the bill, 30 francs on the door – 'le snip!'

The poster also shows Michel Warlop on the same bill, with Django providing the chords. On the recording, Warlop's bold but rather sad attempt at 'Sweet Sue' suffers from poor intonation and just doesn't swing, but he was brave to stand on the same stage as the now-assured Stéphane and got a rousing reception from the home crowd, including his own orchestra.

By July, the Quintet were back in England, where they intended to stay for a few weeks but eventually extended that to four months. This meant a whole mixed bag of appearances, including sharing a top bill at the London Palladium with the cowboy showman Tom Mix. Stéphane remembered Django during rehearsals having a go at Mix's lasso and generally being a little overwhelmed: 'Lew Grade managed to get us there. It's supposed to be the greatest music hall in the World, but it was a dramatic start. The first night, Django didn't turn up! And that was the most difficult thing for me; I can't describe how I suffered, obliged to play with just the three boys. That made it so difficult for me, so I said to Django, "If you do that again, you can find somebody else!"'

This is a stark contrast to another date, which accorded Stéphane the delight of meeting and playing 'Honeysuckle Rose' with Fats Waller. No doubt the violinist was in seventh heaven. The tune remained in his repertoire for the next 60 years.

It was this UK tour that included Lew Grade's booking at the Ardwick Hippodrome on 4 July 1938, and Stéphane kept a snapshot of the billing in his shoebox. BMG writer Charlie Scott and future composer Jack Duarte, 'the Manchester Guitar Circle stalwarts', didn't just watch; they sneaked backstage at rehearsals: 'We found them in a rather small, dingy dressing room. Django spoke no English and we but a little bad schoolboy French. Grappelly did the honours and conveyed our congratulations… Out on the stage, rehearsals had finished and the orchestra played a few desultory bars of the National Anthem. An impish smile flitted across the round swarthy face of Django as his fingers danced across the strings in a deliberately corny but joyous little syncopated caricature of that staid and majestic tune.'

Onstage, meanwhile, 'a packed house has rocked to the broad Yorkshire humour of Albert Modley and relaxed to the "Babbling Brook" songs of Donald Peers. Then from behind the closed curtains comes the ripple of golden notes from a magic guitar, backed seconds later by a solid lifting beat and the resonant, biting attack of a rhythmic violin. A roar of applause surges from the audience… In the centre, on a raised dais, a casual, swarthy figure hunched over a Maccaferri guitar… There, against the contrasting background of the elegant, slim, white-jacketed standing figure of the violinist Stéphane Grappelly, sits this rather nondescript-looking figure…feet clad in street boots…the little French gypsy …a roar of adulation…clap until your hands are sore…chorus follows chorus in a rising tide of excitement and curtain after curtain and repeated encores until finally the elated audience poured out into the dusk of a summer evening.'

British acclaim meant that the Quintet returned to France a success, and this generated a flurry of large-scale promotions. The band took with them the glamorous young English singer Beryl Davis, who claimed to be 14 in order to obtain a work permit when she was in fact only 12 and had the greatest of difficulty finding any bosom to hold up the lavish gowns constructed to make her look more mature. She had no fear of performing abroad, however, having been born backstage at the Plymouth Palace Theatre and touring with Oscar Rabin's band for most of her short life: 'My father, Harry Davis, was a guitarist and former Liverpool docker. My mother a chorus girl and native of Plymouth.' Beryl herself became a child star as an, Ovaltiney, singing in the famous UK advert for a hot malty beverage. She had been suggested as a singer for The Hot Club Quintet by the Collins & Grade Vaudeville Exchange, where Lew knew her work from handling bookings for the Rabin band.

The child-like Beryl caused quite a stir with her romantic repertoire, particularly 'First Affair' and 'Undecided', with their knowing lyrics. Her big influence was early Ella Fitzgerald, 'A Tisket, A Tasket' from the previous year being Ella's first mainstream hit. 'I learned everything from Ella's records,' Davis admits, 'and being so young, I was fearless.' She acted as master of ceremonies for the shows at the Paris ABC and Maginot theatres, speaking in hastily learned phonetic French. Some accounts of these concert describe the audience screaming for Beryl to sing 'En Français', but she remembers learning some songs in French. This suggests that the audience member were, again, not strictly jazz lovers, who might naturally expect American songs to be sung in English. But jazz lovers or not, this young English singer connected with them in a way that transcended language.

That year, 1939, Stéphane returned to France to tragic news. His father, ill for some time, had been admitted on 19 April to l'Hôpital Laribrosière, where he died on 12 May. Stéphane was very close to his father, always quick to tell an interviewer how much he owed to that inspiring and original man.

As Stéphane achieved some success, he had opened a bank account for Ernesto and topped it up regularly for his upkeep. Going through his father's papers, he examined the bank book and discovered that his proud father had never made a withdrawal.

In an unusual move for the time, Stéphane had his father cremated and prepared for his ashes to be returned eventually to his birthplace, visiting Italy in July and painstakingly trying to re-establish connections in Alatri and Nettuno. However, with a gap of 44 years since Ernesto's departure in 1895, and having never met his Italian relatives, this proved a difficult task, one which Stéphane would gently pursue for another 50 years. Throughout that time, Stéphane kept a precious lock of his father's hair carefully wrapped in tissue in his bureau at home, a small photograph adorning the lid, along with some letters in his father's wonderful copperplate handwriting.

Most of the Quintet's 1938/9 engagements, especially in Britain, were music-hall or variety bookings. Stéphane, Django, Louis Vola and various gypsy cousins interspersed quite comfortably amongst jugglers, trick cyclists, magicians and dancing girls, artists such as Dee and Maisie and their 'electric Hawaiian guitars'; Fred Brand, 'the Chocolate Drop from Dixie'; Harry Jerome, 'scientific spoof' – I'm not making this up; these artists all played in support at the Chiswick Empire.

In Europe, 'variety' – literally a variety of entertainment – had grown out of the tradition of music hall, which in turn had emerged from entertainment staged in outdoor pleasure gardens like the Moulin de la Galette and in pubs and inns. The first acknowledged indoor music hall was opened in a pub owned by Charles Morton called the Lambeth, in London's Oxford Street, in 1861. By 1868, there were 200 music halls in London and countless others dotted around the country. Artists could now tour these halls using the newly improved rail and road networks.

Variety 'cleaned up' some of the lewder music-hall sex and comedy content and brought a little more glitz to proceedings. In America, the related art of vaudeville was introduced by European settlers and sprang from the Calvados region of France, where 'vau de ville' meant any form of light entertainment.

Many British entertainment agents aspired to the phenomenal vaudeville success of the American Ziegfeld Follies, the brainchild of French-born Anna Held Ziegfeld, who held her press conferences in baths of milk while singing 'Won't You Come And Play Wiz Me?'. With her enterprising husband, Florenz, they broke all box-office records, and it was an aspiration to equal this success that no doubt led to the Collins & Grade Vaudeville Exchange.

Charles Chilton, who started his career as a messenger boy at Broadcasting House and then became the first ever BBC record librarian, saw the Quintet appear: 'That was the form. Music hall was still being glamorised into variety, and a jazz band was just another act.'

The Quintet's appearance at the gigantic Kilburn State Theatre, an adapted cinema, was reviewed in an August edition of *Melody Maker* as front-page news. Interestingly, this review also favoured Stéphane over Django and covered 'their second triumph, ably compered by Beryl Davis... The white-coated Hot Club Five [opened] with "Djangology", their current theme tune...only surpassed by "Minor Swing", which the fiddler built up to a tremendous climax.

Grappelly showed that he is still one of the sweetest hot fiddlers in the world, and his romantic tone and thoughtful interpretation put him in a class by himself in European music. Beryl Davis sang "Wishing", "Don't Worry 'Bout Me" and a very plaintive and winning treatment of "The Man I Love".' Django goes without a mention. Of course, he may have failed to turn up.

However, in the same week, at a party for the Quintet at jazz hangout the Nut House, Django managed to make his presence felt with some impressive jamming on 'Liebestraum'. Interestingly, also present was George Shearing, and according to the *Melody Maker*, Stéphane was impressed: '[Shearing] is playing some very interesting choruses with a vigorous left hand and he is using a trick of working in the treble with both hands which made Stéphane Grappelly stop and listen with both ears bent.'

This is interesting on two counts, both as the first acknowledged meeting of Stéphane and Shearing but also as an observation of the close-harmony style which was to become the blind pianist's musical signature. For all his fiddle-playing virtuosity, Stéphane remained a pianist at heart, and his appreciation of Shearing's harmony would never dim.

Lew Grade's British success with the Quintet opened the door to other French acts, including the great Edith Piaf, Jean Sablon and Patachou. Agents and promoters particularly like female vocalists as they have an audience appeal beyond their musical talent, and this was exploited then just as much as it is now.

At a session organised by Lew Grade, Beryl Davis recorded with the Quintet at London's Decca Studios on 25 August 1939, delivering 'Undecided' in the straight style of the time, which serves to emphasise the audacity of Stéphane and Django's invention on their instrumental choruses and Django's tasteful counterpoint on the final vocal chorus. The arrangement is full of outrageous detail that lifts a pop song to a different level of interest. There is so much to be learned here about use of dynamics and colour, all enhancing that essential swing feel.

For 'Don't Worry 'Bout Me', Stéphane takes to the studio piano and Django contributes a wistful intro full of musical taste. His audacious second solo features one of his signature one-string runs. Even in support, both Django and Stéphane demonstrate genius.

As the money started to come in, Django saw an opportunity to pursue his love of flash cars. However, his automotive ambition exceeded his income. As Prime Minister Neville Chamberlain made headlines in Munich, losing his battle for appeasement with Adolf Hitler, Lew Grade offered Django a solution. 'It was a terrible thing,' mourned Grade. 'Django wanted to buy a car and he had no money, not enough money to buy a car, [so] I paid for a car and we arranged that I would deduct it from his salary, week to week. Then I woke up in September 1939 and war was declared, and [the Quintet] were due to appear that Monday at a theatre.'

Stéphane also recalled the tale: 'Django called me in my room and said, "We're going back. There's a war on." I said, "Well, I don't care. I'm not in a hurry," so he went away.'

Lew: 'I phoned Stéphane Grappelly and said, "Now you have to stay here and carry on working," and he said, "Django's gone." Django had left and had taken the car with him, so I was stuck with the cost of the car. But Stéphane stayed on and I saw him that night and he was devastated, but I said, "Don't worry. Relax. Everything will be OK." There was no such things as bombs at that time."

This left Stéphane in a quandary. He had just lost his father and the family home in the Rue de Rochechouart. Sylvia had disappeared, taking his baby daughter, Evelyne. In Paris he had just his empty flat in the Rue du Fauberg, while in England he had success, appreciation and potential work. There was little pulling him to a war-torn Europe. He must also have wondered about his fate in Paris as a French Italian. What if, as seemed likely, the Germans took Paris?

In England, his immediate practical problems were soon resolved by Beryl Davis's family, who took him in and gave him food, a bed and some borrowed clothes. Few thought the war would last, and although the air-raid sirens were tested, the Phoney War of 1939–40 seemed to hold little real threat. Safe on this fortress island, Stéphane had his violin, a white tuxedo and a few words of English, but at the age of 31 the former street urchin of Montmartre was once more alone.

12 The War Years

'Stéphane, of Italian descent, living most of his life in France, confided in me that he would really like to call London his home!'

– *Fred R Sharp*

As Stéphane adjusted to his adopted home, there were many practicalities to resolve. He was a French citizen with an Italian name and Italy soon allied itself to Hitler. He must have wondered if he was better off in England as a registered alien or back in France as a French citizen with an Italian name. George Orwell caught the cold reality of this situation when, in Piers Brendon's book *The Dark Valley*, he reported on 'Sicilian coffee bars having bricks hurled through their windows in London's Soho, their owners assaulted on the street'.

When Italy physically entered the war, London restaurateurs the Quaglino brothers disappeared, as did Ferraro, the maître d'hôtel at the Berkeley. Victor Toliano, an Italian waiter, was marched away with a group of his compatriots while a bystander shouted, 'Look at the dirty Germans! Spit on them!' Speaking to *The Sunday Tribune*, Stéphane remarked, 'Italians had a very bad time during the war. I remember the proprietor of the Italian restaurant where I worked in Piccadilly. He was put on a boat with other Italians and the boat sank… This was terrible. That man would not harm anybody but [shrugs] that is war.'

Any foreigner seen consulting a map was likely to be arrested as a suspected spy. *The Enfield Gazette* reported an 'alien' being employed at an ARP centre: 'We are glad to be able to report that the employment of the person in question has now been terminated.'

Stéphane was a stranger with a foreign accent in nervous, angry times. With the Quintet now in Paris, he was also out of work. Django tellingly replaced Stéphane's solos with the less challenging clarinet of Hubert Rostaing. Reinhardt would brave out the war years shielded only by his high-profile fame and a gypsy talent for disappearance.

In London and without recognised papers, Stéphane was in a potentially dangerous position. He reported to the French Ambassador and, following a medical examination, was declared unfit for active service (he had lost a kidney as a result of his earlier privations).* On the work front, however, he was fortunate to have a powerful ally in Lew Grade, a fellow immigrant of reputation and long standing. Grappelly had nothing to declare but his talent, and that was soon snapped up: 'One day I was in Bond Street and a man on a bicycle called me over – it was Arthur Young, who was the first pianist of Jack Hylton['s band]. He asked me what I was doing in London and I told him I couldn't go back to France because it was closed! He then offered me a job – he needed a violin to front his orchestra. He'd been engaged by a company to play in a restaurant during the war...Hatchets in Piccadilly.'

The *Melody Maker* immediately picked up the Hatchets 'coup'. In an article headed 'Grappelly To Star With Young's Band At Hatchets', they reported, 'Arthur Young has secured non other than Stéphane Grappelly as a speciality attraction...doing his stuff to the accompaniment of Arthur's swingy outfit.' Young probably realised the value of a good violin frontman, having worked with Stéphane's old friend Joe Venuti on some recording dates five years earlier. Also, Stéphane was still getting a lot of good press, which is always good for business.

Now with a job and accorded star status, thanks to *Melody Maker*, Stéphane soon settled down and the business of identity papers and work permits was quickly resolved. The way in which he was accepted in London, despite being a foreign national, made a deep impression on him, and until the end of his life Stéphane was always happy to call Britain his adopted home. He found a permanent room at the Piccadilly Hotel, which was slightly run down but convenient for the nightclubs and restaurants that provided work. Quaglino's and the Café de Paris were only 200 yards from Hatchets.

Piccadilly must have been a stark contrast to bohemian Montmartre. Between Mayfair and Soho, it had been a distinguished quarter since it acquired its name in the 17th century from the piccadills – a type of shirt frill – sold at Piccadilly House. Fine clothes for dandies became Piccadilly's stock in trade. The Princess and Burlington Arcades, for example, are Regency shopfronts for Wildsmith & Co Footwear (est 1847) and Milditch & Key, 'shirtmakers since 1899'. At the end of Princess Arcade is Jermyn Street, home to Sir Isaac Newton, 1642–1727, with a tablet affixed in 1908, the year of Stéphane's birth.

All of this would have rung a bell with the *arriviste* Grappelly. This is still the home of Englishness and the heartland of the English gentleman, with his Crombie overcoat and Church's handmade shoes, slipping around the corner

*The kidney loss is attributed to a car accident in another account.

to Fortnum & Masons or sipping whisky in Nell Gwyn's Red Lion pub. Stéphane, with his father's grace and civility, would have enjoyed Piccadilly.

Hatchets itself resided in the basement of a very grand building opposite the Ritz. The four floors and double attic of 1 Dover Street date from 1884, and the building still has a curiously French look about it. The roof, especially, would provide a suitable garret for Modigliani and his comely models, but neither would be able to afford exclusive Mayfair. The façade is graced with mock-Dorian columns and sculpted chimerae: lions with shields. Everything seems to declare, 'pomp and circumstance sold here'. By the 1940s, however, the grand had given way to the refined and elegant, and the intimate space downstairs must have been the ideal spot for a dashing young major on leave accompanied by his fur-clad and bejewelled escort.

The restaurant had introduced dancing as a wartime policy, no doubt a welcome diversion. While performing there, Stéphane was joined by his friend Beryl Davis, now an established broadcaster, and new guitarist Jack Llewelyn.

Aided by Django and Charlie Christian, the guitar was now an established and popular instrument. The BBC Light Programme even broadcast a series title *Guitar Club* in which Jack had a guest spot. Born in 1914 in Blackpool, Lancashire, Llewelyn was the son of a banjoist and had worked for Orlando's Orchestra and Harry Saville before first appearing with Arthur Young in 1939.

The atmosphere at Hatchets was upmarket, as befits the address. Charles Chilton describes it as 'very grand, a nightclub *cum* restaurant, sometimes difficult to get into, but us BBC types were welcome.' His wife, Penny, based like her husband at Broadcasting House, added, 'It was the place to go at the beginning of the war'.

Stéphane quickly acquired a reputation as a flirt, nonchalantly touching up the ladies from the bandstand with the end of his violin bow. No doubt his exotic Gallic charm was a winner with the female patrons. He also boasted that he could 'get a couple to fall in love by wooing the lady with a gypsy refrain'. Indeed, you can catch a glimpse of this table serenade in the 1948 film *The Flamingo Affair*, in which at one point a nightclub gangster's moll is disdainfully cool in response to Stéphane's crooning. (Stéphane was later embarrassed when I mentioned this cameo, but this is no less an insight into his character.)

The Hatchets band had a fluid personnel, especially guitarists, which included Chappie D'Amato, who, according to Charles Chilton, played in the style of Eddie Lang. Also, Bert Weedon, the early British exponent of the electric guitar, was reintroduced to Stéphane after the pair had worked together at the BBC before the war. Weedon took part in the world's first TV service, operated from Alexander Palace and watched live by a few hundred lucky pioneering viewers: 'When I arrived, there were my two idols. I think there was a little jealousy between Stéphane and Django. They were very different – Stéphane was very elegant and spoke some English; Django didn't understand a word I said but just played some amazing things. My two heroes. I couldn't believe it. Later, Stéphane and I were reunited at Hatchets at £15 a week, a very good wage at the time.' Bert went on to become Britain's first television guitar star in the Swinging '60s, while other Hatchets personnel included Bill Shakespeare on trumpet, Dennis Moonan on clarinet and tenor, George Senior on bass and Tony Spurgin on drums.

Soon, the distinctive nasal chug of Arthur Young's Novachord – an early electric keyboard with a limited range of tone colour – pervaded the band's sound. No doubt the instrument's novelty value pleased the crowd. It was preserved on record as quickly as December 1939, when 'The Hatchets Swingtette' recorded 'Alexander's Ragtime Band', a tune that evoked the happier 1920s. The merry opus begins in cheery chin-up-and-don't-let-the-war-get-you-down fashion and remains decidedly quaint throughout. The feel is very British dance-band era rather than anything to do with jazz. On this cut, and not for the first time, Stéphane demonstrates his pragmatic attitude – he's happy to be working, putting a little butter on his spinach. His playing, however, sounds distinctly uninspired, while his friend Beryl Davis sounds reassuring, stylish and very Andrews Sisters in her trumpet 'faldree'. It's simply happy music for bad times. It would soon be needed.

The Phoney War of late 1939 and early 1940, characterised by a lot of talk and very little actual warfare, was dramatically forgotten as Hitler began his airborne siege of London. Between 7 September and 13 November 1940, the capital suffered the Luftwaffes Blitzkrieg every night except 3 November. On 14 October, Piccadilly took its worst hit: 100 yards from Hatchets, the Christopher Wren-designed St James's Church was gutted after incendiary bombs caused a disastrous firestorm.

On the bandstand, throughout, Stéphane didn't confine himself to the lightweight band at Hatchets. Charles Chilton: 'Sometimes we met up with Stéphane at Quaglino's in Berkley Square. The band there was a sextet led by Stéphane… We often had to stay all night because of the air raids.'

The threat was very real. Hatchets' flat roof was the perfect lodging place for incendiaries, and Stéphane was required to do his bit as a fire warden, chasing incendiary bombs with the versatile Chappie D'Amato: 'Everybody was obliged to go on the roof with buckets of sand to put out the fire. Everybody – the maître d'hôtel, the cook, we all took turns waiting for the bombs. My turn came once a week and I managed to go always with my great friend Chappie. He was such a funny man that I was not so afraid. One day, a very stuffy colonel strutting about with his stick and his nose in the air found out I was French and banned me from the roof. That was fine for me!'

The Blitz was an unprecedented horror. This new kind of warfare devastated innocent civilians, tearing apart a culture and its symbols. On a nightly basis, the brave officers of the London Fire Service took on the impossible task of containing the fury of thousands of tons of military ordnance. In Piccadilly, the delicate statue of Eros and his love-inflicting arrows was encased in armour plating. One night, 3,000 civilians died. In total, London received the blast of 18,900 tons of high explosive, which destroyed three and a half million homes.

In the face of this daily horror, Londoners acquired a reputation for grit and determination. The Tube stations became makeshift air-raid shelters for families made homeless by bombs, although many resolute citizens, including Stéphane, refused to be cowed into hiding.

The number of air-raids diminished in 1941, but in March the nearby Café de Paris suffered two direct hits. One bomb remained unexploded while the other killed the bandleader, 'Snake-Hips' Johnson, and several other staff and patrons. A witness, dustman Uncle Tom, remarked tearfully on 'young men in uniforms carrying out their dead girlfriends'.

For Stéphane there was a close and very personal loss. In Stéphane's collection, a photographic portrait by Basil Shackleton of Shaftesbury Avenue shows a raven-haired beauty with the look and style of a '40s film star. This was Gwendoline Turner. Another, more informal snapshot, kept in his shoebox, shows Stéphane and Gwendoline in a club setting with Stéphane embracing Gwen in a shared smile, both staring into the middle distance, Gwen clutching Stéphane's thigh in a gesture of affection, both toasting a mystery wish with half-full wineglasses. Gwendoline died slowly, tragically disfigured by a bomb's initial blast. This, combined with the photographs, is the only evidence that remains. Stéphane could never talk of the pain of his loss, and would never discuss Gwendoline. Most of his closest friends are even unaware of her name. He once remarked that, after her death, he cried intermittently for the next two years. He kept a single curl of her hair

Stéphane's parents, Ernesto Grappelli and Anna Emilie Hanocque, with one-year-old Stephano in 1909 (courtesy of the Stéphane Grappelli Collection)

Isadora Duncan, an evocative photograph for Stéphane (courtesy of the Stéphane Grappelli Collection, photograph by Arnold Genthe, 1916)

Ray Ventura et ses Collegiens, *circa* 1929, Stéphane is first on the left (courtesy of the Stéphane Grappelli Collection)

Hughes Panassié and his saxophone, *circa* 1928 (courtesy of the Patrice Panassié Collection)

Stéphane Grappelly and saxophone (note the large vocal megaphone) in the late 1920s; band unknown (courtesy of the Stéphane Grappelli Collection)

Grégor et ses Grégoriens, possibly on the stage of HMS *Alacantra* bound for Argentina in October 1930 (courtesy of the Stéphane Grappelli Collection, photograph by Don Bishop)

Monte Cristo nightclub, Rue Fromentin, Montmartre, with Stéphane on saxophone! (1934); The Jacque Zarou Orchestra with Don Baird on guitar (courtesy of the Stéphane Grappelli Collection)

La Quintette du Hot Club de France. Photograph taken for the Will Collins and Lew Grade Theatrical & Vaudeville Exchange, *circa* 1938 (© the Grade Organisation)

DJANGO REINHARDT
STEPHANE GRAPPELLY
ET LEUR

QUINTETTE DU HOT CLUB DE FRANCE

VEDETTES DES DISQUES
"LA VOIX DE SON MAITRE"
et "SWING"

PRIX DES PLACES : 10 A 35 FRANCS
(REDUCTIONS AUX MEMBRES DU HOT CLUB)
LOCATION : BOITE A MUSIQUE, 133, Boulevard Raspail – chez MAX ESCHIG,
48, Rue de Rome – à BROADWAY, 79, Avenue des Champs-Elysées – au MUSIC
SHOP, 67, Rue Pierre-Charron – à SINFONIA, 68, Avenue des Champs Elysées;
DURAND, Place de la Madeleine – chez HAMM, 139, Rue de Rennes – au
DISCOBOLE, Galerie des Marchands Gare Saint-Lazare – à la SEMAINE DE
PARIS, 28, Rue d'Assas et à la SALLE GAVEAU

STEPHANE
GRAPPELLY

Swing publicity handout dating from 1937, although the source photo may be earlier (courtesy of the Stéphane Grappelli Collection)

Left: concert poster advertising newly signed Swing artists, 193 (courtesy of *Jazz Hot* magazine

L-r: Stéphane Grappelly, the Norwegian singer Carola Merried and Django Reinhardt, late 1930s (courtesy of the Stéphane Grappelli Collection)

Stéphane Grappelly, Django Reinhardt and 'the first English Quintet' on stage *circa* 1939 (courtesy of the Stéphane Grappelli Collection)

Gwendoline Turner, a victim of the London Blitz (© Basil Shackleton)

Stéphane Grappelly and Gwendoline Turner, *circa* 1940 (courtesy of the Stéphane Grappelli Collection)

Stéphane Grappelly and Django
Reinhardt, *circa* 1938 (courtesy of the
Stéphane Grappelli Collection)

The Hot Club Quintet with Beryl Davis, *circa* 1938
(courtesy of the Stéphane Grappelli Collection)

Stéphane with the Quintet in England, *circa* 1938 (courtesy of the Stéphane Grappelli Collection)

Recording Session, London, 1946. L-r: Django Reinhardt, Allan Hodgkiss, Coleridge Goode, Jack Llewellyn, Stéphane Grappelly (courtesy of *Melody Maker*, IPC Media)

Stéphane Grappelly and his daughter, Evelyne, 1946 (courtesy of the Stéphane Grappelli Collection)

Stéphane Grappelly and Django Reinhardt in London, 1947 (© Erpe)

PHILADELPHIA PETERSBURG
NORKFOLK ROCHESTER
TORONTO CANADA TOLEDO
OMAA OHIO SANFRANCISCO
LINGCOL ENFIN JAIS PARCOURU
PA MAL. ET CE NÈ YUE LA
MOITIES. JE MEUX RAPÈLE PLUS
DES VILLES. A LORS TU TE
RENCONTE DU TRAVALLE.
MON CHÈR STÈPHANE TU
MESCUSERA ENCORE UNE
FOÎT DE PLUS POUR L'OCTOGRAF
MAIS JÉSPÈRE YUE TU CON
PRANDKA. DI BIEN DES
CHOSE GEORGÈTE TU SAIS
LA PETIT DU JOURNALEP
MUSICAL EXPRÉSS A BIENTO
Di Reinhardt

Henry Hudson HOTEL
353 WEST FIFTY-SEVENTH STREET
NEW YORK 19, N. Y.

DEC 1946.
MONT CHÉR
STÉPHANE. JE TÉCRIS SAIS.
DEUX MAUX. POUR TE DIRE
YUE LES A FAIRES VONS
MAGNIFIYUEMENT BIENT. ISI.
TU MÈSCUSERA SI JE TÈ PAS
ÈCRI PLUS VITE. ETANT EN
TOURNÈS JE NAVAI VRAIMENT
PAS LE TENT. LÈSONS SAIS
CHOSE LA DE COTÈS. A NEW YORK
TU È TRÉS ADENDU TOUS LE
MONDE MEÙ. DEMANDES
L'AN VIENDRA TU A LORS MOI

MINTENANT JE VAIS TE ③
DÈCRIRE A LA VITÉSE LA
TOURNÈS. SAIS FORMIDABLE
NOUS AVONS UN PULMMANE
POUR L'ORCHÈSTE. TOUS LES
MUSICIEN SONS COUCHÈT. ET
DUKE ET MOI NOUS AVONS
UN PETIT LIVIG ROOM. A DEUX
LIT. DUKE SAIS LE PLUS
GRAND MUSICIEN. SOUVEN A
PRÈS LE CONCÈR. DUKE ÈCRI
LA MUSIYUE. DANS LE PETIT
LIVIG ROOM. A LORS SAIS
MÈRVÈLLES SAIS VRAIMENT
FORMIDABLE DUKE VIEN DÈS
CRIRE GRAND OPÉRA. SAIS FOUS
ENFIN JE VAIS TE DIRLES
YUELYUE VILLES. BUFALO CLAIVE
LAN. KASAS CITI CINSINNATI
CHICAGO BOSTON DÈTROIT

JE LEUR RÉPOND. YUE TU ②
VIENDRA BIENTO. A LORS
TOUS LE MONDE È RAVIS.
MAIS YUELYUE JOUR APRÉS
MON ARIVÉR. JE ME SUIS
INFORMÉS POUR LE YUINTÈTE.
A LU NIONS IL MON DI YUE
SAIS INPOSIBLE. A LORS JE
ME SUIS DI SAIS PAS LA
PÈNE. DE. TROT LEUR PARLÈS.
DE TOIT. IL SONS. TRÉS DUR
MAIS TOUT CA RENJERA
YAN MÊME. CA DURERA PETÈTRE
LONTENT MAIS TU VIENDRA
AUX USA. MON CHÉR
STÉPHANE JE. NE VOIS PLUS.
GRAND CHOSE A TE DIR

Django's letter sent to Stéphane Grappelly whilst touring with Duke Ellington, December 1946 (courtesy of the Stéphane Grappelli Collection) in his bureau in Paris in an envelope marked 'Final letter of Papa and *cheveux* Gwen'. Her studio photograph he had copied as an oil painting, but it remained locked away from all eyes but his.

The loss of his father and lover in such a short span of time precipitated health problems for Stéphane, and in August 1941 he was admitted with kidney problems to the Collindale Hospital in Hendon. During this time, the Musicians' Union helped him through a difficult financial situation as, being an alien, he had no immediate right to hospital care. He was subjected to two operations in a fortnight and at one point, with seven doctors in attendance and a temperature of 105 degrees, things were touch and go. Ill health plagued Stéphane throughout his career, worsened perhaps by the malnutrition of his urchin days, but he always made light of his condition and it rarely stopped him from giving a concert.

By October, the *Melody Maker* was able to report that Stéphane was again picking up his fan mail, apologising for not replying to all his well-wishers, and pictured him reading his get-well cards. Once more, Stéphane kept a copy of the original photograph in his shoebox collection.

The Grappelly luck appeared once more in the shape of a Hatchets customer, Dr Jack Harrison. Stéphane had few real friends, but Dr Harrison and his wife, Audrey, came to mean a lot to him. Their acquaintanceship started in hospital but developed with an invitation to their Devon home in order to convalescence. Stéphane was sufficiently entranced by this first experience of the English countryside to seek his own retreat in that same county, which he found in the peaceful village of Lustleigh. His cottage there, Underwood, became a frequent bolthole, even as his health returned.

It was at this stage in his life, with his first real home to furnish, that Stéphane began his lifelong passion for collecting antiques. English village antique shops have a reputation as Aladdin's caves, and amongst the white elephants and junk there are often hidden treasures spotted only by the informed eye. From this point on, Stéphane developed his collector's nose for a bargain, buying perhaps a dozen apparently anonymous china plates in order to secure one hidden gem, often to the surprise of his travelling companions, to whom Stéphane would proudly present the dross – 'A little something for your wife's scullery' – having first extracted the hidden booty secured for a few pennies as part of a junk pile.

The antiques continued to fill his every home. In Paris, there were glass cabinets overflowing with trinkets: snuff boxes, Japanese dolls, assorted silver and a preponderance of miniature violins of every shape and size – some ceramic, others of gilt and pewter. It's a collector's whim that he shared with his later collaborator and similar Anglophile Yehudi Menuhin.

More substantial objects in Stéphane's collection included directoire cabinets and music chests, overstuffed sofas and Queen Anne-style chairs. A favourite was a wooden music stand, more likely to carry a glorious Romanesque art book full of gilded angels than a dusty manuscript.

However, he also loved exquisite miniatures, whether paintings or *objéts d'art*, and those examples in his collection often displayed a filigree nature akin to his own more delicate musical creations, like his harmonic flourishes at the end of a ballad. Indeed, the broadcaster Michael Parkinson was later given to remark, 'Stéphane was incapable of playing an inelegant phrase.'

Elegance in music relies to some extent on a sure foundation, of course, and despite the wartime struggle, Stéphane continued to refine his violin technique, no doubt still harbouring a slight jealousy for the conservatoire training of his friend Michel Warlop. Stéphane was not the sort of man to languish in inadequacies, and despite his fame he sought out a teacher. According to the pianist Alan Clare, Stéphane consulted the distinguished classical virtuoso Alfredo Campoli.

Born in Rome but now based in London, Campoli was two years older than Stéphane and had given his Wigmore Hall debut in 1923, having more recently performed Paganini's *Violin Concerto in D Major* at the celebrated Henry Wood Promenade concerts. Campoli was already a household name for his performances of light music and radio broadcasts, which may explain his meeting Grappelly. The classically trained violinist's Italian citizenship meant that he was banned from the radio in 1940, which also perhaps explains why he would need to teach. Another possibility is that as they were both giving concerts for the troops, maybe even appearing on the same bill.

However it came about, Stéphane seems to have learned a considerable amount of technical polish; Yehudi Menuhin said that Stéphane had 'a perfect classical technique'. Although impressed by Campoli's famous *bel canto* phrasing, describing it as 'pure luminous tone and effortless grace', Grappelly soon found the classical approach inhibiting his freedom and reverted to his auto-didactic approach.*

Back at Hatchets, Stéphane took advantage of Arthur Young and Jack Llewelyn's military call-up to make some very musical changes: 'When Arthur was called up to the army, I became the *chef d'orchestre*, the director.

---

*Campoli's Stradivarius violin, the Dragonetti of 1700, would no doubt have given these two 'Italians' something to talk about. The young Stéphane would have dreamed of one day owning a great violin.

I was obliged to replace him. Somebody told me he knew someone, a young man who played the accordion, and he played the piano too, very good, but he is blind. I said, "So what, if he plays well?" So I went to Battersea to the pub where he was playing and it was George Shearing. So I engaged him and he was very pleased. He started to play with me and we went seven years together. We formed a group together – two guitars, bass and a drummer, a funny man who was very amusing.' The funny man was either Dave Fullerton or Ray Ellington.

Again, the 1948 film of Stéphane and the Quintet shows the prime suspect to be Ray, who seemed to enjoy a winning combination of Satchmo's scat and Louis Mitchell's contraption-drumming antics. However, it's interesting to note that for the film Ray plays a very modern bop drumkit of the type associated with American star Gene Krupa. Throughout his long career, Stéphane always liked to surround himself with forward-looking players, often much younger than himself.

The anecdote concerning Stéphane's 'discovering' George Shearing in a pub is a good story but perhaps not as accurate as it might be. The two men had clearly met earlier at the Nut House, as the *Melody Maker* observed in 1939, when Stéphane acknowledged George's accomplished jazz piano. Whatever the truth behind the story, Stéphane knew good chords when he heard them and he responded immediately to George's more sophisticated harmonic web. George's style looked to the future and the birth of 'cool' West Coast jazz. He was also a composer, which helped the band shape an identity beyond the familiar standard repertoire.

Bert Weedon was struck by Stéphane and George's perfect pitch: 'George was marvellous, though completely unknown then. Stéphane would change key and George would instantly follow, despite not being able to see a thing. They could play anything. They were very happy days.

'I remember going into the band room one day and the bulb had gone in the light fitting. The room was in complete darkness and I fumbled around when a voice said, "Are you all right, Bert?" So I lit a match and there was George sitting in the corner, reading a book in Braille. He didn't care whether the lights worked!'

Introduced via BBC radio sessions, Coleridge Goode, a wonderfully innovative bass player, also worked with George and Stéphane at this time. Born in Kingston, Jamaica, in 1914, Goode had travelled to Britain in 1934 and pursued parallel careers in electrical engineering and music. The paths of the musicians had crossed when Coleridge became the first bass-viol player to experiment with home-made amplification.

The need for amplification had arisen as overstrung pianos and modern drumkits became louder and, in jazz, larger brass instruments replaced clarinets and cornets. Dance bands and small combos were getting louder as relatively expensive big bands were increasingly forced out of business. The pre-war depression had already seen off many larger bands, and the trend continued as war took many players into uniform. The audience, however, still expected the dynamic kick and thrill of loud music. In their relatively quiet and small combo, Coleridge enjoyed watching Stéphane working with George. 'Though I started on violin,' he reported, 'there were very few people playing jazz on fiddle at that time, so I switched to bass, which I did very early on. After a lot of club work, I was delighted to be asked to broadcast with these two distinguished players. Stéphane was unique and fantastic in his very distinctive French way.

'George, because of his blindness, depended on his hearing for his existence, which gave him a very focused ear. He also had the technique to transfer his musical ideas to the keyboard. He had his own harmonic ideas, different from a standard dance-band player. Stéphane would hear George's ideas and instantly be able to write them out on manuscript. It was fascinating to watch.'

On a personal level, the two principals became true friends. Stéphane took George's blindness into account and helped him negotiate the late-night trains to south London, while George reciprocated by guiding Stéphane through the compulsory blackouts. Tiring of the long journey home in often disrupted trains, Stéphane eventually introduced George to the nearby YMCA hostel. Stéphane remembered using the YMCA facilities in Paris for *gymnastique* as a boy. For George, it not only meant a home near to work but also led to a happy relationship. 'George liked his cups of tea, so we went together to the YMCA, and I saw a young woman there washing the floor, and I introduced them,' recalled Stéphane. 'Six months later, he says, "I'm getting married" – and it was the same young girl!' This was George's initial encounter with his first wife, Trixie.

In 1942, as Stéphane started to branch out into other work, Chappie D'Amato became the Quintet's bandleader, while according to the *Melody Maker* he was also a guitarist, vocalist, 'scriptist' and football-club director! Under his leadership, the band continued to change its personnel – the trumpet-playing Dennis Moonan had departed, taking with him the musical charts, and another guitarist appeared, Frank Deniz, along with bass player Joe Nussbaum and vocalist Diana Decker. Stéphane remembered, 'Many celebrities came down to Hatchets [presumably many of them from the Ritz, over the road]. One night, Lew Grade came down and suggested we could make better money out on the road as a touring variety act.' Initially, George was reluctant to try this, but by September 1943 he had also given up his post and became part of Stéphane's touring band with vocalist Beryl Davis.

Beryl was convinced that the Luftwaffe were on a personal vendetta: 'Everywhere we went, the bombs fell: Coventry, Liverpool, Scotland – there was no escape.'

Stéphane particularly remembers one night at the Shepherd's Bush Empire: 'It was the time where the Blitz was on very solidly, and we were playing that week at the Shepherd's Bush Empire. One night it was so bad – *boom! boom! boom!* – George Shearing was trembling. So I went to see the stage manager – he was in full dress; in those days, they wore full dress – I told him we should stop because of the bombs and all the people were flying away. I said, "Now, you promise me we stop – there's nobody in the house!" Anyway, he was drunk, and he said, "You're kidding. You play to the end. We are in England here. England will never die." So we were obliged for that bloody cheque to play to the end.'

George Shearing remembered the spirit-of-the-Blitz humour:* 'Musicians felt responsible not to provoke panic in the public. If the sirens sounded, we left the stage in a dignified way and went like everybody else to take refuge in the shelters. Life was difficult, sure, but the English didn't lose either their composure or sense of humour. I still remember the entertainers jokes: If you go out tonight, watch out; they're not throwing tomatoes but bombs. More deeply, people made it a point of honour to live as though nothing was happening. Music, I believe, also had a therapeutic quality. In order to forget – if possible – the horrors, the privations, the public wanted to have a good time and to laugh. When the words that Beryl Davis was singing rolled up behind us on a screen, the public took up the chorus with warmth.'

George was also perceptive in his observations of the man behind the fiddle: 'He knew a minimum of English. When one of us said we were angry, he'd say, "Oh yes, I'm hungry."

'Stéphane was an ideal companion, his mood always even, always playful. He loved to tell stories, notably about Django Reinhardt. With musicians, he conducted himself with kindness and an everyday respect. We were all much

*George Shearing quotes taken from *Stéphane Grappelli: Mon Violon Pour Tout Baggage* (see 'Bibliography').

younger than he was and a lot less well known, but if you swing, then no problem. There was no sense of seniority or hierarchy; you were one of his peers. He [treated] you as an equal.

'I believe there wasn't a shadow of vanity in that man. Not that he didn't know his own worth, but he didn't need to make anything of it. You hear it when he plays and that's enough. In three strokes of the bow, he stops time.

'When I discovered Stéphane was also a pianist, I was stupefied. When he played for the first time, *Reflets Sur L'eau*, by Debussy, I knew that he wasn't only a good violinist but a complete, authentic musician. He was particularly a man who knew a lot more about music than he wanted to say. Behind his modest and discreet air was hidden a very sensitive, a very refined Stéphane.'

Stéphane liked to do his bit for morale, and music was recognised as a potent force. In 1943, the *Melody Maker* carried the story of 'Grappelly's Troop Gesture'. After a gig in a provincial theatre, Stéphane and his band, along with vocalist Gloria Brent, ventured for miles deep into the blacked-out wilds to give a special concert for the troops. Starting at 10:30pm, they played until midnight and then, in response to applause, gave a quarter of an hour of encores. The gig was in February and the band then struggled back to their digs through freezing country lanes whose signposts had been removed as part of a national invasion-scuppering strategy. More than likely, this free gig was one of many – Stéphane kept some of the letters from grateful military officers.

Stéphane continued to return to Hatchets until August 1943, but his appearances became more sporadic as Lew Grade's variety tours and many broadcast dates filled out his diary. Glasgow, Bristol, all the Empires and Hippodromes from Land's End to John O'Groats – The Grappelly Swingtette was in demand. Always, however, he returned to Piccadilly.

In all, 15,000 people died in London's Blitz. There's a plaque up now in what I think of as Stéphane's Piccadilly:

THE GARDEN ON THIS BOMB-DAMAGED SITE WAS GIVEN
BY VISCOUNT SOUTHWOOD TO COMMEMORATE THE
COURAGE AND FORTITUDE OF THE PEOPLE OF LONDON
IN THE SECOND WORLD WAR 1939–1945

The garden is that of the restored St James's Church midway between Hatchets and the Café de Paris and virtually opposite the Royal Academy of Art. Inside the church, the marble font, which saw the baptism of William Blake, is serene and calm, despite its depictions of the Garden of Eden lost to a serpent Devil. With Stéphane's developing passion for elegant architecture, he would have loved this garden. Indeed, as his talent later took him around the world, he always liked to spend his free time exploring, and churches, cathedrals and castles held a special fascination for him. Despite the constant threat of the war, London's Piccadilly is where Stéphane first refined the sense of history and taste that he had acquired from his elegant Italian father.

13 Victory Celebration And Reunion

FOR KING AND COUNTRY
VE DAY – IT'S ALL OVER
'All quiet till 9pm, then the London crowds went mad in the West End.'
– The Daily Mail, *Tuesday 8 May 1945*

Wonderful contemporary colour film shot by visiting American servicemen catches the spirit of these fantastic times and the sheer unbridled joy of the celebrations in Piccadilly Circus. As all traffic came to a standstill, the shocked and unbelieving citizens of London literally danced in the streets. Young nurses paraded in a conga, a schoolboy relished a rare ice cream and thousands of revellers swarmed around the armour-clad Eros, their sense of euphoria palpable. Yesterday, these people had merely survived one day at a time. Now they could believe in tomorrow.

This was a time for music. As all-night revelry kept the clubs and restaurants busy, Stéphane joined his adopted country in the triumphant streets of Piccadilly, and on the BBC airwaves. The world was changed by the war, and music was changing too. Coleridge Goode made an interesting observation about their radio engagements: 'We never used any of the material that Stéphane had recorded with Django in the pre-war days of The Hot Club Quintet. He had moved on to new things by then.'

The fiddler soon secured his own radio series, *Sophisticated Swing*, broadcast on Thursday mornings as part of the BBC Home Service. Starting in September 1945 and featuring his 'exotic fiddlesticks', he was accompanied by George Shearing, the great showman drummer Jack Parnell, Jack Llewelyn and Charlie Short on guitars, with vocals provided by Denny Dennis and Anne Lenner. A war that had started with Grappelly a lone foreigner, out of work and destitute, ended very differently for him.

After six years of war, the economic depressions and escapist art of the 1930s must have seemed very distant. The Holocaust, the Blitz and the million other individual horrors brought by the conflict had left the survivors with a thirst for a new life. Stéphane had to adjust, move on. The post-war world had new values and new aspirations, and as an entertainer and artist Stéphane had to reinvent himself.

Many, however, were still looking back. For his 38th birthday, Stéphane remembered a surprise: 'One evening, when I returned to the Piccadilly Hotel, I found Charles Delaunay and Django waiting for me. It was in January and they were there to wish me a good anniversary [sic]. I was pleased to see them after five years, and the reason was that Delaunay wanted to reunite the Quintet as before the war...so I agreed. Why not?'

In Stéphane's version of events, the redoubtable Charles Delaunay had brought Django and his now-official wife, Naguine, to London after having been married by the mayor of Loir-et-Cher in 1944.* The Quintet's leaders had been separated for nearly seven years. In Delaunay's version of the musical reunion, given in his book *Django Reinhardt*, it was Stéphane who rang Delaunay in Paris, keen to get back together: 'And, when the "business" is finished, talked on the phone with Django for almost an hour, punctuated by roars of laughter.'

In this version of events, the BBC plays a big part. During the war, both musicians worked separately for the corporation, which was apparently keen to broadcast a series on the reunited group. BBC representatives travelled with Django from Paris (Django's reputation for disappearance, perhaps?) along with the guitarist's 15-month-old son, Babik, whose father was welcomed back by none other than England's guitar guru Ivor Mairants.† A contemporary photograph with Ivor catches the mood, with Django caught in a broad smile, hands aloft in appreciation, everybody – including Naguine – sharing a joke or perhaps just *fromage* for the camera.

The two chroniclers of the reunion agree at least on the form of musical celebration. The Quintet leaders, overcome by emotion and patriotism, apparently burst into a spontaneous rendition of 'La Marseillaise'. But there

---

*This unusual move for the Manouche was probably prompted by the birth of Babik, his son, although another factor could have been the legal attribution of royalties from Django's wartime hit 'Nuages', which he often joked would keep his wife forever.

† Born on 18 July 1908 in Rypin, Poland, Ivor Mairants arrived with his family in the United Kingdom in 1913. He took up the banjo at the age of 15 and was working as a professional musician by the time he was 20. During the 1930s, Mairants was a featured banjoist, and then guitarist, of many of Britain's leading dance bands, including those of Ambrose, Roy Fox, Lew Stone, Geraldo and Ted Heath. He also became a prolific columnist in several leading music journals, including *Melody Maker*, *BMG* and *Classical Guitar*. His guitar quintet broadcast regularly in the late 1950s on the BBC's *Guitar Club* series. In total, he spent over 50 years as a professional guitarist, teacher, composer and leading UK retailer of musical instruments and devoted the last few years of his life to composing and writing for the guitar. He died in London on 20 February 1998. His comprehensive study of jazz guitar, *The Great Jazz Guitarists*, is available from Sanctuary Publishing in two volumes (see back page for ordering details).

was work to do; in the enthusiasts' journal *Banjo, Mandolin & Guitar*, the guitarist Allan Hodgkiss[*] writes, 'At Grappelly's place in Piccadilly…that night we sketched out the recording sessions we did for Decca and HMV.'

Jam sessions in the rather war-torn hotel[†] were one thing, but recording the new Quintet presented contractual problems. Django was signed to the Swing label and Stéphane to Decca. There were also obligations to Pathé-Marconi label in Paris.

While a contractual compromise was being negotiated, Django went off in search of music. He found himself at London's Caribbean club, where Stéphane's friend Coleridge Goode was the resident bassist. Said Goode, 'I was at the Caribbean club one night and a very unusual person walked in. He was dressed as one would expect a mountain climber to be dressed – he had huge mountain boots on. But this person was none other than Django Reinhardt. He had a reputation of never playing anybody else's instrument, but fortunately our guitar player had an instrument with an especially wide fingerboard, and when he saw that, and we invited him to play, he did. It was absolutely fantastic.' That guitarist at the Caribbean was Lauderic Caton and the pianist was Dick Katz. Together with Coleridge, they made up The Caribbean Trio.

Meanwhile, a compromise was reached over record contracts: the Quintet would record for both Swing and Decca labels. On 31 January 1946, with Coleridge Goode and English guitarists Jack Llewelyn and Allan Hodgkiss, the Anglo-French Quintet recorded 'Coquette', 'Django's Tiger' (a thinly disguised 'Tiger Rag'), 'Embraceable You' and 'Echoes Of France', the last being a hastily assumed release title for an irreverent version of the French National Anthem. While this last track was obviously performed in good intent, it wasn't always received in that way by traditionalists. This was the 1946 equivalent of The Sex Pistols recording 'God Save The Queen' in the 1970s. The controversy was masked by the adoption of the fake title.

The EMI recordings were licensed to the Swing label and the sessions took place at that magic north London address 3 Abbey Road. Built in 1830, this converted town house became the property of the Gramophone Company in

---

[*]Guitarist Hodgkiss joined Stéphane at Hatchets in 1943, following three years with the Royal Berkshire Regiment. Born in London in 1917, his parents were both keen banjo players, and he showed early promise on the guitar before meeting and working with Django in 1937. In 1945, he toured with Stéphane and so was an obvious choice for the 1946 sessions at Abbey Road. He also worked the Paris Jazz Festival in 1949, as well as freelancing with Henry Hall and Joe Loss. He died in 1986.

[†]Coleridge remembers that the reunion between Django and Stéphane took place at the Athenaeum, overlooking Green Park, 'where Stéphane had a comfortable flat'.

1929 and in 1931 was inaugurated with a session by Sir Edward Elgar and the London Symphony Orchestra.

The Quintet recorded in the legendary Studio 2, later the creative home of The Beatles. Ironically, little changed in the intervening 16 years before the Liverpudlians' arrival in 1962, other than the advent of tape recording; in 1946, even that technology was denied the Quintet, and their state-of-the-art recording consisted of one take, direct to disc. A team of white-coated engineers supervised everything from the placing of the huge but fragile ribbon and condenser microphones to the extraction of the waste swarf from the precious groove of the 78rpm master. Musicians were expected to arrive fully rehearsed, sit quietly and, when the red light came on, deliver the goods, preferably in the first take.

This process sounds a bit cool and clinical, but in fact it lends a spontaneity and adrenaline to the recordings, giving these legendary cuts a certain edge. In a sense, these direct recordings are live performances, the audience unseen but immortal. And as long as people enjoy music, they will return to these captured moments of time. There are no overdubs, no edits, no fixing it in the mix or any other of the varied post-production techniques that are now everyday fare for artists from Nashville cats to Simon Rattle recording Mahler. In 1946, when the red light came on, the band performed and whatever happened in the following two minutes became the released record. There's an honesty about these primitive recording that sets them apart, and perhaps that's why they're valued so much.

I've been party to hundreds of such sessions as musician, engineer and producer. As producer, you can only try to create an atmosphere and environment in which artists can relax and give their best. This varies from commissioning a musical arrangement to fetching cups of coffee. As engineer, you prepare the studio and place the microphones for optimal effect. As musician, you practise your intro, plan your solo and take a deep breath. Then, as the red light comes on, the producer is powerless – he lights the blue touch paper and retires. The engineer, however, retains some control – he can vary the amplification on the microphones or alter their tonal response.

Meanwhile, the musician inhabits a strange other world were every nuance of that fleeting moment is captured under a microscope. He might play something slightly different than had been rehearsed, a nuance of dynamic or a flourished chord might appears out of God knows where. His partner might respond with something also new, and suddenly both might play something they didn't know they could play. Stéphane's young disciple, the violinist Ric

Sanders, refers to 'improvisation transcending technique'. A lot of this alchemy occurs on Grappelly recordings. John Etheridge and Joseph Oldenhove have both remarked on Stéphane's quiet, slightly withdrawn moments prior to recording, and yet when the red light comes on, in Yehudi Menuhin's words, 'it's as if you could stand next to a volcano and capture its energy coming from deep, deep in the Earth'.

Stéphane lived through every advance in recording technology, from cylinder to disc to tape to digital hard disk, but for 99 per cent of his output over 68 recording years he retained his practice of recording one take live, maybe two.

The day after the recording session, 1 February 1946, the Quintet regrouped at Decca Studios to record 'Nuages', 'Love's Melody', 'Belleville' and 'Liza', the first track giving Stéphane his first taste of the wartime hit. Allan Hodgkiss was impressed: 'In the recording studio, Django surpassed himself in the haunting melancholy "Nuages".' The Reinhardt composition, his most famous, had been first recorded in November 1940, with a clarinet instead of a violin, and it was also turned into a popular song, 'The Bluest Kind Of Blue'. The tune remained in Stéphane's repertoire for the rest of his life.

This first Grappelly version has one of those remarkable enigmatic introductions that Django seemed to conjure from nowhere, with *rasguedo* chordal clouds creating an atmosphere of tension before the sun breaks through. Stéphane then 'sings' the melody, first alone and then complemented by Django's tasteful counterpoint. It says much that Django hardly refers to the melody, leaving this, his most gorgeous melody line, in Stéphane's capable hands. In contrast to the version Django had recorded earlier during the war, without Stéphane, this version has none of that recording's comic cowbell percussion and jaunty, defiant strut. The clouds have passed over and better days lie ahead. There is certainly an air of nostalgic optimism, especially when Stéphane and Django play their unison refrain and Django plays his favourite trick of coming in early with a tremolando to create tension under his friend's melody. This is a happy reunion of two musicians driving each other to deliver their best. As ever, Stéphane imparts taste to Django's wild adventure and Django challenges Stéphane to stare over the chasm and leap into the dark.

A feature of the infamous 'Echoes Of France' is Coleridge's characteristic bowing of his double bass.* A common enough technique in classical music, Coleridge remains one of its few jazz exponents. This bowed intro was Coleridge's idea, and his memory of that gives a little insight into the freedom and spontaneity of those sessions, despite their 'red light discipline': 'I like to use the bow, and

*Coleridge plays a beautiful Mittenwalde of 1860 which he used for all his Hot Club Quintet recordings and those of the 1947 Grappelly Quintet. He was still playing it at live gigs in 2003.

it occurred to me to play the long note with the bow as an accompaniment to the introduction. Then the tempo went up and it really swung.' Coleridge got another chance to solo with his bow in the Decca versions of 'Belleville' and Gershwin's 'Liza', on which he was very impressed by Stéphane's playing: 'His intonation was perfect and he had a subtle approach to notes; he wouldn't hit them straight in the middle but would caress them, draw them out, swooping into them like Johnny Hodges with Duke Ellington.'

Coleridge caught the mood of these sessions perfectly. Sitting in his music room in Notting Hill in August 2000, looking at the back of his perfectly preserved 78rpm copy of 'Nuages', he remarked, 'For me, the title sums it up. "Love's Melody" – there was a lot of love and a lot of melody.' Certainly Stéphane's playing surpasses anything he recorded during the war. He was back on track, playing music with lasting value, way beyond dance band and dinner-dance duty. Charles Delaunay remarked, 'From the very first note, it was as though they had never ceased playing together. They rediscovered the miraculous communion of old... Nothing seemed impossible. From time to time, Stéphane cast a glance of confidence – of gratitude, even – towards Django, who for his part was no less moved to find the man who could best express his ideas, playing with him once again.'

Stéphane however found 'another Django, mature, and yet more abrupt than ever. I was astonished at how changed he was.'

Even Delaunay had to admit, 'Something was broken between them.'

Despite this, the English Hot Club Quintet – minus the cousins on rhythm guitar – was a success, reviving a sense of past and happy times, and the press were enthusiastic for their prospects. Stéphane, meanwhile, carried on with his established commitments, which now included a residency at the London's distinguished Berkeley Hotel.

Inevitable changes aside, the reunion with his dear friend Django was a happy time for Stéphane, though more crucial, personally, was his re-establishing contact with his daughter, Evelyne. On his return to Paris, he first visited his pre-war flat at the Rue du Faubourg, which had been looted during the war. Stéphane had lost absolutely everything and was devastated, not by the material loss but by the very personal items that were stolen, including some of his late father's letters, including one from the cardinal prefect of Paris congratulating him on his work for the National Library. More devastating still was the loss of two items of his mother's: a lock of her hair and a small jewel she liked to wear. Amidst this tragedy there was a stroke of good fortune, however – Stéphane had given his first three-quarter-size violin to a repair shop for attention in 1939, and on his return to the shop six years later he was overwhelmed to find it not just intact but fully strung and in perfect working condition: 'I keep that, you know, because it's the only thing I have where my father put his hands.'

Stéphane then arranged to meet up with his old girlfriend Sylvia and daughter Evelyne at the Esplanade des Invalides, the home of Marcel Foucret, who had been Sylvia's partner during the war. The atmosphere was no doubt a little strained.

Speaking of these times in 2002 in Cannes, Evelyne Tanasesco-Grappelli was still conscious of how she was informed of her father's return to her life. One day in 1946, her mother, 'in the same matter of fact tone as if she might have been asking her to pass the salt and pepper [announced], "Your father is coming to visit."' In 2002, by that time a spry 67 and herself a mother of two, Evelyne bore a striking family resemblance to her father and remembered fantasising about him *in absentia* during the difficult war years and during the jubilation of the Paris Liberation. She imagined him as 'a mysterious silhouette, a schoolgirl's Prince Charming', having been only four when the war separated them. At their reunification, she remembered being impressed by this handsome 38-year-old, fashionably dressed, a musician whose records she had heard.

Evelyne also remembered her preparation for the meeting. She had revitalised an old printed cotton dress, even this a great luxury following the privations of the war years. She was anxious that her long-imagined father 'would find her beautiful'. Her anxiety was soon forgotten, though, as Stéphane embraced her as if they had left each other only the previous evening. His modesty, simplicity and sensitivity immediately impressed her. With her mother's reluctant consent, arrangements were soon made for Evelyne to spend a year with her father in London.

For this exciting childhood adventure, Evelyne travelled by small aircraft, the airport coach dropping her in a mysterious part of central London. Speaking no English, she hailed a black cab and asked for Piccadilly. The happy cabby turned the car around and dropped her on the opposite side of the same street, at the Piccadilly Hotel, Stéphane's residence. In her one small valise, she bore a special gift for Stéphane, who, starved of good food by wartime rationing, was overwhelmed by Evelyne's contraband: a full leg of French lamb.

As a treat, Stéphane immediately took Evelyne on a steam train to his new love, the Devonshire seaside, the precious lamb travelling with them. Indeed, it was that joint of meat that occasioned Evelyne's first encounter with Stéphane's rare but explosive Gallic anger. His well-meaning Devon housekeeper boiled the lamb instead of roasting it, shattering all of Stéphane's culinary dreams. But his anger soon evaporated into characteristic mirth.

On that visit, Evelyne 'felt like a character from Alice in Wonderland'. By day, she visited theatres, music halls and radio studios with her father, but by night, she was tucked up in bed, 'like a good Italian girl', and left to the care of an English maid. She lived in Piccadilly with her father for a year, keeping up her schooling at the London Lycée.

Evelyne treasures her many photos from this period, one of which shows a proud father with Brylcreemed hair, gently protective of a sweet 11-year-old, all Minnie Mouse hair ribbons and Peter Pan collar. The two smile into the middle distance with all the '40s glamour of a Hollywood publicity photograph for *From Here To Eternity*. These are posed photos of which Stéphane kept several, obviously feeling that the occasion deserved the attention of a professional. There are many similarly composed publicity photos of Stéphane from this era taken by Baron of 2 Brick Street, Park Lane, an up-market choice.

More revealing, perhaps, are the more informal snapshots that Stéphane kept in his cardboard shoebox that depict Evelyne still beribboned but with a warm overcoat against England's chill and a small brooch adorning her lapel. Stéphane smiles warmly, a dapper handkerchief tucked in his jacket pocket, an arm embraces his shy but happy daughter.

Evelyne remembered visiting the pianist George Shearing and his wife, Trixie, in a nearby basement flat and remarking that all of her father's post-war band seemed to have 'special needs' (George was obviously blind and other band members were otherwise disabled). An 11-year-old wouldn't realise, of course, that this was the nature of many bands formed during wartime, and she probably wondered if all bands were like this. Like many children growing up in the 1940s, Evelyn had no memory of a world without war, but she did remember enjoying the band's swinging music. In an uncharacteristic overtly emotional gesture, Stéphane wrote a tune for his rediscovered daughter, which he would later record with both Django and George Shearing.

Evelyn's happy sojourn was eventually ended by Sylvia, who telephoned constantly, insisting on her daughter's return to France. Stéphane reluctantly complied, but Evelyne soon found herself not in the care of her mother but returned once more to her maternal grandmother.

These immediate post war years were punctuated with dilemmas for Stéphane. The public seemed keen on Hot Club Quintet revivals. The *Melody Maker* fanned interest in this, and by November 1946 *The Accordion Times And New Musical Express* was drawn to banner headlines espousing, 'Reinhardt And Grappelly Will Reunite – The Hot Club Quintet To Be Reformed In America.'

The rumours had resulted from a chance encounter outside the Bag O' Nails club. The embryonic *NME*'s news editor had met up with Django, jamming again with a borrowed guitar at the Caribbean club, and together they met with the drummer Ray Ellington. Suddenly, out of the London fog Stéphane appeared. The two Frenchmen went inside and engaged in an intense discussion.

Django was bound for America, where he was billed to appear at last with Duke Ellington, but a strike at Orly Airport had meant a diversion via the newly opened Heathrow. Django and Stéphane both seemed keen to reunite once Django had fulfilled his already-fixed solo engagements. The reporter seemed confident that Django would be a great success in America, particularly at Carnegie Hall. If Stéphane had his doubts, he didn't share them with the newspaper.

The following night, Django jammed again at the Caribbean, this time with Coleridge Goode and George Shearing. Django even asked Coleridge to come to America but, like Stéphane, he declined. There was great talk of the wonders of the USA, and no doubt George's hopes were as high as Django's. A quote from Django in the *Melody Maker* of 2 November is very revealing: 'I intend staying in America for three years and hope to clinch movie contracts with two well-known film companies.'

As it turned out, Django's American sojourn was fraught with difficulty. The guitarist didn't take a guitar with him, expecting the American manufacturers to fall over themselves to equip him, and he eventually had to buy a Gibson, one of the new electric archtops. Although the height of musical fashion, the narrow necks of these modern guitars were a great hindrance to Django, with his deformed left hand. He also had little experience of the unique characteristics of the electric guitar. Commenting in the *Melody Maker* on his recent concerts in Basle, Switzerland, Ellis Gruber noted, 'Django used an electric guitar the whole time, feeling that it was easier for the audience to appreciate his performance, when they could hear it without straining. Some of his subtleties were lost as a result... Personally, I missed the swing violin, which used to blend so well with Django's guitar.'

To the layman, the electric guitar, particularly the archtop 'cello type, appears to resemble the acoustic guitar, the only apparent difference being the amplification afforded by the pickup and amplifier. To an acoustic guitarist making the switch, however, there is a shock in store: the electric guitar has a completely different character. Whereas Django's acoustic Maccaferri responded best to a solid attack with a heavy plectrum, the electric guitar responds best to a light touch and a minimum of attack. Where the acoustic guitar sang to Django's violent gypsy rasguedos and tremolandos, the Gibson would just balk and its primitive amplifier distort.

Even Gibson, the leading American guitar manufacturer, recognised technical difficulties with the revolutionary instrument. The strings of an acoustic plectrum guitar are metallic and therefore able to trigger the magnetic electric pickup. However, on these early models, the different gauges of the strings from high to low all had different magnetic responses, resulting in unpredictable volume changes from one string to the next.

For the players of these early electric guitars, this sometimes meant strange results as the amplified chords sounded in unpredictable inversions. Notes that were sounded evenly by players of acoustic instruments sounded uneven when played on amplified guitar. Eventually, pickups were redesigned and special electric strings were produced, but this was years in the future. The great American jazz guitarist Barney Kessel commented, 'I was one of the lucky ones, starting with the electric instrument from the beginning.'

While Django's technique was built on the virtues of the acoustic guitar, in America, Charlie Christian, a wonderful young guitarist, had forged a whole new approach. For almost ten years, since 1937, Christian's pioneering style with a patented pickup on a Gibson ES150 guitar had exploited the power of the electric guitar to soar over the jazz orchestra in effortless single lines.

Django, meanwhile, was booked to play with Ellington's big band, where there would be little scope for being heard with his acoustic Selmer, even if one could be found. The Maccaferri was a uniquely European instrument.

In a tribute to his musicality, Django soon adapted to the electric guitar and its vastly different dynamic. By the time he reached the Chicago Civic Opera House on 10 November, a compromise had been found: Django appeared with the Ellington band as a featured soloist, set apart from the band on a separate dais. (Trades unions had previously taken issue with the classification of electric guitarists – the Musicians Union argued that they should they be in a different union and therefore, as 'electricians', play on a separate stage.)

Despite these difficulties and Django's own unpredictability, turning up three hours late at Carnegie Hall, the tour's surviving acetate recordings show that Django played well and in a whole new style. But the New York date received very mixed reviews, some critics comparing Django unfavourably with the great American innovator Barney Kessel. If the audience had turned up to hear The Hot Club Quintet sound, made familiar by their records, they would have been surprised and probably confused; Django had learned quickly, assimilated the new styles and moved on.

As often happens, audiences are slower to change than musicians. The Duke, however, knew that he was dealing with a fellow genius and accommodated Django, despite having to weave his appearances into an itinerary that had been planned without him. Duke remembered, 'We would just hit him with a pin spot and he'd be sitting there. Black out the whole stage. He'd state some theme – every night it was a different theme. He'd play these wonderful things and just sit there in that one soft spot and just play and play. So much happening there. It was a gas. But you had to stay with him every minute because, if a chick went by, he'd be behind her. If somebody was coming down the elevator and he sees a sharp chick, oh man! He'd get in the cab with her. Django was too much, man!' The Duke, in common with his contemporary Count Basie, was struggling to keep a big orchestra together financially and still had to subsidise the touring band with his royalties from composing.

Back in England, Stéphane received a surprise letter* from his Manouche friend. This would have been especially heartening, as it was Stéphane who had started Django on the road to literacy. 'I began showing him the letters of the alphabet,' Stéphane recalled. 'As it was a difficult matter for him, I taught him just the capitals. I began, naturally enough, with "Django", and [he] took so long on that word that I said, "Never mind the Django. D will do just as well." At first he was insistent on the whole name – he really liked the name Django. Finally he got tired, too, and agreed with me that D would do. That was all right. The great job came when we started on 'Reinhardt'. It is a complicated name, and spelling meant nothing to Django. Still, he was a painter who could remember a shape, and at last he got it... It was worth the effort because in his face I saw such pleasure.''

In this letter from America, Django described the Ellington tour and the many wonderful cities he was seeing – Cincinnati, Detroit, Kansas etc – magical-sounding places in 1946, evocative no doubt of everything the two had dreamed of in 1931. He wrote enthusiastically of the Duke's private train carriages, a reference to Ellington's solution to the problem of racism. In 1940s America, hotels were still divided between whites and non-whites, and in many towns there were no hotels for non whites. The Duke took his 'Pullman Hotel' with

*See photographs.

the band wherever they went and parked it in a railway siding, well away from racist taunts, and Django had shared his carriage. Of all Django's comments in the letter, however, most intriguing is his revival of the idea of Stéphane joining him in America.

His tour over, Django remained in New York to perform some club dates. The Hollywood offers and the Gary Cooper salaries he dreamt of remained dreams. Only musicians like Les Paul and Barney Kessel saw Django's potential. 'If Django wanted to stay in the States and learn the language, I'm convinced he would have altered the course of contemporary jazz-guitar playing,' affirmed Kessel, 'perhaps even the course of the music itself.'

Despite the optimistic letter to Stéphane, Django returned from America despondent and confused after America failed to take him to its heart. He told his wife Naguine that no one understood him any more, that luck was against him. A disillusioned man, he preferred to fish by the Seine and play billiards.

In Paris, this was also a turning point for the French Hot Club movement as Hughes Panassié, the original founder, had fallen out with Charles Delaunay. According to Patrice Panassié, this was more about a power struggle than a musical difference: 'Delaunay wanted to be the head of *Hot Jazz* and Panassié was above him and so they fell out. My father also regarded bebop as a new kind of music set apart from jazz.' From that point on, there would be two Hot Clubs: the original, now run by Panassié, and a new breakaway 'Federation of Hot Jazz', run by Delaunay. All of Stéphane's allies and advocates were divided and weaker.

Wisely, Stéphane understood the wave of change that was encompassing jazz. Big-band swing was already perceived by many as yesterday's music. The giants of bebop were travelling a whole new road with small combos featuring Charlie Parker and Dizzy Gillespie. There was still a place for Stéphane and Django's brand of swing but it certainly wasn't in the American mainstream.

In the basement clubs on New York's 52nd Street, the bebop pioneers were paring jazz down to its harmonic components. Charlie Parker and Miles Davis were exploring the melodic skeleton of the jazz framework while drummers Max Roach and Elvin Jones were stretching the rhythmic boundaries. The happy dance music of a New Orleans marching band was no longer revered, and the Young Turks of New York and Philadelphia were aspiring to creating art with a capital J. This was the beginning of a new take on jazz, reaching beyond its roots in Mardi Gras, dance music and light entertainment.

In April 1947, Stéphane once more checked out the Paris music scene and saw that things were bleak. There was talk of an exchange scheme, with French musicians swapping engagements with English bands, but heavy tax arrangements in the UK soon scuppered that idea. By November, 70 per cent of the local Paris musicians were reportedly unemployed.

This is all part of a wider picture of post-war austerity. World War II had left a legacy of international debt. Industry was decimated – bombing had destroyed many factories and shattered national dockyards. The factories left unscathed by bombing were more fitted to produce bullets and tanks than anything instantly saleable. Rationing persisted until the early 1950s and returning soldiers were too busy trying to pay for food and shelter to think much about leisure.

In Paris, Stéphane recorded a number of pieces for the Hot Club, including 'Loverman' and 'R Vingt-Six'. In November, despite the slump, he and Django gave a concert for Charles Delaunay, reuniting the original Hot Club Quintet line-up at the Salle Pleyel. Writing in *Jazz Hot*, even Delaunay had to admit that Django's vanity had been punctured: 'Some of Django's choruses recalled the splendid improviser we once knew so well…and yet somehow the old flame, the old urge to create, seems to have left him.'

Stéphane remarked to Geoffrey Smith, 'He was so affected by his flop in America.'

Django and Stéphane were once more at a crucial crossroads.

14 1947–53: Band Slump In Paris

'High taxation, particularly on champagne, means many Paris cabarets are now closed, with a consequent high unemployment figure amongst musicians... The Hot Club is to present a special "Nuit de Jazz" for the benefit of Latin Quarter students who cannot afford the high prices charged at nightclubs and dance halls.'

– Melody Maker, *22 March 1947*

As the above bleak article was published, the French post-war economy had worsened. A week earlier, Stéphane had received the saddening news that his friend and fellow violinist Michel Warlop had died in the small town of Bagnères-de-Bigorre at the age of only 36. Constantly frustrated by his failing jazz aspirations, Warlop had latterly reverted to composition. During the war, he had even conducted the Orchestre Symphonique de Paris in his ambitious *Noël du Prisonnier*. Some say that the young musician died from despair and a descent into alcohol, partly hastened by his frustration in trying to emulate Stéphane. His premature death began a legend, and the violin Warlop lent to Stéphane during his time with Grégor et ses Grégoriens has become a powerful symbol of the French jazz-violin tradition, having been passed ceremoniously amongst French players until very recently.*

In April, a new musical strategy emerged in Paris when the ambitious but unemployed pianist Guy Luypaerts formed a 53-piece jazz orchestra. The idea was to stimulate a new interest in jazz by presenting large-scale concerts on the radio. The first was to be an all-Gershwin programme using Luypaerts' own arrangements. Back in 1947, it was obviously still difficult to obtain original scores, and Stéphane's old bandleader Ray Ventura appealed in the music papers for anyone who might have the music for *An American In Paris*. This move back to the classical jazz experiments of the 1920s is interesting but suggests a certain confusion and perhaps even desperation.

Stéphane responded with his familiar pragmatism, staying in England and touring music halls with George Shearing. At the East Ham Palace, the duo

*The Warlop violin is now kept at the Musée de Musique in Paris with two of Django's guitars. Stéphane was seen playing it with Duke Ellington in 1960. (See Appendix: 'Instruments'.)

played 'The Old Lamplighter' and 'Open The Door Richard', songs demanding imaginative playing and inventive arrangement. A critic of the time commented, 'It isn't what you play, it's how you play it,' before going on to praise 'Stéphane's silken tone…and Shearing's tasteful work on the keyboard, all so expressive and effortless'. The sheet music for 'The Old Lamplighter', advertised in the same journal, was the current 'nation's favourite', according to Irvin Dash Music Publishing, and you could 'add dash to your programming' for as little as 2/6d for a set of musical parts. A snip.

When Grappelly and Shearing played the Kingston Empire, in the audience was a 13-year-old guitarist brought along as a treat by his father Harry Bream. The young Julian would never forget the delight of seeing Stéphane Grappelly and George Shearing live.

A surprise feature at the East Ham venue were Stéphane and George's piano duets, warmly received by the audience. The same critic's report ends with a recommendation to catch the next week's show at the Croydon Empire and a revealing caveat: 'Shall I be accused of encouraging two such wizards of le jazz hot to wallow in commercialism?'

This remark is further evidence of the changing attitude to what jazz was about. Stéphane was never one to intellectualise his own playing, but he must have found this particular wind of change very uncomfortable. Jazz had been popular music, *la musique du jour* – the popular song 'The Old Lamplighter' was once valid jazz material, just as 'The Lambeth Walk' had been 15 years earlier – but now it was suffering an identity crisis. The question began to be asked more and more: If you remained commercial and popular, were you of necessity selling out in the pursuit of the art of jazz?

Stéphane, of course, came into music as the humblest of buskers. He progressed to the silent cinema band and thence to music hall and jazz fame with The Hot Club Quintet. Throughout – and certainly from 1930 onwards, as the first recordings show – his playing had a distinct Stéphane Grappelly sound. People came to him for the secret of that sound, including Grégor and Django Reinhardt. He'd survived the war and prospered, topping polls consistently as Best Jazz Violinist or Best Soloist On Another Instrument. More than any of this, he was making a living, and his insecurities about that can never be underestimated, given his beginnings in the gutter. 'Jazz is my life, really, but I cannot be a real purist because I like good living too,' he once confessed. 'I have learned that you have to put water with the wine sometimes.'

Was he likely to give up his hard won security in the pursuit of musical innovation? The temptation must have been there – he was still a youthful 39, he could hear and understand the harmonic changes on which the new style of bebop depended, but ultimately he didn't always like the results. Ironically, Stéphane's uncertainty is more difficult to understand with the 20–20 vision of hindsight. It's important to remember that Stéphane's survival as a swing musician was the exception; of his swing contemporaries, only a handful had a career beyond the 1950s, and many died tragic and early deaths, discarded and forgotten.

Like that of his hero Louis Armstrong, Stéphane's style was rooted in melody, the great standard American repertoire of everybody from Berlin to Gershwin. From these melodic gems, he could weave spontaneous magic of his own. With his violin, itself created in Italy and to be used in a song-like *bel canto* style, he could take a melodic fragment, turn it, embellish it and, more than all of this, make it swing with that indefinable quality remarked on by Armstrong – 'If you have to ask what it is, you don't have it!' – and the Duke – 'It don't mean a thing if it ain't got that swing.'

Stéphane could certainly swing, but he had yet to find a place for himself in a world where swing was slowly becoming a quaint historical term from a world before the war. He had never courted fame or commercialism; he was simply a musician who enjoyed playing for people. Even 50 years later, at the age of 87, he always seemed to me happy with his success but faintly bemused by it, believing, 'We play simple music, you know, but it's *how* we play it that counts.' His variety agent, Lew Grade, would naturally err towards a world of entertainment and not what he would have probably called 'musicians' music'. Even the musicians' bible, the *Melody Maker*, was full of stories of the world of bandleaders Billy Cotton, Jack Hylton and Henry Hall, a contemporary scene a long way behind America. In April 1947, a *Melody Maker* feature titled 'Around The Halls' extolled the success of *Oklahoma!*, a new musical at the Manchester Opera House, while the Victoria Palace was advertised to feature the comic antics of The Crazy Gang, with music from The Radio Revellers. 'Is Bill Cotton corny?' asked the reporter, 'Yes, but terrific,' came the reply.

With his roots in music hall, Bill Cotton was already a legend, his band and its act personifying the notion of 'all-round entertainer'. 'Playing hits like "Toy Trumpet",' the reporter continued, 'his musicians are immensely professional, the musicianship impeccable, with individual hints of jazz as varied as Benny Goodman, Louis Armstrong, Gene Krupa and the Glen Miller Band.'

Henry Hall was also a major force, his show at the Empress Brixton 'taking commercialism a step higher than Cotton (but with similar steady success with family audiences). He builds his programme upon well-scored, well-played, modern melodies and without loss of contact with his public.' Tellingly, Stéphane kept a signed photograph of Hall in his 'shoebox' collection.

In the 'Around The Halls' article, Ivy Benson, leading her all-girl band, felt, 'The bands must make their shows more of a variety act and not a concert. Just sitting on a stage with a dull face, playing music, is not enough.'

At this time, Stéphane took all kinds of work. On the wireless – still the prime source of home entertainment – he became a light-entertainment regular and Charles Chilton booked him for the BBC show *To Town On Two Pianos*. He didn't have to play the piano, however; that role fell to George Shearing and an unpredictable Arthur Young.

Scripted by Roy Plomley, the deviser of the remarkable *Desert Island Discs*, *To Town...* featured music interspersed with comic sketches. With the programmes live, straight-to-air broadcasts, if an artist was late arriving, the announcer had to improvise. Stéphane nearly dropped his violin in laughter when a sketch about Arthur Young, 'dressed as a woman to escape his creditors', turned out to be true, the pianist turning up late at the BBC in full drag.

Clearly, the scene in England still had a pre-war feel about it, with many of the individual musicians sharing Stéphane's roots in the 1920s. Wartime in Europe was no time for artistic innovation, after all; it was more about survival. For America, the war had been distant, remote, 'over there'. With the conflict on the other side of the Atlantic having had less domestic impact, American jazz had continued to move on.

At this time, Stéphane received first-hand accounts of the American scene from George Shearing and Beryl Davis. Visiting the country late in 1946, George enjoyed America and felt that he could make the break there. Beryl, who crossed by steamer in January 1947, was surprised to find herself billed as a 'sweater girl' and 'the UK's most important rival to Jane Russell'. Her regular reports in her *Melody Maker* 'Letters From America' column were equally confident, even if she came across as being somewhat overawed by skyscrapers, central heating and multicoloured cars, all innovations unknown in make-do-and-mend Britain'. Most tellingly, she remarked, 'Here people don't dance, they just sit around listening to the sensational music.' This Atlantic rift largely evaporated with better communications. The countries 'divided by a common language' would eventually be pulled together by the popular media of television and the international appeal of rock 'n' roll. However, these innovations were effectively still a decade in the future.

Stéphane must have wondered which way to turn. Should he chance his arm in America? He knew that the Americans had their own swing fiddlers, having heard Joe Venuti and Stuff Smith and having recorded with Eddie South. Was he better off in his own small pond? Was it worth alienating an established audience at home in Europe for the pursuit of a new one with no real base? Despite some Paris concerts by Dizzy Gillespie, bebop fans in Europe in 1947 must have seemed a tiny clique, with no clubs to attend and therefore no commercial viability for a professional musician. Initially, Stéphane took some safe work at the Athenaeum Club and even returned briefly to Hatchets, pragmatic as ever, riding out the slump.

In Britain, Stéphane remained a minor celebrity, invited to provide musical input for two films. Initially, director Horace Shepherd needed in-vision bands for his *The Flamingo Affair*, a seedy British gangster film to be filmed by Inspiration Pictures in Kensington. Stéphane put together one of two filmed combos – his is the most forward-looking; the other is much more a dinner-dance outfit. They are billed here as 'Stéphane Grappelly And His Quintet'* with Dave Goldberg (borrowed from Ted Heath's band) on guitar, Coleridge Goode on bass, Ray Ellington on drums and featuring 'the celebrated blind pianist' George Shearing.

The film proper provides a glimpse of what late-1940s nightclub life might have been like in Soho. The band are seen playing for dancing, and Stéphane even indulges in a little tableside gypsy serenading. The violin twirl he effortlessly executes at the end of a number is too practised to be new.

Filmed at the same time, on the same studio set, is a remarkable little 17-minute film 'soundie', a sort of *MTV Unplugged* for the 1940s. Soho is the traditional home of Britain's tiny film industry, and the wizards of Wardour Street of that time had been under considerable political pressure to ape the American success of short musical features. There was a tax on the showing of American films in British cinemas in the 1940s, and the president of the Board of Trade, Sir Stafford Cripps, leaned heavily on producers to consider these British shorts as a way forward.

The short film in which Stéphane appears has the same musical line-up as *The Flamingo Affair* but is recorded with better sound and the set is purely of Stéphane's own choosing. He remarked at the time, 'The director himself is a

*The DVD *Stéphane Grappelli: A Life In The Jazz Century* contains a transfer of Stéphane Grappelly And His Quintet on this occasion, complete with restored sound. *The Flamingo Affair* was given a release date of 1948, the short film a date of 1946. Presumably filming for both occurred in late 1946.

former musician and has given me free rein… This has resulted in the ideal atmosphere for playing the sort of jazz we all like.'

Here, the band plays a happy little quickstep – 'one of Stéphane's best-known compositions', according to the film's announcer – which catches the spirit of the by then 13-year-old 'Evelyne'. Stéphane states the theme, George improvises in an inventive, forward-looking way and Goldberg similarly stretches out on a very futuristic custom electric guitar – the guitarist had obviously heard records of Charlie Christian and perhaps Willie Dixon's guitarist Bernardo Dennis. He and Ellington form a modern rhythm section, complete with ride cymbals, hi-hat and off-the-beat bass accents, the whole aspiring to a much more sophisticated feel than the distinctly 1930s Hot Club Quintet sound. Indeed, the announcer, Ronald Waldman, congratulates Ellington on his scat solo: 'I hope he feels better now having got all that "rebop" [sic] of his chest.'

The film's only drawback is the reliance on one camera. Other angles were shot later, but without sound synchronisation there are some silly edits were unsynchronised shots show Coleridge playing pizzicato while he's seen with a bow, and vice versa. Nevertheless, it remains an extraordinary record of a little-documented period in popular music. Stéphane is billed as 'violinist and composer' and introduced in Waldman's marvellous BBC received-pronunciation voice, while the opulent set is all art deco on a budget, with lots of shadowy palms hiding the cracks in the scenery.

The remarkable film also features 'The Stéphane's Blues', a polite, stylised affair a long way removed from the Mississippi Delta. (Stéphane had produced a much rawer take on the blues in his 1937 'Stephan Blues', with just Django as a foil.) The other titles are 'Piccadilly Stomp', 'Wendy' (written by Shearing for his daughter) and 'Sweet Georgia Brown'.

It's interesting to note that here Stéphane is at the top of his profession, all of the members of his band featuring in the Top Ten of the recent *Melody Maker* polls. The film, made at Viking Studios, now resides at The British Film Institute.

This was to be Shearing's parting shot. In November 1947, at the Lansdowne Hotel, he put down his swing accordion for the last time and returned to the United States with a telling comment: 'Naturally, it is the ambition of every dance musician to play in America, and it would be a wonderful break for me and for British dance music. About my future plans… Well, they depend on what happens when I get over there.'

George took his wife and daughter and began a new and dazzling career. He was an immediate success on New York's 52nd Street and packed them in at the Three Deuces, Art Tatum's old haunt. He soon developed his concept of close instrumental harmony, employing the new colours of the electric guitar and combining them with vibraphone and piano. This distinctive innovation soon becoming known as 'the Shearing sound', and his eventual hit 'Lullaby Of Broadway' was so American that it defied his Battersea roots. However, George never lost his connection with England and returned every year for a summer holiday in the Cotswolds. When I last saw him, in 1988, he continued to be fascinated by innovation, sitting in his garden and marvelling at the sound of my new digital tape recorder. The Shearing sound continues into the 21st century, and Stéphane would always miss George's adventurous harmony, constantly searching for pianists who could match his inventiveness.

Returning to Paris, Stéphane led a 12-piece band for a month at the prestigious Sa Majesté nightclub, where his performance – polished for these type of venues at the likes of Hatchets – was very well received.

In October, Stéphane revived his Hot Four for the Swing label. This session had a very unusual line-up, including Joseph Reinhardt on electric guitar. On the recording, Django's brother comes across as assured and relaxed in the company of regulars Roger Chaput and Reinhardt bassist Emmanuel Soudieux.* It's unclear whether Django forgot to appear or, as Stéphane implied, he was genuinely giving his younger brother a chance to shine. Stéphane, in typical style, delivered a violin solo on 'Oui Pour Vous Revoir', playing a nice obbligato intro with Joseph. In the same session, he recorded two piano solos, including his long-time favourite 'Tea For Two' and ' Rebop Medley', but the acetates for these solos were damaged and so there's no way of knowing how his piano playing was developing at this time.

Django eventually showed up in November, and Stéphane took the opportunity to play 'Evelyne' again, this time with the more liberating line-up of acoustic guitars and bass, and this version features some nice interplay between the old friends. Meanwhile, on 'What Is This Thing Called Love?', both seem much more pre-occupied with the arpeggio style of bebop rather than their old melody-based style. Then, on 'Ol' Man River', both turn on the invention, coming up with interesting modulations and plenty of fire. 'Diminishing', from the same session, is very modern sounding, an enigmatic Reinhardt tone poem a world away from the cheery Quintet sound of 1934.

Later that same month, the Quintet – with Eugene Vees and Joseph on

*Born in 1919, Soudieux had a musical background in the musette and tango tradition. He was probably Django's favourite bass player and worked with him for 11 years, on and off. He later worked steadily for the singer Yves Montand before eventually retiring in Paris.

guitar and Fred Emerlin on bass – gave similarly forward looking performances for the Paris-based RDF radio station's programme *Surprise-Partie*. The feel on this recording is very jazz concert, with no concessions to light music, and many die-hard pre-war fans must have felt alienated by this daring new Quintet. 'For Dinah' has become an Impressionistic romp, and Stéphane is just as far out as his fellow musicians. Clearly this was an attempt to impress the bop audiences, even if the two rhythm guitars do pull everything back into the 1930s. Nevertheless, 'Tiger Rag' is so far from New Orleans that its composer probably wouldn't recognise anything beyond the first chorus. It's only the two guitars that remind the listener that this is the same band. The leaders must have wondered how to modernise the rhythm section without resorting to the drum kit and its resulting problems of acoustic balance.

In February 1948,* the Quintet played at the ABC in Paris, where they were visited by bop bandleader Dizzy Gillespie, whom Emmanuel Soudieux reported 'jammed' in the backstage lounge.

Then, at the last minute, the Quintet was added to the bill at the Nice Festival. This first real French jazz festival was promoted by the Hot Club and was an important event featuring Louis Armstrong, Earl Hines and Jack Teagarden, but the Quintet seemed to be added as an afterthought to make up a decent French presence. Summoned by fast train, they appeared on the very last night to a lukewarm response.

The surviving private recording of that performance on 28 February is startling for the silence that greets their stage announcement without the merest hint of applause. Django sounds furious as he first makes a shocked, hesitant start to 'Swing 42' and then attacks his guitar in a real I'll-show-you-a-thing-or-two attitude. The applause that follows is lukewarm, and the loud chatter continues throughout an electrically amplified 'Nuages' in which Stéphane sounds very uninspired as Django launches into more angry chords over his solo chorus.

The critics were scathing. 'The same old story for the umpteenth time,' according to Boris Vian for *Jazz Hot* and *Combat*. There was no doubt by that time that the French group were considered by many French as old fashioned. Django himself, still smarting from his New York critics, was despondent in the face of the disapproval of so many Americans.

Curiously, the revival of traditional New Orleans-style jazz began to make its mark at this festival, with Claude Luter's band making a big impact alongside legendary drummer 'Baby' Dodds and even Henry Godwin, a veteran of the

*The guitarist John Etheridge was born on 12 January.

1925 *La Revue Nègre* band. Jazz was increasingly divided and the Quintet's brand of swing was becoming lost in the middle of two historic extremes.

Brought back to England again to perform a variety turn, the boys met with another kind of disaster. Booked for the Hackney Empire on 15 March, they checked in at their hotel, storing their luggage and instruments behind the bar, then went for dinner, only to return to find all of their things stolen. The rhythm section apparently took umbrage and departed for home, while Django was amused in his inimitably fatalistic manner and apparently had the Tottenham Court Road policeman rolling about in laughter. Typically, Stéphane hired some dress clothes from a second-hand-clothes shop and, together with a hastily arranged rhythm section, got on with the show.

This concert was critically praised for its 'non-commercial' approach (that word again). There were no flashing lights, no glamorous guest vocalists, just 'Django's incredible guitaristics and Stéphane's pleasant personality and nimble violin playing', according to *Melody Maker*. Most significantly, there was '[nothing] ultra-modern or in any way rebopish'. This time Stéphane was the right side of the increasingly divided jazz camp.

The change of musical line-up was partly disguised by careful stage lighting, but presumably no one had paid to hear the rhythm guitars and bass. Stéphane, however, was quick to praise the remarkable British musicians Alan Mindel and Malcolm Mitchell on guitars, along with Teddy Wallmore on bass. (Their vocalist, Beryl Davis, was still in America, appearing on radio with Frank Sinatra and destined to never return.)

Banned from ballroom appearances by a Ministry of Labour edict, the Quintet had to cancel their major appearance at Earls Court, which had been promoted by Butlin's as 'the golden ballroom of the resorts'. The edict allowed 'foreign' acts to give concerts but wouldn't allow them to stage balls! Stéphane wasn't alone in this – his distinguished friend Coleman Hawkins suffered a similar fate. The Ministry of Labour spokesman said, 'Under the Alien Act of 1920, permits to admit alien performers are not issued to unlicensed clubs or bottle parties.'

The Anglo-French Quintet did, however, perform on some experimental television appearances for the BBC. Sadly, these were of course live to an audience of less than 100 lucky possessors of what was then called a 'Televisor set'. Although still dismissed as a novelty and despised by BBC founder Lord Reith, television had arrived and from now on would play an increasingly important part in Stéphane's career.

In 1948, the Quintet's British rhythm section stayed with the band when they returned to Scandinavia for the first time since the war, pushing onto Copenhagen. Then, thanks to Django and Hubert Rostaing's experimentation with the wartime invention the magnetoband, or tape recorder, a concert staged in Brussels became one of the first live performances to be taped. Amateur recording was becoming popular and tape recording clubs were fostered amongst young people, who were now being referred to as *teenagers*.* These amateur recordings and the various radio discs acquired importance later as Django, depressed perhaps by his reception at Nice, would refrain from recording officially for three years, until 1951.

However, popularity for the Quintet continued abroad, and in early 1949 Stéphane found himself in Rome, where he and Django – billed as 'Three Fingers Lightning' – appeared with three local musicians at La Rupe Tarpea, playing as an intermission act in the restaurant and for dancing in a separate dancehall. It was here that Stéphane made a new and lasting friendship with Mario de Crescenzo, a Roman doctor who had first heard the Quintet on the radio. 'It was a Sunday afternoon in the winter of 1936,' he remembered, 'and I tuned in to French radio and heard this fantastic group playing "Dinah" and "Sweet Sue". I thought I must be dreaming – they had such a fantastic swing, and swing is the essence of jazz. I was confused because the French were not the jazzmen *par excellence*. At that time, the fascist regime prevented us getting jazz records in Italy, but I managed to obtain some in Britain.'

Mario remained a fan throughout the difficult war years, when jazz was banned, but had never managed to see the Quintet live. Then, one night in 1949, he had a surprise: 'It was one o'clock in the morning and I was at a party when somebody told me that Stéphane and Django were playing at La Rupe Tarpea. I said, "Are you sure? This is not the place for these top people." And so I rang the place and they said, "Yes, we have two foreigners playing, but if you want to know more you have to come along." So I descended the stairs and there was Django with a plate of spaghetti and a bottle of chianti. I asked if I could embrace him and he said, "I have to go and play!" So he went to the small room, where they had about 12 tables and a space for dancing. Then in came Stéphane Grappelly and an Italian rhythm group. Somebody made the point that, when you have the privilege of listening to musicians like these, you don't dance, you listen, so we started rearranging the chairs like a concert. A Dominican billionaire with two models on his arms embraced the spirit of the occasion and ordered drinks all round, and the band jammed until three in the morning. It was fantastic.'

*The new teenagers had their own BBC Television programme with guests including, on 9 August 1948, the teenaged classical guitarist Julian Bream, who grew up playing Django Reinhardt for his dance-band-musician father, Harry Bream.

Mario visited the restaurant every night and got to know the musicians: 'Stéphane was very precise, very humble, modest and kind to everybody, unlike Django, who went missing when they needed to catch a train to Naples. Stéphane was always dealing with one catastrophe or another. When it came to contracts, Django always wanted the same fee as Gary Cooper, the movie star, so often they lost the contract, whereas Stéphane would have accepted something more modest.' Despite this criticism, Mario and Django also became friends. As Django withdrew from music, he took up painting, and Mario is one of the few lucky people to own one of the guitarist's rare pieces. Like many of his works, this portrait of a woman has a hint of Paul Gaugin's Tahitian period.

Mario and Stéphane's friendship grew through their mutual admiration of the piano work of Earl Hines. Stéphane would improvise for hours on Mario's baby-grand piano, often playing through the night until the Rome dawn chorus. He even taught Mario a little piano, insisting on more adventurous chords for standards like Duke Ellington's 'Satin Doll', his rich, jazzy flattened fifths and added sixths replacing many of Mario's common triads. For the duo of Stéphane and Django, meanwhile – for this was the musical reality – a group of Italian musicians providing a competent but uninspired rhythmic bed.

Then came the opportunity to broadcast for the Italian radio station RAI, and broadcast they did – in January and February 1949, Django and Stéphane laid down 50 separate titles, encompassing everything from their 1930s hits 'Minor Swing' and 'Honeysuckle Rose' to 'Lover Man' and 'La Mer'. But this was no revival band; both soloists had moved on. Stéphane sounds ever more sophisticated, if perhaps a little too tamed by his war years at Hatchets, while Django is back on his acoustic Selmer guitar but light years way from 1934. He sounds futuristic, a musician reaching out with adventurous harmony and fragmented melodies which presage Miles Davis and John Coltrane.

Most importantly, it's clear that the two musicians have moved apart. The old magic, where they anticipated each other's direction and each spurred the other to greater heights, is replaced by a more modern sparring approach: my solo, your solo, my solo, and the whole thing, rather than developing the original synergy, instead feels uncomfortable. The greatest sadness is that Django sounds like a prophet without disciples – his guitar suggests all kinds of futures, but he's lost. Sadly, even today the whole gypsy-jazz industry seems based on the Reinhardt of 1939 when even in 1949 he was reinventing himself for an audience not yet ready.

Stéphane, meanwhile, has become the sophisticated stylist, immediately recognisable with a beautiful tone, fantastic phrasing – especially in his daring harmonics – and, more than any other jazz violinist before or since, always immaculately in tune.

This was to be the pair's last recording together. After 18 years, the mighty duo of 1931 was now too big for them both to occupy the same small space. They parted as friends.

In May, Stéphane returned to London to lead an eight-piece band at the Milroy, an exclusive Mayfair nightspot. An eight-piece band! In the face of all the austerity of 1949, when even the distinguished veteran Henry Hall had had to disband, this must have seemed like an orchestra. The Milroy's unusual band had Stéphane on violin along with four saxophones, bassist Russ Allen (doubling as comedian!), pianist Frank Baron and an unnamed drummer.

It seems unlikely that Stéphane was booked for his jazz; more likely, the club were legitimately trading on his celebrity, allied to the sure knowledge that this distinguished gentleman would deliver polite standards with a polished swing. A publicity handout from the Milroy bills him as 'Stéphane Grappelly (of Hot Club de France) and his orchestra with Russ Allen'. Stéphane is pictured in a debonair white tuxedo alongside his co-stars 'Francisco Conde, Monte Tyree and their Latin-American music'. Francisco and Monte are kitted out in the enormous rouched sleeves and flamboyant kerchiefs that were then fashionable for Latin-tinged dancing, and Monte is pictured with his bongos. (Stéphane was familiar with the Latin craze, having shared a recent series on the BBC's Light Programme with the fashionable star Edmundo Ross.) A Mayfair telephone number is given on the handout, for those wishing to make table reservations, alongside a cartoon of a wine waiter in full dress. If swing was on the way out, the busker of Montmartre was making plans.

Stéphane took rooms at 55 Troy Court, Kensington, and for a lucrative while doubled his duties at the Milroy with a similar gig at 96 Piccadilly. At this venue, the pianist was Alan Clare, a brilliant musician whom Stéphane compared to Debussy for his harmonic sensitivity. In contemporary photographs, the nightclub audiences seem a mixed bunch of spivs and debutantes, but Stéphane is as happy as ever, turning a tune for a paying crowd. However, he wouldn't be taken for granted or pushed around, and resigned from the Piccadilly when the manager dictated that a tango should invariably follow every interval. Stéphane always preferred to play what the customers wanted, and no entrepreneur could read an audience like the seasoned professional he now was. He quickly found a new job at the Empress, stealing away Marion Williams, whom the *Melody Maker* described as Johnny Dankworth's 'dusky' vocalist.

Stéphane was in good company as a variety entertainer. Nat 'King' Cole, Lena Horne and the 'jazz' vocalist Frank Sinatra were all due to perform in London, brought over by Lew Grade and Val Parnell, owner of the London Palladium. The Palladium was, of course, the 'variety palace', and Sinatra's desertion of swing jazz wasn't without its London critics, one of whom reported, 'You can hear every word he sings…which is sometimes a pity, considering his material. It's like being force fed with treacle.' Nevertheless, Stéphane treasured his signed photograph, on which Frank had dedicated, 'To Stéphane Grappelli, a wonderful artist.'

As the 1950s loomed, Stéphane decided to take his talents to a warmer climate. He was 42, dogged by ill health and his chosen style of music was increasingly considered *passé*. He wisely decided to put comfort and lifestyle first. After all, if you're going to play for dancing, you can do that just a well in Nice or Cannes as you can in foggy London. These were the worst years of London's smog, when Battersea Power Station and millions of coal-burning homes poisoned the air on a daily basis. Thousands were dying either directly from air pollution or from associated respiratory problems.

The Mediterranean was a different world, and the Club d'Angleterre and the Excelsior Hotel provided Stéphane with comfortable work and seaside air. The Croisette was a vivid crescent of white sand next to the perfect azure of a yet-unspoiled Mediterranean. Here he would later meet one of the most important companions of his life: ex-RAF section officer Jean Barclay.

Stéphane later told Joseph Oldenhove of these Riviera days: 'In the '50s, because of his daughter, he liked to stay in France – for instance, a season in St Tropez. He also stayed in Nice, at the Hôtel Angleterre . On the Riviera, he met a British woman who had two daughters, quite a wealthy woman with a house on the Croisette at Cannes, a private home with a garden. In those days, the Croisette was quite attractive, not so spoilt like today. They became good friends, and one of the daughters was Jean Barclay. Jean was very cultured – she recited Verlaine and played piano and they became very close though, I think, platonic friends. He had close friends like us for much of his life. Jean was often in Ireland, where the family had a beautiful estate on a lake.'

Jean Barclay's sister, Pamela Reid, revealed more about her younger sibling. Five years younger than Pamela, Jean was born on the 31 October 1919 in London, the Irish town of Conamara considered too remote: 'The Irish house has amazing views over the lakes and mountains but no heating, having been built as a summer home in 1910. This is where we spent our childhood. Our mother was Katherine Willcox, an American born in Paris but bought up in Europe. Our father was Arthur Barclay, from Surrey but with family in Scotland.'

Twenty years old when war broke out, Jean immediately joined the RAF, where she became a plotter at Fighter Command, tracking enemy-aircraft activity at Bentley Priory, Stanmore, during the Battle of Britain before going to Lincoln and becoming an intelligence officer at the bomber stations there. During the war, Jean spent her leave with her American grandmother in Dublin and a photograph taken at the time shows a smiling young woman in uniform, cap at a chic angle, confidence in her eyes.

Jean kept a rare journal of her life with Bomber Command, and the tragedy of the daily losses of her many friends and colleagues are published collectively as *The Brave Never Die*, 'dedicated to the gallant aircrew of Bomber command who failed to return'. Preserved in the library of the Imperial War Museum, this personal record offers a rare glimpse into the life of one young woman faced with the horrors of the nightly air attacks on Germany, 'a scene of unbelievable courage, hope, desperation, deadly terror into which one could not intrude but be overpowered by one's own shyness and hopeless inadequacy, caused by never having the chance to feel what it is like to live always on the brink of annihilation...'

In the dawn light, Jean would have the job of interviewing the surviving air crews, searching for clues and vital intelligence on enemy action and guns that might save the lives of the next evening's flight. Pamela remembers Jean finding civilian life difficult after so much pain: 'After the war, Jean found it very hard to settle. She certainly didn't want to marry. She went to a Paris finishing school and spoke fluent French and Italian.

'She met Stéphane in 1952 when in the south of France with her grandmother for a couple of months in the winter. She had various jobs down there but couldn't really settle. Jean had played piano from a child and became very good. She had a good ear; she could come back from seeing a film and play all the music by ear. She would accompany Stéphane a good bit in hotels in Nice or Cannes [and] was quite a good pianist. Stéphane once said that it was Jean who introduced him to opera.

'Their relationship was a great friendship. I think it was a romance at first, perhaps later. They didn't mind being apart for months on end – in fact, it suited them. She never went on tour with him or appeared at parties; she was determined to keep in the background.

'I think they were very fond of each other. Jean had had at least one heartbreak in the war and perhaps thought she could never find that again. She was certainly very devoted to him and spoke very affectionately about him.

'She worried a lot. His health was a big concern to her – he worked too hard and rushed around too much. But they had a lot of laughs together – Jean could be very funny; she was always good at telling funny stories. She also said they had flaming rows which didn't mean anything... [but] she understood these and they used to blow over. I remember her saying that "neither of us could live with anyone all the time. The arrangement suits us very well."'

Eventually Jean found an apartment in a block in Cannes: 'She did a lot of odd jobs for estates, looking at old houses that could be restored. She and Grandma took a flat in the Parc Continental, which used to be a big hotel. He also had an apartment in the same block. Stéphane lived in the old part, on the top right, with a beautiful view of Cannes.

'[Jean and Stéphane] were together for 30 years and built together a small house in Castagniers, Aspremont, near Nice. Stéphane had many country houses, even a small château near Limoges, but he never slept there because he bought it with 25 acres and found it difficult to get it restored – the workers never turned up – so he got rid of it. He had a house in Chartres, where he spent a lot of time with Jean. He liked to repair country houses and organise their decoration.'

Another joy for Stéphane in Cannes was meeting the singer Jean Sablon again. They were very close and always got together whenever possible. Sablon had a lot of respect for both Stéphane and Django, and they had of course all worked together in the 1930s. Cannes was coming to mean 'family life' for Stéphane, home to Jean Barclay and his daughter, Evelyne, and also a resting place, a haven from an increasingly busy schedule.

St Tropez and Rome were next on Stéphane's itinerary, after which he moved on to the Shaker Grill in Naples, then Rome again and Milan. In the vernacular of the time, he was becoming a celebrity jet-setter.

All of this playing for dancing, however, left Stéphane with the problem of his violin's losing battle with the increasing volume of modern rhythm sections. Drum kits now featured in all of his bands. The polite calfskin snare drum and wire brushes of the 1940s were increasingly out of fashion. New plastic drumheads, introduced by American drummer Sonny Greer, were durable and could be played longer and louder, while the ride and hi-hat cymbals of the new bop kits, made fashionable by Gene Krupa and Buddy Rich, were designed to cut through behind the brass section. For Stéphane, they cut right across the violin's range making him sound thin and weak.

Leo Fender, a radio repairman from Fullerton, California, had caused a stir in 1949 with an electric guitar made from one solid piece of wood and with no resonating acoustic soundbox. Instead, a magnetic pickup and a converted radio amplifier provided all the volume any guitarist could wish for.

In 1952, the jazz band led by Lionel Hampton featured bass player Roy Johnson, who could be heard in any venue. Jazz journalist Leonard Feather in a *Down Beat* magazine article remarked, 'There was something wrong with the band. It didn't have a bass player, yet we heard a bass.' He headlined his article 'Hamp-lified Fiddle May Lighten Bassists' Burden'.

This demonstrated something closer to Stéphane's dilemma: a solid bass guitar, a compact but loud version of the traditional bass viol. This was another Leo Fender innovation. But this quiet start heralded a revolution.

Holding his fiddle close to the inadequate microphones of the time was clearly not working for Stéphane, and he was keen to know more. Still occasionally touring in British variety with his acoustic violin, fourth on the bill to 'cheerful Charlie Chester', but still billed higher than 'television's spotlight Reg Varney', in November 1952 Stéphane headlined once more in *Melody Maker* under the title 'Now The Violin Can Find A Real Place In Jazz'. The article – billed as a comeback not just for Stéphane but for his American jazz counterpart, Eddie South – reports, 'Stéphane feels that in jazz his new electric violin will be his instrument's saviour... The instrument Stéphane advocates is also American, a solid, heavy instrument necessitating steel strings for its magnetic pickup. "It isn't easy to play at first, but once you have mastered this fiddle, it is fantastic. There is all the difference that you find between the electric guitar and acoustic instrument, but to me this has a better sound than the electric guitar."'

On the existing records of Stéphane playing his electric fiddle, the instrument certainly doesn't sound as good or as compelling as his acoustic sound. The primitive electronics of the period mask some of his subtle dynamic and the tone is colder, less human.

However, Stéphane's flirtation with the electric instrument to me offers some insight into the man himself. In these middle years, he was always insecure and just wanted to do what he did best – entertain, charm, beguile with his invention – but his ordered world of swing success was under threat. Everywhere he looked there were people younger with new ideas about what jazz was about and where the future lay.

Stéphane never looked back, though. He was always interested in the next new thing, even though he was uncomfortable with music that strayed beyond recognisable melody and harmony. He must have felt that he wasn't being heard enough, and perhaps felt that being louder was the answer. On one occasion, he confided to Joe Venuti at the Nice Jazz Festival* that the whole area of amplification was a mystery to him. There were so many issues with a simple microphone – the audience could hear him but he couldn't hear himself. (This, of course, was a long time before sophisticated onstage monitoring.) Furthermore, in outdoor festivals the pianist couldn't hear him for the drummer: 'This electric fiddle is definitely better than the normal one for jazz playing. There is no comparison. For solos it is powerful and exciting and you can play along with the sax, the trumpet and the clarinet... It means that the violin can take a full part in the jazz orchestra at last. It's no longer a little voice; it's more like four fiddles.' His summation, though, was prophetic: 'But of course the sound is not the same. In fact, it is an entirely new sound and eventually it will add tone colour to jazz recordings... People are slow to change. I know and it may be a long time before the electric fiddle replaces the other one...but I believe it must come for dance music and jazz... Really, it is a new tone. Yes, it is formidable.'

That prophecy would come true with Jean-Luc Ponty, Regina Carter and Ric Sanders, but that was in the '60s, the '70s and the 21st century, not 1952.

Stéphane closed his interview with comments on bop jazz: 'I am always interested in new techniques, new ideas. I feel like that about jazz. That's why I have to like bop, because it is advanced... It is an absurdity to say there is nothing in bop. A lot of dance musicians say it is dead, but it is already in the arrangements they play.'

When asked about which he would put first in a list of jazz components – swing, improvisation, technique or feeling – he replied, 'Feeling. What can you do without that? Jazz is not study but feeling. It is a thing of the heart. If you have it, you have it. The rest comes later.'

In the early 1950s, the music press was still dominated by matters of the jazz and dance-band scene. However, in November of the same year, *The Accordion Times And New Musical Express* carried an innovative feature, a 'Hit Parade' of top-selling records, introduced by new owner Maurice Kinn. For the first time in Europe, popular music would have a league table of success.

*Recorded by Bill Bacin, courtesy of AB Fable archive. © Allardyce, Barnett, Publishers, 2003.

Stéphane was an unlikely candidate for the Top 20, but clearly his world of popular entertainment was changing.

Despite an almost four-year absence, though, Stéphane hadn't forgotten his friend Django. From yet another nostalgic promoter with dreams of a 'Hot Club Quintet' revival, he received an offer for them both to visit America. The still-cautious violinist visited Paris, but Django was elusive, probably either in Switzerland, were he had enjoyed some success, or fishing in his adopted village of Samois-sur-Seine. The guitarist had found a new friend in Les Paul, the New York inventor and guitarist, and the pair had been seen together in Paris in September.

Despairing of his search in the spring of 1953, Stéphane departed once more for Italy, where he was scheduled to perform with a radio orchestra. At least in that restrained setting he would have no need of primitive amplification. Working in his father's homeland, perhaps his thoughts turned to Ernesto and the fourth anniversary of his death on 12 May.

15 Django Is Dead

'If I had a friend in my life, it was him.'

– Stéphane Grappelli

In May 1953, long-distance telecommunications were still rare. Urgent and usually bad news came by telegram. The reputation of these flimsy but notorious slips of paper was such that their arrival would always be greeted with trepidation. Stéphane's radio assignment in Florence was interrupted by a uniformed runner with a hand-delivered message. With Naguine Reinhardt unable to write, the record producer Charles Delaunay had assumed the sad responsibility of informing Stéphane of the sudden death of his still-young friend Django. Stéphane was emotionally crushed: 'By the time I received the telegram, Django had already been buried two days.'

A hastily put together Paris benefit concert clashed with Stéphane's radio commitments and he brushed the offer aside – he could think of nothing he wanted to do less than perform music. For Stéphane, music was a celebration, and there was little to celebrate in this loss: 'I could not feel like going into a happy atmosphere to play jazz in tribute to a dead friend.'*

His Italian commitments completed, Stéphane travelled to Paris and then took the one-hour journey to Samois-sur-Seine. Sixty kilometres southeast of the French capital, this sleepy little village remains a peaceful haven. The town's quiet square, with two cafés, a patisserie and a pharmacy, has changed little over the past 400 years.

Django's house at 3 Rue du Bas Samois sat 20 metres from the river, a terraced artisan's cottage with stone walls and a wood-burning stove. It was the perfect hideaway for an artist and fisherman. Here Django indulged his passion for painting, played billiards at the village club and, when a journalist insisted, would pose by the stove with his Selmer guitar, now bearing a shiny chrome pickup.

Django had suffered a bout of headaches during a recent trip to Switzerland. His suspicion of doctors, prompted by the fire incident of 1928 and their

Melody Maker interview, February 1954.

suggestions of amputation, meant that he didn't seek help beyond the traditional folk remedies of his clan. On Saturday 15 May, he complained again to Naguine of a headache and numbness of the hands. A doctor was eventually summoned and Django transferred to the hospital at Fontainebleau. The diagnosis of a brain haemorrhage came too late for intervention and he died in the early hours of 16 May 1953.

Django's funeral, at Samois's little 11th-century church, was well attended, although of the original Hot Club Quintet only his brother Joseph and Roger Chaput could attend. Two hundred Romany were amongst the 500 mourners present, many of them musicians, including Arthur Briggs, Andre Ekyan and Bill Coleman. Some local citizens turned out to mourn with the entourage – obviously Django had made an impression on this small traditional community. There were also floral tributes given by the billiard clubs of which he was a member. The funeral costs had been partly donated by the great American guitarist Les Paul, and Naguine entrusted him with one of Django's guitars.

Stéphane visited the grave with Django's widow, Naguine, and their eight-year-old son, Babik. Even in death, Django suffered the ignominy of wrong spelling, with Djengo Reinhardt carved on his headstone for over 20 years.

In tribute to their long friendship, Naguine gave Stéphane the red silk scarf in which Django had wrapped his own violin. For the next 44 years, after each performance, he would ritually wrap his own violin in that same scarf.

Stéphane occasionally returned to Samois to attend the annual Django Reinhardt Festivals hosted by the village. Sometimes he would perform with Babik, who became an accomplished electric guitarist, but he would have found the serene village, with its tree-lined riverbanks and slumbering sea-going barges, too sombre, too laden with memory, for him to be truly comfortable there.

Stéphane's Django was the wild, abandoned youth of the 1930s, ever searching for the new harmony and outrageous guitar fills. In 1954, he described his friend as 'the Paganini of guitar...a genius in the real sense. He had genius and it found expression through music, particularly jazz. He did more for the guitar than any other man in jazz. His way of playing was unlike anyone else, and jazz is different because of him. There can be many other fine guitarists, but there cannot be another Reinhardt. I am sure of that. Although he was well-known musically, Django himself was known by very few people. He was the most reserved fellow I ever met in my life. He almost never spoke, and his abruptness of manner didn't help. I knew him for more than 20 years and came to understand him... To me Django was more than a good musician, more than a friend; he was like a relation. He made me feel he was part of my family.'

Stéphane also commented on the changes in his friend's character that he observed after the American trip. Perhaps Samois was the place that this older, disillusioned Django came to forget, where – according to one friend – even his guitar strings became rusty with neglect.

However, as late as March 1953, Django was recording great music, clearly ahead of his time. His version of the Cole Porter melody 'Night And Day' recorded at this time with drums, bass and piano pre-dates the classic 1960s recordings of Wes Montgomery. Django had absorbed the electric guitar's ability to sustain a melodic line but took his invention further, sprinkling his new sound palette with tone clusters and a surprise ending. With Django's death, for many musicians jazz guitar became stuck in a middle-of-the-road rut and didn't take a significant step forward until Joe Pass came along. Pass himself commented, 'I was first inspired by Django. I'd never heard anyone play like him, so flowing and modern. I wanted to play with exactly the same expression.'

Ironically, many of the musicians that now annually frequent the Django Festival at Samois celebrate a gypsy-jazz style still revolving in a 78rpm groove stuck sometime in 1939. On the vast canvas of 21st-century music, gypsy jazz has since become a sub-genre with its own enthusiastic cult following, partly out of nostalgia, partly out of respect and a great deal to do with the sheer joy of making music. Django, however, would have long moved on.

These days, with digital media and improved communications, there's a place for every kind of music. We now enjoy a popular musical scene that encompasses everything from world music to medieval plainsong. However, in 1953, at the age of 45, there was a much narrower range of musical availability, and consequently the potential market for a musician of Stéphane's adventurous nature was much more limited. He somehow had to pick up the pieces and move on. He and Django had invented a new form of music: Django gave it gypsy fire and an eccentric, unpredictable inventiveness while Stéphane had given it form, elegance and wit. It had been a 22-year on-and-off adventure, but now it was over. In Stéphane's words, 'I'm often asked when the Quintet finished. The answer is that it died with Django's death... If he had lived, the style would have moved with the times... If Django were alive, it would still be modern.'

In old age Stéphane had little to say about Django's death. However, in a quiet moment, without the television cameras and the radio microphones, he shared one deeply felt thought: 'He was up in the air, then ten minutes later he was normal. I think he was suffering inside, not only physically but his brain. He was always ill, always had something. He wouldn't see anybody – the only thing he accepted was to stay in a hospital in London for seven weeks. But he was in such a state that he could not be cured immediately. Medicine wasn't perhaps what it is today. I obliged him to go, and when I visited the surgeon recommended an operation because he couldn't go on like that. Of course, when you are in so much pain, you are not in good humour, and that was deflected onto his entourage. It was not amusing. And I was younger and didn't understand his philosophy like I do today.'

In 1996, Stéphane and I even discussed the possibility that perhaps Django was one of the first victims of a fierce modern plastics fire, with all of the then-unknown consequences of its noxious inhalations.* We'll never know. But there was little doubt Stéphane missed working with his old partner, a musician who only found himself when immersed in his guitar. In an extensive set of articles he wrote as a tribute to Django for the *Melody Maker*, Stéphane affirmed, 'He was in the main an assured person, confident in himself and in his ability as a guitarist. And his confidence was reassuring to those who worked with him. I was never nervous with Django. Playing violin with him, for example, it felt as easy as though I was sitting in my own drawing room. In fact, I used to wonder if he ever felt like the rock of Gibraltar, that man always so serene on the stage… Emotionally he often seemed adolescent to

---

*Carl B Margereson, senior lecturer in Adult Nursing at Thames Valley University, observed the following about the possible after-effects of such a fire that Django might have been suffering: 'There are three considerations here that reach far beyond the medical practice of 1928. Django may have suffered some degree of pulmonary fibrosis as a result of lung damage. This is difficult to detect by the non-specialist even today but may have contributed to worsening symptoms such as breathlessness and fatigue. Resulting disability can lead to loss of independence, frustration and long-term stress. Secondly, Django suffered an extreme physical trauma in late adolescence, a difficult time for any youth. The effects of such physical trauma, in some, can lead to psychosocial difficulties, and mood changes are not uncommon, with changes in self-concept perhaps due in part to a distorted body image. We know Django was extremely self-conscious about his scarred body hiding his hand whenever he was not actually playing his instrument. Resulting negative cognitions can influence behaviour and emotions, with depression and anxiety experienced by some individuals. Nowadays, where such distorted cognitions exist, cognitive behavioural therapy can often help individuals to re-evaluate their life, allay frustration and help them cope more effectively.

'The third issue involves insights gained from the science of psychoneuroimmunology. The ongoing chronic psychosocial stress Django suffered may have had a detrimental effect on his overall health. The raised cortisol levels, together with other stress hormones found in those who are chronically stressed, can have a negative effect not only on the immune system but also the blood. It is suggested that these changes can increase individual risk of brain and heart disease due to blood-vessel damage.'

me, but I was always being astonished by a nobility in his character. Despite what would be called "poor birth", Django had the stuff of a *grand seigneur* – instinctively he liked elegance. This, I think, was an atavistic streak in his nature, but of course it took time to develop as a caravan life does not easily lend itself to elegance. I shall never forget the first day Django put on evening dress with bright red socks. It took some time to explain without injuring his feelings how red socks were not the right thing. Django insisted that he liked it that way because red looked so well with black.

'Before the Quintet days, he was absolutely broke, living with his second wife and his mother in a little room in an ugly Montmartre hotel. But it never taught him to attach much importance to worldly things. Immediately he got hold of some money, he would spend the night in a café and lose it all at cards.'

In the same interview, Stéphane also offered some insight on Django's approach to music: 'Django was not keen on arrangements, social or musical, but in fact he had an extraordinary memory for music and could remember quite complex pieces. Of course, he preferred to make up original stuff. To begin with, he was far too lazy to learn to read music – he liked to stay in bed. I wonder if, in his young days, he even knew that printed music existed. Then again, he didn't wish to play arranged music, in any case. He was naturally an improviser, one of the finest I've heard in my lifetime.

'An essential part of Django was his love and appreciation of any good music. Music would bring him anywhere and, though he might be ignorant of the work and the composer he was hearing, he would absorb and sympathise and understand.

'I should explain that, despite his childish conceit, Django was fundamentally very humble. About art he was humble and curious. I cannot forget watching him listening to the music of the old masters, never talking, never criticising, always listening. He liked great things, and I believe he experienced them in the way they should be experienced. To see his expression in the glorious church of St Eustace in Paris, hearing for the first time the Berlioz *Requiem*, was to see a person in ecstasy. This admiration, coming from a man like him, who knew music better than most people did and was himself a great musician, spoke of his true simplicity and humility. It was the finishing touch of a real artist.'

The relationship between Stéphane and Django constituted one of 20th-century music's great interdependent partnerships. For sustained listening, the solo violin needs a harmonic and rhythmic foil over which it can sing, and Django provided this with an imaginative flair. With the melodic sensibilities of a fellow violinist, he brought out the young Stéphane's personal best.

The solo guitar is a challenge to any player, even those blessed with five fingers. But Django also needed a foil. His rare unaccompanied solo excursions are fascinating but they lack the sparkle of his many collaborations. Compare 1937's solo in 'Tea For Two' with what happens when even just Vola's double bass is added. The rendition of 'You Rascal You' from the same session is a perfect illustration: with the merest anchor, the guitarist can soar. Much of the joy of the Django-Grappelly duo is the true rubato that they used, the playing with time that is the essence of swing. For this to succeed, the listener needs a reference, a pulse, and this they provided for each other.

Stéphane also gave Django a concept of musical structure. The solo guitar recordings 'Improvisation Number One' and '…Number Two' show Django's spontaneous invention, which, although dazzling, lacks shape and arrangement, something that the Quintet achieved via Stéphane's self-taught musical literacy. Stéphane also had the harmonic sensibilities of a pianist, something that Django learned from him and admired. Django once commented to Delaunay, 'The harmonies, that's what I like best of all in music. There you have the mother of music… That's why I like JS Bach so much – all his music is built up from the bass.'

Stéphane summed up the character of his lost friend thus: 'In Django there was a mixture of everything: intolerance, dissatisfaction, jealousy, sensibility, arrogance, shrewdness and the restlessness, the mild craziness, of genius.'

No man expects to lose his youthful friends so early, and all this untimely looking back brought out a gesture in Stéphane. Only days from Django's death fell the anniversary of Ernesto's death, and the recent trip to Italy had perhaps planted a thought in Stéphane's mind. From that point on, he would be reborn a Grappelli. Whereas the Quintet had featured him as a 'Grappelly', the new Stéphane would be his father's son.

Returning to London in July, Stéphane paid five shillings for a driving licence. Typed inside was the name of 'Mr Stéphane Grappelli, 55 Troy Court, Kensington', so ingrained was the habit that he signed it with a Y! Having used the old spelling in print for over 20 years, it was 1969 before it finally officially disappeared.

A month earlier, on 2 June, a new Elizabethan era had begun in Stéphane's adopted country. The Coronation of Queen Elizabeth II of England was watched on television by millions of people worldwide. For many people, from now on, history would always acquire its reality on television.

In March 1954, Stéphane returned to Nice, where he received a happy telegram from the editors and staff of *Melody Maker* congratulating him on holding his place at the top of the readers' poll. At least his popularity remained intact.

However, once more the emotional trauma of bereavement had a physical effect and Stéphane found himself in hospital with gall-bladder problems. Perhaps frightened by Django's early demise, Stéphane found the funds to set himself up in a private hospital. As he put it to Max Jones, 'My dear, this is the only gall bladder I've got!'

Fully recovered, the intention was for Stéphane to remain in France, but he would never neglect his adopted home, returning regularly to feature in TV variety shows and radio guest spots. His first major commitment was in Paris's Latin Quarter, at the Club St Germain, the equivalent of New York's 52nd Street, if a little behind the times. This was real jazz work. Recordings of Grappelli's style of jazz were few, as the record companies' jazz budgets were being spent on bebop, which meant the American stars Dizzy Gillespie and Charlie Parker.

In 1950s Britain, popular light entertainment – which once marketed jazz as swing – adopted the attitude 'It's trad, Dad.' This approach consisted of the New Orleans bands of the 1920s reinvented for a new audience, which curiously included beatniks and existentialists. Ken Colyer and Chris Barber led a spirited revival, complete with banjos and even the occasional sousaphone.

In the '50s, many young people aspired to be 'modern', trying desperately to throw off at last the grim, grey world of post-war austerity. Women were so desperate for the fashionable new nylons that there was a black market. When the liner *Franconia* docked in Liverpool and was impounded by customs, her inner hull turned out to contain £80,000 worth of 'fully fashioned' contraband American hosiery. Everywhere, style was emerging from the drabness of rationing, and that meant chrome on cars, plastic chairs and architecture that heralded a sleek, clean space age.

The UK launched the decade with its Festival of Britain, which saw futuristic 'skylons' probing the smog and television promising a convenient, gadget-filled future. New York had the United Nations and a growing Manhattan skyline, the French had St Tropez, Brigitte Bardot and more chic than any one Paris courtier could dispense.

In the summer of 1954, Stéphane returned to Bricktop's, now fashionably established in the Rome glamorised by that year's hit song and film *Three Coins In The Fountain*. Then, in 1955, he enjoyed a season at St Tropez's L'Escale, and his collection later contained a snapshot of himself outside the club, cool in shorts and sunglasses. That winter, he spent as much time as he could in the South of France, eagerly awaiting the birth of his first grandchild, and his joy was doubled when, at Stéphane's own birthday party on 26 January 1956, Evelyne gave birth to a boy, who unsurprisingly became known as 'young Stéphane'. For Stéphane Snr, Cannes would from now on be eponymous with family and a delight in his young namesake.

Also in 1956, in the town of Hove in Sussex, England, another cool violinist took his first breath, Nigel Kennedy, who, merely six years later, would begin his study with the household name Yehudi Menuhin.

In the meantime, Stéphane's rare '50s ventures into the studio displayed a calm virtuosity, showing that he was equally cool with the modern vibraphone and shuffling wire brushes. For some inexplicable reason, the engineers recorded his electric violin directly into the recording console, with no room acoustic to give the sound life, and the results are dry and lack subtlety. On 'Improvisations' from 1956, Stéphane is the consummate professional, but the usual wit and cheek are suppressed by a suave and contrived red-velvet sophistication. (He may have insisted on playing the electric instrument, wallowing in its modernity and volume.)

The contemporary publicity photographs of Stéphane at this time – taken again by Baron – show a cravat-wearing, debonair gentleman with a pickup and volume control now fitted to his acoustic violin. He even felt able to contribute an album of solo piano, bass and drums. 'The violin, you know, is only my gimmick,' he would say to Martin Taylor in 1980.

Remarkably, Taylor, this other 'adopted grandson', was also born in 1956. While Stéphane was wowing the new Riviera jet set, Martin quietly arrived in Harlow, Essex. His mother, Rhoda, would bring him up to the sound of Nat 'King' Cole and Frank Sinatra. His father, a keen amateur musician, soon bought a Hofner jazz guitar and a small amplifier. Martin still remembers the luxurious smell of that flamboyant 1950s icon: a blond electric guitar. *One day*, he dreamt.

Stéphane's guitarist in the 1950s was Henri Crolla, another Django disciple. His band's recordings, however, were critically damned with the most condescending of faint praise, considered by *Jazz Hot* to be 'light, melodious...[for] connoisseurs'.

The good news, however, was the arrival of the long-playing microgroove record. Having initially a 10" and later a 12" diameter, these 'unbreakable' vinyl wonders not only contained more music – up to 45 minutes' worth – but the sound reproduction quality was also a marked improvement on the 78rpm shellac. 'Full-frequency range reproduction,' claimed the manufacturers. And soon the discs would also be available in stereo.

Although the British inventor Alan Blumlein had patented the stereo process in 1931, the fragile shellac 78rpm record could hardly accommodate its mechanical requirements. With advances in technology, however, Stéphane's fiddle was soon better recorded, and that increase in quality became available in the shops. Initially, the record companies focused on reissuing his back catalogue, which meant that, for the first time, whole albums of Hot Club Quintet material were arranged as suites or sides. The resulting publicity created a new audience for Stéphane, although already another trend was beginning: the legend of Django Reinhardt.

Dead, Django became a myth, a fate that would later befall James Dean and Marilyn Monroe. His musical talent remained without question, but mythology is a favourite and potent marketing strategy. To his annoyance, Stéphane soon found titles they recorded as a partnership sold as 'Django' records.

The mythology was given a further impetus by Paul Paviot's 1957 film *Django Reinhardt*.* Although featured on the soundtrack, Stéphane is largely absent until the end. Together with Joseph Reinhardt, Henri Crolla and Eugene Vees on guitar, Emmanuel Soldieux on bass, Gerard Leveque and Hubert Rostaing on clarinet and Andre Ekyan on alto sax, Stéphane contributes a spirited 'Minor Swing'. The performance provides a rare chance to see Joseph Reinhardt on solo guitar, and his playing is inspired and modern, even on an acoustic guitar. Andre Ekyan is similarly inventive and the two clarinets sing, but the whole thing is intended to be nostalgic, with a pair of two-beat rhythm guitars and a clear tribute to Louis Vola in Soldieux's short solo. The film, and Stéphane's performance, is an early mark of a coming trend; although nostalgia marketing wouldn't take a proper hold for the Quintet for another 15 years, this is the first glimpse of post-Quintet gypsy jazz.

'Hot Clubs' had been established all over Europe since the mid-1930s, but with Reinhardt's death they took on a new significance. Everywhere

*See the Music on Earth DVD *Stéphane Grappelli: A Life In The Jazz Century* for significant excerpts of this film, including 'Minor Swing' played in its entirety.

enthusiastic fans swapped rare pre-war Quintet recordings and exchanged snippets of information. A whole cottage industry of Djangomania was fanned by home-made magazines and newsletters, and Charles Delaunay became the font of Django memorabilia and anecdote. In 1954, he published a pamphlet of Django memoirs in *Jazz Hot*, and this edition was soon snapped up and became a collectors' item. Stéphane was asked to address meetings and memorial concerts and guitarists everywhere pressed him with inquiries about his mythic friend. Stéphane was uncomfortable, too old for bop and too young for nostalgia.

Meanwhile, in Britain popular music was evolving fast, and another offshoot of the trad-jazz fad was skiffle. This home-made music shared the banjo with trad and was rooted in American folksong and blues. Diz Disley, a young man from Yorkshire then in his 20s, had come to the guitar via records of Django, but like the Manouche he had started out on banjo and found work playing skiffle in the coffee bars and pubs of Soho. Like famous skiffle player Lonnie Donegan, his banjo could also double as a rhythm instrument for the trad bands, Donegan with Chris Barber's band and Diz with Alex Welsh and Kenny Ball. In Liverpool, Diz played the Cavern with The Yorkshire Jazz Band, and when the jazz bands took a break, skiffle groups such as The Quarrymen and The Eddie Clayton Skiffle Group provided a fill. The former band had a pushy guitarist called John Lennon, while Eddie Clayton's skinbeater was a bearded beatnik called Richard Starkey. Too young for the Cavern, a schoolboy called George Harrison was also keen to learn. 'My dad had played guitar when he was in the merchant navy,' recalled Harrison in *The Beatles Anthology* (see 'Bibliography'). 'When I started playing, he said, "I have a friend who plays..." He'd show me new chords and play songs to me like "Dinah" and "Sweet Sue" and Django Reinhardt or Stéphane Grappelli sort of tunes...* By this time, I'd met Paul McCartney on the bus coming back from school.'

The same cellar-club enthusiasts who craved real New Orleans trad also championed performances in Europe by authentic black American bluesmen. In the 1950s, London, Liverpool and Paris played host to Leadbelly, Big Bill Broonzy and Josh White. The black musicians had a political standpoint as an oppressed minority, the blues being the music of affirmation of a people whose identity had been crushed. This politicisation of music struck a nerve amongst

---

*Harrison would later record the 1935 Reinhardt-Grappelly number 'Sheik Of Araby' as a vocal for his Beatles audition for Decca in 1962. His interest in the tune was probably revitalised by Joe Brown's version from the TV show *6-5 Special*. (In his *Beatles Anthology*, Mark Lewisholm wrongly assumes this song to have been first heard in 1940.) George remained a Hot Club Quintet enthusiast and even booked Ian Cruickshank's Gypsy Jazz to perform for his private parties.

early civil-rights campaigners and particularly with the ban-the-bomb lobby. The first Aldermaston Marches featured a trad-jazz band and folksingers. Popular music was changing, reaching beyond entertainment and taking on a political message.

Stéphane couldn't relate to skiffle or its affected bohemia, which must have seemed to him a little contrived, having experienced the real bohemia of 1920s Montmartre. For his generation, however, the real shock was yet to come.

In 1956, rock 'n' roll hit the airwaves of Europe, slightly sanitised by white marketing executives and still issued on 78rpm discs but targeted at a youth market craving its own 45s. On the surface, the new music was electric powered, modern and loud. In truth, this music was a white-bread version of black rhythm and blues; in the marketing process it lost most of its sexual innuendo, retaining just enough to drive the newly invented teenagers wild.

This alienated Stéphane even more. The field of popular music and variety were changing beyond recognition. Agents and venues were quick to adapt – the new youth market had a little money and didn't mind standing. Theatres everywhere were soon filled with hastily compiled rock 'n' roll revues. If the punters were lucky, there might even be an authentic American rock 'n' roller topping the bill, but more often old variety acts were revamped into soundalikes and old swing musicians who needed the cash combed back their Brylcreemed hair and made a noise.

There was no place in any of this for a jazz violin, least of all one played by a dinner-jacketed 47-year-old. Stéphane's youth following, still intact in the Milroy photographs of the early 1950s, had now found a music that was theirs alone. For the first time, young people could identify with a new set of musical heroes of their own age.

Continental Europe, meanwhile, was slower to change. In Paris in May 1957, the black-American jazz violinist Stuff Smith appeared as part of Norman Grantz's *Jazz At The Philharmonic*. Smith was for Stéphane a jazz musician with as much power as Django or Louis Armstrong, but the French public weren't so impressed; they had grown up with Stéphane's sophisticated swing and were shocked by this American growl.

Born Hezekiah Leroy Gordan on 14 August 1909 in Portsmouth, Ohio, Stuff was an exact contemporary for Stéphane. Like Grappelli, he'd also been supported by his father, who not only hand-made him a violin but also gave him a job in his band. Stuff grew up in the mainstream of American jazz with a spot at the Onyx – 'the cradle of swing' – on New York's 52nd Street, and in his style it's possible to hear strains of Stéphane's hero Louis Armstrong. (On 'Onyx Club Spree' from 1937, for example, the violinist even sings like Satchmo.) Stuff swings with an authenticity that's in his blood and, unlike Michel Warlop, he could play blues. Stéphane loved Stuff's phrasing and his *moto perpetuo* riffs, while his use of the low strings in a ballad has all of Stéphane's emotion and vocalisation. In the upper register, however, he eschews Grappelli's full-bodied tone, instead screaming expressively like a horn player where Stéphane always preferred to sing.

Nevertheless, Stéphane sprang to Stuff's defence in the French press, and they went on to record together for the album *Violins No End*, the supposedly 'lost' tapes of which were not to surface for 25 years, which was unfortunately too late for Stuff, who died prematurely in 1967. The mature Grappelli would assimilate much of Stuff's swing.

Stéphane carried on mixing his jazz work with his usual forays into hotels, like the Paris Claridge's, and even recording some light-music albums with strings. Here the classy arrangements were by a young Quincy Jones.

The confusion that dominates jazz in the '50s is characterised in the rejection by many die-hard 'modernists' of that now-canonised icon Louis Armstrong. Looking back on the jazz century from a new-millennium perspective, Louis can be seen as a wellspring, one of the true pioneers, maintaining his dignity in any costume, on any stage. But films like 1957's *High Society* saw him cast as a Hollywood entertainer, and he also became associated with State Department tours as 'an American cultural ambassador'. For some, in a still deeply segregated nation, he was regarded as a political Uncle Tom, a sell-out.

Stéphane would have felt for Louis and no doubt saw a parallel dilemma. Where do you turn when your talent and craft outlasts fashion and social change? In the *Saturday Review* of 17 May 1958, Richard Gehman wrote, 'Grappelli pulls out a rhythm of his own, and above it he plays some of the most exciting jazz I've ever heard in my life... On ballads he is overcome by romanticism. He turns down the lights and plays moodily and ruminatively, as though picking over some old affair. I got the feeling that he misses his friend and musical companion much more than he will say. Perhaps that is what makes the sad tunes so astonishingly effective.'

Django's ghost would remain at Stéphane's elbow for the next 39 years.

16 Meeting The Duke

'It don't mean a thing if it ain't got that swing.'
– Edward Kennedy 'The Duke' Ellington

The 1958 Newport Jazz Festival was accidentally immortalised on film by Bert Stern as *Jazz On A Summer's Day*.* As well as creating a fascinating record of the event, Stern caught a snapshot of jazz on the brink of the '60s. Here, performing before an upmarket, sophisticated crowd in summer hats, posh frocks and pearls is Thelonious Monk at his peak, 'unconcerned by any opposition to his daring quarter-tone experiments'. Stéphane's friend George Shearing wows the crowd, playing in a Latin mood. Louis Armstrong seemingly, immortal at 57, duets with Jack Teagarden, Satchmo giving the crowd his full range from vocal charm to a riotous 'Tiger Rag' that harks back to New Orleans.

The strangest item, however, is a token nod to the fledgling rock 'n' roll, with Chuck Berry performing 'Sweet Little 16', complete with a jazz-clarinet solo break and a bemused Jack Teagarden. The festival repertoire features all of the staples that Stéphane used for the rest of his life: 'Sweet Georgia Brown', 'Tea For Two' and a range of what were coming to be called 'standards'. The documentary ends on a Sunday with 'the greatest gospel singer in the world', Mahalia Jackson, performing a musical interpretation of the Lord's Prayer.

What the festival best illustrates is how the jazz umbrella was now sheltering a complex mix of music too complicated to package and market, and so increasingly nobody did. But rock 'n' roll, the amusing side show of 1958 – now that had potential, surely? From that point on, the packaging and marketing of popular music would increasingly drive the 'industry', for that's what it had become. The 19th-century convergence of popular folk musics into the music halls had begun the growth of a series of global empires.

Meanwhile, in Duluth, Minnesota, a 17-year-old Robert Zimmerman had run away from home to visit Woody Guthrie, the composer of the Dustbowl Ballads, in hospital. The time were a-changing, and the restless young man would soon change his name to Bob Dylan.

*Stern was trying to make a low-budget feature film set at a jazz festival but instead made this fascinating documentary.

Stéphane didn't get an invite to Newport that year, but he was earning a reasonable living in Paris and London, still juggling a mix of venues from variety to straight-ahead jazz. Then, in 1959, he lost another friend, Sidney Bechet, who, based in Paris for the last ten years of his life, had often met with Stéphane to play in the basement clubs of the Latin quarter. Stéphane kept two affectionate photos of them relaxing together, possibly taken at Le Caveau de Hutchette. The two musicians shared a love of an earlier stage of jazz, its first flash of 1920s brilliance, and Bechet, a jazz original, left a thought for his contemporaries: 'The music has come a long way and it's time now for it to come out from round the corner; it's got to come up and cross the street. If I would believe it would do that, I wouldn't worry... All I want is to sleep and don't worry...that's the big thing. And that's what's holding the music back from this step it has to take. It's still worried. It's still not sure of itself. It's still in the shade and it's time it just stood up and crossed the street to the sunny side.'

In New York, Miles Davis took jazz on a new journey, exploring a cool modal approach, finding his place 'on the sunny side' with the orchestrations of Gil Evans on 'Kind Of Blue' and 'Sketches Of Spain'. Davis's jazz would eventually acquire a bold, in-your-face confidence, but not in the maelstrom of 1960.

Popular music in 1960s Europe began with red electric guitars and dreams of conquering space. In Britain, 'Apache' by The Shadows and 'Telstar' by The Tornados, launched a form of instrumental pop, borrowed from America, and both records shot to the top of the Hit Parade. Both groups featured electric instruments, The Shadows a matched set of guitars by California's Leo Fender and The Tornados an electric organ by the American inventor Laurens Hammond. However, the distinctive sounds of both groups were attributable in part to the amplification techniques developed by the British innovator Jennings and his Vox company. Electronic sound was becoming an important factor in popular music.

Throughout the Western world, the spirit of the technological age was epitomised by the silver space satellites launched from Florida's Cape Canaveral, which featured in film newsreels viewed on expensive but popular monochrome television sets. The satellite Telstar promised an age of global communications, represented for now by a barely recognisable face allegedly beamed across the Atlantic. The transatlantic pop music buzzed and crackled from miniature Japanese transistor radios in garish-coloured cases made from new-fangled and highly brittle new plastics. It was wonderful.

Both 'Apache' and 'Telstar' were British recording productions inspired by the American records that dominated late-'50s popular music. The new producers were striving for a hit sound, Norrie Paramor at Abbey Road for The Shadows and Joe Meek in a converted bedroom over a London shop for The Tornados' 'Telstar'. This producer-led approach marked a change in the recording of popular music, which took the artists' performances as being just the starting point.

The 'hit sound' started out with just the liberal addition of artificial reverberation and delay effects. Many of these were introduced by having the relatively new valve-amplified tape recorders record a selected instrument and then, milliseconds later, play it back. These 'effects' were then added to the live performance. The new teen stars talked of echo chambers and double-tracking.

Norrie Paramor, then Britain's most successful producer, came from the old school of A&R (in this context, arrangers and recorders). His productions were subtle enhancements of what remained essentially a live performance. At the other extreme, Joe Meek, the first independent British producer, piled on the new effects, creating in 'Telstar' an orgiastic blast from the future.

As the decade progressed, the number of recording effects available increased. With the additional aid of multitrack tape recording, invented by Les Paul, performers were soon able to add instruments and vocals to the initial performance and later mix these multiple performances to achieve a finished master. Innovators like The Beach Boys with Brian Wilson and, much later, Jimi Hendrix with Chas Chandler would soon take recording technology into the realms of psychedelic imagination.

At the other extreme, 'trad Dad' jazz had calmed to a level that saw bowler-hatted clarinetist Acker Bilk topping the Top 20 with 'Stranger On The Shore', a soothing, melodic anthem that epitomised what was soon labelled MOR (middle of the road). Popular music was diversifying in the search for different markets – MOR was for squares; pop music was the clarion call of the with-it generation.

The '60s also epitomised a social revolution, characterised in the English courts by the shift in legal status of DH Lawrence's novel *Lady Chatterley's Lover*, a frank and moral account of a love affair between a high-born woman and a gardener. Prosecuted for it's apparent 'depravity', it was now deemed 'fit for the eyes of wives and servants', and its Penguin paperback version, priced at

3/6d, gave many their first access to classic literature. Throughout Europe, liberal socialism was driving home the argument for accessibility to art and equality of education.

The deeply rooted class institutions of Europe remained, however. The class war wasn't over, but there were cracks in the divides. In Britain, people with real regional accents were appearing on the television, in radio programmes and films. The soap opera *Coronation Street*, set in a northern English town, acknowledged the existence of swearing and domestic violence. In France, 'new wave' films dared to represent real life in all its stark detail. European theatre applauded a whole new breed of angry young men with plays about the previously unspeakable subjects of sex, divorce, adultery, abortion and racial inequality. Entertainment in all its forms started to concern itself with the marketing mix.

In 1960, Stéphane was 52 and looked 39, but his checked sports jackets, tartan shirts and brown cardigans set him apart from the Swinging '60s. When it came to recording music, studio techniques remained for him a literal representation of a live performance, just as they had in 1929. This division between the straights and the freaks applied to matters across the board – clothes, music, art and morals. Stéphane was clearly and happily a straight.

As the first '60s teenagers took jobs, they became the first consumers and began to drive the market in fashion, style and all forms of popular art. As a direct consequence, pop records, once sold in plain brown paper bags, now had sleeve art, with glossy portraits and glamorous settings full of aspiration. Elsewhere, with their artists wrapped up in music rather than marketing and much happier out of the limelight, many jazz labels took the alternative route of abstraction and minimalism.

At this time, Stéphane started recording for one of the hippest jazz labels of all, Nesuhi Ertegun's Atlantic Records, his first record for whom adopted the abstraction of the time and appeared as *Feeling + Finesse = Jazz*. Ironically, in America the album was called *Django* – the legend was beginning to grow. However, Stéphane challenged Ertegun's concept of revisiting some of Stéphane's partner's old material; he was clearly in no mood for revivalism. The violinist insisted on a whole new approach, with the modern rhythm section of bass and drums replacing the plodding two-beat guitar trio. One of the guitarists on the album, Pierre Cavalli, was also a modernist.

On this release, alongside the familiar 'Minor Swing' and 'Nuages', Stéphane offers a tune from New York saxophonist Sonny Rollins. Stéphane admired the tenor player's tendency to spontaneous melody, avoiding too much spiky bebop. 'Pent-Up House' has Stéphane swinging on top of Daniel Humair's rustling wire brushes. The bass of Guy Pederson is competently unobtrusive, but Cavalli's guitar, with a distinctly electric twang, almost evokes the country flavour of Nashville. Again, the sound of Stéphane's electric violin is a little dry and one-dimensional. Commenting in the *Melody Maker*, he had completely changed his mind about the subject of amplification, considering it 'a necessary evil, distorting the violin's tone and making it sound like a clarinet... Personally, I don't like it.'

Thankfully, on 'Django', a John Lewis tune made famous by The Modern Jazz Quartet, there is either a microphone recording Stéphane's acoustic violin or the producer has discovered the potential of a little tasteful reverberation, and the difference is astonishing. With all his dynamic and tonal nuance restored, Stéphane sounds fresh and invigorated. In the up-tempo sections, he dances across the strings in an affectionate tribute to his Manouche friend, while accomplished drummer Humair has the good taste to use his modern ride cymbal only against the electric guitar and not the delicate fiddle.

For the closing theme of the piece, Stéphane switches gracefully to a rhapsodic gypsy style, his portamento slides literally moaning into the note. Whatever tests Django might have imposed on Stéphane's patience, nine years later it's clear that his loss remains an open and emotional wound.

'Minor Swing' and 'Daphne', meanwhile, demonstrate a still-growing virtuosity. Here Stéphane clearly presents his young band with a challenge and they respond with vigour. He may be out of fashion but he is playing better than ever. For a musician still growing, striving for his peak, these must have been difficult days.

In February 1962, at the Playhouse Theatre in Manchester, a young beat group passed an audition for the BBC. The producer for the occasion, Peter Pilbeam, described them on the audition sheet as 'an unusual group, not as "rocky" as most, more "country and western", with a tendency to play music', and went on to book them for the Light Programme series *Teenagers' Turn*. The band were apparently from Liverpool, where they had a considerable following at a jazz club called the Cavern. Their manager, Brian Epstein, a pushy record-store owner, was sure that they'd do well if he could only get them to cut their hair and dress properly. The young boys admired Buddy Holly, recently doing well in the now well-established *Melody Maker* Hit Parade, and with reference to his Crickets the Liverpudlians adopt another insect name, The Beatles. It's February 1962 and the pop-music landscape will soon change forever.

As 1962 turned to 1963, the Liverpudlians honed their craft in the German city of Hamburg, while in the same year the freelance compere Diz Disley introduced them for the BBC to a London audience. At that time, everybody in the pop business except George Martin, an EMI comedy producer, felt that guitar groups were finished and expected the fuss to blow over any day. Dick Rowe, head of Decca, famously remarked, 'Guitar groups are on the way out, Mr Epstein.'

In Paris, oblivious to the revolution that was taking place across the Channel, Stéphane revelled in the delights of a second grandson, Gilles, born to Evelyne on 5 April 1962. He was also preparing to meet one of his lifetime heroes, somebody also experiencing the wind of change: 'I was playing at the Hilton Hotel with the pianist Raymond Fol, a close friend of another pianist, Billy Strayhorn. Billy arranged a tea party and I remember being welcomed by Duke Ellington, a great gentleman and a very kind person. I was terribly proud to know him.'

The Duke was now taking work as a record producer for Frank Sinatra's Reprise label. Frank had launched Ellington's new venture with a huge press launch at Chicago's Ambassador West Hotel. (Ironically, the label's first album, recorded the very next day, was titled *Will The Big Bands Ever Come Back?*) Almost immediately, the Duke departed for a hectic European tour.

Stéphane was flattered by the audience with the Duke and the offer of a recording: 'I did a record with him, in fact with three violinists: his own, Ray Nance, [whom] I liked very much, a very nice man, also my old friend Sven Asmussen from Denmark, and myself.' The album would suffer a long gestation due to internal changes within the record company and the colossal impact on the pop-music world of what came to be known as Merseybeat. The times, according to the Dylan song of that year, really were a-changing. Eventually, the vinyl album *Duke Ellington's Jazz Violin Session* did appear, but 13 years later, in 1976, and on the Atlantic label. Even so, this remains one of the Duke's rarest records, still unavailable on CD, and Stéphane remarked in 1996, in a typically philosophical mood, 'I never received a record and I'm terribly curious to hear it.'*

The ultimate irony is that Stéphane's solo contribution, on Ellington's 'In A Sentimental Mood', is the clear high point of the record. He revels in one of

---

*Even the BBC gramophone library are without a copy, and, try as I did, I still regret never managing to obtain a copy for Stéphane. In 2001, the Ellington Society lent me their precious vinyl copy for eight hours. The recording features on the Music on Earth DVD *Stéphane Grappelli: A Life In The Jazz Century*.

the great rhythm sections of the 20th century, with the Duke himself on piano, Ernie Shepherd (one of Ellington's favourites) on bass and the legendary Sam Woodyard on drums.

After an *ad lib* introduction, with a vocal quality that would do credit to Billie Holiday, Stéphane takes flight *a tempo*, free at last to soar, while Ellington's sparse chords and Shepherd's apt counterpoint provide a delightful minimalism. Woodyard then enters with assured taste, pointing up the rhythm with brushes, hi-hat and sizzle cymbal, relaxed and clearly never confusing sentiment with plodding. As Stéphane gives one of the most tasteful and virtuosic performances of his life, the Duke seems to play less and less, paring his chords to the cleanest of ivory.

Stéphane had waited 16 years for this moment, and he was clearly enjoying it. It's only a shame that his friend Django couldn't take the next chorus. There are echoes in Stéphane's interpretation of the Duke's version, featuring Johnny Hodges soprano saxophone, which he first heard in 1935. He particularly borrows Hodges' style of swooping into the note with a bluesy glissando.

Here, Ellington has retained his sparse modern mood from his recent *Money Jungle* album, made with giants Max Roach and Charles Mingus. In the same week, he recorded the groundbreaking *My Favourite Things* album with John Coltrane, and Stéphane would no doubt have discussed this with Duke as Stéphane loved Coltrane's soprano-sax work on the album. This was an interesting juncture, two legends, both clearly hearing the shape of the new jazz, and yet revisiting their memories of swing.

The other *Jazz Violin Session* tracks pale in comparison. Ray Nance is an occasional fiddler more comfortable on trumpet. Born in Chicago in 1913, he'd been with the Duke on and off for over 20 years, providing when required that respectable fiddle that denoted 'orchestra'. Stéphane is a hard act to follow, though, and Nance sounds a little thin on a pared-down, Impressionistic 'Take The A-Train', but he can clearly swing.

Most out of water is Asmussen, playing viola here for reasons of contrast, uncomfortable and never quite in tune. The Danish fiddler is better heard in other settings. Born in Copenhagen in 1916, he enjoyed a classical training and formed his own Venuti-styled outfit in as early as 1933, and his 1940 take on 'My Melancholy Baby' demonstrates a fantastic versatility. His *pizzicato* violin is delightful, his vibraphone futuristic and his laid-back vocal pre-empts Chet Baker by a clear 20 years. His 1944 recording with his quartet, *It Don't Mean A Thing*, certainly swings.

For the Duke, Stéphane delivers the goods as the man he dubbed 'the world's greatest swing fiddler'. Once again, the French wizard kept a proud collection of photos from this session, recorded at Barclay Studios. In one snap, taken in the control room the Duke shares a joke with Stéphane while in the studio Billy Strayhorn clarifies a routine. Lined up for the trio recordings, the three fiddlers look a little inhibited, heads stuck in the dots. The Duke and Sven also frown while Steph casually puffs on a Galouise. In a fifth shot, the dots are thankfully abandoned as the engineer adjusts a microphone ready for a take. The photos capture perfectly the mood of the record, a strange brew for a difficult period in jazz.

For this session, Stéphane used his famous Warlop violin by Pierre Hel, the one he famously played for Grégor et ses Grégoriens. Perhaps in playing for Ellington, Stéphane was looking back to those heady days when he first recorded 'It Don't Mean A Thing' and 'Solitude', the hits he played 30 years earlier at Bricktop's in Montmartre.

The Duke, of course, could look back even further. Nine years Stéphane's senior, born in 1899 in Washington, DC, he acquired his title early as a reference to his teenage elegance. Ada Smith, alias Bricktop, had heard the regal young man in his home town and, in 1923, recommended him to the manager of the Barrons club, thus securing for him his first important New York gig. He went on to record in 1924, played the Cotton Club in 1927 and by 1933 was famous enough, via his records, to visit Europe. On 12 June in that year, he topped a music-hall bill for Jack Hylton at the London Palladium, where his support included 'the original Snake Hips girl Bessie Dudley' and 'the world's most sensational acrobatic roller skaters' The Three Whirlwinds. Bottom of the bill was 'Cheeky Chappie' Max Miller, but with admission at ninepence nobody was complaining. The Duke was shocked to receive a ten-minute ovation so far from home.

On the same 1933 tour, the Duke had played the Salle Pleyel in Paris, where one planned show turned into three due to popular demand. He soon became a key figure for the French jazz hot movement, appearing in an early issue of *Jazz Hot* magazine* which also promised to devote a special 'number' to him. Dated April 1935, the magazine also includes a transcript of 'Here Comes The Duke' by Spencer Williams and Pat Castleton, complete with the lyric 'Hail the greatest swing director/Greet the greatest Swing injector...for he's the potentate of syncopated swing'.

Stéphane had caught up with Duke's sophisticated swing in the same year

---

*In the same issue there is an Ultraphone advertisement for six different Grappelli 78s, two of which received reviews by Hugh Panassié.

and had recorded his own version of 'It Don't Mean A Thing', the hit that had taken Ellington back to his roots, playing music that was intended for dancing. Although he gives a spirited performance on this rendition, it wasn't until he recorded Ellington's brilliant ballad 'In A Sentimental Mood' in April 1937 that Stéphane really came to grips with one of the century's greatest jazz composers.

Quite how much Stéphane's playing had matured by 1963 is clearly heard on *Duke Ellington's Jazz Violin Session*. It must have been exasperating for Stéphane to be surrounded all the time by copious reissues of his inferior '30s work and yet be unable to obtain a copy of this latest advance. Nevertheless, he fulfilled a lifetime's ambition in recording for the Duke. Not a note was wasted.

In 1964 Stéphane suffered a small accident, breaking the little finger on his left hand in a fall following a misplaced step on a concrete stairwell. For most people, this would be an inconvenience; for Stéphane, it might have ended his career. He told a friend, 'It's OK. I have a little piece of silver in my finger now. I can't sustain the pressure on it so I play faster. It's like a little souvenir from Django to me. If he can take it, I can take it too!' He could usually find a bright side. After the poverty of Montmartre, this was nothing.

The effects of his injury were soon tested on the 1965 album *Stuff And Steff*, and here he sounds as assured as ever. It's perhaps at this stage that Stéphane perfected his extremely light touch, remarked on by many violinists. In his excellent book *Jazz Violin*, co-written with Stéphane, New Yorker Matt Glasser observed, 'Stéphane keeps his fingers in a gentle curve. He comes into notes almost parallel with the string, as opposed to hitting them from above. This minute slide into every note lands him on the fleshiest part of his finger, which is one of the factors responsible for his clear, rich tone. Very light finger pressure is another Grappelli trademark; just enough to get the job done, no bearing down unnecessarily on a note. This allows Stéphane to play at incredibly fast tempos.'

Stéphane kept up his radio appearances but moved on from the rather staid BBC Light Programme and French Public Radio to be a featured artist on Radio Luxembourg, or FAB 208, as it became known. In the 1960s, the independent commercial station Luxembourg broadcast mostly at night in order to bounce its signal off the Earth's ionosphere. Pre-dating satellite radio, 'Luxy' was about as groovy as you could get. Although the station signal faded in and out as the ionosphere shifted, all over Europe this was the place to listen for popular music.

Stéphane recorded his contributions in London with a new friend, Laurence Holloway, whom he had met in the early '60s. 'I was in Cyril Stapleton's Orchestra in about 1960 and Steph was a friend of Cyril's,' recalled Holloway. 'We did a series called *The Melody Dances* which was from Finsbury Park Ballroom. We had guests on every week and one week it was Steph. Cyril wondered if I was up to playing with Stéphane. I was a young kid then, aged 22. Anyway, I was up to it. I was living in a caravan at the back of a petrol station in Harringay at the time.

'Stéphane then was asked to do a radio series for Radio Luxembourg…13 weeks [of] quarter-hour programmes, compered by Steve Race. He had a studio in Hertford Street near the Hilton Hotel. Stéphane liked the way I played so he asked me to put a trio together. So with Joe Muddel on bass and Jock Cummings on drums, [we] did 13 programmes, and then they asked if we could do another 13. We eventually did 39 quarter-hour broadcasts.'

Laurie Holloway, as he has come to be known, was born in 1938 in Oldham, Lancashire, and worked with Stéphane on and off for the rest of the fiddler's career. They became friends, and in the mid-'60s Laurie visited Stéphane at his family base in Cannes, where Evelyne and her husband were now running a restaurant known as the Arch Door, which Stéphane helped set up in the Souquet district, 'up a cobbled street and quite small and dark', according to Pam Reid, who visited in 1966 to see her sister, Jean Barclay. Stéphane would greet celebrity guests there and even occasionally served on the cash register, totting up the bills.

'I went to the Arch Door with my wife, Marion Montgomery, and stayed with Evelyne,' recalled Holloway. 'According to Pam, both Stéphane and Jean spent a lot of time with Evelyne. Jean always got on very well with Gilles – she and Steph tried to grandparent the boys. Young Stéphane was a very nice boy; he came to stay with us at Ashton. Our son was about the same age and they played together with the model railway.

'I first met Evelyne in 1966 and saw her again in 1970 briefly, but I never really got to know her. Stéphane worried about them, especially when they were trying to get the Arch Door off the ground – money was terribly tight, so I gather. It was a bold venture. I remember going to eat there. It was very nice. They had some signature dishes. Quite a lot of showbusiness people went there because they were quite discreet.'

Back at work in September 1966, Stéphane set off for Switzerland to work for Radio Basel on their series of concert recordings *Jazz Im Fauteuil*, a performance which later appeared on vinyl as *Violin Summit*, where his fellow bandmembers included a young Jean-Luc Ponty. At this time, he was also reunited with his old friends Sven Asmussen, from the Ellington sessions, and Stuff Smith.

The *Violin Summit* recording was the second time that Stéphane benefited from the superb bass playing of Niels-Henning Orsted Pedersen. One of the world's greatest players, and still only 20 years old at the time, he had originally met Stéphane in 1965 on a *Festival* album with Asmussen. Stéphane especially appreciated the Dane's instant counterpoint and irresistible swing, a sentiment common to many fellow artists from Count Basie, whom Pedersen famously turned down, to Oscar Peterson, with whom he would tour for years. One of the highlights of the album is Pedersen's solo on 'Pent-Up House', where he plays with drummer Axel Riehl, pianist Kenny Drew and other rhythm players, all borrowed from Club Montmartre in Copenhagen.

Stuff Smith, by this time a resident in Copenhagen, had clearly developed a close affinity with Sven, and they are obviously enjoying themselves on 'Timme's Blues' with Stuff's relaxed vocals breaking up the violin duels.

On the Ellington track 'It Don't Mean A Thing', the quartet of fiddles achieve their best ensemble and all solo effectively, but it's clear that the best time was being had by the audience. It must have been fantastic to have been there and seen this unique summit, but it's not great music in any lasting sense.

Stéphane sounds most at ease on his solo contribution, 'Pennies From Heaven', doing what he does best and being warmly received with shouts for more. The marked contrast of sound between Steph and Stuff is never clearer than when the latter plays 'Only Time Will Tell', digging in, in his inimitable way, the complete opposite of Stéphane's lyrical approach.

More difficult was Stéphane's response to Jean-Luc Ponty. The fellow Frenchman was only 24 at the time but seemed poised to take the violin into a new age. For Ponty, there was no dilemma over amplification; for him it was the only way. In that year, he seemed to be Stéphane's natural successor, winning the *Down Beat* international critics' poll. Born in Avranches the son of a violin professor, he had already won the first prize at the Paris Conservatoire for his classical playing. He came to jazz through seeing Stéphane and Stuff in Limoges, and Stéphane had taken time to encourage him, along with Kenny Clarke and others.* 'In 1961, alongside my classical work with symphony orchestras, I liked to frequent the jazz clubs in Paris with professional musicians from America and France,' recalled Ponty. 'I learnt one day that Babik Reinhardt,

*Jean-Luc Ponty quotes taken from *Stéphane Grappelli: Mon Violon Pour Tout Baggage* (see 'Bibliography').

Django's son, and Stéphane Grappelli wanted to meet me. Stéphane invited me to go and see them with my violin at his flat in Montmartre. After we chatted for a while we went to a bar-club in Saint Germain des Près for me to play with a pianist, Raymond Fol. After he had listened to a few jazz standards, he paid me a compliment, in particular to the originality of my improvising. I was not quite 19 at this time, and this compliment from such a great, celebrated musician had a profound effect on me as it confirmed to me that I had found my voice and a style I felt comfortable with.'

Nor was this all one-way traffic: 'Stéphane invited me to return to his house, where he asked me about classical technique exercises. Being *auto-didacte*, he wanted to know about my classical technique. We played exercises together, which was very stimulating. When not on tour, Stéphane often asked me to show him some exercises to loosen the fingers. After these exercises, Stéphane announced, "Now we can go and play the bible!" He had the Bach concerto for two violins in D minor.

'We played in the classical style very seriously, and after the first movement Stéphane took out a bottle of whiskey to reward our great effort. We didn't need much for the second movement, which was a slow one, but Stéphane estimated that we had earned another drink for double effort. But the third movement was very fast, and if my memory serves me correctly, we never finished it. After several bars, the whole thing collapsed and Stéphane put down his violin and installed himself at the piano and we played some jazz together. Apart from these spontaneous piano-and-violin duos, we never played jazz like this together.

'We were both very different people. In a world of jazz, it is necessary to experiment properly with your individuality, and it is this that is of most interest to the public and the musicians, in my opinion.'

Eventually, Jean-Luc ploughed a whole new path, exploring every effect and process for which his electric fiddle could provide a source. His Coltrane-like horn approach found him a place fronting a concerto for eccentric American guitarist Frank Zappa. Stéphane was bemused and perhaps a little saddened by the direction of his former protégé.

But Ponty's direction is perfectly in keeping with the times. In 1966, Jimi Hendrix literally blazed his guitar at the Paris Olympia, the British supergroup Cream were pioneering a new kind of free-form rock and The Beatles were ensconced at Abbey Road creating a concept album, the groundbreaking *Sgt Pepper's Lonely Hearts Club Band*, launched to almost universal acclaim the following year. Young people everywhere dressed in floral outfits and the rock music many jazzers hoped would go away seemed to be stronger, louder and, for Stéphane, increasingly more alien. Even cool jazz exponents like Miles Davis were employing electric guitarists and experimenting with production. The stage was set for the Summer of Love.

Stéphane's closest early encounter with flower-power came from an unlikely direction. The celebrated film composer Henry Mancini had been hired to score the Albert Finney/Audrey Hepburn vehicle *Two For The Road*, a touching little comedy taking the form of an early road movie that saw the trendy couple take a long odyssey through France, love, marriage, infidelity and liberation. Hepburn was dressed fantastically in the outrageous floral mini-dresses and gargantuan sunglasses of high-'60s fashion while Finney affected a James Bond-like cool in an assortment of sports cars.

On the soundtrack, Mancini added a French flavour to his essentially American approach to scoring, his trademark lush strings augmented by a musette accordion and the quintessential French fiddle of Stéphane Grappelli. The love theme is further imbued with French credibility by Stéphane's plaintive solo. However, Stéphane never gets the chance to improvise, and this probably explained why he basically shut down when quizzed about the project, no doubt resenting the straitjacket of the written theme. At the mention of Mancini, he professed that he couldn't even remember working with him.

A common phrase during pop-music recording sessions of this era was 'no jazz'. For many people, jazz was old-fashioned, undisciplined and unpredictable. In the soundtrack for *Two For The Road*, Stéphane clearly played what was written, but it's a testament to his talent that his distinctive sound sings through. It's a good little film, a vignette of an era.

Despite his earlier memory lapse, Stéphane did keep a couple of posed studio photos of him and the great Henry in his shoebox. Tellingly they are shown alongside a huge stopwatch, the signature of the tightly disciplined, professional film composer.

In September 1967, Grappelli lost yet another friend, his recent collaborator Stuff Smith, who had enjoyed his last few years in Denmark. Together with Sven Asmussen and Jean-Luc Ponty, Stéphane gave a memorial concert for the Ohio fiddler in Copenhagen.

As the '60s love affair with pop blossomed, The Beatles sang 'All You Need Is Love' to the world's largest ever television audience, the Vietnam War escalated and student unrest erupted in Paris. It was clear that Dylan had been right. Jean-Luc could have the limelight; Stéphane was content with somewhere to ride out the storm.

17 A Hilton Retreat

'Those people on the stage are making so much noise I can't hear a word
you are saying.'

– Henry Taylor Parker, American music critic

Ever the pragmatist, Stéphane spent most of the years between 1967 and 1972
providing dinner entertainment at Le Toit de Paris. This restaurant, 'the roof
of Paris' on the tenth floor of the Hilton Hotel, was a convenient place to eat
for the socialites of Paris and today is the first choice for many American visitors
to the city.

Stéphane had a small band with guitar doubling vocals, bass, drums and
himself on fiddle, with the occasional saxophone taking a few solos. Recalling
his cinema days, he would sometimes also play the intermission music on solo
piano and challenged himself by performing his favourite standards in fiendishly
difficult keys. The aristocrat of the fiddle didn't mind the anonymous nature
of the gig, where, according to many visitors, he wasn't even mentioned in the
foyer hoarding. 'We would see him in Paris on occasions,' Laurie Holloway
remembers. 'I went to see him at the Hilton with my wife…just a restaurant
job. A bit sad in a way.'

Stéphane did mind the clatter of knifes and forks, however. If anyone had
the gall to complain about the volume of the band, he would retort, 'You can
move. I'm stuck here!'

Was he stuck? Probably. There were no record deals for middle-period
swing jazzers in the late '60s. Records generate gigs, or rather the promotional
departments of record companies insist on gigging bands out on the road,
pushing product. Stéphane, meanwhile, had no product to push. The last album
specifically under his name had been released on an obscure label in 1963. But
his restaurant job was what musicians call a nice little number: steady work,
not too strenuous, regular hours and offering safety in a precarious profession
for which security is a rarity.

The Hilton Band can be heard on the album *Le Toit de Paris*. Packaged as the perfect Paris souvenir, the sleeve shows Stéphane against a backdrop of the Eiffel Tower, his name misspelled as the old 'Grappelly', accompanied by a note: 'The roof bar of The Paris Hilton. All the natural grace and elegance of Stéphane Grappelly echoed by the finesse of Raymond Fol.' Alongside Fol's piano, Stéphane had Jack Sewing on bass, Tony Ovio on guitar and Andre Hartmann on drums. The sound is the epitome of much cosy jazz of the '60s – light, frothy and unobtrusive, like a well-made cappuccino. The brushes swish on a polite snare drum, the piano tinkles with an elegant tonal grace, the bass hums along in a steady, relaxed stroll and Stéphane gilds the lily with a little *chocolat*. This is music to wash your cares away and it's the best of its kind. Ironically, Stéphane's here is incredibly virtuosic, playing better than ever, but the musical content is light years from what's really happening in jazz. There's nothing of the challenge of Thelonious Monk at Newport or Miles Davis's contemporary album *Filles de Kilimanjaro*. Stéphane has his head well below the parapet.

Not touring had its plus points. Stéphane would be 60 in early 1968, having spent 40 years on the road living out of a suitcase. He'd been bombed by the Luftwaffe, and stranded by the airlines, lost in France and frozen in Norway. Most people retire at about his age; why not sit out a few dances while a cold wind whistles around a tenth-floor window?

The closer you look at the late 1960s, the more hostile the environment must have been for a 1930s jazzer. World communications had vastly improved and news of the world's tragedies travelled fast. When John F Kennedy was assassinated on 22 November 1963 and television reported the news virtually instantly, for many people the shock was almost physical. Two days later, millions watched on live television as Jack Ruby killed the president's alleged assassin, Lee Harvey Oswald.

As the Vietnam War escalated, news programmes every night showed the massacre in barely censored gory detail. Riots were seen in Northern Ireland as bombs shattered a Catholic church. Russian tanks entered the Czech capital of Prague and the Cold War crept ever nearer to Armageddon. Many felt that all-out nuclear war was inevitable.

In April 1968, the assassinations of civil-rights leader Martin Luther King and, in June, Senator Bobby Kennedy added to the sense of a world gone mad. In Britain, the Conservative politician Enoch Powell gave his provocative speech on the impact of immigration and warned of a potential violence and 'rivers of blood'. President Nixon came to power in America and the musical *Hair* rocked the entertainment world with its full-frontal nudity and dramatised free love.

Meanwhile, in May 1968, 30,000 students took to the streets of Paris to participate in the worst riots ever witnessed by a modern city. Général de Gaulle, the French president and a national hero, warned of the threat of a takeover by a communist dictatorship. Then a general strike involving ten million workers plunged the nation into chaos. De Gaulle postponed a national referendum and finally resigned in April 1969, prompting the Prime Minister to declare, 'A new page has been turned in the history of France.'

By this time, Stéphane had moved into a new apartment at the Rue Dunkerque, a small but very respectable address that no doubt required a big mortgage. His Quartier remained the same, however, and he could still hear the bells of the Sacre Coeur, in neighbouring Montmartre. Ironically, he was living in the sort of bourgeois respectability that he could only dream of as a child. The courtyards that surround the apartments and the Parc d'Anvers were precisely the pitches he'd sought 50 years earlier as a busker. The need to maintain some steady work must have been particularly clear to him.

The carpet-quiet Hilton had crisp white linen and crystal, elaborate flower arrangements, champagne and ice sculptures – these were the accessories. The décor was '60s sparse, with floor-to-ceiling drapes masking massive picture windows. The daytime view was spectacular, as was the company; one of Stéphane's photographs shows him sunning himself on the Hotel roof with Twiggy, whom the rapidly expanding mass media had made into the first supermodel. In the tabloid-style photo, both are sipping cocktails from straws, breakfasting under a sun umbrella, Twiggy probably telling Stéphane that her mum had all his records.

The nights on the little platform stage were no doubt long, but this imposition was alleviated by the passing trade. At the Hilton, Stéphane collected a small mound of happy photos for his shoebox collection. In one photo, Dizzy Gillespie can be seen blowing a few choruses while Stéphane smiles ready to deliver a more than respectable response. In a conservative suit with a kipper tie and a sober shirt, beside him Diz is in polka dots and paisley. Were the clientele impressed by these apparent superstar jams? Possibly not, as these photographs were probably taken after hours as the stars returned from their paying gigs to their hotel, seeking a quiet drink and a jam with that brilliant fiddler in the bar.

In another photograph, Stéphane is seen taking a song request from star actress Julie Christie and her handsome beau, a uniformed wine waiter hovering nearby. In yet another, Teddy Wilson, Billie Holiday's favourite pianist, has the biggest kipper tie in the world and seems set to take a chorus, while Count Basie is drinking a toast and the maître d'hôtel smiles fit to bust. Stéphane is clearly enjoying himself, staying put as the world's greatest musicians come and jam. They suffer the suitcases and the airports; he walks home.

In June 1969, the great American guitarist Barney Kessel was in town. Born in 1923 in Muskogee, Oklahoma, Barney had worked on film with artists as diverse as Lester Young and Elvis Presley. His late recordings with Billie Holiday and Ben Webster were already classics and in many ways he was the direct successor to Charlie Christian, the father of electric jazz guitar, who had in fact given Kessel three days unofficial tuition. Kessel was also a Django fan and the two guitarists had met in 1953, when Barney first toured with Oscar Peterson. He and Stéphane had much to talk about as they jammed at the Hilton. There was soon talk of a record, and on the 23 and 24 June they made it into Studio Davout, Paris.

For this recording, the emphasis was again on Django Reinhardt, and Barney clearly based his 'I Remember Django' on the gypsy's famous tune 'Nuages'. Following Kessel's turn, Stéphane responds in a sensitive and elegiac way. The two then whip through 'Honeysuckle Rose' and 'Undecided' as if the '30s had never gone away. Kessel's electric guitar is never quite as compatible as the acoustic in this role, certainly not with the technology available in 1969, and causes Stéphane's violin to sound a little colourless, although only on the swing tunes, where he occasionally resorts to his electric violin. On the ballads, Kessel's subtle chords give Stéphane plenty to work with. The recordings were popular enough to merit a reissue in 1991 complete with extra, previously unreleased tracks.

Stéphane's protégé Jean-Luc Ponty had by this time introduced an American audience to the concept of jazz violin. Although still to tour the states, Jean-Luc was topping American critics' polls. This, combined with George Wein's conviction that the true original of the French school could succeed stateside, convinced Stéphane to take a risk: 'In 1969 I remember being engaged by George Wein to put my feet at last to America. I did my little bit with George at the piano and some musicians I never played with except some fabulous vibraphonist, and when I finished up I got down from the stage and there was somebody there all dressed in blue jeans and long hair and he said, "Hey, man. You play all right." I was very pleased to hear that and I said, "Are you a musician?", and he said, "Yes. My name is Miles. Miles Davis."'

Despite his delight in meeting Miles, Stéphane hated Newport. In the spirit of those heady times, the management gave in to the inevitable. With jazz interest at an all-time low and rock firmly in the ascendant, Stéphane had to share the bill with heavily amplified rock bands and the air was thick with drugs, dissent and a general distrust of anyone older than 25. To the dismay of the police, 22,000 people crammed into an area normally confined to 18,500. *Down Beat* magazine, the voice of jazz, reported, 'Newport 1969: Bad Trip'. 'It was not a concert; it was a revolution,' said Stéphane, reporting to Geoffrey Smith in 1985, 'It was cold it was raining all the time. It's a crazy place. I played 12 hours late and I don't like to work like that.'

The brilliant vibraharp* player Gary Burton was also at the festival but didn't meet Stéphane. He recalls, 'I was only familiar with his name, not his music. I just knew from my knowledge of jazz history that he had been part of The Hot Club Of France group and had played decades earlier with Django Reinhardt. At that time I was in the midst of my hippy jazz-rock phase, complete with long hair, beads and fringe jackets.'

Stéphane wasn't bothered by the clothes, but the vibraphone,[†] which he'd previously encountered played by the jazz innovator Red Norvo, intrigued him – 'There was a fabulous vibraphone player. I think it was Gary Cooper [*sic*].'

The vibraharp, as Gary Burton preferred to call it, was, like so many of the Newport instruments, electric, a sort of electric xylophone with metal keys that can't function without power for its motor-driven vibrato. (Burton also liked to work with electric guitar and Leo Fender's electric bass.) However, like the violin, the vibraharp is a delicate instrument, best suited to subtle textures and lilting rhythms. In Burton's hands, stretched out with four mallets, the instrument provided a rich chordal Impressionism.

Burton was entranced: 'I learned later that, while my quartet was playing our set, Stéphane was having a conversation with George Wein, complaining that he was always getting stuck playing with old musicians. Why couldn't he sometimes play with the young guys, playing newer music? George said, "Like who?" Stéphane pointed to my group playing on the stage and said, "Well, I like Gary's group, for instance." So, when we finished our set, George came up to me backstage and started talking about Stéphane. He asked if I would want to play with him. I said I didn't really know his playing, just that he was one of the old-timers – Stéphane was 61, I was 26. But I

---

*The vibraharp player that Stéphane worked with at Newport was probably Red Norvo.

[†]A patented bar metallophone known by its USA tradename as a Vibraharp (Deagan of Chicago). Its metallic bars are arranged keyboard fashion and amplified by tubular resonators that are alternately opened and closed by revolving vanes, producing a distinct and variable vibrato.

said I would be interested in finding out if there was any common ground between us.

'George and I walked over to Nesuhi Ertegun, the co-president of Atlantic, my record company then. It turned out he'd spent his teenage years in Paris and knew Stéphane's playing well. Nesuhi was all for the idea of us doing a record together. I was unsure about committing to a project with someone I'd never even heard play, so we worked out a plan. My group would be touring Europe a few months later, with a concert in Paris on the schedule. We left a couple of days open and agreed to get together and rehearse for a couple of hours to see if we could play [together]. If things were comfortable, we would go into the studio the following day and make the record.' Of course, none of this could happen until November and Stéphane returned to Paris, amidst the space-race fever of the times.

On 21 July at 3:56am BST, as half the world watched, a man stood on the Moon for the first time and a new perspective on our world was revealed. The Apollo 11 mission brought back colour photographs of an Earthrise. All who saw those images of a frail blue planet in a vast universe of inky black were moved. The power of that image helped establish a foundation for the new ecology movements.

Meanwhile, eccentric Beatle John Lennon championed the peace movement by staying in bed at the Amsterdam Hilton, singing 'Give Peace A Chance' while millions sang along. The global perspective had arrived, and this was first reflected in popular music.

Stéphane was disappointed by America. All his life he'd admired jazz, the only distinctly American art form. He had striven to perfect his own style of the genre and was in awe of its gods, particularly Louis Armstrong and Art Tatum. The reality he experienced was a muddy field and hordes of disaffected youth. It must have seemed that the USA had forsaken its own music in pursuit of a fast buck. Stéphane had no idea then that those surfing the new wave were interested in him.

Ironically, Stéphane had met jazz's new crown prince, Miles Davis, before Newport in 1950s Paris. Then Miles had been a besuited advocate of 'the birth of the cool'. By 1969 – as Stéphane's shoebox photograph shows – he was still with his French girlfriend, Juliet Greco, but by now the suit was replaced by denim and the eyes smouldered behind huge fly-eye shades. Stéphane understood cool jazz, even loved it in the hands of Gary Burton, the new evangelist of the vibraharp, but Miles had already moved on.

Born in 1926 in Illinois, Miles Davis had grown up with the bebop of Dizzy Gillespie and had featured in the crusading bands of Charlie Parker. Since the late '50s he'd ploughed his own furrow, experimenting with brass textures and orchestral sound. With Gil Evans he'd made jazz popular, his albums *Kind Of Blue*, *Porgy And Bess* and *Sketches Of Spain* bringing a whole new audience. His arranger, Gil Evans, was one of those who stayed at the Paris Hilton and marvelled at Stéphane's style, but even Evans was now left behind as Davis's restless experimentation and modal exploration replaced bebop's playing-over-changes approach. By 1969, the seductive electric sound world had drawn him to the electronic piano of Chick Corea and Joe Zawinul and the electric guitar of John McLaughlin. He took his place at the forefront of what became known as *fusion* and *jazz rock*. Stéphane could probably relate to the delicate textures of albums like *In A Silent Way*, but *Filles de Kilimanjaro* and *Bitches Brew* were a very long way from 'Tiger Rag'. There would be no direct Miles collaboration, although Miles did famously say during the *Sketches Of Spain* sessions, '[Sometimes] the melody is so strong there's nothing you have to do with it. If you tried to play bebop on it, you'd wind up being a hip cornball.'

Safely back in Paris, Stéphane's old friend Joe Venuti came to town in October as part of George Wein's Newport all stars. Stéphane was pleased to see his old friend again: 'Joe was Italian…and I speak a little Italian. We managed to speak together. We had worked together before. I showed him around Paris. He was a funny man and we had a good time together. I showed him the museums and churches and he became a great friend. When I visited his hotel, he was crying, in a right mess – somebody had stolen his violin. So I lent him one of mine.'

With a replacement violin arranged for Joe, he and Stéphane ventured into the studio with George Wein again at the piano, Barney Kessel on guitar, Larry Ridley on bass and the Don Lamond on drums: 'The record was organised by George Wein, the promoter of the Nice Jazz Festival,' recalled Stéphane, 'but I tell you, I never got to hear it.'

This telling remark is typical of Stéphane. He listened to his records only if people sent them to him. His flat at Rue Dunkerque had many but certainly not all of his hundreds of albums. His live approach meant that this album, *Venupelli Blues*, was recorded in one day on 22 October 1969. Not hearing his records doesn't mean he was dismissive or uncaring for the results, however; as he said, 'It's just over when it's done and let's move on.'

In fact, Stéphane did remember one particular track from Joe, 'I'll Never Be The Same', remarking, 'I accompanied him on the piano and only he can play like that.' The sleevenotes' writer, Trevor Salter, wasn't informed of the change of pianist, however, and, thinking that it's George Wein playing, remarks that 'the [pianist] managed to extricate his hands from the cuffs of his jacket'.

That track sounds like two old friends having a ball. On violin they were miles apart, but this way, with Stéphane on the keys, they found some common ground. It's all a little sentimental, but if two Italians by extraction can't be sentimental at the ages of 61 and 66, they never can. When comparing these two giants on the violin-duo tracks, it comes down to a difference of dialect and accent. Both are demonstrably Italian in their love of melody. Joe's sound has a distinct Philadelphia accent: brash, American, in your face. If Joe asks, 'Why, buddy?' Steph asks a gentle 'Pourquoi, mon ami?' Stéphane's accent is Parisian – he never leans on a note like Joe and always slips around the beat, searching out the poetry. Joe's sound is influenced by the jazz horns that have always dominated his American landscape, while Stéphane's sound skips around like the Paris musette.

On Stéphane's feature number, 'My One And Only Love', he displays all his long-won taste and virtuosity. There is real feeling in his playing, as if Gwendoline – lost in the war, her likeness sealed in his hidden oil painting – is present in his thoughts. This is one ballad to which Stéphane often returned.

It's significant that Stéphane, perhaps contemplating his own 'retirement' at the Paris Hilton, was working again with the man who had started it all over 40 years earlier at the Ambassador in 1928, with Paul Whiteman and Eddie Lang, back when Stéphane had first seen a way to be part of jazz. Now both so alienated from the current mainstream, here were two jazz violinists swapping choruses on *Venupelli Blues*.

Back on the scene after a long gap, Joe pulled out all the stops for his revival. On the title track of this album, he even included his signature trick, first featured in 'Four-String Joe' in 1927, involving him threading his violin bow through the strings to play sequences of chords, sounding all four strings simultaneously.

This musical stunt was typical of Venuti's humour. Stéphane had many stories of practical jokes played by his Italian buddy, whose repertoire included pouring flour into a tuba players horn, resulting in an onstage snowstorm; tacking an overzealous soloist to the stage with a hammer and nails; and ringing up 20 double-bass players, offering them a gig at the same club and then watching the resulting mayhem from a convenient hotel room. Sadly, alcohol had done its worst and the clown prince of the violin was already in his last decade. After the album, they went on one last tour together, with Duke Ellington in Italy, where the crowd identified so strongly with Grappelli and Venuti, the prodigal adventurers, that the Duke gave them their own 15-minute spot.

For Grappelli, *Venupelli Blues* is an important album. His track 'My One And Only Love', for instance, is the first real display of his resolved, mature style. His playing is seemingly effortless, as if he has nothing left to prove. Musical fashions would come and go, but from now on there was only one Stéphane Grappelli. For another 28 years he would refine this signature sound. Significantly, from 1969 onwards, all of Stéphane's albums carried the Grappelli name with the Italian spelling, with an I.

The record session over, Joe and Stéphane jammed together at the Hilton to the delight of Jean-Louis Ginibre, the editor of Paris's trendy magazine *Lui*, who enthused, 'There are musicians whose youth endures on and whom maturity continues to approach perfection. They not only remain in full possession of those means which originally enabled them to build their renown during their youth but they even succeed to master these means more each year. The violinist Stéphane Grappelli is one of those men.'

In the following month, Gary Burton arrived in Paris, as promised, and the two musicians, separated by 35 years, an ocean and a culture, at last had the opportunity to speak. 'The tour went as planned,' recalled Gary, 'and we eventually found ourselves meeting Stéphane for the first time; I hadn't so much as laid eyes on him at Newport. We had brought along some lead sheets to songs we were used to playing, and we knew Stéphane was going to provide some pieces of his choice. That was the concept for the repertoire. We were a bit nervous that Stéphane would have difficulty playing over the more complex harmony structures of more contemporary pieces and we started on the first piece – Steve Swallow's 'Falling Grace', one of our favourite compositions – with some hesitation. Well, Stéphane read through it as if he had played it all his life, and we knew this was going to be a piece of cake.

'These days, you can hardly picture making a record in one day, but both the technology and the approach to recording was simpler in 1969. We were in the studio about ten hours and completed everything. It was a very primitive scene [with] a pot-bellied stove in the middle of the room.' This was Gary's intro to the European way of recording at Studios Europe Sonor on a cold

Paris on 4 November: 'I couldn't believe they didn't have heat in a recording studio! It turned out that three of us were so-so piano players – myself, Stéphane and Steve Swallow – so the usual approach to working up each tune was that one of us would take the lead and sit down at the piano and demonstrate the song and suggest some sort of arrangement. It was a very efficient way to work, and we moved steadily through our list of songs, alternating with Stéphane's choices. By the end of the day, I knew we had a great record and I said goodbye to Stéphane eager to play it for the record company back in New York.'

Stéphane particularly enjoyed working with Gary's bass player, Steve Swallow, who had recently made the move to electric bass and empathised with all the problems of amplification of stringed instruments, along with the general trend to play louder. On Steve's 'Falling Grace', Stéphane and Steve play a perfect improvised counterpoint with Gary providing a tasteful harmonic underpin, sparse and reminiscent of Duke Ellington's role for Stéphane six years earlier. Only the drummer seems locked into some kind of overbusy jazz-rock nirvana of his own. The key is listening – Stéphane had great ears and is always hearing and responding, whatever the setting. This sounds obvious, but there's a lot of music made by people who don't really listen.

Stéphane chose to play Django's tune 'Daphne' and sounds 29 again as he bounds through inventive stop choruses, duelling with the crazy beaded and becapped young dudes. In fact, the session photo has them all clad in the trendy capes of the era, snug against the cold.

Stéphane's real triumph, however, is the ballad 'Blue And Green'. Let loose at last on Miles Davis's tune and Coltrane's canvas, he wails like he was born to the blues. His cascading arpeggios inhabit a time-world of their own, light years ahead of anything from Joe Venuti, Stuff Smith or Eddie South. Grappelli's sheer musicality, his perfect intonation, his taste and grace all scream 'Listen! I'm here!' Stéphane shows again that the Hilton is just a refuge, that his genius is intact, a phoenix awaiting rebirth.

At least two books have since been written on the impact of Miles Davis's seminal album *Kind Of Blue*. Stéphane made his acknowledgement in 1969, ten years after Miles walked out of Columbia's 30th Street studios but 30 years ahead of any book. Stéphane didn't need a book; he just listened and soared. In paying his dues to Coltrane, Stéphane was making a statement about his potential for anybody able to hear. Plenty of musicians were listening, but the public would once more have to wait. Fate and the mood of the times were working against him.

'Back in New York, I sat down with Nesuhi at Atlantic Records,' Gary Burton continues. 'To my surprise, he had experienced a change of perspective about the project since that night in Newport. Now he was worried that releasing a more traditional jazz record like this would conflict with my developing image as a jazz-rock innovator, so in spite of my protests he decided not to release it. Sadly, I resigned myself to the possibility that it would never get to the public.

'Years later, I heard a very charming story from a Paris musician about something that happened the night of our record session in '69. It seems Stéphane had left the studio and gone to one of the musicians' favourite bars and was socialising with some of the other local players. I was told he was talking enthusiastically about the record session he had just done with "this great American vibraphone player – Gary, uh, Gary Cooper". I laugh every time I think of this story because it captures so well the kind of likeable, affable personality he possessed.

'When we had our Paris Encounter in 1969, Stéphane's career was in something of a lull...no longer touring or recording on his own. But within a year or two, his life had taken a new turn... Within a few years he was having the time of his life and the career success he had always dreamed about.

'I have always treasured a piece of manuscript he sent to me a year or so after our recording session. He composed a song in my honour and titled it "Gary" and sent me a hand-written copy, which I framed and put up on my wall. It struck me as a great irony that over the years that the ink faded and the paper turned brown, all the while Stéphane was still continuing to tour and perform. I loved the idea of his career outliving that piece of faded paper.'

The delayed release of *Paris Encounter* makes perfect sense, considering the frenzy of popular music in 1969. That August, back in the hippie wilderness of America, music had witnessed a revolution. In Woodstock, New York State, a farmer called Max Yasgur hired out his land to a bunch of hippy entrepreneurs for them to stage 'the Woodstock Festival of Music and Arts'. Billed as 'three days of peace and music', the event saw half a million hippies gathered together as a self-declared nation. On the festival site, two people died and three were born. In an anti-war protest, Jimi Hendrix crashed through a version of 'The Star Spangled Banner', a 10,000-watt sonic depiction of war. It was all a long way from Bricktop's cabaret of 1937.

Stéphane's brand of swing jazz had originally been mainstream popular music; Woodstock now gave an electric snapshot of the current popular scene. Just as jazz had diversified in the '40s, pop now splintered. At the centre was rock, exemplified by Hendrix and Carlos Santana, while Santana's band also absorbed Mexican and Latin beats and blues. Meanwhile, Joan Baez represented the folk revival and Stephen Stills and Arlo Guthrie represented the singer/songwriters. Most importantly there was a tolerance, an open anything-goes attitude. Many record companies were slower to pick up on this than the fans, still mostly managed by straights like Stéphane, but they would finally come to understand their audience's open minds, and it would eventually work in Stéphane's favour.

Woodstock became a phenomenon, spawning a triple album of music, a major feature documentary and an attitude that ricocheted through popular culture and social attitudes. There were mini-Woodstocks staged throughout the world, reverberating in celebration of a newly discovered diversity of music and multiculture.

Meanwhile, in December 1969, Stéphane was still ensconced in a twilit world of men in sports jackets with leather patches at the elbows, the uniform of the European jazz's old guard. Having once met the legendary pianist Teddy Wilson at the Hilton, BBC television now asked him to perform with Wilson at Ronnie Scott's, London's premier jazz venue. The director of the proposed TV programmed thought that Django's tender 'Nuages' – a tune still prominent in Stéphane's repertoire – would be appropriate for this intimate venue. But Stéphane was in for a shock: I remember that Teddy didn't know that tune, so I said, "Don't worry. I will write the chord symbols."' Turning up for rehearsal, Stéphane was astonished to discover that Wilson couldn't get his head around Django's chromatic changes. It's a reminder of the gulf that still existed between original American jazz and its European offshoots. 'The Americans had their own system, and he couldn't get it,' exclaimed Stéphane. 'I was so amazed.'

Teddy Wilson was about as original as you could get. Born in 1912, in Austin, Texas, he had a classical training on the violin. From 1929 onwards, he worked in Detroit and Chicago with Louis Armstrong and Benny Carter. before moving to New York and taking up with Benny Goodman and becoming Billie Holiday's favourite pianist. He and Stéphane had a lot to talk about.

On the programme recorded at Ronnie Scott's, the host himself* introduced the veterans to the audience: 'Now two musicians who amazingly enough have never played together before, but I think their styles are really very similar. They're both very sophisticated and both have impeccable taste – the great French violinist Stéphane Grappelli and, at the piano, the immortal Teddy Wilson, playing an old standard, "Tangerine".'

*Tenor-sax player, club owner and promoter Scott was said to employ bouncers to throw people into his establishment.

We then see a suave, debonair Stéphane slink through the changes with an effortless flair. He's definitely a straight; in December 1969, only bank managers and accountants were still wearing dark conservative suits. Wilson, meanwhile, contributes a consummate chorus and the rhythm section are quiet perfection, but it's going nowhere special. It's another missed opportunity, Grappelli just running through the changes with some veteran buddies. 'Nuages' would have given Stéphane the chance to stretch out, to show his new relaxed freedom.

Nevertheless, Stéphane was pleased to work officially with Wilson, another hero of his: 'It was a pleasure to work with him such a nice person and a great artist, such excitement to work with such a pianist. Good enough for Benny Goodman, good enough for me!'

However, this performance was typical of the European mainstream jazz scene in the late '60s – comfortable, easy, riding out the storm. Stéphane deserved more of a challenge, but he would have to wait.

On his return to the Paris Hilton, a surprise awaited Stéphane. In early 1971, Paul Simon, an American musical adventurer had split with his long-time partner Art Garfunkel, with whom he enjoyed great success exploring English folk music, particularly his reworking of 'Scarborough Fair'. The pair had also experimented with Andean music alongside Los Incas, reinterpreting 'El Condor Pasa' as part of *Bridge Over Troubled Water*, an album that won six Grammys and sold over 11 million copies. Now once more a solo artist, Simon sought new inspiration. Stéphane met him in Le Toit: 'He'd been in India, Germany and Italy, and every place he visited he asked somebody to do something with him. In France he did something with Marcel Solial and then he asked me to do something with him. I was very pleased to be asked to work with this man who sold millions of records. So we arrive in the studio and nothing happened; he was not on form. The people who were doing the record, they were getting nervous – they want something – so I told him, "If you like, we play the blues and you can call it what you want." So I put down the chords C, F, G. It's easy. We manage to do it.

'A few months later, he came to the Hilton with his manager, very sympathetic. He said, "I've come here to sign a contract with you for our composition" [which Simon worked into 'Hobo's Blues'], because he was honest, you see. He'd played what I told him to do, but he wanted to share that with me. He had 20 tunes in the record and he gave me half of one of the tunes. I said, "That's very kind for just playing C, F and G – it's not complicated." And I still receive a few dollars from time to time.'

This humble little tune is interesting on several counts. Firstly, it's not really blues. Secondly, it starts with Stéphane playing a harmonic figure reminiscent of the old Reinhardt-Grappelli opus 'Daphne'. Here, Stéphane is once more in a Paris studio with a guitarist, and together they use a few 'found fragments' to construct a composition. Humble a ditty as it might be, the cheery character of the piece, with its acoustic guitar and swing feel, is once more redolent of the sound of The Hot Club Quintet Of France.

The jazz rock violinist Ric Sanders, then a Birmingham teenager but later frontman for Soft Machine and Fairport Convention, two of the most innovative bands of the 1970s, soon learned 'Hobo's Blues': 'Steph says it's just a blues, but it's a little gem of perfection, just perfect the way he moves through the chords the chromatic movement. It's the perfect blues.'

Like many artists of the time, Paul Simon was slightly lost for direction, a folk-rock singer/songwriter, the self-dubbed 'rhyming Simon'. The recording he made with Stéphane was eventually released as part of his solo album *Paul Simon*.

Another guitarist to seek out Stéphane in Paris was Diz Disley, an ardent Django Reinhardt fan. A performance Diz gave in 1958 at London's Wood Green was reviewed in the press at the time under the heading 'Django Rides Again – The Dauntless Disley Attempts The Impossible'. The accompanying photograph shows a bearded, guitar-wielding beatnik youth in a sharp shirt and skinny tie. Diz had progressed from The Yorkshire Jazz Band and playing skiffle at the Liverpool Cavern to recording albums of folk music with Martin Carthy* and fiddler Dave Swarbrick, doyens of the late-'60s folk revival.

In his heart, though, what Diz really wanted to do was reform Le Quintet du Hot Club de France. He'd mentioned this to Stéphane back in 1964 at the Django Reinhardt Festival in Samois, but that was in a world embroiled in Merseybeat. In 1970, however, he visited Stéphane at the Hilton and once more expressed his enthusiasm.

Stéphane encouraged Diz by inviting him to appear on his album *Stéphane Grappelli And Friends*, along with the Hilton pianist Marc Hemmeler, bassist Lennie Bush and drummer John Spooner. Ironically, this first record with Diz features a rare vocal outing for Stéphane, and it's awful, a joke. 'Darling, Je Vous Aime Beaucoup' is so bad that the band are heard laughing in the background. In fairness, Stéphane was probably 'takin' ze piss' in true music-hall tradition, but it's a rare insight into Stéphane's sense of humour and the fact that he did something badly is gratifying; genius can be so intimidating.

*Coincidentally, it was Martin Carthy who taught Paul Simon 'Scarborough Fair'.

This light-hearted session is a reminder of the truly liberating effect of the work then going on at Abbey Road with The Beatles and their producer, George Martin. On their pioneering and experimental musical work, The Beatles also managed to incorporate their irreverent humour. This anarchic approach was an inheritance of the BBC Light Programme and its surreal *Goon Show* and *Round The Horn* comedy, itself straight out of the music-hall tradition. Indeed, one of the reasons that The Beatles gave for working with Martin was his credibility in this area. When John Lennon sang 'For The Benefit Of Mr Kite' and Paul McCartney 'Your Mother Should Know' and 'When I'm 64', they were unconsciously evoking their heritage of family knees-ups and a tradition of 'doing the halls'. To a new generation they were saying, 'It's OK to have a laugh. It'll do yer good.' This unself-conscious approach – the perfect antidote to emerging heavy rock – worked just as well for hard bebop and would ironically open new doors for Stéphane, a musician who knew these entertainment roots well. Music hall was quietly alive; it had just gone underground.

Elsewhere on the *Stéphane Grappelli And Friends* album, Diz sounds crisp and precise, the sort of rhythm guitarist everybody values. He even plays a Maccaferri guitar precisely like Django's.

For 'How High The Moon', Stéphane swings like crazy, but his sound on electric fiddle is narrow and nasal – electronics still have a way to go in capturing Stéphane's range of timbre and dynamic. Diz, meanwhile, is enthusiastic and inventive in support, exhibiting hints of Django's wild tremolando chords. For their version of 'More', Diz is allowed an introduction and a couple of solo choruses and Stéphane dazzles with some signature harmonics while the piano plods throughout.

On the same album, the band include 'Sweet Georgia Brown' and 'I Got Rhythm'. Something is obviously cooking. Maybe another of Stéphane's *étrangers providentiels* has planted a thought…

18 Michael Parkinson's Good Idea

'The Africans are right – music is magic. It puts us in touch with the spirits of the past and also of the future.'

– Yehudi Menuhin*

In the early 1970s, still holding down his steady job at the Paris Hilton, Stéphane was reunited for recordings with his old partner, the English pianist Alan Clare, with whom he'd previously worked in 1948, at 96 Piccadilly and The Milroy. Stéphane was delighted, considering him 'a marvellous pianist. In England they used to call him "the musicians' pianist"... His speciality was chords for the ballads. You'd think you had Debussy or Ravel behind you.' Born in Walthamstow in 1921, Clare had been a child prodigy and if not for the Depression and World War II would probably have studied as a classical pianist. Classical music's loss, though, was Stéphane's gain.

The fruits of their partnership were recorded first on two tracks of the *Stéphane Grappelli And Friends* album, but the pair really shine on the albums they recorded for Pye and RCA in 1970, which also feature the brilliant drummers Tony Crombie[†] and Kenny Clarke. Stéphane was now mixing with the British session-music elite, a fate he shared with many great jazz players of this era – they could play brilliantly with little rehearsal and many could read music and so, as London became one of the music capitals of the world, they soon found themselves in demand for hundreds of television and recording sessions in an ever-increasing variety of studios.

BBC Television was itself enjoying a peak. Bill Cotton Jnr, who was the son of the renowned music-hall star, regularly gave the public a feast of popular light entertainment, and one of his protégés was Michael Parkinson, a journalist from Yorkshire who, following success in regional television, was at the time hosting the British equivalent of *The Johnny Carson Show* on prime-time TV. Michael, a cultured man and perceptive interviewer, also loved swing music and particularly Stéphane Grappelli: 'When I started doing the talk show, I was determined not to have on that show "pop pap". I wanted to have music that I liked. So when the chance came to get Stéphane, it was

*From The Music of Man, *Yehudi Menuhin and Curtis W Davis (see 'Bibliography').*

[†]The drummer famously quipped, 'A Pye record - if you don't like it, you can eat it!'

like meeting your hero. And it just happened by chance – we were going to do an interview with Yehudi Menuhin.'

Yehudi was expecting to do a conventional interview for the show, probably covering familiar ground. His career had blazed a meteoric trail across the classical-music firmament – just the previous year he had dazzled classical audiences with his interpretations of JS Bach's solo partitas. For many, Yehudi epitomised the 20th-century violin virtuoso, his talents acknowledged as early as 1932 by Sir Edward Elgar. Famously, when Menuhin was about to première his *Violin Concerto*, Elgar had stopped him after 30 bars of rehearsal to say, 'I can add nothing. It cannot be done better. You need not work on it any longer… Let's go to the races instead.' He later had works written for him by the great composers Béla Bartók and Sir William Walton. For many he was 'the musician of the century'.*

Michael Parkinson, not an expert on classical music, prepared assiduously for all his interviews, and this was no exception: 'My researcher came back from seeing Yehudi in Hampstead and said, just by way of conversation, "This strange thing happened," he said. "On his desk there was an LP of Stéphane Grappelli." He said "Are you a fan?" Yehudi said, "I don't know who he is. They tell me he's a marvellous musician," and I laughed at this and I said, "Wouldn't it be marvellous, therefore, to bring them together?"'

Yehudi, however, was in for a shock. 'I was prepared for the BBC call,' he remembered, 'well prepared in one way and totally unprepared in another. It was the morning of Christmas Eve, I think. They called and said, "Tonight you're going to play with Grappelli." I said, "I've never played jazz! I've never improvised. I'm totally unprepared!" I couldn't stand the test. "Well, we know you love Grappelli," [they said], because I had spoken about him, and they said, "You're going to come, you're going to do it." And there is something in me which cannot resist an adventure, something new, the suppressed improvising streak that hasn't come out through my violin.'

Michael Parkinson: 'We contacted Sir Yehudi, who said yes, he'd love to do it, and then we got Stéphane. Now, Stéphane was playing in some nightclub in Paris [and protested], "I'm a fiddle player! I cannot play – he's a genius, a maestro. I'm just a fiddle player."'

In 1996, Stéphane remembered, 'I thought it was a joke. I said, "Look, I'm not classical; I'm not a great violinist, in any case. [The BBC protested], "Well, we asked Menuhin, who's enchanted to do that with you," so I felt, if he's pleased, why not?'

Classic magazine CD tribute, May 1999.

Michael: 'Eventually we talked money and Stéphane came. He arrived at the BBC in the morning, like a child – he has this wonderful child-like quality. We had breakfast with him and he had to go up to Hampstead to rehearse with Yehudi Menuhin. The thought terrified him to the extent that we put two minders in the car with him to make sure that he went. "I cannot play. I mean, he's the maestro. I am a fiddle player" – all this stuff. So we said, "Look, come straight back and you tell us exactly what you think."'

Yehudi was also anxious: 'I've never been more nervous in my life than when I turned up and there was Grappelli with his rhythm group – the double-bass player and the percussion. They had asked me on the telephone: "Isn't there anything you can remember, a song of the 1920s or so?" I said, well, I did remember of course "Jealousy" – it's a tango that my mother had my sisters and me learn to dance to…in California in 1936… It's sufficiently gypsy, too, and tango and Spanish.'

Stéphane was appalled: 'They asked Menuhin what kind of jazz tune he knows, and Menuhin didn't know what to say – he said "Jealousy", which is the contrary of a jazz tune… When we met, we did "Jealously". It was OK.'

The two violinists also had an impromptu stab at Gershwin's 'Lady Be Good'. Michael recalls, 'Four hours later, at the BBC bar, Stéphane came through the door with his face wreathed in smiles, just again like a child. We said, "You had a good time?"

'"Good time?" he said. "Tell me, four bars into "Lady Be Good", who's the maestro?" And of course he was right. Four bars into "Lady Be Good", Yehudi Menuhin didn't know where he was going, but Stéphane did very clearly. That was the beginning of it.'

On 19 December 1971, Stéphane and Yehudi played 'Jealousy' to an enraptured light-entertainment audience. With hindsight, Yehudi was amused and honest: 'In practical terms, I committed my part to memory. I then played it as well as I could and responded to Grappelli, of course. But I didn't actually improvise – that was beyond me. I would have given one eye tooth to have been able to match him. But we each have our sphere, I suppose. At least I've bridged it. And each time I felt as one would feel having received some kind of pep injection, you know? Just the feeling for every note, the feeling that every note was an event, every note had a meaning, a savour which the shop-worn and the packaged and the frozen cannot have.'

This fascination with the mystery of improvisation is the key to Yehudi's enthusiastic involvement. Improvisation, the spontaneous composition of music, is the essence of jazz and has fascinated classical players since its birth on the streets of New Orleans in the late 19th century, when, according to musicologist Alan Lomax, 'a new kind of music emerged. Basically it was counterpoint in polyrhythm. No music had ever been so complex. European composers were absolutely amazed. They had been doing counterpoint, but suddenly here were these people doing counterpoint in polyrhythm, and all the parts were improvised jointly… In New Orleans, these sophisticated people, these "African Frenchmen", got hold of those European instruments…and started to play them with a new approach – "That's an African orchestra; no European orchestra plays that way…" They studied European counterpoint and they had the whole African tradition available to them. They put it together and out of it came the most complicated music that the human species had ever produced.'

What Stéphane and Yehudi cooked up was merely an impression of that jazz tradition with the improvised parts written out. 'Everything was written…by a great arranger called Max Harris,' confessed Stéphane. 'He managed to get Menuhin to play jazz and me to play classical!'

For Max, an established arranger, this was nevertheless an intriguing commission: 'The first time I met Steph was on the Michael Parkinson show, when he first met Menuhin. The initial commission was to do the arrangement and I was warned, "Don't write anything too difficult for Stéphane because he's a jazz violinist and we don't think he can read." But when I saw him run through what I'd written as though it was a like a sort of morning biscuit, I realised that he had a lot more potential for sight-reading than people gave him credit for, which gave me an insight into what to write for him in the future.

'Menuhin was…showing off how good a tone he had and his technique. He had trouble with his elbow a lot of the time. Grappelli would keep the bow on the strings all the time, but Menuhin did the reverse so it always sounded a bit jumpy… But one or two places I thought it worked quite well, and there were a few places where I felt that, unless you knew a bit about jazz, it would be difficult to say who played what, which pleased me.

'The whole arrangement was written by me, but the Menuhin jazz solos were also my own – he wasn't an improviser. Steph didn't help out – I think Steph was trying to assert himself as much as he could. He was quite extraordinary.'

Max, of course, was present for the first rehearsal at Yehudi's home: 'They were both completely in awe of each other, but it didn't take long, and within a few minutes Menuhin was talking in French and, like all musicians, they were soon comparing instruments. Before long they were just two musicians who were interested in their playing and the quality of their instruments. Once it got off, it all happened. It was lovely...an historic occasion. It was the first of its kind, really, the meeting of the ways, classical with jazz, and with no hint of snobbishness on either side.'

It's important to remember the rather stuffy climate of the time, when the jazz and classical worlds rarely crossed paths. In 1971, this collaboration was considered a daring venture. Fortunately, the experiment was warmly received and, as Michael Parkinson recalled, 'it was the beginning of not just a marvellous programme, because it worked out really well; they admired each other. It was the start of a relationship that led to half a dozen records and a huge response from the British public, which was very good indeed for music.'

So it was that a chance encounter turned into one of the most remembered musical events in British television. It's fascinating now to watch the video recording of that first historic meeting and to consider the context in which it has become such a potent memory for thousands of people.

Michael Parkinson first introduces the musicians with due portent: 'Stéphane Grappelli and Yehudi Menuhin joined together, need I say it for the very first time, to play their version of "Jealousy".' The two giants on their distant podium then launch into an introduction with a hint of gypsy *czardas*. (This itself reminiscent of Menuhin's party trick in which he occasionally performed as a tease in restaurants, joining the resident gypsy serenaders whom he so admired.) He and Stéphane then swap *ad lib* arpeggio phrases with lots of flourish and panache, ending with a screaming harmonic from Yehudi. Menuhin then takes them into tempo with even more *bravura* and lots of bow. The rhythm section -- comprising drums, bass, piano, vibes and Latin percussion – provides a steady tango rhythm and together the violinists establish the melody straight. Then the fun begins.

The two violinists are playing from written music. For Yehudi, this is the norm, while the virtuosity of his part is not. (Jazz when annotated looks terrifying – the rhythmic complexity, natural to the ear, takes on a stark intensity on paper. The seasoned session musicians call this bewildering notation 'birdshit', the page a mass of almost indecipherable black and white.) Yehudi is challenged but coping, his part also committed to his prodigious memory.

Stéphane, meanwhile, is wearing glasses and reading music, the latter a rare concession. He is the anchor around which Yehudi's florid decorations are carefully draped. As the performance unfolds, the intonation gets increasingly more approximate until the end, when the relief on the faces of both violinists is visible as their final pizzicato flourish leads to a nearly coincident ending. Despite the performance's shortcomings, the occasion is forever locked in millions of minds as a triumph.

And it was a triumph, but not of jazz nor even the tango. It was a triumph of the human spirit, which is probably why so many remember it so fondly. Great memories are often carved out of circumstance, and it's easy to remember the core of an event but, without the context, fail to understand it. Here were two bold adventurers, Stéphane, at 63, the undoubted jazz-fiddle king and Yehudi, at 55, a legend in the world of classical music.

The world was a violent place at the time, full of conflict and division. The Irish troubles had escalated amid threats of a Christmas pub-bombing campaign, Pakistan and India were at war over Bangladesh and Stanley Kubrick's new film *A Clockwork Orange* had painted a grim urban future. Closer to the hearts of musicians, the legendary Louis Armstrong had recently died. But amidst this bleak news and London's freezing December winds, the fact these two giants from traditions worlds apart could find some common ground, could engage publicly in a courageous dialogue, was cause for hope. The British nation took them to their hearts, and so the next day did the French and, later, the Americans, who were treated to televised re-runs of their success in England. Together the two violinists had struck a chord, and the public embraced them for it.

Many have since questioned the musical validity of this event, even Michael Parkinson, who remarked, 'For me it didn't really work musically, but what can you say?', yet Yehudi remained inspired, professing, 'It was a most exciting moment, one of the great moments of my life.'

Whatever the finite musical worth of the venture, there's no doubt that these two men showed an extraordinary display of courage and wit. Menuhin, particularly, revealed the depth of his beliefs as a great humanist and philosopher and remains the greatest human being I've ever had the pleasure to work with.

I was lucky enough to interview Menuhin at his home, keen to hear first hand about that great adventure. The interview was originally conducted for broadcast television, with all of the paraphernalia of wires and lights and microphones that that entails. Menuhin made a quiet unheralded entrance and calmly inspected the chaos that was once his elegant antique-furnished sitting room. Unflustered at the age of 81 and having just finished his daily yoga session, he was incredibly humble, introducing himself individually to every sound assistant and lighting gaffer personally. When asked, 'How shall I address you, Lord Menuhin?', he replied with the warmest of smiles, 'My friends call me Yehudi.'

Here I was confronted with a man who had played Elgar *for* Elgar, who proceeded to calmly denigrate himself for his inadequacies in the face of Grappelli's improvisation. Here was someone with nothing left to prove but still wishing to learn, confessing that he'd been as baffled by jazz as any classical musician of his generation. Although classical music had originally been partly improvised, with Bach, Vivaldi and Beethoven all renowned extemporisers, the art has been largely lost. With the introduction of increasingly sophisticated musical notation throughout the centuries, composers became more proscriptive, demanding less improvisation, and the art was certainly not taught in Yehudi's youth. Consequently, for him and for most early 20th-century maestros, improvisation was an unfathomable mystery.

But it wasn't just jazz improvisation that had intrigued Menuhin. For the five years before the Grappelli encounter, he had been experimenting with the north Indian tradition of raga. This came about through his appearance at the Bath Music Festival, where he had met the great sitar virtuoso Ravi Shankar and together they had performed the daring concerto *West Meets East*. 'Perhaps the most moving and exciting quality of Indian music is the innocence of its rapture,' Menuhin noted, 'the ecstatic and spontaneous delight which binds performer and audience... It is this immediacy of experience, the electric instantaneousness which fuses cause and effect...bypassing all theories, treatises, all rituals concerned with the study of the formal exposition of a studied script; it is these living values, expressing an immediate spiritual and physical state of being, which distinguish Indian music.'

Ironically, although not written in manuscript, there are more rules to be observed in Indian classical music than jazz, which is probably why Yehudi's raga experiments were more successful. In his recording from 1966 with Shankar's tabla player Alla Rakha, of Prabhati, he had to observe the strict priority attributed to the notes of raga Gunkali. Amongst the many complexities of raga, at the very least these rules define how each note may be approached in ascending and descending passages. Freedom always being the most heady of wines, this raga discipline may have sat easier with Yehudi's conservatoire approach.

Certainly this experiment and some others with the jazz composer John Dankworth left Yehudi in no doubt about the formidable skills required by an improviser, and indeed this is one of the issues that he addressed with his own

Yehudi Menuhin School, a training ground for musical prodigies that he had established in London in 1963. What Yehudi had learned from experience is that a pupil can learn to play a Western classical piece quite mechanically, without actually engaging with the music itself. He learned that, in order to succeed in recreating music, 'You don't just play the notes that are on the printed page, because they're just symbols and you can play them correctly without any sense of the music whatsoever.'

These mechanical dangers are especially true for the piano, the centrepiece of Western classical-music education in the 1970s.* As an antidote, Yehudi passionately championed string instruments as a way into real musical engagement, also founding a string orchestra. And although he saw the European string tradition as being under threat, he felt that Britain presented the best climate in which to nurture a new generation.

This brings things back to Yehudi's fascination with Stéphane, who was not only a string player but also a great improviser. Yehudi discovered that jazz, in common with many other improvised music, is very much more difficult to bluff. He felt that, in order to give life to music, 'you have to be trained in that way, to follow the germ, the cell – the rhythmic cell, the melodic cell, the harmonic cell – as it unfolds'. He saw that his classical students could benefit from the jazz musician's direct and instinctive engagement with real music: 'When [music is] played with the feeling of improvisation – which is what the composer felt when he was creating that work – a totally different work emerges.'

Yehudi realised that the jazz musician had to know the *music* – not the notation, that inadequate map, but the melody and how it flowed, the harmony and what it implied and the rhythm and how it developed. Without this understanding, reaching beyond intellectual analysis and existing in real time at the level of instinct, there could be no improvisation, no magic.

For Yehudi, Stéphane offered a way forward for new students and, ironically, a way backward to the improvised classical cadenzas of the 18th century. Towards that goal, Stéphane epitomised a combination of profound musical knowledge, allied with an instinctive musical understanding. This was the road, perhaps, to a Grappelli-like freedom of expression. Of his own improvising, Stéphane once said, 'The movement is like water. I always visualise that.' For him, like Einstein, 'creativity should be like falling off a log'.

*The very mechanical nature of the way in which the piano creates sound, in tandem with the scientific application of the rules of musical notation, can easily result in a mechanical realisation of sound as it is written, but this was not Yehudi's idea of music. He was familiar with the common problem of 'too many pianists, not enough musicians who happen to play the piano'. The violin, of course, is far more unforgiving than the piano - you have to actually hear the note in order to make it, and there are no mechanics to provide an instant middle C.

25 years later, Yehudi was still amazed, still reeling from the impact of their encounter: '[Grappelli] just plays. He picks up his violin in the most nonchalant way, as if it were part of his body, and plays away – but always with a control, a control of the spontaneous. It's as if you could control a volcano and bring out little bits of energy for specific purposes out of something which draws its power from deep, deep in the ground.'* Clearly Stéphane, the great jazz improviser, was more skilled with the real material of music than most conservatoire graduates, prompting Yehudi to invite Stéphane to inspire his pupils.

This gesture has to be understood in the context of musical education at the time: Yehudi was a quiet revolutionary. I myself studied music at this time and, strange as it now seems, even performing Renaissance music at college was considered extra-curricular and a bit risqué. Jazz and popular music didn't enter the British music curriculum until the late 1980s, so Yehudi was really an intrepid, risk-taking adventurer.

By 1971, the Yehudi Menuhin School was relocated to Stoke D'Abernon, Surrey, where it made fine use of a former business-management school. When Yehudi invited him there to teach improvisation to his pupils, Stéphane took with him the dependable pianist Alan Clare for moral support, as he was a little nervous.

Unknown to Stéphane, amongst Yehudi's prodigies was a young man from Hove, an undoubted talent who, following the unhappy childhood separation of his parents, had immersed himself in his violin. This was the young Nigel Kennedy, for whom hearing Stéphane was a profound revelation: 'It was just one of the most mind-blowing experiences I'd ever had as a child. I was about 13 or something when he came there. Just to hear such fluency and such beautiful sound quality, great intonation, something which most classical players would be wishing they might have once in a lifetime… Stéphane displayed those qualities which make it just a pleasure to hear every note…that in two notes you can really identify who it is, the personality of a player.

'So he was playing there and he kind of blurted out this question a little bit out of nerves – I think he was nervous about being confronted by all of us snotty little accomplished violinists – but he had no need to be because he could teach us 1,001 things about violin playing in just one phrase. But he blurted

---

*There is something about improvised music that reaches a very special place in the human psyche. From my work with Stéphane I'm beginning to understand something of this, and I have my suspicions that improvised music taps into a very primal area of human consciousness – a wild, pre-ordered, pre-rationalised area that equates to our wild, free, roaming hunter-gatherer roots. When we share the journey of a musical improviser, we may be riding back in time.

out, "Does anyone want to join in?", and I had my violin already out of the case underneath the seat there and got up before he could say no.

'We ended up doing impromptu renditions of "Sweet Georgia Brown" and "Honeysuckle Rose". It was just a great moment of my life. I remember going back later into the little hall where he played in front of the kids, on my own and thinking, "Wow! I've played with Stéphane!"'

Nigel's awe went back a long way, to a dusty family collection of 78s of Le Quintette du Hot Club de France. This thirst for jazz meant that he was delighted when Stéphane took him under his wing, even inviting him to London's Ronnie Scott's. 'Playing in Ronnie's also was, like, one of the great jazz venues,' enthused Kennedy, 'so for me to be making my Ronnie Scott's debut with Stéphane, that was another memory which I'll always cherish.

'And he was the first person to actually pay me any money for playing, which also gave me hope for the future – that I might be able to actually do something and be paid for it. [He gave me] about ten quid, I think, which was a vast amount of money – I was on 25 pence a week pocket money, which was already quite good within the realms of boarding school, but ten quid was definitely a round of drinks.'

Yehudi no doubt approved of Stéphane's teaching style. 'He's got such a great attitude,' remembered Nigel. 'He didn't come on all high and mighty like he's got to be a teacher telling people what to do; he just let us play. And the learning experience for me was just through the experience, not through being told. He was a great, great guy.'

The two soon developed a mutual admiration, Stéphane noting that Kennedy 'plays jazz quite well, and on top of that he's got a fantastic knowledge in classical music. I admire him for that, and he's an amusing person, always kind to me.'

Stéphane and Nigel remained friends and often appeared together onstage, even when Nigel became one of the world's great violin soloists.

Meanwhile, the public's response to the Menuhin-Grappelli duet on *The Parkinson Show* led to EMI suggesting that the pair make a record. The original concept was that Stéphane would jazz up some classics and Yehudi would classic up some jazz! In the event, the traffic would go only one way. The first album was again arranged by Max Harris, and the violinists were surrounded by a stellar team, with Alan Clare again on piano, Lennie Bush on bass and Chris Karran on drums. It was a small line-up, a small financial risk and a low-risk experiment – if it hadn't worked, it would no doubt have been no great loss to EMI.

Stéphane was happy to be back at Abbey Road Studios after so long, having last been there with Django in the 1930s and 1940s – since then The Beatles had come and gone, their acrimonious split selling newspapers by the bucketload. Now, Stéphane the survivor was back making records, one of 11 albums that year – not bad for someone who really knew the meaning of Lennon and McCartney's 'When I'm 64'.

With the album release, the Grappelli-Menuhin partnership once again caused controversy. Many of the hardened jazz fraternity were upset, looking on the recording as a travesty of jazz. Stéphane, however, was unconcerned – he never called it jazz; this was just another episode in a lifetime of pleasing his audience. He loved working with Menuhin, Clare and Harris – they were skilful and sensitive artists – and at least in the studios where Yehudi had once stood with Elgar there were no clattering knives and forks to distract him. Once again, Menuhin praised Stéphane's inventiveness, describing him ironically as 'a wonderful juggler who throws plates and pots into the air and miraculously catches them again'. Very music hall.

During the session, the merry fiddlers re-recorded 'Jealousy' and combined it with a mixture of standards: 'A Fine Romance', 'Love Is Here To Stay', 'Night And Day' – familiar ground for Stéphane, and not a hint of the suggested jazzed-up classics. Stéphane had presumably had enough of that with Eddie South in 1937, and such an experiment would no doubt have had little appeal for Yehudi.

The standards that they played for the session are fun and all very tongue-in-cheek. This was quality easy listening for anybody who liked that sort of thing, and millions did. For those who really missed Mantovani, Yehudi provided the project with respectability – the public could buy an easy record without embarrassment – while Stéphane endorsed it for the old swing fans. The public enjoyed the fun, and as Stéphane put it the records sold 'like hot cakes all over the world'.

This meant that Stéphane at last had a good record deal with a major record company – his first, no less, and with EMI, then the world's biggest recording organisation – and would start to receive royalties. In fact, he hated many of his early recordings, partly because he rightly felt that his playing had now improved but also because many of his early recording deals had been one-offs, with no expectation of sales longevity, which often meant no commitment from the record company in terms of ongoing royalties. There were dozens of his albums being sold around the world for which Stéphane received nothing.

At the age of 64, he may have been concerned for his pension, which would be in the form of royalties alone.

Max Harris thought that the deal had come at a good time for Stéphane: 'I remember how thrilled he was. I don't think he was financially very well off at that stage. He'd just got his bus pass, and I think it was like being left a small fortune. And he was thrilled at being able to go on the buses for free!

'He was playing in Paris for quite a long time, more or less tied to a contract he couldn't get out of, playing tea-time music, everybody rattling cups and so on. It couldn't have been very pleasant for him.'

The huge popularity of the first album, *Jealousy*,* released in 1973, inflamed a demand for more, and Stéphane found that he needed a London base again. His relationship with Jean Barclay was still going strong and they both shared a love of buying and refurbishing property, and so later, in 1975, they took a lease on a property at 303 King's Road. Max would visit Stéphane at the flat, where they discovered a mutual admiration for Art Tatum and other jazz pianists. 'Stéphane was a really gifted pianist,' said the arranger, 'a wonderful stride piano player, and I used to meet him to discuss what titles we'd do – it was all left to Stéphane and myself. We met in Chelsea – he had an electric piano there, and we'd discuss things. And he'd get on the keyboard and I'd say to him, "Come on, Steph. Give me some Fats Waller." He could emulate any pianist he liked. He was brilliant, very florid.'

Max had been born in 1918 in Bournemouth, although his father was Polish and his mother from Latvia. He'd studied piano at The Royal Academy of Music, but his life was transformed by a chance radio transmission: 'I heard an Art Tatum piano solo during my teens. Lucky for me… I felt this was real music.'

With Harris's help, the Grappelli-Menuhin partnership blossomed, the duo recording albums every couple of years until 1980. This success spawned other record deals, and Stéphane particularly enjoyed these outings, usually again with Alan Clare, who constantly encouraged him to get out and perform concerts, which he eventually did. Alan was also keen that Stéphane should quit the Hilton and play for an appreciative, paying audience.

The invitation that Stéphane received to play the 1972 Royal Variety Show may have been the last little push – he acquiesced, and after his performance he was delighted to meet the Queen and to find himself again a star. Soon he had another photograph to keep in his violin case – the street urchin of Montmartre and the Queen of England. In the words of another famous turn, George Formby, 'Turned out nice again.'

*Ironically, one of Django's bass players, the now-distinguished classical composer John Duarte, wrote most of the sleeve notes for these records. He observed that they received sensible budgets.

19 Desert Island Celebrity

'Ladies and gentlemen, God is in the house.'
— *Fats Waller, referring to Art Tatum*

The British have a strange broadcasting ritual: they dispatch their celebrities to a mythical desert island. Such is the appeal of this tradition that it's alleged that prime ministers and film stars alike secretly keep lists of their 'desert island discs', the eight records they would take with them should the coveted call from the BBC ever come.

First broadcast on 29 January 1942, *Desert Island Discs* – the world's longest running radio show, developed by the radio innovator Roy Plomley – remains immensely popular. Along with their records, the 'castaways' are allowed one luxury item and a single book and are then asked to explain their choices. All of the castaways are allowed the Bible and the complete works of Shakespeare.

The programme may appear superficial, a gentle piece of light entertainment with the mood of a friendly fireside chat, its signature tune – 'By The Sleepy Lagoon' – a warm bath in limpid strings, as cosy as a comfortable hammock in the shade of a rustling palm, but the programme's strength lies in the revelations it offers into the characters of the castaways. As the celebrities talk, they often offer glimpses of their personalities. It's no coincidence that for many years the programme alternated with another called *In The Psychiatrist's Chair*; ironically, the desert island revelations are often less guarded and perhaps more revealing, than any confessions given to a professional analyst. These days, celebrities are said to consult their public-relations officers about their choices and consider the spin that any offbeat selections might suggest.

In May 1972, in more innocent times, Stéphane was interviewed by the series' originator. He and Roy Plomley were old acquaintances, having worked together in 1946 on the light-entertainment show *To Town On Two Pianos*, written by Roy and produced by Charles Chilton. During the interview, Stéphane was relaxed, comfortable, his appearance on the show perhaps seen as the summation of a 52-year career.

After introducing Stéphane (his surname still spelled 'Grappelly' in the BBC script), Roy immediately asked him if he could endure loneliness. 'Yes, I can,' Stéphane replied. 'I am quite happy sometimes to be alone. Maybe I'm supposed to have a bit of imagination. That helps you a lot to suffer to be alone.' Indeed, Stéphane liked time apart to reflect. He would sit very still, apparently in deep contemplation, even when there were visitors in other rooms of his flat.

On the desert island, Roy asked, 'What would you be happiest to have got away from?'

'From the cold.'

Although he'd performed there from the 1920s onward, from the late 1950s Stéphane always returned to the south as often as possible, specifically to Cannes, on the French Mediterranean Riviera. The jazz festivals at Juan le Pins, Antibes, Nice and Monaco were obvious magnets for Stéphane, and some of his appearances at these venues are preserved in television recordings. It was good to have Paris and London as a work base, but he needed some warmth in his half-southern bones.

Stéphane had a modest apartment at Le Parc Continental, an unpretentious residence on the outskirts of Cannes several miles from the glamour of La Plage de la Croissette, where Brigitte Bardot and other starlets sashayed, but it was warm, surrounded by palms and grandiloquent scented pine trees. It had a private entrance and the air of a little money but was far from luxurious. The view, however, was grand, with a clear panorama of the coast and the distant mountains. Stéphane furnished his little refuge with a mixture of antiques and oddities – a Baroque cherub in weathered rock next to a sturdy modern coffee table happy with the weight of large format books.

Cannes itself is an odd mixture. The grandeur of the Riviera of the 1920s survives in the Hôtel Carlton and the sweep of the sandy crescent beach, but elsewhere there is a slightly faded elegance as McDonald's culture and the worst excesses of the annual film festival increasingly dominate the Cote d'Azur seascape.

Stéphane always avoided visiting during the crowded festival weeks. His Cannes was probably more the memory of Django's huge 1930s cars outside the Hôtel Splendid and dukes and duchesses taking the air on the palm-lined promenade. He would retreat during the festival to his friend Mario de Crescenzo's house at St Paul de Vence, a medieval walled town 15 kilometres from the coast on the road to Nice. As we've heard, they had met in 1949, when the last incarnation of The Hot Club Quintet performed at a Roman restaurant, and they remained great friends, sharing a love of the great jazz pianists, particularly Earl Hines and Art Tatum.

Through Stéphane, Mario met Jean-Luc Ponty, probably at the tribute concert immortalised as *Violin Summit*, where his drummer had immediately suggested that Mario would be at home in a 'magical village' he had discovered. This turned out to be Vence.

When Stéphane first visited this enchanted citadel, he was charmed. Built on a hilltop surrounded by gnarled olive trees, cypresses and pines, the tiny houses of Vence are circled by a bastion wall. Mario had converted a granary and stable to a modest studio, and soon after his arrival Stéphane had the medieval stone reverberating to 'Tea For Two ' and 'Sophisticated Lady'. On one memorable birthday, filled with the culinary delights of Provençale and a good wine, Stéphane played the piano until dawn. The neighbours were apparently delighted.

Occasionally the two friends would improvise together, Mario happy as long as the key was E major and Stéphane equally content to eat huge platefuls of Mario's pasta. Stéphane paid for the pasta by giving Mario piano lessons, still teaching him to be more adventurous with his harmony, introducing minor seconds and flattened fifths to Mario's renditions of 'Satin Doll'.

Vence was a perfect refuge for artists – indeed, it still is – and Stéphane enjoyed the sculpture, oil paintings and tapestry for which the town is now famous and kept a photograph of his Italian friend sunning himself in this idyllic retreat. Evelyne, his daughter, also enjoyed the climate of the Cote d'Azur and has lived here most of her life.

Back on his desert island, Stéphane's first choice of music was the surprisingly Germanic Beethoven's *Sixth Symphony*, the 'Pastoral'. He selected the first movement – 'Erwachen Heitere Gefuhle Bei Der Ankunft Auf Dem Lande' ('Feelings Of Joy On Arriving In The Country') – under the baton of Herbert von Karajan, then the conductor of the Berlin Philharmonic in its new home in West Berlin. His choice was probably not particularly significant; Stéphane surely enjoyed Beethoven's sentiments, although he is reported to have found the countryside disconcerting, with too many open spaces. Paradoxically, however, Joseph Oldenhove, his last personal manager, reported that Stéphane often hankered to live in the country, and of course he had once owned a cottage in the Devon countryside.

This paradox is not untypical of Stéphane. His restless spirit always wanted to be home when touring and on the road when at home. Certainly, he would have enjoyed Beethoven's apparently effortless harmony and the flow of seamless melody. The wit in the rhythm and the obvious but glorious modulation are traits that Stéphane brought to his own audiences. He may even have heard the symphony with his father as a child on one of their many outings.

This is the inference that Stéphane gave to his next choice, Debussy's *Prelude à L'Àpres-Midi d'un Faune*, a piece forever linked for Stéphane with Isadora Duncan and his time at her school in 1914. Stéphane chose the version by Charles Munch and the French National Radio Orchestra. Indeed, when asked for his favourite pieces, Stéphane always referred to French classical music, and the sumptuous harmony of Ravel and Debussy is clearly never far from his thoughts: 'My father was very musical but he didn't know anything of music. He loved music, though, and we often went to Sunday concerts.'

Asked when he decided to be a musician, he retorted, 'Well, I didn't decide anything. My father decided that for me...when he came back from his military service.' This is obviously a reference to his first violin, that three-quarter-size model that his father acquired, although by this time Stéphane had already been dabbling on café pianos.

When asked about his first jazz leanings, Stéphane launched into a version of the 'Stumblin'' jukebox story, although this time the jazz musician was Bix Beiderbecke, described by Stéphane as 'more known as a trumpeter than a pianist, but he's the first modern pianist, in my opinion. The way he played "In The Mist" in 1928... He is the father of all modern musicians.'

This extraordinary record from September 1927 exemplifies Stéphane's ideal for improvisation ('it flows like a river'). The opening is Impressionistic, suggesting the influence of Debussy (perhaps Bix's boss, Paul Whiteman, brought some French records back from Paris?), but despite its syncopation the track leaves ragtime behind and, as Stéphane observed, is astonishingly modern for New York in the late 1920s. When Stéphane doodled on his piano at home at the Rue Dunkerque, this was his idiom. In choosing Bix, he was harking back to the very beginnings of jazz.

Stéphane went on to mention briefly to Plomley his sojourn at the silent cinema and his busking era. Then, when asked, 'What was the first important thing to happen in your career?', he replied, 'Well, the important thing was when

I get away from the misery and when I meet Grégor And His Grégorians…the top orchestra in France, [as famous] as Jack Hylton in England,' before going on to tell the story of Grégor insisting that he went back to the violin. The Armenian eccentric – Stéphane's first real boss – had died in the previous year in Malente, Germany, at the age of 73.

Going on to recall the Django Reinhardt years, Stéphane revealed that Django discovered his passion for billiards and snooker in London: 'He was very happy to play that, so he forgot to be at the première at the Palladium!'

Then, in a brief chat edited out from the BBC broadcast, Stéphane told Roy about Hughes Panassié and Le Hot Club du France: 'Well, there is no club at all – it's a letter box, to my opinion. That's all.' Here he was presumably referring to a mail-order PO box where readers could order a copy of *Jazz Hot* magazine, as opposed to a working club. Ever the pragmatist, for Stéphane a working club would have been of more use to a musician in the midst of the economic depression of the 1930s.

For record number four, Stéphane opted for Satchmo, his first choice of all jazz musicians: 'When I was about 18, I heard for the first time Louis Armstrong, and that was a great shock for me. The only title coming to my memory is "I Can't Believe That You Are In Love With Me". He put so much heart in it.'

This record, released in 1930, marks an interesting transition for Louis. What Grappelli heard at the age of 18 in 1926 would have been the great Hot Five and Hot Seven records, which saw Louis leading his own small groups in this first great blossoming of jazz. By 1930 and 'I Can't Believe…', Louis was fronting a big band for drummer Willy Lynch as The Coconut Grove Orchestra and being billed as 'the greatest trumpeter in jazz'. Ironically, though, as he later told Humphrey Lyttelton, it wasn't the trumpet playing that so impressed Stéphane: 'It was the way he was singing. I couldn't understand the words, but he brought such joy to a generation.'

On listening to the track, it's easy to understand why Stéphane was so deeply affected. Louis' vocal phrasing is all Stéphane aspired to in a career with the fiddle. Satchmo dances across the rhythm, walking a tightrope, always in danger of losing the musical thread, but he never does, yet he's late in and early to finish, pushing and pulling the phrases, all with an apparent lack of effort, always masking the art. Most of all, there is pure joy in just making music. In these epochal recordings, Armstrong redefined jazz. Louis' bass player of the time, Arvell Shaw, put it like this: 'Before Louis, the musicians would play the melody and heavily syncopate it. What Louis started doing was improvising

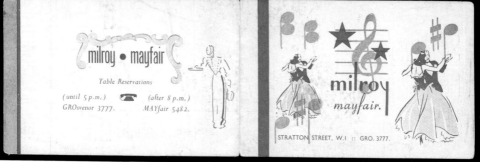

Milroy brochure produced in Stéphane's dinner-and-dance days in Mayfair, 1949
(courtesy of the Stéphane Grappelli Collection)

Stéphane and Marion Williams in the early 1950s, possibly at the Empress Club
(© Baron Photo Centre Ltd)

Manchester Hippodrome variety poster from the late 1950s (courtesy of the Stéphane Grappelli Collection)

Stéphane Grappelli with Joseph Reinhardt (centre, seated), taken from the 1957 Paul Paviot film *Django Reinhardt* (courtesy of the Stéphane Grappelli Collection)

Sidney Bechet (left) and Stéphane Grappelli (centre),
mid '50s (courtesy of the Stéphane Grappelli Collection)

Stéphane Grappelli and Dizzy
Gillespie, mid '60s, at the Paris
Hilton (courtesy of the Stéphane
Grappelli Collection)

Clockwise from bottom: Ray Nance, Sven
Asmussen, Ernie Shepard, Duke Ellington
and Stéphane Grappelli, 1963 (courtesy of
the Stéphane Grappelli Collection)

Stéphane at the Duke Ellington violin
session, 1963, with Sven Asmussen,
the Duke, Ray Nance and bass player
Ernie Shepard (© Interpress)

Stéphane Grappelli, 1970s – the era of the 'glorious' shirts begins (© Allan Warren)

Stéphane Grappelli and Teddy Wilson, early 1970s (courtesy of the Stéphane Grappelli Collection)

L-r: Yehudi Menuhin, Max Harris (arranger) and Stéphane Grappelli at Abbey Road in 1972 (courtesy of the Stéphane Grappelli Collection)

Stéphane and HRH
the Queen with Sacha
Distel at the 1972
Royal Variety Show
(© Joe Matthews)

George Shearing and Stéphane,
August 1976 (© Mark Mander)

L-r: Phil Bates, Diz Disley,
Stéphane and Ike Isaacs, *circa*
1976 (courtesy of the Stéphane
Grappelli Collection)

Stéphane dressed for the 1978 film *King Of The Gypsies*; he loved the hat! (courtesy of the Stéphane Grappelli Collection)

Her Royal Highness, Her Majesty, Queen Elizabeth, the Queen Mother, with Stéphane and other stars at the Royal Variety Show, 1986; Stéphane kept this shot in his violin case (© Doug McKenzie)

Stéphane and the Suzuki violinists on *Roy Castle Beats Time*, 1978 (courtesy of the Stéphane Grappelli Collection)

Jean Barclay with Stéphane in the King's Road apartment, *circa* 1978 (courtesy of the Pamela Reid Collection)

Stéphane Grappelli and Miles Davis, late 1980s (courtesy of the Stéphane Grappelli Collection)

Above: Stéphane and Edward Baxter, who looked after Stéphane's British engagements for over 15 years, 1990 (© Marc Marnie, Stagefright Photography)

Stéphane with (l-r) Martin Taylor, Jack Sewing and Marc Fosset, 1990 (© Marc Marnie, Stagefright Photography)

Stéphane still performing in 1996
(© Andrzej Szozda)

Stéphane Grappelli and Nigel Kennedy at the Sydney
Opera House, 1991 (© Bob King)

Stéphane receiving the
second degree of the Légion
d'Honneur, the Commandeur
de l'Ordre du Mérite, from
President François
Mitterrand, 4 March 1993
(© Louys Riclafe)

L-r: Stéphane, Joseph
Oldenhove and
Dr L Subramaniam
(courtesy of the Stéphane
Grappelli Collection)

on the chord structure. By himself he made jazz into a soloist's art.' Everything about Stéphane as musician and communicator is illuminated in this simple choice of Desert Island company.

Roy's next question was about Stéphane's time in London at the outbreak of the war, and Stéphane recalled his need for an operation. It's known that he did suffer a bout of ill health then, but before this time he had never mentioned an operation. Beryl Davis, whose family took him in at the time, didn't recall hospitalisation either. This is just another unsolved little enigma.

Stéphane was consistent, however, about meeting bandleader Arthur Young on a bicycle in Bond Street, apparently while the latter was working as an air raid warden, while on his discovery of George Shearing in a Battersea pub he said that he was very impressed with the blind musician's skill, 'even on an accordion'.

The pair then went on to discuss Stéphane's recent duet with Yehudi Menuhin on *The Parkinson Show*, and the violinist voiced his pleasure about the event and further revealed that he had also worked recently with the very fine guitarist Sacha Distel. This is particularly interesting as Sacha is only really known outside France for his pop singing, as characterised by his vocals on the Bacharach tune 'Raindrops Keep Falling On My Head', his 1970 cover version of part of the soundtrack to the western *Butch Cassidy And The Sundance Kid*. In France, however, Distel is a respected jazz musician and session guitarist, and has worked with Dizzy Gillespie, Stan Getz and Lionel Hampton. At that time, he and Stéphane were working together at London's Duke of York Theatre.

For record number five, Stéphane recounted another surprise: 'Oh, a great *shock musicale*... Art Tatum in 1935 – that came late for me, but since I heard him I never changed my mind. Art Tatum has such a wide imagination, and I bring with me on the island "Humoresque".' Indeed, Tatum's portrait hung over Stéphane's piano at his Rue Dunkerque apartment, and Stéphane often made reference to the Fats Waller remark, 'Ladies and gentlemen, God is in the house.' In Cannes, Stéphane kept a vinyl LP box set of Tatum's *The Complete Capitol Recordings*.

But what was it about Tatum that Stéphane so admired?* Certainly his virtuosity. Born in Toledo, Ohio, in 1909, Tatum had been almost completely blind for most of his life and learned piano by ear from piano rolls, some of which replicated the playing of three or four hands, leading Art to attempt the technically impossible and frequently achieving it. Famously, Stéphane first heard Tatum's 'Tiger Rag' on a beach in Deauville in 1935 and, mishearing

---

*See the DVD *Stéphane Grappelli: A Life In The Jazz Century* for examples of rare Art Tatum material, edited from the film rushes shot at Chicago's Three Deuces.

the radio announcer, thought it was two musicians, 'Art and Tintin'. Discovering it was a soloist, Stéphane allegedly despaired: 'I was so astonished and disturbed by his genius that I temporarily lost my enthusiasm for the piano and determined to concentrate on the violin.'

Beyond the technical accomplishment on 'Humoresque', Tatum's playing exhibits a level of imaginative improvisation that is almost beyond belief. Stéphane would forever aspire to Tatum's audacity and, indeed, often achieved it, and once revealed to Geoffrey Smith that 'hearing Tatum helped me to play with Django'. Certainly Reinhardt shared the largely untutored wildness of the best of Tatum's playing, and the Baroque-like filigree of Tatum's decoration is also evident in Stéphane's solo cadenzas.

Tatum was also admired by Sergei Rachmaninov, who said, 'I can repeat your notes, but I can't hold the tempo at the same time.'

Revered by Horowitz and Paderewski, other classical concert giants of his day, Tatum shared Stéphane's love of the classics and hence Stéphane's choice of 'Humoresque', a dazzling improvisation on the theme by the Czech composer Antonin Dvořák.

For his next choice, Stéphane remained with Tatum, selecting 'My One And Only Love', also featuring the great saxophone innovator Ben Webster. Stéphane liked to play the tune himself, and indeed he'd recorded it recently with Joe Venuti. It had perhaps a special meaning in its sentiment, again alluding to Gwendoline Turner.

Musically, Stéphane would have admired Webster's big tone, his rubato and his apparently effortless invention – all Grappelli virtues. Webster shared Stéphane's admiration of Tatum, and so the unlikely partnership works. (Interestingly, *Melody Maker* had recently described Stéphane as 'the Ben Webster of the violin'.)

Webster is an almost exact contemporary of Stéphane and shared his background in silent cinema orchestras. Born in Kansas City in 1909, he is rated next to Coleman Hawkins as one of the first great tenor-sax players and cut his teeth working for Stéphane's heroes Duke Ellington and the singer Billie Holiday. After moving to Copenhagen in 1964, he became an important part of the European jazz scene. At the time of this broadcast, Stéphane had just paid tribute to him in his own 1970 composition 'Dear Ben', recorded on *I Hear Music* with Kenny Clarke and Marc Hemmeler.

Stéphane's chosen interpretation of 'My One And Only Love' is an absolute joy. As the great jazz writer Benny Green said, 'By the time he entered his last phase, of which the Tatum tracks are a perfect example, the sound he was making had grown so sumptuous that it seemed almost to possess a tactile quality, duping the listener into thinking he might reach out and run his fingers through the timbre... But something else had happened too. Ben had finally arrived at that nirvana of the jazz soloist, the stage where he could create authentic jazz just by playing the tune, for his tone was so redolent of the jazz spirit and his sense of time and rhythm and harmony so profound that he could take a ballad...and, merely by rocking it gently in the arms of his style, squeeze more jazz out of it, [unlike] a great many young men who cannot play the tune at all without introducing into its structure passing chords and substituted chords, which would have caused George Gershwin to raise his eyebrows, not in horror but in pity.' Of course, this isn't a Gershwin tune, but the sentiments apply. Stéphane knew what it was to rock a ballad in the arms of his style, and his tone was unmistakable.

Stéphane's seventh record is still not a violinist but another saxophonist, the giant step to John Coltrane. It's an unusual choice, with 'Trane playing the classic tune 'Body And Soul', usually linked to Stéphane's old friend Coleman Hawkins and a tune that Stéphane and Django had recorded together in April 1937. Stéphane: 'I heard Coltrane play so well on "Body And Soul" and in a different way... He is recognised as the father of the new school of modern saxophonist and he is greatly helped by a marvellous pianist there.'

The drummer on the track was the incomparable Elvin Jones while the pianist was McCoy Tyner, and Stéphane harboured a secret ambition to work with the latter, often half-joking that his violin was his 'gimmick' and that at heart he was a pianist. The help Tyner gives Coltrane on 'Body And Soul' is a thread that pervades Stéphane's work – 'I need good chords to inspire me.' Stéphane often returned to this message, always craving imaginative harmony from all of his sidemen.

This version of 'Body And Soul' was recorded in 1960, when 'Trane was only 34 and, tragically, had less than seven years left to live. Drug-related illness had recently cost him jobs with Johnny Hodges and Miles Davis. Despite this, the Coltrane legacy is as important as any in jazz. Stéphane would have loved 'Trane's time-defying runs and apparently effortless decorations to the melody that slither from his horn like a hypnotised serpent. This search for harmonic richness, stringing out every note in each chord, became a Coltrane trademark and was described as 'sheets of sound'. Of 'Trane's 'Body And Soul', the distinguished jazz critic Nat Hentoff once said, 'He opens new dimensions of getting into, of becoming part of those standards.'

This is what Stéphane strived for and, indeed, often achieved, apparently without effort – the elusive art of concealing art – making it seem as natural as breathing. This throwaway quality evident in many of Stéphane's best musical performances is informed by listening to John Coltrane with what the jazz fraternity refer to as big ears.

Stéphane's last record choice surprised Plomley: 'I'll take one of my own with me.'

Roy: 'One of your own?'

This wasn't unprecedented – the castaway Elizabeth Schwarzkopf took seven of her own records – but it was unusual, implying a sort of vanity.*

'Why not, if it's good?', Stéphane replied, shrugging – not arrogant, just genuinely puzzled.

The piece that Stéphane chose, 'Gary' – dedicated to 'one of the greatest musicians I met in my life, Gary Burton' – appeared on the 1970 album *I Hear Music*, significantly alongside another track called simply 'Coltrane' and the aforementioned 'Dear Ben'. For the latter track and 'Gary', Stéphane multitracked himself on piano and violin. The American guitarist Les Paul had pioneered this idea in the early 1950s, but outside the world of pop music it was still quite an unusual technique. Stéphane of course was taking the idea to extremes playing such disparate roles.[†] At the opening of 'Gary', Stéphane paid tribute on the piano to Burton's famous four-mallet vibraphone technique, producing similar shifting patterns of block chords.

For most of the record Stéphane depended on his Paris regulars: Marc Hemmeler on piano and organ and the great Kenny Clarke on drums. As another surprise, their version of 'Body And Soul' has the drummer making his recording debut on piano, Clarke's sparse chords inspiring Stéphane to stretch out and bridge the gaps, conspiring together to an enigmatic coda.

Stéphane's bassist on the track was Jack Sewing, who would appear at the fiddler's side in many future bands. The Dutchman had been born in the year of the first Hot Club Quintet, 1934, in Rotterdam. A versatile musician, he had previously played accordion and guitar, settling in Paris in 1965. From 1968, he had joined Stéphane at the Paris Hilton.

Also on *I Hear Music* is Stéphane's tune 'Flower For Kenny', unusual in the lexicon of jazz as the only tune credited to a fiddler that turns out to be a drum solo!

---

*Stéphane was one of few artists who could bear to listen to his own records. Usually, artists' comments are full of misgivings about past endeavours – 'I wish I'd played better', 'I had a cold that day', 'The drummer put me off', etc. Apparently he took to listening to his own recordings only in his later years. Age has its own perspective.

[†] In the 1990s, Stéphane repeated the trick for French TV, this time playing piano and violin in split-screen video.

In a standard question, Roy then asked Stéphane which of the records he would keep if a disaster took seven of them away. Stéphane liked them all equally and settled to leave it to fate.

When asked which luxury item he wanted to take with him, 'an object of no practical use, which would give pleasure to have with you?', Stéphane plumped for an extravagance: 'A lovely jewel, in case I get away from the island.'

Roy: 'A diamond, for example?'

Stéphane was very specific. He wanted an extravagant object: 'The Koh-I-Nor.'

Wherever his music took him, Stéphane liked to explore. The museums and art galleries were often on his agenda, and no doubt he had viewed the Koh-I-Nor in its place as part of the Crown Jewels at the Tower of London. Its name literally the 'Mountain of Light', the oval diamond has a carat weight of nearly 109 and was valued at $700,000 when Queen Victoria displayed it at the Great Exhibition of 1851. Stéphane would have seen it mounted in the Coronation crown of Queen Elizabeth, the Queen Mother. Once the property of the Mogul Empire, the diamond is priceless, very beautiful and very Grappelli. Typically, it wasn't the largest nor the most valuable of the Crown Jewels – that was the Cullinan, over twice as big at 317 carats. Stéphane clearly knew what he liked.

Meanwhile, his choice of book to take to his island was both prophetic and practical and he laughed as he told Roy, 'A good atlas, to get away from the island!'

Desert Island Discs featuring Stéphane Grappelli was broadcast four months later, on 12 August 1972.

Stéphane was now a celebrity again, largely due to the Yehudi Menuhin association, and in 1972 Atlantic records at last released the album he recorded with Gary Burton, *Paris Encounter*. Burton was understandably pleased: 'I got word that they were releasing *Paris Encounter* – their name, not mine, though it's perfectly acceptable. So finally, the record came out, albeit belatedly, and, I'm happy to say it got great reviews. It didn't seem to conflict with my image, and it sold pretty well, too.' Indeed, the album was still selling as a CD at the time of writing.

Fairport Convention violinist Ric Sanders first heard swing as a child: 'My dad had a great selection of 78s which he'd acquired during the war working on an American airbase, "Tuxedo Junction" and Gene Krupa's "Drummer Man" with some Beryl Davis-style vocals. Then Jimi Hendrix and Miles Davis opened the door to jazz and I watched *Jazz Scene* on BBC2, and there was Stéphane with Teddy Wilson playing "Tangerine". It was a defining moment in my life. The supreme eloquence and beauty and excitement Stéphane's playing blew me away… That led me to the two *Ace Of Clubs* records, the old Decca recordings. Those records were amazing and I started to learn that repertoire. With my first amateur group, The Fishnet Tights Swing Orchestra, we played the folk clubs of Birmingham, playing The Hot Club Quintet repertoire: "Minor Swing", "Stomping At Decca", "Nuages", all completely by ear.

'When I was 19, I had only played the fiddle for two years. Steph was playing in Ronnie Scott's. I got there at nine o'clock, first in…and we watched the Steph sets. I was agape, paralysed. He was, as the Americans say, awesome.'

Also in 1972, Stéphane made an appearance at London's Queen Elizabeth Hall, a large and prestigious venue. Ostensibly, he was booked to appear with his old friend Alan Clare and run through a few standards before handing over to The Alex Welsh Band, a group of New Orleans revivalists led by a passionate Scotsman. That would have been that, if not for the persistent Diz Disley. Together with his guitarist friend Jim Douglas, Diz pushed Stéphane to perform a couple of Hot Club specialities, and the audience loved it. Stéphane, though, wasn't convinced; as the 50th anniversary of his career loomed, he was his own man.

In January 1973, Stéphane reached his retirement age of 65, and French Television celebrated the occasion in style. Stéphane had joined the CGT union in 1923, and to celebrate his golden jubilee in the business they hired not just Duke Ellington but the great Canadian pianist Oscar Peterson. A photograph taken at the event shows Stéphane smiling, holding his Warlop violin. For the rehearsal stills, Stéphane is seen comfortable in an old cardigan, while for the studio shots he appears wearing a flamboyant kipper tie and the Duke seems ready to join Sgt Pepper's Band, sporting a zigzag-patterned tie with a collar designed for aerodynamic lift. The old swingers are apparently going psychedelic.

Since their last meeting in 1962, the Duke had suffered the loss of his right-hand man, Billy Strayhorn, and soloist Johnny Hodges, and was becoming more and more committed to religious music. According to Ruth Ellington, 'He spent the last ten years of his life writing music to the glory of God, from which everything came. That's all that's important.'

That year, the Duke had given a vast choral concert in New York's cathedral with another planned for London's Westminster Abbey in October. The television photographs show a real empathy between him and Stéphane – no doubt they played sympathetically on 'Satin Doll' and 'It Don't Mean A Thing' – yet the Duke looks very ill, already suffering from cancer and only a year away from dying in New York's Presbyterian Hospital the following May. It's a remarkable tribute to Stéphane that he made this late trip to Paris.

The French TV show that gave Stéphane his last meeting with the Duke also featured Bill Coleman and reunited Stéphane with Yehudi Menuhin, but perhaps his most significant musical encounter was with Oscar Peterson. Stéphane had known the Canadian pianist and his work with the touring Jazz At The Philharmonic since the 1950s, and indeed they had played together briefly in 1957, along with Stuff Smith. This time, however something gelled, and they planned to be in the recording studio by February with a rhythm section comprising Kenny Clarke and the propelling swing of Niels Pedersen.

In January, Britain had joined the European Economic Community – Stéphane's second home was on its way into Europe. Nevertheless, the quartet met again in Paris, staying away from the British miners' strike with its nine-hour blackouts and three-day weeks.

This first Peterson-Grappelli recording is a landmark. The same intelligent Abbey Road engineers that produced the Menuhin sessions have cured Stéphane of his electric violin, having shown him that, if properly recorded, the acoustic violin can soar over anything, while Menuhin has since taught Stéphane that he is special, unique. The praise and respect from somebody he had known only as a distant maestro obviously meant a lot to Stéphane. He had always had to find his own way, and he now acquired a new confidence and a relaxed approach born of his age. Indeed, he could have retired – he had nothing to prove, free at last and with musicians around him that were the best in the world.

On the recording Peterson is Stéphane's perfect foil. In 1973, he was only 48 but had been hailed as a prodigy from the age of six and had absorbed the influence of George Shearing and Teddy Wilson and had shared with Teddy the delight of accompanying Billie Holiday. Like Art Tatum, he loves the classics and has also provided a harmonic bed for Stéphane's other hero, Ben Webster. Aptly acclaimed as 'the Franz Liszt of jazz', he had great admiration for Stéphane and still plays him to his protégés: 'I'm going to play some Stéphane to a young pianist because of [his] grace. There was grace to his playing that is seldom found in many other so-called ballad players in the jazz world. That's one thing I admired about him.'

Kenny Clarke, meanwhile, was one of the great innovators of post-war jazz, a musician who happened to play the drums. Born in 1914 in Philadelphia, he worked with Louis Armstrong and Ella Fitzgerald before moving to Paris in 1956, where his sensitivity had made him the perfect first drummer for those founders of 'chamber jazz' The Modern Jazz Quartet. Stéphane met him through his sometime bassist Pierre Michelot. Initially, the violinist had thought him too loud, but that was a decade before the time of this recording, when Kenny had come fresh from Dizzy Gillespie and the first flush of bebop. Known as 'Klook', the mature Clarke was the musician's drummer.

In 1973, Niels Pedersen was still only 27. Born in Denmark, he had been the house bass player at Copenhagen's Montmartre Jazzhus at the age of 15 and had since worked with Ben Webster, as well as Roland Kirk and Bill Evans, and was another bebop mainstay. Despite his youth, he had taken Ray Brown's seat with Oscar's trio. His bass solos were famous, often in the highest reaches of the instrument, and he could bow like an orchestral master.

Stéphane had lost the Duke but for this session he was playing with a prince, and he knew it. From the first notes of 'Them There Eyes', he is out of the gate running with Oscar providing an intelligent, sparse harmonic frame and Klook and Niels driving like an overdue express. Peterson provides the most challenging solo choruses Stéphane has ever experienced and the French wizard bounces back with delight. This is breathtaking post-bop swing.

On 'Flamingo', Stéphane croons like a gypsy on speed, although this is probably due to his usual 'secret weapon', a dram of Chivas Regal. His signature portamentos throw an inspired line to Peterson, who comes back with a limpid cascade that Ravel would have been proud of. Stéphane returns, throwing a mirror to the Canadian master before restating the theme in dazzling swoops and perfectly tuned double-stops. Stéphane is clearly having the time of his life, offering up a message for those jazzers disappointed by the Menuhin outings. His jazz heart is obviously alive and well and has never been healthier.

The best is yet to come, though, as Stéphane recalls his *Desert Island Discs* choice 'My One And Only Love'. Here, he and Oscar, freed of the old pop-music tyranny of the three-minute single, give us a nearly ten-minute rendition. Oscar is boundlessly inventive in solos and support as Stéphane explores to devastating effect the limits of both his instrument and his technique. In fact, with the freer tempo adopted here, the emotional pitch is even higher than the version of their two heroes Tatum and Webster.

No doubt Stéphane and Oscar talked of Art Tatum. Unlike Grappelli, Peterson had met him and even dedicated a four-stanza poem to him, the first of which ran, 'I once knew a man whose mind was so quick/That to run through eight bars was like playing one lick/I once knew a man whose hand were so fast/He could skate over the keyboard as though it were glass.'*

In Oscar, Stéphane had found the perfect musical partner and they would remain friends and colleagues for the rest of his life. Ironically, though, he never told Oscar that he played piano and was clearly too in awe of Oscar to play in

*From Oscar Peterson's book *A Jazz Odyssey*, reproduced here by kind permission.

front of him. 'I couldn't envisage him playing piano,' confessed the pianist on hearing this. 'When somebody is so talented on another instrument, you can't envisage them playing a second instrument. I think the violin was his calling. I never heard him play piano and I'd say from the things I heard him do on the violin that that was his instrument.'

Back in England, in March 1973 Stéphane took an unlikely trip to the picturesque village of Denham. Famous for its film studios and acting community, the village also possessed a sound-recording facility. Designed for recording a complete symphony orchestra for film synchronisation, that spring Anvil Studios echoed to the most intimate sound of one piano and one violin. The pianist was Alan Clare, who had just been described by Stéphane's new friend Oscar Peterson as an 'insider', 'a player that looks to plumb the very vitals of a song and whose deepest pleasure is to savour the lushness of beautiful harmonies and subtle lines'.*

The album recorded here, *Talk Of The Town* (nothing to do with the famous nightclub of that name), is something of a tribute to Stéphane's new status. The spacious reverberation of Anvil Studios is perfect, surrounding Hoagy Carmichael's 'Stardust' with acoustic moon glow. The engineers Eric Tomlinson and Michael Hook have clearly heard a violin before and record Stéphane with an all-too-rare sensitivity. (This may seem a small point, but some of Stéphane's '50s and '60s recordings are abysmal; in the '20s, '30s and '40s he suffered the technical limitations of the 78rpm disc, but he later faced a lot of cloth-eared engineers who had clearly had too much rock 'n' roll for breakfast.)

Inspired, Stéphane wrote two originals for the album: 'Amanda', a tender dedication to an unknown woman, and 'Tournesol', Grappelli's take on 'Sunflowers', complemented by an almost orchestral evocation of pizzicato violin and staccato piano. The folk song 'Greensleeves' also appears, with Stéphane cheekily accompanied by Alan's no doubt spontaneous discovery of an orchestral celeste.

A rhythm section in this cathedral acoustic would have ricocheted off the walls like gunfire. Did the acoustic inspire the choice of a repertoire consisting solely of ballads or was this a long-held ambition? Whatever the reason, it's a treat, all recorded, as ever, in one day. The newly confident Grappelli gives us everything he knows and makes it all sound effortless.

The album resurfaced in 2000 as *Stardust*, a 24-bit remastering with additional takes and outtakes, making sensible use of the extra length of the CD format. It's interesting to note the profusion of takes – 17 for 'Greensleeves'

*From Oscar Peterson's book *A Jazz Odyssey*, reproduced here by kind permission.

and eight for several others; Stéphane and Alan were obviously striving for a kind of perfection in one of their final meetings. However, Stéphane is clearly happy with his virtuoso pianists – this was already his second album of 1973.

In July, Stéphane was reunited with his European band at the Montreaux Jazz Festival to stage a performance that was recorded beautifully by producer Alan Bates and engineer Carlos Olms. Here, Stéphane seems completely relaxed, despite his high-profile appearance at one of the world's most prestigious festivals with pianist Swiss Marc Hemmeler, bassist Jack Sewing and drummer Daniel Humair. He astounds the crowd with his rhythmic sparring with Humair on 'More' and his very delicate take on 'Misty', having recently met the ballad's composer, Errol Garner.

Two months later, Stéphane entered London's Chappell Studios with the drummer Mel 'The Tailor' Lewis to record an album that was released in the US as *Parisian Thoroughfare*. Born in 1929 in Buffalo, New York, Lewis acquired his nickname for his knack of pulling together good bands without fuss, and his 1973 recording with Stéphane was no exception. Roland Hanna on piano and electric piano and Jiri Mraz on bass provide Stéphane with plenty of challenge.

A novelty on the album is Stéphane's interpretation of Chopin's popular prelude number four in E minor. Stéphane had recently been to Majorca and been deeply moved on visiting Chopin's cell at the abandoned monastery at Valldemossa, where this prelude was composed in the dark, storm-plagued winter of 1838–9. At this time, the Polish composer was already dying of consumption and was rejected by the Mallorcans, no doubt scandalised by his relationship with Georges Sand. Chopin described his music as '*zal*', a polish word best translated by Liszt as having 'all the tenderness all the humility of a regret borne with resignation and without a murmur'.

Stéphane injects his own special pathos into this unusual choice of material. If his reason for selecting the tune had been sought, Stéphane would no doubt have responded, 'Why not?' For the great improviser, melody had no classification beyond good and bad.

Parisian Thoroughfare became a further American ice-breaker, receiving a five-star rating in *Down Beat* magazine. Stéphane's star was clearly crossing the dateline.

Altogether in his 65th year, Stéphane made 11 albums and also recorded a film score. The guitar was conspicuously absent from many of the bands he played with and he seemed very happy with these diverse pianos. No doubt he was thinking, 'Who needs guitar players?'

20 Along Came Diz

'It's all folks music, as far as I can see. I ain't never heard a horse sing.'
— *Louis Armstrong*

At the beginning of the 1970s, there was a growing openness and crossing over in the world of popular music. Huge music festivals like Woodstock, Monterey, the Isle of White and Montreux featured an ever-widening range of musical styles. Traditional jazz festivals such as Newport were starting to feature rock bands while rock festivals hosted folk-rock band such as Britain's Fairport Convention and Steeleye Span. In France, pop festivals were staging traditional Celtic music, a movement spearheaded by the Briton harpist Alan Stivel. The word on the street was *eclectic*.

There was also a growing in interest in what was then termed 'international music' – ie music from outside the American and European mainstream. Thus the folk festival at Sidmouth, Devon, became the International Music Festival, featuring artists from Africa and South America alongside English morris dancers and traditional balladeers.

For the growing number of record buyers, listening habits were also changing. The notion of the single – a double-sided 78rpm record developed in the '20s and '30s – had evolved in the '50s into the 45rpm microgroove record and monophonic sound had been superseded by stereo. This microgroove technology, with its slower speeds and narrow groove, enabled the evolution of the LP, which allowed the recording of perhaps six tracks on each side of the disc, totalling 40 minutes of music in all. For popular musicians, this extended playing time enabled them to explore the concept of the album as a musical form. The Beatles' *Sgt Pepper* album and The Beach Boys' *Pet Sounds* had blazed a trail in the late '60s, and by the 1970s – when the album started to outsell the single for the first time – it seemed that every artist had a concept album in development.

These albums, with their longer lengths and loosely designed structures, lent themselves to considered listening way beyond the three-minute attention span required for the singles in the Hit Parade. Many of the musicians producing these albums employed an element of improvisation in their songs, with rock music particularly stretching beyond the basic song structure to accommodate extended solos and collective jams. British groups Cream and Led Zeppelin pushed back the boundaries, racking up 39-minute versions of three-minute songs. This was good for Stéphane as improvisation, his speciality, once again became a language familiar to the vast majority of young listeners.

Television responded with shows like the UK's *The Old Grey Whistle Test*, a show devoted to album-only artists. For the first time, many popular musicians eschewed releasing singles – many thousands of people became album collectors and treasured their expensive discs, playing them back on ever more sophisticated hi-fi systems. Stéphane, in common with most jazz artists, was naturally an album act (his last single was probably 'The Marseillaise' in 1946, and the BBC had banned that!). The album became a musical form in itself, and in that sense it provided a unification, a common denominator.

The album-buyers of 1973 were offered an eclectic mix of jazz, psychedelic rock, heavy metal, folk rock, international, singer/songwriters, easy listening and pop, as well as a dozen other categories that came and went with the tide. This rich mix was good for musicians, as it meant that audiences came to a gig with open ears. The big question was no longer, 'What do they play?' More likely, the festival crowds asked, 'Is it good?'

Even ageism was on the way out. Popular music in the '60s had been increasingly dominated by artists in their teens and 20s, but in the '70s bewildered blues artists forgotten for decades were revered for their roots. BB King and John Lee Hooker were suddenly appearing onstage alongside The Rolling Stones and The Grateful Dead. Miles Davis, approaching 50, could suddenly headline a rock festival.

All over the world, a whole generation listened, their minds open to almost anything. And folk festivals even had room for a little jazz. Diz Disley recalls, 'In 1973 I was doing a folk club up in Cambridge and Ken Woollard, the guy who ran the Cambridge Folk Festival, came to see me and asked me to play at his festival and then said, "Come back and have a drink." I said, "No thanks, I'm going to Ronnie Scott's to meet a young lady and we're going to hear Grappelli, who's playing there... There's a good idea! Why don't you ask him to be a guest at the Cambridge Folk Festival?" This was the ninth festival, held in the grounds of Cherry Hinton Hall from 27–29 July.

'[Woollard] said, "That's a good idea. Ask him." So I asked Grappelli in Ronnie's office and he said, "Yes, all right. Who's on piano?"

'I said, "There isn't a piano. We're doing the Cambridge Festival. It's in huge tents, out in the field. Camping and so on. There's no piano. We've got a couple of guitars. Everything will be all right! So he says, "Oh, I'll leave it to you, my dear."

'I fixed up [Stéphane's appearances] the week before in folk clubs. The first one was Jasper Carrott's club in Solihull on the Monday night, and then there was the Surbiton Assembly Rooms...then two nights in Norwich and a television appearance at Anglia Television.'

It's extraordinary but typical of the time to imagine Stéphane playing a small folk club in suburban Birmingham. There was even a surprise appearance by Stéphane's new protégé, and this was spotted at one show by the *Birmingham Evening Mail*, who touted, 'United They Swing – Stéphane Grappelli Star Guest Last Night At Solihull's Boggery Folk Club.

'The master, his hair silver long but thinning...the pupil, his hair a boyish chestnut mop....David and Goliath... The scene stealer was 16-year-old Nigel Kennedy of Park Road, Solihull, sounding almost more like Grappelli than Grappelli himself and shared in a thrilling sequence of question-and-answer choruses, backed by the Hot Club-sounding Diz Disley trio.'

The 'remarkable and memorable evening' was hosted by Jasper Carrott, a then-unknown comic singer who would go on to huge success, later hosting his own television series and receiving an OBE in January 2003.

Diz, meanwhile, marched his reluctant hero to battle. 'Finally we got to Cambridge. Well, Stéphane feared that it was like one of these French student concerts that he'd been compelled to do from time to time, which are apparently the worst type of torture you can imagine – all these idiots and boneheads all shout and scream and jump over the seats and show off to one another all the time and don't pay any attention. But he was amazed when we got to Cambridge and he saw all these tents full of nice, well-behaved young people. He calmed down and didn't worry about it."

Stéphane's memory of the event wasn't quite so calm, however: 'We go to an enormous marquee. You can get 10,000 people inside, but not seated – sitting on the floor! It was young people and I said, "If they see me, they will kill me." Diz said, "No, don't worry. Everything will be alright."'

Diz thought it was time for the Chivas Regal: 'While we were waiting to go on, we went in the beer tent and somebody got us a beer in and he started playing away, so he was relaxed by then…and then we went on in the big tent, which was packed out.'

In the programme, Stéphane Grappelli and The Diz Disley Trio were top of the bill, preceded by celebrated guitar innovator Davy Graham and talented singer/songwriter Harvey Andrews. The four took the 11pm-to-midnight slot and were introduced enthusiastically by folk singer Tony Capstick. Pushed onto the stage, the terrified Grappelli gave his best on a Hot Club Standard, and then even Diz was surprised: 'They all went nuts! Everybody stood up, screamed and clapped and cheered. Thousands of people. Stéphane was flabbergasted, thrilled to bits.'

In popular culture, timing is everything, and suddenly the mature Grappelli had found a whole new audience. People in their teens and 20s who had never heard of the original Hot Club Quintet were enjoying the sounds. Long-haired, jean-clad groovies dug this swinging grandad. Tune in, man, turn it up!

These modern-day festivals were loud. A whole new industry of PA companies had grown up to service events up to 10,000 strong. Innovators like Brits Jim Marshall and Charlie Watkins, with his WEM company, and American Cerwin Vega were providing sound systems that meant acoustic guitars and feeble violins could be heard for miles. Suddenly Stéphane was being heard by more people in one day than he could have reached in a year at Ronnie Scott's or the Paris Hilton. These sophisticated new sound systems with front-of-house mixing desks contributed to the rebirth of acoustic popular music in the 1970s. As the systems became ever better, a whole new generation of listeners and musicians grew up with acoustic music, which turned out to be as dynamic and exciting as electric music. The trend escalated, eventually culminating in the '90s with MTV's *Unplugged* series, featuring a broad cross-section of popular musicians without the overt aid of electricity.

Stéphane suddenly found himself with a broad audience appeal, a marketing manager's dream ticket. There were connoisseurs listening to his Menuhin collaborations, jazz fans listening to him working with Oscar Peterson and vintage records with him and Django, all bolstered now by a direct line to a whole new young audience of hi-fi-owning record buyers eager to expand their collections.

An archive film of the 1974 Cambridge Folk Festival – one year after Stéphane's debut – evokes the flavour of the times, showing a huge rural campus with several giant marquees. Anglia Television proudly proclaimed the event 'the greatest folk festival in the world'. The atmosphere seems electric, with thousands of young people enjoying the spirit of the time. There's a tangible sense of revelry, freedom of expression and, above all, that anything-goes attitude to music. The local television footage shows jam sessions in tents dotted around the campsite played by wild eccentrics with star-spangled sunglasses and flowing, Merlinesque hair. There are pet mice in the beer tent and children dancing like fairies around a maypole. It's a sort of mini-Woodstock.

The organiser, Ken Woollard, comments for the camera and catches the spirit of the age of Aquarius: 'We're putting on a festival. We're not in the *business* of putting on a festival, which makes a lot of difference.'

There are lots of fiddles being played, interest in the instrument being fanned by soloists such as Fairport Convention's brilliant Dave Swarbrick.

The band line-up at Stéphane's Cambridge debut had been classic, comprising Denny Wright and Diz on acoustic guitars, 'Brillo' David Ethridge on bass and Stéphane on violin. With no Manouche family politics to appease, the third guitar was unneeded, but it was certainly guitars to the fore.

This must have been a very ironic situation for Stéphane. For the last ten years he had been cultivating a mature style built on a sophisticated approach to harmony. As a pianist himself, he loved working with piano, enjoying that distinct keyboard approach to harmony, particularly when stretched out in a ballad, the subtle movement of the inner parts within a chord, the change of bass note with its implied harmonic shift. On the guitar, this was technically difficult and consequently there were few players who could provide that kind of support. Stéphane's first question to Diz in Ronnie Scott's had been, 'Who is on piano?'

Unwittingly, Diz rescued Stéphane from a dilemma. By the 1970s, the sound often associated with jazz – that of the piano trio, with its slick chords, walking acoustic bass and clever brushwork – was becoming rather tired, often drifting into a sort of cocktail-hour cliché. The best players managed to spice the trio with enough musical challenge to avoid this, but many didn't. And besides, however good the players, by now that sound had no appeal to a generation raised on the colourful output of Memphis, Tennessee, and Abbey Road Studio 2.

By 1970, of course, the guitar was the most popular instrument in the history of music. With its infinite variety of forms and sounds, it was also the common denominator for all these new festivals of jazz, rock and folk.

Luckily, Diz knew a British guitarist by the name of Ike Isaacs who could provide Stéphane with the subtlety he required. Ike had been born in Burma in 1920 and had enjoyed a long career in jazz, including 12 years with The Ted Heath Orchestra. Under his own name, he had recorded an album of the music of Michel Legrand.

Very soon after their meeting, Stéphane and Diz's ensemble recorded an album at Villengen, West Germany, to be released under the name Stéphane Grappelli With The Diz Disley Trio. On this recording, Stéphane is perhaps mourning the loss of his friend Duke Ellington as they play his composition 'Solitude'. Here the two guitars of Diz and Ike more than make up for the loss of a piano. Meanwhile, 'Shine' has Diz reinforcing the Hot Club Quintet connection, contributing a Django-esque solo on a Maccaferri guitar. But Stéphane really shines on 'A Nightingale Sang In Berkeley Square' with some of his best harmonic choruses, subtle double-stops and fantastic playing with time, while Ike and Diz contribute their own bell-like chorus. On the album *Violinspiration*, or *Shades Of Django*, the melodic bass player is Isla Echinger, one of many musicians that the trio employed at this time (probably pick-up players booked on an ad-hoc basis as the band toured).

Ike Isaacs can also be glimpsed in a BBC local news film at Ronnie Scott's with Stéphane, Diz and Nigel Kennedy. Ike displays a firm command of the proceedings, keeping a close rein on what was obviously another impromptu jam session.

Diz tells an amusing story about Denny Wright, clearly another astute player, and occasional bandmember: 'Sometimes Grappelli was very forgetful. He would do an introduction and then go off into another tune. We had to be ready for this and get stuck in and follow him. Sometimes it was quite funny. There's even a record of this happening. It's a South Bank concert in London, and in the middle of this concert he started playing "Flamingo" – he was supposed to be playing "Old Man River". You had to be very quick. Denny Wright realised immediately being a very bright and sharp player and just joined in with him, and that's on the record.'

Wright had known Stéphane from his Hatchets days (clearly that venue got through its share of guitarists). Since then, he had played in the skiffle boom with Lonnie Donegan and on pop records with Johnny Duncan And The Blue Grass Boys. Together they had a minor hit record with 'The Last Train To San Fernando'.

The 'Flamingo' incident, Diz recalls, most likely took place at the Queen

Elizabeth Hall on 5 November 1973, traditionally Guy Fawkes' Night in England, celebrated with fireworks. Certainly, on the accompanying live release Stéphane delivers an intro to 'Flamingo' brimming with sparkling imagination. In fact, *Stéphane Grappelli Live In London* can be recommended as a wonderful example of the early line-up of 'The Hot Club Of London'. The character of the acoustic instruments is beautifully captured and the producer, Alan Bates, makes the most of the concert-hall reverberation, adding life to the sound.

Although the quartet with Diz was a success, Stéphane still appeared and recorded with a range of musical partners, including earlier that same year the piano genius Earl Hines. They had originally met in Paris in 1948, yet it took them 26 years to fix a recording date. When they eventually did, it was again produced by Alan Bates and the resulting record – released on CD as *Stéphane Grappelli Meets Earl Hines* – is a masterpiece. The two giants came from wholly different musical perspectives, but their genius is evident in the way they leave each other space.

Born in 1903 in Duquesne, a suburb of Pittsburgh, Hines was of a similar age to Stéphane. Despite acquiring a reputation as a bebop innovator, he shared Stéphane's love of Louis Armstrong, and indeed had performed with Satchmo in the 1920s and was a member of one of the original Hot Fives. The Armstrong connection continued through reunions in the All Stars of the early 1950s and a tribute album in 1971, recorded only a few days after Louis's passing.

For his recording with Grappelli, Hines allegedly taught Stéphane the classic 'Manhattan' in just ten minutes, after which the violinist performed it as if he'd known it all his life. Stéphane couldn't resist this dalliance with the keyboard masters, and if anyone has the slightest doubt of his jazz credentials they need look no further. Even an unlikely jazz tune such as 'Somewhere Over The Rainbow' bends to the duo's very different but equally potent treatments. Then, in 'Moonlight In Vermont', Stéphane is stretched by the pianist's sparse harmony, responding inventively, often challenged but never defeated.

Despite these sojourns with other artists, increasingly the British guitar trio was Stéphane's musical base. Diz, with a background as a commercial artist and *Melody Maker* cartoonist, even provided the tour posters, billing Stéphane as 'The World's Greatest Jazz Violinist'. The press latched on and very soon the headlines were full of phrases such as 'Jazz Violin Genius', 'An Old Master Gets Better' and 'The Ageless Stéphane Grappelli'. Suddenly everything fell into place: a receptive audience, the publicity of the Menuhin albums and television appearances and a sudden and increasing variety of available Grappelli recordings.

As if this wasn't enough, Stéphane was then asked to perform on the soundtrack for the film *Les Valseuses*, an early outing for French megastar Gerald Depardieu that caught the flavour of the times. The title translates roughly into the 'The Dickheads', and that's just about as highbrow as the subject matter gets as the actions follows two likely lads travelling around France and causing havoc, mostly of a violent or sexual nature. Directed by Bertrand Blier, it's an odd film for Stéphane to work on, but at least his unmistakable sound gives this French *Saturday Night Fever* a home-grown character. The swing idiom is a strange anachronism amongst all the bell-bottoms and hippy hair, but it works well during the road-movie sequences. Stéphane really comes into his own, however, with his theme for Jeanne Moreau, who plays a fading vamp; his seductive violin is the perfect foil for the *ménage à trois* sequence. For this project Stéphane was supported by a French-Belgian band comprising Maurice Vander on piano and harpsichord, Guy Pedersen on bass, Daniel Humair on drums and Philip Catherine providing some very '70s guitar. Stéphane's pizzicato main theme is one of his best movie pieces.

Through the film Grappelli was again revealed to a young audience and was quick to respond to them, soon adopting their flamboyant clothes. At that time he was living in Chelsea, surrounded by the hippiedom of the trendy London set. It seems odd now but Stéphane went from the grey suits and cardigans of 1969 to his 1970s dandy image virtually overnight. One press comment at the time refers to 'an eccentric maestro who has chosen to wear bell-bottomed trousers and a heavily flowered shirt'.

The new high-profile Stéphane was soon in demand, and his entrepreneurial guitarist Diz saw an opportunity to make the new Hot Quintet Of London an international attraction: 'I went down to Ronnie Scott's office one afternoon to pay some commission, and I was talking to Brian who worked in the office. He said, "We're going to Australia," and I said, "Well, you might be interested in us, because we're doing quite well at the moment." In the end we made a deal and signed up for this tour – it was called Jazz From Europe. That was the Ronnie Scott Trio and Stéphane Grappelli And The Diz Disley Trio.

Down under, they were received warmly. The 16 September 1974 edition of *The Melbourne Sun* headlinined, 'Grappelli Is An Absolute Marvel,' and praised 'some of the most exciting and lyrical music heard since Errol Garner was here two years ago'. The *Sydney Morning Herald* led with 'Jazz Violin At

Its Nimble Best', noting 'it was not only the quality of the musicianship that was so special but the verve and enjoyment of these great jazzmen.

Despite this popular acclaim, Diz was astounded at Australian impresario Clifford Hocking's next move: 'We went to America and he took a chance and booked Carnegie Hall, and that was quite a success. So that's how all that foreign travelling started.'

The audacity of this Carnegie Hall debut is astonishing – Stéphane had last been to the States in 1969, and that was to play at a jazz festival to a captive audience. Nevertheless, the gamble paid off. 29 September 1974, $7 on the door and the delights of Ronnie Scott as support on tenor sax, Mike Carr on organ and Bobby Gien on drums.

Stéphane no doubt enjoyed the famous natural acoustic of this 3,000-seat hall, inaugurated by no less than Pyotr Tchaikovsky in 1891. Perhaps he realised that, until 1898, it was called a 'Music Hall'. With Diz and Ike Isaacs on guitar and Len Skeat on bass, he gave the New Yorkers his all.

The Jazz From Europe tour might have been a little like taking coals to Newcastle, but it set the European adventurers up nicely for a week at Buddy's Jazz Spot, starting the very next day. Stéphane's conquest of America had begun in style.

The appeal of this ageing father figure with his eccentric clothes and swinging music seemed to be universal. Everywhere they went, Stéphane would attract a curious audience ranging from teenagers who thought he was 'the next big thing' to older fans who perhaps knew The Hot Club Quintet but had never had the opportunity to hear them live.

Clifford Hocking, impressed by the standing ovations at Carnegie Hall, suggested more touring, which was no problem with Diz, who was enjoying the ride: 'New Zealand, Mauritius, Honolulu, all over the States, Canada, Martinique. Fiji we went to – that was a terrific experience. And successful everywhere. Nowhere was there a duff performance or a poor audience.'

From the Jazz from Europe tour, on which they shared the billing with The Ronnie Scott Trio, Stéphane suddenly became what his old friend Lew Grade would call 'a headliner'. In 12 months he'd gone from Surbiton and Kingston Folk Club ('75p admission plus late bar') to a sell-out gig at New York's prestigious Carnegie Hall. Once more, Grappelli proved himself to be 'the perfect antidote'.

As the '60s dream faded in a disappointed cloud of political assassinations and escalating war, people needed an escape. Rock music had lost its way, with audiences and music critics becoming increasingly disillusioned by pretentious triple-album concepts, rock operas and extravaganzas on ice. Mainstream pop, meanwhile, had become more of a sideline, with the glam-rock craze for teenyboppers more about sequins and make-up than music. Once more Stéphane picked up a following as audiences turned to the Grappelli brand of unpretentious escapism, the simple charm of swing and melody.

In England, Stéphane was enjoying his flat on the King's Road. This was on a shared 20-year lease with Jean Barclay and had a nice little garden, a rare luxury in central London. There are charming photographs of Stéphane and Jean from this era, shown relaxing like an old happy couple surrounded by the comforts of home. The only sadness was a burglary, which robbed them of some valuables.

At home in England, Stéphane had an extraordinary encounter with the new rock cognoscenti. Together with Phil Collins, Brian Eno, Alvin Lee and Gary Moore, he was asked to work on a recording of a rock version of Sergei Prokofiev's children's music odyssey *Peter And The Wolf*. Stéphane's violin would play the cat. On this revisionist version, 'The Cat's Dance' is a blues accompanied by Alvin Lee's wah-wah guitar and the bass guitar of Dave Marquee, but riding on top of this novel backing in the swing department, Stéphane soon leaves the rockers behind. For another track, 'Cat', he plays the famous Prokofiev melody this time with just the bass guitar. The narrator for the album was the surreal Viv Stanshall from The Bonzo Dog Doo-Dah Band and the whole project was doubled up in French by Pierre Clementi, with other versions in German, Spanish and Italian. It was a bold venture and demonstrated once again how Grappelli was fitting into the new, more open world of music.

Also in 1975, President of France Valéry Giscard d'Estaing acknowledged Stéphane's new status by awarding him La Légion d'Honneur. The award had originally been established by Napoleon, and Stéphane went straight to the Commander level, the third degree of 'honneur'. A photograph taken at the time shows Stéphane receiving the medal at the Paris Hilton, of all places, besuited for the occasion with collar and tie but with his silver mane trendily over his collar. With the president pinning the medal to his chest, Stéphane is grinning broadly. It's clearly a big day for a self-taught street urchin.

Stéphane was also now a man of property. For a short while in 1976 he had a house in Flonville, France; a small cottage in Aspremont and his King's Road flat, all at the same time. Pamela Reid, Jean Barclay's sister, remembered, 'Jean had a flat in Nice and we stayed with her at 8 Rue Massenet. She and Stéphane used to cycle around Nice to get away, and they were building at Aspremont, which was on a steep hill behind Nice. There were a few houses and a small restaurant with some sort of a round castle… It was very pretty, with a wonderful view back down the Var Valley.

'[The cottage in] Aspremont at first had no conveniences, and then after a few years they put in a bathroom. Basically, it was a room with a view. They also bought another small tower, a folly. Jean was very busy in those years, dealing with the builders, the masons, the tilers and so on… They made it extremely nice, added another room eventually and built a garage hut over the road because the cottage itself, while it was very nice, there was no access by car.

'Then, in about the middle '70s, they bought a one-storey house at Flonville, near Chartres. That was originally a Norman house with a huge garden. Very pretty. It was near a railway line and Jean used to wave Stéphane off.'

Back at work, Stéphane continued to go back to his tried-and-trusted pianists, at least on record. Reunited in San Francisco after 30 years with his old friend George Shearing, they decided to revive their old partnership. Eventually they fixed a date in April 1976 in Villingen, Germany, to make a recording appropriately entitled *Reunion*.

Here, in their interpretation of 'The Folks Who Live On The Hill', Stéphane and his old piano partner clearly have a ball. Shearing delivers those delicious chords that Stéphane loves and the fiddler rhapsodises with a broad approach, perhaps borrowed from Yehudi. As if to show they aren't too serious, Shearing then gives one of his signature musical riddles, contriving to turn Oscar Hammerstein's serenade into a parody of a '50s teen ballad, complete with a chopsticks piano bass and a calypso lilt.

In 1976, George was 57 and an established star, having successfully crossed the line between jazz and popular entertainment. His 'Lullaby Of Birdland', with its signature block harmonies provided by piano, vibes and electric guitar, made him a household name in the isolation of 1950s America. On the recording, it's evident that the duo have both come a long way from wartime Hatchets, and with the able support of Andrew Simpkin's bass and Rusty Jones's drums they show a confidence and *élan* both rare and wonderful.

After this brief foray, Stéphane returned to the guitar trio and continued touring. The casual informality of these early trips is caught in a letter Stéphane wrote to Diz at his new home in Garrucha, Spain, in August 1976 from his apartment in Cannes:

My Dear Diz,

I thank you very much for your letter… I hope you are well. I was thinking you were in Spain? Right you are to prepare some more tunes and a new repertory. I hope to catch you quickly. I am going tomorrow to Tunisia and I'll be back here on the 14th…so we can't do the England tour for the time being. I'm glad you send me the dates for the USA because I didn't receive nothing so far. Keep on prepare some new things with Ike and please give him my best regards, also to Moira.

I'll be pleased to see you soon my dear Diz….

Ta ta for now,

All the very best,

Stéphane

The Moira here refers to the wife of Ike Isaacs, who stayed on for most of what turned into a world tour. That summer included three dates in New Zealand and 17 in Australia, everything from Perth Concert Hall to Woolongong Town Hall. This was followed in October by a trip to South Africa.

Ray Hopkins, a journalist for *The Daily Star*, caught up with the band at this time and covered them in an article headline, 'Diz Deals It Out Like A Giant'…before going on to devote most of the review to Diz, which is a reminder that at this stage it was Stéphane Grappelli And The Diz Disley Trio. Ike gets praise for his 'superb musicianship of the elegant and sophisticated modern school'. Indeed, Ike profoundly understood Stéphane's musicianship, once telling New York writer Matt Glasser, 'Stéphane is really a pianist on the violin because he thinks both vertically and horizontally. He has a wonderfully receptive mind, musically. When I play with him *colla voce* ['freely'], he responds instantly to chord variations. He has a great harmonic sense and very acute ears.'

However, Ike was of an older, mainstream school of playing and Diz was about to make changes that he felt appropriate and commensurate with the appeal to a younger audience. Via a vibraphone player called Pete Shade, Disley was recommended to fusion-rock band Soft Machine's lead guitarist, John Etheridge, whom, according to John, Pete had seen on television. The guitarist was a little surprised by the call: 'Late '76, I was approached by Diz to join Steph. That's how it would go with Steph – he didn't pick the band, but he had a veto. The same system, in fact, that Louis Armstrong used. He was very relaxed about who was in the band. As long as they were good enough, that was OK. So I said to Diz, "I don't know if I can do this. I'm already in a band…" so Diz became more determined to get me.'

John, a Londoner, had originally studied History of Art at the University of Essex. Influenced largely by Hank Marvin, Eric Clapton and Joe Pass, before Soft Machine he was big in Japan with the rock band Wolf. He had travelled to Hamburg to meet Stéphane. 'I sat around in this hotel for what seemed like days, though it probably wasn't,' he recalled. 'No sign of anybody. I didn't even have an acoustic guitar. I borrowed one… I was basically an electric guitarist.

'Then Diz said, "We'll have to buy you a shirt, a fancy shirt." So he took me down to this market and he made me buy this bright pillar-box-red shirt. And he said, "You've also got to have a dangler," so we got this big block of wood on the end of a leather string and he said, "Go back to your room and put your clothes on and wait there."

'So I sat in this room, me and my guitar, and finally there was a knock on the door and Diz said, "Come next door." And there was Phil Bates,* the bass player. We sat there and then Stéphane appeared, looking very annoyed. I don't think he knew Ike wasn't coming until then, and he wouldn't even look at me. Stéphane sat on the bed putting rosin on his bow and rocking and I was thinking, "This is the great Stéphane Grappelli! This is amazing!"

'So Stéphane says to Diz – not me! – "Does he know 'Them There Eyes'?"

'So Diz says, "John, dear boy, do you know 'Them There Eyes'?"

'I said, "I think so." I'd heard Django play it, but I hadn't boned up or anything. So we start playing and for the second chord I played D7 and Stéphane didn't look at me but said, "Oh, what is that horrible chord?" I muttered, "I think that's what Django played." Stéphane was appalled. "He would never play that! *Alors*, A7!"

'We carried on and it went all right, and then Stéphane said, "Ask him if he knows 'Manoir de Mes Rêves'." So Diz says, "John, do you know Manoir de Mes Rêves?" And I thought, "God! Well, slightly!"

'So we started playing and he was flying about all over the place and I was gamely attempting to follow. I'd never really done a jazz gig. Stéphane said, "No, no, no," but we eventually got through it and Stéphane said, "Now we are going to do Stevie Wonder, 'You Are The Sunshine Of My Life'." And I thought, "I know this," and he waved to me to do a solo, so I played a couple of flashy runs.

'At the end, he finally spoke to me, very enthusiastic: "I like that, what you

*Bass player Phil Bates was a jazz veteran of The Tubby Hayes Band and also Ronnie Scott's. He also toured with Sarah Vaughan and folk Singer Judy Collins.

did there. I like it! I like that fast business you do. It amuse the tourists!" Then, to Diz, "I like him. He's a nice boy." And that was it. I was accepted after that.'

But the new boy still had to adjust to non-rock 'n' roll stage etiquette: 'There were one or two incidents on the same gig. My shoes, for instance, caused concern. We were just about to go on to perform on and he stopped: "Your shoes! You are not on a farm. Clean them!" So I went all around this complex, trying to find some black shoe polish without success. Eventually I went back and Stéphane gave me his... But eventually he accepted me.'

In fact, Stéphane soon remarked to an Australian reporter, 'This newcomer has been a great help to me. He gave me the opportunity to open the door of a world I didn't know before.' Among other things, this open doorway accorded him a fresh view at the popular repertoire, and soon Stevie Wonder and Lennon-and-McCartney tunes appeared on Stéphane's set lists.

John was typical of some of Stéphane's new younger audience: 'I heard Django in 1964 on my father's 78s. I was playing Shadows tunes at the time and I was blown away hearing Django... In the '60s, of course, the past didn't really exist, so the Hot Club Quintet records weren't readily available, but I thought they were incredible when I did manage to hear them. So with a friend I experimented on 'Blue Drag' and 'Swanee River' on a Spanish guitar with two steel strings! I knew about the Quintet, which was unusual at the time. I worked in a factory as a schoolboy and nobody had heard of Django, but all these old dears remembered dancing to Stéphane Grappelli during the war.

Initially, John Etheridge must have seemed an odd choice as a bandmember, but the Soft Machine connection proved to have great credibility with a younger audience and the average age of the band went down two decades at a stroke.

At this stage the new quartet was very much a co-operative, with no real management structure and no official representation. It was a fusion of Diz Disley's Trio and Stéphane's individual talent. Together they harked back to the Django era.

John found Stéphane fascinating, if different than expected: 'I've always felt that the paradox between Django the uneducated, natural man and Stéphane the bourgeois Parisien is so wrong. What separates them vitally is that Reinhardt, being brought up in that gypsy background with the men surrounded by doting females, left him with a great sense of himself and extremely confident.'

This is interesting, considering Stéphane's own comments on working with Django: 'To me Django was more than a good musician, more than a friend.

He was like a relation. His confidence was reassuring to those working with him. I was never nervous with Django. Playing violin with him it felt as though I was sitting in my own drawing room.'

John continues, 'Stéphane was desperately insecure in many ways, he really felt that music was his way of "making himself". He felt music was the thing that stopped him being a street urchin. Music was the innate gift that he employed to make his way in the world rather than something he took to and wanted to explore. That's why he wasn't the sort of person who practised for hours every day. He didn't have that kind of mentality towards music at all... He would say, "I'll do anything for money, me."

'But paradoxically, however much of a jobbing musician he may have consciously felt himself to be, he had this deep musical integrity. So when he picked up the violin, it was never schmaltzy. It's so easy for the violin to sound saccharine and sentimental, but his integrity took over. In some ways he thought of himself as a court jester, someone who was just there to please the public...but the wonderful thing, part of the magic, was that when he picked up the violin, it was so princely and so immaculate.

'There is a lot of smoke and mirrors surrounding Stéphane. People became very attached, but he never opened up to them. We all felt that. But he was still loveable. I used to think, "Why is this bloke so loveable?" I've worked with lots of celebrity musicians, and after a time it's the personality that you're responding to, and he had an incredibly engaging personality. It was incredibly unself-conscious. That's why he was so engaging, almost like a child.'

This is the same childlike quality that Michael Parkinson observed during the Menuhin television encounter. However, it was a quality that could have repercussions in the day-to-day life of a touring band. 'Just like a child, you couldn't rely on him emotionally,' remembers John. 'He wasn't there for you, perhaps because he'd never been to school and had never been subject to that normal social pressure to conform. This early environment encouraged him to be a loner. He had a tendency to anxiety offstage – he would rock in his chair and you could tell he was worried about something. But as soon as he was playing he was fine. Both my parents came to the airport the first time I went on a world tour with Stéphane, and there he was, rocking over his trolley, which my mum noted immediately as a classic sign of anxiety.'

Musically, John also had to adjust to Stéphane's very distinct style: 'His music has a distinct Gallic quality. He doesn't play a straight-eight, always having a natural tendency to swing jazz. He isn't a blues player; he has no blues inclination at all. He's very Euro in that sense. Perhaps because of his life, he doesn't want to go into the dark side – he's a major-key player.'

John remembers Stéphane's first encounter with the dark modal nature of north Indian classical music, something that was rising in popularity due to the 1960s experimentation of The Beatles and Yehudi Menuhin: 'Clifford Hocking had just been touring Ali Ackbar Khan [the great Indian Sarod player], and he put on a track for Stéphane. [At first he listened]: "Oh, it's interesting." Then, after about ten seconds, "Oh, take it off. It gives me the *bleu*. There are no chord changes." That's very Parisian, wanting to move on, not wanting to go down. Maybe that was also related to the insecurities of his background.

'If people have self-confidence, they go consciously into the dark side, because they feel they can face it. I think perhaps with Stéphane he always wanted to move on, keep it buoyant.'

There was little time to dwell on such matters, though, as the popularity of the band continued to grow. In 1976, the world of popular music had again been turned on its head. Punk rock arrived in a barrage of graffiti-driven publicity, the movement characterised by spitting punks with green mohican hairstyles and safety pins for facial jewellery, the complete antithesis of everything conventionally musical. Many young people felt betrayed as this anti-music force took hold, and once more Stéphane inherited a following from an unlikely direction. Even his young protégé Nigel Kennedy would acquire a new image, punkish but still playing music.

'We did a whole load of world tours,' remembers John Etheridge of the time, 'tours of England every year, two tours of America and some gigs in France. Ed Baxter fixed the gigs in England and Clifford Hocking and then Abby Hoffer fixed the tours in America.'

In England, Stéphane needed a permanent agent and he found Edward Baxter. Born in 1926, Baxter is a straight-talking Scotsman who never confuses a spade with a garden implement for digging holes, and Stéphane clearly admired his directness. Their paths crossed when Ed was a teenager during the war: 'I remember as I kid I used to go and see him at the Theatre Royal in Edinburgh. Shearing played with him then. It was around 1942, when Steph toured the music halls – two shows a night, 6:35 and 8:30. His agent at the time was Lew Grade. I used to go and see them for sixpence up in the gods.'

Much later, in 1972, a journalist friend questioned Ed on the lack of jazz at the Edinburgh Festival: 'My wife, Eileen, and I were in the box office in Edinburgh at the Usher Hall. John Gibson, who was the entertainment critic at *The Edinburgh Evening News* said, "There never seems to be any jazz around at the festival."

'John said, "Well, as a matter of fact I'm going down to London next week to see and hear Stéphane Grappelli at Ronnie Scott's."

'I said, "You mean he's still playing?"

'"He's playing at his absolute peak."

'So he got me the name of the agent at the time, London Management. The only thing I'd promoted was the year before, two concerts for Sid Lawrence, and I got the bug. So I got in touch with the agent and said, "What about Mr Grappelli at the festival next year?"

'Not too long after, he called me back to say yes, Mr Grappelli would be delighted to come and play at the festival. We talked about it and I asked what kind of a fee they'd be looking for the week – seven nights with an 11 o'clock start. [We paid] £1,500 for the week for the four of them. The boys paid the accommodation, not me, and they travelled up and back and I didn't pay for that. I did pay Steph's hotel – he stayed at the King James in Edinburgh and he used to take them all, The Alan Clare Trio, up to the concert by car – Tony Crombie on drums and Len Skeat on bass. The gig was a rip-roaring success and went into *The Evening News* the next night.'

The following year, Stéphane returned with Diz, Ike Isaacs and a mystery guest: 'On the first night,' recalls Baxter, 'a young chap came along to the box office for a ticket. He had a violin case with him. Eileen was at the box office so she charged him for the ticket, and at the end of it he came along to the dressing room: "Do you think I could see Mr. Grappelli for a minute? I know him personally, you know." So I said yes, by all means, and said to Steph, "Steph there's a young man here to see you."

'"Ah yes, Nigel, come in."

'I had no idea who Nigel Kennedy was. Steph said, "You going to play with us?" And so they played "Lady Be Good" and "Tiger Rag", and that one hit the headlines again.

'We could have sold twice the number of tickets every night, easy. People wanted to hear Steph play with this young lad. Nigel was staying at the YMCA in Edinburgh and I used to take Nigel back there every night after the concert. At the end of the week, I said to Steph, "What do you think I should give Nigel, Steph? He's helped a bit here and there. He's not played much or anything." Steph said £30. Nigel was absolutely delighted.

'The following year, I arranged one or two things for Steph, not a great deal, and Disley had still been arranging gigs and folk clubs. I spoke with Steph on the phone and he said, "You know, I like the way you do the business – the set-up, the little concert halls and stuff like that. Do you think you could maybe do some more?"

'"Yes, I think so," I said. "Give me maybe a week or two on it and I'll come back to you." Which I did. And of course I knew nowhere in England, or anything about halls, so together with Jim Crawshaw, who was the orchestral manager for Sid Lawrence, we arranged a tour of about ten concerts and Steph liked it...and it just went on from there.'

This was all part of the huge growth in popularity for Stéphane in the 1970s, from his 75p-on-the-door folk-club gigs to sell-out tours with separate agents and promoters in four key territories. Ed gradually took informal bookings in the UK while Abby Hoffer handled Stéphane's arrangements in the USA, Clifford Hocking covered Australasia and Michel Chouanard took France.

By 1977, Stéphane wanted Ed to take over officially, although, as Ed recalls with pride, they never had a formal contract; it was always a gentlemen's agreement: 'Lo and behold, Steph says, "I want you to look after the business for me in the UK." I have a letter dated 1977 that went out to the media – BBC, ITV, to the contract department, to *Melody Maker* and stuff – [saying] that I was his UK rep. I was on trial 'til then... That's the only contract we ever had between us.'

Throughout the world, the band with Diz and John became very popular on television light-entertainment shows, particularly after further stints on Michael Parkinson's chat show. One appearance from 1979 has The Hot Club Quartet in its full floral-shirted glory, Stéphane complements his flamboyant shirt with a pair of lime-green trousers so flared that they almost obliterate his trendy white shoes. The rest of the band – Diz, John and bass player Phil Bates – fall into line and the transformation is complete; it's difficult to equate the near-retirement cardigan-and-spectacles Stéphane of 1971 with this reborn phoenix. The band proceed to bounce through 'Let's Fall In Love' with a *joie de vivre* that people wanted to hear. Musically, for Stéphane, it's a simple jaunt – no Earl Hines or Oscar Peterson, just the unpretentious thrum of the guitars and Diz playing a Django-esque solo in the swing spirit of 1939.

After their turn, Parkinson back-announced, 'Stéphane Grappelli demonstrating the meaning of style' – and stylish it was for the mid-'70s, a time when no shirt collar could be to big and no trousers too tight. In the era that saw the release of films like *Saturday Night Fever*, with its disco anthems, and ABBA getting camper with every pop video, Stéphane had again found himself a place in the mainstream of entertainment.

Michael recalled an amusing incident behind the scenes after his show: 'The thing I remember most about Stéphane, he had this extraordinary business about mopping up the Green Room after the guests had left. I wouldn't say Stéphane was a mean man, but he was careful – and I say this fondly because I have nothing but fond memories of Stéphane. When he did the show, he'd come back to the green room and we'd have sandwiches and buns and so on. At the end of it, he'd get a little bag and go around the room, pick up all the leftover sandwiches and take them back to his suite at the Savoy and eat them.'

(In fairness, I doubt if it was the Savoy, as the BBC had more modest ideas about accommodation for their artists.)

'This came to an extraordinary conclusion one day when a publicist called Theo Cowan – who had the same habit – and Stéphane were both working on the same show and sharing the same Green Room. They actually collided in the middle of the room! He'd been working one half and Theo had been working the other and they met in the middle with both their separate bags of goodies to take back to their places to eat.'

According to a great friend, Stéphane couldn't eat before performing and invariably, by the time they got back to the hotel, the kitchen would be shut, and so this, coupled with his dislike for waste, was his solution. Eccentric perhaps, but also very pragmatic, very Stéphane.

In re-establishing the Hot Club sound, Diz Disley had set Stéphane off on a new path, one that was profitable and enjoyable and Stéphane would never forget Diz, despite their frequent differences of opinion. In 1996 I'd been trying to trace Diz for inclusion in a BBC radio programme and I mentioned his apparent disappearance to Stéphane. 'I hope he is OK,' he replied. 'Diz was a very amusing guy, but so sympathetic, and in any case he's the man who put me in my new position and I thanks him, I thanks him very much.'

21 A Life On The Road

'I don't like living in one space. I don't like doing the same thing every day. Meeting new people and seeing new places all the time keeps me young, it keeps me interested and it keeps me healthy.'

– Stéphane Grappelli

In January 1978, Stéphane celebrated his 70th year and 56 years in the business with a spectacular three-hour live broadcast on French national television. Joining him were the great jazz-Bach exponent Jacques Loussier, the singer Gilbert Becaud, the violinists Salvatore Accardo, Sven Asmussen and Didier Lockwood and the ORTF Symphony Orchestra. The show also featured Stéphane's now regular trio.

Stéphane remained ambivalent about the guitar band. He later told me that the guitars were often better on tour because the house pianos were frequently out of tune, and of course you couldn't often fix that – problematic if you have perfect pitch! But the guitar you can easily tune up. Even so, John Etheridge told me, 'Stéphane worked best with pianists, especially Alan Clare. He liked to hear nice chords on the guitar and he appreciated being accompanied well, but his ear was really tuned in to the piano…and he was very critical of pianists. Art Tatum was the only music he really listened to. When the cassette Walkman came out in the late '70s, he got this recording of Art Tatum playing "Paper Moon" and he worked out how to go back and forth on the tape. There was one chord change he particularly liked – he just loved it, and he played it over and over again on the way to the gigs with his headphones on in the back of the car. He would never do that with a guitar player.'

Working on *The Michael Parkinson Show*, Stéphane was reacquainted with another great pianist, the resident musical director, Laurie Holloway. A superb musician and a sensitive accompanist, Stéphane was pleased to be able to bring him in on the latest Menuhin-Grappelli album.

For this third set of violin duos, Stéphane returned to George Gershwin, ideal melodic inspiration for a now-established formula. However, even Laurie, aided by Pierre Michelot and Ted Heath's drummer, Ronnie Verrell, couldn't stem the drift into easy listening. Stéphane was of course giving a section of his public what they wanted. 'Why not?' he would say. 'Jazz could be played elsewhere.' He was well aware, though, of what happens to people who spend too long in the middle of the road. But with 50 years of practice, he somehow managed to juggle jazz and light entertainment.

This was the Stéphane Grappelli I would meet for the first time in 1978. He was 70 and I was 27. Like millions of others, I had admired his musicianship from afar. I'd been a musical teenager, and as a schoolboy I'd made a record as a guitarist for Decca's Ace Of Clubs label. Later, working at a gap-year job in a record shop, I discovered another Ace Of Clubs record sitting next to mine in the shop's storage racks. This quaint old record with its 1930s graphics and playing-card logo featured Stéphane and Django. I was intrigued by the sleeve photograph of a strange gypsy with an unusual guitar, his dangerous-looking 'brothers' and a dapper young violinist.

I came to enjoy The Hot Club Quintet Of France and played their record on sunny weekend afternoons, their evocative sound often drifting through the open window of my student flat. Somehow The Hot Club Quintet's unmistakable sound was nostalgic of a time I didn't know – but of course, in Yehudi Menuhin's words, 'music is magic'. At that time, my own music world encompassed an eclectic mixture of '60s and '70s styles, including playing the cellar clubs of Liverpool as a rock drummer, touring the UK and appearing on television in Germany and England. I had also appeared at festivals very much like the Cambridge Folk Festival playing contemporary folk and was at the time studying classical guitar.

At my music school, I discovered that violinists were in awe of Stéphane's free-flowing improvisation. Together we tried to conjure the Hot Club spirit at end-of-term concerts, but it was elusive, distant, from a long time ago. As a student, I couldn't afford a television set, so I missed the whole early '70s Grappelli revival, including his duo with Menuhin on *The Parkinson Show*.

Leaving college, I joined the BBC at their Pebble Mill Studios and trained as a sound engineer, specialising in music recording. It was a fantastic and privileged time, full of surprise. You could arrive innocently at work, hear a distant piano, turn a corner and find yourself face to face with Vladimir Ashkenazy. This happened a lot.

One morning in 1978, I was tapped on the shoulder, by a distraught Frenchman: 'Excuse me, I 'ave a difficulty. I must warm up. Can you 'elp?' I have to admit, I was taken aback – Stéphane looked older than he did in 1937, but the glint in the eye was very much there. To me, he was a picture on a faded album sleeve, a musician on a mono 78rpm record, a part of music history. Even by Pebble Mill standards, this was a big surprise. Quickly recovering my composure, I decided that 'oui' was the right answer.

I found Stéphane an empty radio studio, and this cavernous space soon reverberated to the best fiddle sound I'd ever heard (this from a man who turned a corner one day to find the Amadeus String Quartet!). Stéphane carried on playing all day. When the need to speak arose, his mumbled Anglo-French formed a stuttered counterpoint.

I would later discover that, during this week, Stéphane had acquired one of his precious 18th-century Italian violins. After years of relative obscurity, he had recently found his renaissance and several new audiences. New fame brought money, and money bought dream violins. His manager told me, 'Stéphane played almost all his life on good-quality but very ordinary violins, not Stradivarius, Montagnana or Amati, but he knew about those violins. He would visit violin makers all over the world, perhaps for running repairs. The main violin-making friend was Etienne Vatelot in Paris. In the '70s, Stéphane was told by one of his agents to invest in a good violin. He visited Vatelot and bought the 1742 Gagliano.*

That day at Pebble Mill, I chatted to Stéphane and told him how much I admired his new violin. Then Diz let me play his Maccaferri guitar, which had so fascinated me on those early record sleeves, and John Etheridge and I discussed the ongoing problems of acoustic-guitar amplification. Etheridge then had a novel instrument called an Ovation, which was partly made of plastic and had built in electronics.

Stéphane performed live on television that day and it was a brilliant performance, strikingly better than any of his 1930s output. Indeed, everyone was ecstatic except the television director, the lighting man and the sound supervisor, my boss; 18th-century violins are sensitive objects, and having found a new friend Grappelli wasn't about to be parted from it. In protecting it, he set in motion a chain reaction of television disaster.

It was a sunny day and everyone in the country enjoyed a sunny day except lighting men on *Pebble Mill At One*. The programme was broadcast from an entrance foyer with glass windows for a backdrop rather than a studio wall.

*Alessandro Gagliano was the founder of the Neapolitan school of violin-making, producing violins and cellos between 1700 and 1735. His work is considered to have great character and generally followed the classical model, and he was renown for using magnificent varnish. After the 1730s, his sons Nicolò and Gennaro abandoned their father's varnish in favour of an inferior, spirit-based recipe and mainly followed the Stradivari form.

As daylight increased, the lighting men had to turn up their lights to compensate or the guests would have appeared as moody silhouettes against these vast glass walls.

There is, of course, no light without heat, as anyone who's burnt their fingers changing a 100-watt lightbulb will know. Well, the bulb illuminating Stéphane Grappelli was 10,000 watts. Fuming with anger, the fiddler was ready to leap on the next cross-Channel ferry with his fragile Gagliano. As a pragmatic compromise, he stayed in England, but a significant metre to the left of his appointed studio position where it was cooler.

In the television control room, however, the temperature rose. This was live television, and so there could be no retakes. As Stéphane edged left in moody, Expressionistic gloom, he left his microphone behind. The camera followed Stéphane and so spelt doom for all the director's planned images. In desperation, the lighting man turned up his lights even brighter and Stéphane edged even farther to the left. Soon the control-room air was thick with French and Anglo-Saxon expletives. Two minutes sometimes seems a lifetime, but as they say in live television, 'no life lost'. The music ended, the studio audience – oblivious to the drama – applauded enthusiastically and we all went home. Fade to black.

A new day faded up on the lighting man's dimmer board. Yesterday's *Pebble Mill* script was recycled scribbling paper for the local playschool. Older but not necessarily wiser, I turned up for work once more.

''Ello, monsieur le sound.'

It was that man again, now safely ensconced in a television studio with real walls. That day Stéphane guested for the talented entertainer and musician Roy Castle, hosting a children's music programme. As a surprise Roy had arranged for an emotional Stéphane to be surrounded by a troupe of Suzuki violin students. The children processed around Stéphane with their tiny violins.

Grappelli was in tears. 'I must 'ave un picture!' So off I went to find the staff photographer and everyone posed for a couple of snaps. Stéphane scribbled his address on a piece of scrap paper and again we all went home. *Un homme de mon mot*, I duly sent Stéphane the snaps and thought no more about it.

What a happy surprise, therefore, when a few weeks later Stéphane sent me a signed photo of himself with a note thanking me for his snaps. For the next 19 years, he sent me postcards from Singapore, Cannes, Australia and all the far-flung places Stéphane's talent would take him. (Stéphane loved sending postcards; according to John Etheridge, when on tour he might send 80 a day!).

My curiosity about this remarkable 70-year-old musician was aroused and I quickly read everything I could find. Fortunately, he was in the press a lot that year.

For that *Pebble Mill* show, Stéphane had played with his famous line-up containing John Etheridge and Diz Disley, and it was interesting to observe the slick rearrangement of their music to precisely fit the television time slot. 'It was almost a rule that he wouldn't play tunes we'd rehearsed,' reveals Etheridge. 'We would go round to his flat in the King's Road, were he had an electric piano, and we'd start going through a tune and he'd get down on the keyboard and get really intricate with the harmony. We'd work out a really fussy, harmonically rich arrangement and then we'd get to a gig and I'd suggest we play it, and because of his memory he'd forgotten or he'd be nervous about forgetting so he wouldn't want to play it. So we only played tunes that we hadn't rehearsed properly! He didn't have a good retentive memory. One of the things that forces you to be a good improviser is if you can't remember an hour and half of music.'

Yehudi Menuhin also mentioned this to me in connection with their record sessions: 'It is the fact that the moment becomes a creative moment. You're not listening to something that has already been written or played or that you know already and have heard 1,000 times…it's a new revelation. And the extraordinary thing, when we recorded Stéphane never repeated himself. I don't think he could.'

For John Etheridge, this creative memory failure led to some interesting moments: 'It was San Francisco, very late at night, second set at a club. On "How High The Moon", Stéphane would play 64 bars unaccompanied. He did his 64 bars on the changes of the song and then he started to break it down. I was listening to this, thinking, "This is great. Stéphane goes free." He was wafting all over the instrument, all the harmonics and all his Bach quotes. The audience must have thought this was absolutely immaculate, great, this lyrical violin. So I gave him the thumbs up – "Yeah, yeah, this is great," and so on – and he was looking at me out of the corner of his eye, trying to tell me something and I couldn't think what. He carried on with this and moving towards me and also trying to keep the violin somewhere near the microphone and he gets close to my ear and he says, "What are we playing?" So I had to tell him. He'd completely forgotten. But the audience loved it.'

For John, Stéphane's approach to improvising was unusual but appropriate: 'He had a wonderful way with a melody. He almost made the accompanist redundant because he played his own fills, probably because he'd played with so many pick-up rhythm sections.'

Often those fills implied the harmony of the tune, but Stéphane excelled as a creator of spontaneous melody. John: 'That's one of the timeless things about his playing, the way he played a melody. With jazz musicians, we tend to concentrate only on their solos, but his respect for the melody was fantastic. Among the two most popular soloists are Stéphane and Stan Getz, both of whose playing doesn't address the chords in a detailed and fussy way – the notes are in the key, but it's a melody – as opposed to say John Coltrane, where you attack every chord and play off it.

'I've discussed this with other violinists. The violin is a melodic instrument, so Stéphane played it melodically. The piano is a harmonic instrument, and he played that very harmonically. On the violin he played through the changes, but he didn't necessarily address all the changes, and that seems a natural way to play the violin. Violinists who get more fussy harmonically seem to lose something and are not as popular. If you analyse a Stéphane Grappelli solo, he plays on top of the changes, but that's just natural to the instrument.'

Above all, John felt that Stéphane was completely himself: 'He's unique in the way that jazz musicians are supposedly always unique, in that they are themselves. But really, it's very rare for a musician to be so authentically himself, and…he was always completely relaxed, unhurried, and the flow of ideas was totally uninhibited. He was completely himself, and this is really what jazz should be about and so rarely is. It's not a self-conscious thing; it's just there. There's a tendency to think that it's something the character achieves through conscious effort, but unfortunately – and in a way, it's a pessimistic view – it seems to me people either are or aren't. Stéphane Grappelli always was himself.'

John felt that Stéphane often joked about the fact that he would do anything for money, but in fact, whatever he might have consciously tried to do, Stéphane's integrity ran deep: 'He had within him this uncompromising integrity. That's what was so memorable and loveable. I've known lots of so-called "characters" that you don't remember. The character is a sort of adjunct, developed to be amusing or something. He didn't try to be amusing; he just was amusing.

'With a genius, it's said you can't tell anything of the overt personality from the product. I remember looking at him once, very early on…and the initial impression was of a rather anxious old guy and thinking, "This playing is nothing to do with this old French character. It's something else. Something's happening when he's playing." And that's one of the defining things of genius – something comes through. People like myths but there is an element of truth in there.'

One myth that Stéphane had to deal with was the ever-present shadow of his old gypsy friend Django. For Dave Grisman,* while he was composing the music for the film *King Of The Gypsies*, Stéphane's gypsy credentials were only part of the story: 'In the summer of 1977, Federico de Laurentiis sought me out and hired me to write music for a film he was producing called *King Of The Gypsies*. He wanted real musicians playing the music live in the film and put me in charge of hiring them. After a month or so of scouting Hungarian restaurants in search of a gypsy fiddler, I had a brainstorm – why not Stéphane? The film people had never heard of him, but fortunately he had an engagement in New York and they went and heard him and agreed that he would be perfect for the film. I'll never forget our first meeting to work on the music. It was on my 33rd birthday, 23 March 1978. The thing that amazed me was that Stéphane had a bit of difficulty playing the tunes…something I never would have expected. We became friends and he invited me to sit in with his group at another Great American Music Hall gig a short while later.'

King Of The Gypsies, an evocative but ultimately shallow adventure, tells the story of an American gypsy family in mid-20th-century America. Stéphane appears in vision after just seven minutes as part of a live gypsy band at a nocturnal celebration. His face fills the screen, brimming with happiness but looking far more like Stéphane Grappelli than any gypsy. Wardrobe and make-up have done their best, but this podgy Franco-Italian is no swarthy Romany. Diz Disley, however, is born to the part – with his hat and moustache, he is typically Manouche. The band, with Dave Grisman on mandolin, give a spirited atmosphere to a film-makers cliché of swirling skirts and rattling tambourines.

David Grisman: 'One of the music scenes was filmed at around midnight, out in a field in New Jersey. It was very cold and late. They spent a lot of time filming the dancers without music. Then it was finally our turn, and we played the song once and they said, "That's it." The next day, when I saw the rushes, I heard that the recording was distorted. I asked Stéphane if he could duplicate his solo in the studio to the film. He told me it would be impossible. But I had

*Born on 23 March 1945 in Hackensack, New Jersey, by the age of 15 Grisman developed an interest in bluegrass music and took up the mandolin. By 18 he had made his first recordings, as both a producer and as a player. In 1975 he formed The David Grisman Quintet to play his original compositions in the style he calls 'dawg', a synthesis of jazz, bluegrass and other forms. He has also collaborated with Sven Asmussen, Jerry Garcia, John Hartford, Tony Rice and Martin Taylor, as well as many other artists. David is considered one of the great mandolin players of his time.

my violinist, Darol Anger, transcribe Stéphane's solo and he *did* play it note for note, without distortion.'

Next in the film is a birth celebration, and Stéphane and Diz turn up again, gypsy kings of the Technicolor screen. Interestingly, in playing the music for the film, Stéphane adds a few gypsy nuances to his playing. Its not overt, almost as if he's drawing something out that is already there, something buried deep in his playing, or perhaps in the nature of his instrument.

Stéphane enjoyed making this film. It's so far from his previous in-vision appearance in 1946's *The Flamingo Affair* that it's hard to believe it's the same Grappelli. Ironic it must have seemed that he finally made it to the big American movie whereas Django, his gypsy partner who wanted that so much, never did.

Back in England in August 1978 Stéphane received the sad news that his friend and fellow jazz fiddler Joe Venuti had finally lost his long battle with cancer, passing away in Seattle at the age of 74. For Stéphane, Joe was one of the funniest men he had ever met and he would regale friends with stories of his many pranks. There were few enough jazz fiddlers in the world and Joe was certainly the one who had started Stéphane on his long road, way back in 1928.

In December, Stéphane's adopted home celebrated his 70th birthday, not just in London but also in Edinburgh and Liverpool. The Scots celebrated first at Edinburgh's Usher Hall on the tenth, and this was followed by a Liverpool show at the Empire Theatre on the 14th. In between was a televised spectacular recorded at the Royal Albert Hall.

The joint programme for these concerts is an extraordinary document. The cover features a painting of Stéphane by David Naseby, a psychedelic impression of him in lime-green and blue. Inside there is a whole page of newspaper clippings: 'Bon Anniversaire, Stéphane Grappelli' from *Le Figaro*, 'A Jazz-Violin Genius Makes California Debut' from *The Times*' Leonard Feather, 'The Ageless Stéphane Grappelli' and 'Grappelli As Hot As Ever' from *The Vancouver Sun*. Then, under the simple heading 'Stéphane Grappelli', there is this observation from the radical American rock journal *Rolling Stone*: 'Today, at 70 years of age, Stéphane Grappelli is at the height of his imaginative and technical powers.'

Sadly, the archive footage of the concert, recorded for BBC2, has long since been erased,* but John Etheridge has managed to get hold of a domestic video recording. As seen in this rare recording, the programme opened with Stéphane giving an introduction on a hotel balcony: 'This is my first time at the Royal

---

*Although perhaps not. In 2002, the BBC didn't seem to be sure.

Albert Hall, the most fabulous concert hall I've ever played in my life, and with George Shearing, Julian Bream, Niels Pedersen, Didier Lockwood and David Grisman.'

With Stéphane again in his famous lime-green, flared trousers and a flamboyant shirt, the concert then starts in a spirited way with 'Let's Fall In Love'. Stéphane is accompanied the now-regular duo of Diz and John but augmented by the American bassist Brian Torff. He is immediately generous with his birthday space, however, and makes way for new boy John Etheridge, who delivers a fine extended solo with a very modern approach, including some blistering harmonics. Stéphane then takes up the baton and develops John's ideas, demonstrating that this septuagenarian veteran was always listening and learning.

Next, 'After You've Gone' sees Diz in fine form, urging his Django Reinhardt Petit Bouche Maccaferri into a busy double-tempo solo, complete with spirited stop choruses.

Here, Stéphane plays with the energy of a teenager and the composure of a Mandarin. After a couple more tunes, he introduces his latest violin protégé, Didier Lockwood, confiding to the audience that he sees Didier as part of a long line starting with Joe Venuti and encompassing Stuff Smith, Eddie South, Ray Nance and Sven Asmussen. With Phil Bates now on bass, the two violinists rhapsodise on 'Autumn Leaves'. With the enthusiasm of youth, Didier trades phrases with Stéphane and then launches double-tempo into every hot lick he knows. This is the Royal Albert Hall and he's riding with the king, and, bowing vigorously with shoulder-length hair and flowing scarf, Didier is playing to impress. This has nothing to do with 'Autumn Leaves', so Stéphane pulls him back down to earth by simply playing the tune. The fun then continues through 'Tiger Rag'.

Stéphane then recounts his American adventures on *King Of The Gypsies* before introducing David Grisman, the composer of the score and a remarkable mandolin virtuoso. Following a brilliant 'Limehouse Blues', Grisman tells the audience, 'For *Gypsies* we needed a violinist, and the first violinist I always think of is Stéphane Grappelli, so we got to do this movie together.' Grisman, in full beard and '70s floral shirt, then announces a title from the film, 'The Tipsy Gypsy', which includes wonderful unison and thirds writing for the violin and mandolin, all in Romanian-sounding modes. Together they have a ball and the audience end the first programme with thunderous applause.

The second programme, shown the following day, is one of the most infamous televised music concerts in popular-music history. In the archive footage, it all starts calm enough, with Stéphane's 'Bonsoir, Mesdames et Messieurs' continuing with a swinging rendition of Gershwin's 'Fascinating Rhythm'.

Then the fun begins, all at the expense of unsuspecting guitarist Julian Bream. Born in London's Battersea in 1933, Julian's father had first introduced the young Julian to the recordings of Django Reinhardt. Showing early promise as a classical guitarist, Julian had been thwarted at every turn – in 1948 there were no classical guitars available, no classical-guitar teachers and a dearth of suitable music. Undaunted, the teenager played a borrowed Maccaferri, took lessons on the piano and had new music written for his chosen instrument. By 1978 he was the instrument's acknowledged master. Benjamin Britten, William Walton and Igor Stravinsky had all written music for him. As a concert maestro from Carnegie Hall to the Sydney Opera House, he was guaranteed a full house.

However, he remained a Reinhardt fan, admitting, 'I admire Django more than Segovia,' so when the opportunity came to play with Stéphane he accepted with alacrity, if a little anxiety. A rehearsal at Stéphane's King's Road flat went OK, and from Grappelli Julian even learned a new harmonisation of 'Nuages', which he accepted with grace. Then, on the day of the Albert Hall concert, he rehearsed 'Belleville' – another Django opus – with Diz and John Etheridge. Julian remained apprehensive but bold.

On the night of the concert, Stéphane was supposed to introduce Julian Bream, who would play some JS Bach and a solo Spanish guitar piece, and indeed that's what Julian does – at the time, he was the greatest classical guitarist in the world and this was the Royal Albert Hall. However, Stéphane has, according to Diz, been introduced by his young entourage to the delights of 'wacky baccy', and in an authentic hippy daze he has forgotten all about Spanish guitar solos.

After introducing Julian, Stéphane immediately announces that he will play 'Nuages', completely wrong-footing the nervous maestro. Decked out in dinner jacket and black tie, he's set to enthral with Bach and Albeniz. With good grace, however, he plays an eloquent introduction to 'Nuages' and together he and Stéphane play two free choruses, with Julian supplying some inventive and inspired chords.

Julian takes the lead next, playing the melody with wonderful decoration, tasteful and appropriate, boldly going where classical guitarists rarely dare to tread, after which Stéphane supplies a beautiful violin chorus and ends with a dazzling cadenza. Then Julian consolidates things with a firm G major chord and the audience erupts in triumphant applause.

In an interview with Tony Palmer,* Julian revealed that, during the performance, he was stirred but not shaken: 'It occurred to me that, well, this must be my solo spot – but not a bit of it. Grappelli announced that I would now do a number with his group, and before I knew where we were he glanced across at me, indicating that he wanted a four-bar intro. This I provided. After the initial 32-bar chorus, he glanced over to me again, which meant that I should take the first solo, which I did. I wasn't making such a bad fist of it when Grappelli walked over to me and said, "Take another." I thought this was pushing it a bit, but there was nothing else I could do but comply.

'By this time my powers of improvisation, such as they were, were beginning to ebb rapidly. All the little riffs and embryonic ideas I had thought over in the dressing room vanished from my fingers, and in the final eight bars of the second solo I was reduced to simple arpeggios on block chords, sounding not unlike Giuliani on an off night. Worse was to come. As I finished the second solo, Grappelli walked over to me and muttered, "Take another." And that, I can say, was the most embarrassing moment of my life.

'When I finished and I thought at long last the moment had come to do my solos, Grappelli just said, "Thank you very much, Julian Bream. Now we'll get on with the show." So I plodded offstage in complete disarray. Christ, that was a nightmare to end all nightmares. I could have killed him.'

The scene of Bream's embarrassment was 'Belleville', introduced by Stéphane as 'not a very nice district of Paris'. Watching the videotape of the concert recently with the guitarist, I was struck by the warmth of the crowd. Whether Stéphane had been given a whiff of marijuana or was just having a senior moment, who knows? Many in the audience seem to realise Julian's dilemma and Stéphane's mischief. As Julian leaves the stage, there is a roar of support for his bravery under fire and Stéphane even brings him back for a second bow.

In 2002, Julian was philosophical about the whole affair: 'It was a case of rounding the circle – that's where I started out with The Hot Club Quintet records. And it was a wonderful thing to do, even if I couldn't do it as a jazz musician.'

As an interesting postscript, Stéphane drew Julian aside at the end of the concert and afforded a rare accolade: 'You know, Julian, you are a jazz musician!' Even Yehudi could never have received that from Stéphane.

For the televised broadcast, the BBC recorded Julian's classical pieces

*Tony Palmer, *A Life On The Road* (Macdonald & Co, 1982).

separately and inserted them into the second half, but on the live occasion Stéphane next introduced 'My dear old friend George Shearing. We played together in music hall and for the troops in the war, after which he went to America, but now he's back, accompanied by one of the greatest bass player in history.' And then, calamitously, Stéphane forgets his name. '*Mon dieu!* Niels Pedersen!' The film then shows Stéphane giving George a generous slot, with Pedersen providing a great counterpoint and amazing solo on a Ravel-like 'The Lamp Is Low'.

George then announces, 'Just as many of you may not be aware that Julian Bream is also Django Reinhardt, Niels Pedersen is also a composer,' and the band then launch into Pedersen's 'Cowboy Samba', with the bass having the tune from the top.

This virtuosity demonstrated, George goes on to introduce his most famous composition: 'It's nine or ten months now since The Shearing Quintet broke up after 29 years. People say this sound is just as fresh as when they first heard it. You know why? They don't have to play it every night!' He then plays the intro to 'Lullaby Of Birdland' and is greeted with applause. Even if they don't know the title, everyone in the audience knows the tune.

Taking the rapturous applause George, next brings back Stéphane: 'It's so marvellous to be back after all these years with my very good friend, the birthday boy.' He then sings 'Happy Birthday' with the full house of the Royal Albert Hall. Stéphane is visibly moved.

The three of them – Grappelli, Shearing and Pedersen – then perform 'La Chanson de la Rue' from the recent album *Reunion*. Stéphane plays this simple tune beautifully, a little man in a blue spotlight, his single violin filling the vast hall – this is a long way from the street corners of his childhood – while Shearing provides support with some gentle and very appropriate Debussy-like chords. They play one more piece as a trio and then Stéphane invites everyone back for a jam session on 'Sweet Georgia Brown' on which each player takes a solo, with Pedersen and Shearing shining but with some wonderful solos also from John Etheridge and Diz, who experiment with some Django-esque single-string runs. Stéphane and his protégé Didier then swap choruses, then finally he pulls them all back to the theme and the crowd goes nuts.

Looking at the musicians taking their bows, the question remains, who else could have brought this esteemed gathering together? The Albert Hall gig was a triumph, and Stéphane, at 70, was clearly at a peak.

★

A rare vinyl album from 1978 catches the spirit of Grappelli at this career summit. Proudly labelled 'Made In Scotland', the live album *As Time Goes By* consists of a miscellany of tracks recorded in concerts given that year. The completely acoustic Grappelli band is truly staggering, particularly on 'St Louis Blues', while the recording as a whole has the quality of classical chamber music in its intimacy, and the band is incredibly tight. It's fascinating to hear the Disley and Etheridge band freed from the restrictions of their frequent three-minute TV spots. On 'St Louis Blues', Stéphane's violin choruses give over to John Etheridge's harmonics and West Coast style of break-it-down jazz.

Then Stéphane further demonstrates his fantastic ear by picking up on John Etheridge's improvisations and echoing them in his own. The rhythmic style takes on a tango feel, then switches to straight swing, and guitar harmonics lead into Diz performing some more Django-esque single-string runs. He then passes things over to John, who breaks the chords down into breathtaking runs that echo Stéphane's flippant but honest remark at his audition: 'The tourists will love that fast stuff!' John then breaks the tune down further into harmonics and diminished arpeggios. The guitars and violin swap phrases until finally Stéphane pulls them all back to the melody, concluding the ten-minute epic, all the while underpinned by Phil Bates' inventive acoustic bass.

In the sleeve notes, the 70-year-old violinist reflects revealingly on his health, travel and his approach to performance: 'I don't like living in one space. I don't like doing the same thing every day. Meeting new people and seeing new places all the time keeps me young, it keeps me interested and it keeps me healthy.

'I used to smoke a lot but gave it up in 1970 and now my brain is clearer. I must say one thing that helps me through when I'm playing is a couple of malt whiskies before I go onstage [what he earlier refereed to as '*mon arme secrète*']. When I'm at Carnegie Hall, for example, I get a little nervous. It's normal, but when you must attack – *bang!* – you need a little support.

'Practice is good for the fingers but not good for the imagination. Therefore I play very little before a performance. Of course, I choose repertoire and make decisions about who should take certain solos and naturally we warm up before a concert. Because improvisation forms the basis of what I do, I prefer not to expend all my energy and imagination in practice, or in the rehearsal room. It is my hope that, on every occasion I play, the music is as fresh for the audience as it is for me.'

Diz Disley keeps many souvenirs from these Stéphane years, amongst them many set lists. These scribbled notes on the backs of hotel bills and miscellaneous stationery tell the quiet story of an artist trying to reach an audience with variety and also keeping the musicians' imagination fresh with a changing programme of tunes. Some selections seem mandatory; the 'Gershwin Medley', 'How High The Moon' and 'Old Man River' crop up a lot, as does 'Piano', Stéphane's solo spot where he put down his 'gimmick' and played the piano in his own idiosyncratic style. 'I like my programme to have something soft, something energetic, something slow, something blue, something red, something burning,' he revealed. 'It's quite difficult to do that with just two guitars, string bass and violin.'

He was always searching for that elusive perfect acoustic tone that every violinist strives for in his inner ear: 'We are a bit victimised by the new aspects of electric music. I don't dare to say that I'm playing like Heifetz; I play my own style. But I'm trying to get that sound. Those classical guys go very fast, but I go fast in my music as well. Why not? It keeps you alive.'

In 1978, Stéphane was more alive than many teenagers.

22 Stéphane Grappelli: This Is Your Life

'Retire? Why should I retire? I make music with my friends and I get paid for it. I'm OK.'

– *Stéphane Grappelli*

By 1979, Stéphane was again a well-established celebrity, and this inevitably led to very public surprises. The UK and US television show *This Is Your Life* celebrates the great and the good as their fame peaks. In its early days, it was almost a prelude to retirement, a reflective look back at a career, with nostalgic input from friends and family. Part of the fun for the audience is an element of surprise for the subject, and according to agent Ed Baxter this was certainly the case for Stéphane as the fateful hour arrived: 'He believed he was doing a concert and kept asking for Diz. He hadn't a clue. He thought he was going to the Dorchester and Diz would be along. And Steph was tuning up: "Where's Diz? Where's Diz?" We'll get Diz in a minute Steph, but let's take a walk round here for a minute, OK?'

On the Thames Television recording, Stéphane leaves his hotel to be greeted by the show's host, Eammon Andrews, and a surprising chauffeur, the singer Petula Clark. Stéphane looks bemused but happy as Eammon tells him, 'Tonight Stéphane Grappelli, this is your life.' Stéphane then turns to Petula and chuckles, 'But what kind of life?'

Driving through the snow-covered London streets, the entourage arrives at the studios and Stéphane is escorted by Ed and Petula through a delighted audience. Stéphane clearly hasn't had time to prepare and is wearing a shirt straight from the laundry bag with neat, square creases in all the wrong places. According to Petula, Stéphane even asked, off camera, 'Who is this Eammon Andrews?', and, worried about missing his concert, 'Will I get my money?'

It transpires that Petula has flown over especially from Geneva to chauffeur her old friend. 'I've been a fan for many years,' she tells the television audience, 'and first saw him at Club St Germain as part of the audience with my then-husband-to-be, Claude Wolfe.'

Eammon Andrews then brings on the current band – Phil Bates on bass and John Etheridge and Diz Disley on guitars – reassuring Stéphane that he hasn't missed the concert, and then reminds the audience that Stéphane has recently been awarded La Légion d'Honneur. He then introduces Stéphane's countryman Sacha Distel, currently famous for his pop success with 'Raindrops Keep Falling On My Head', who it turns out had met Stéphane during his years at the Paris Hilton and brought him to London to work the Palladium together.

Stéphane's next surprise is the offstage voice of Louis Vola, which he clearly doesn't recognise, but all is forgotten in Gallic embraces when Stéphane immediately recognises the face of his old friend. (It later transpires that Vola had issued the *This Is Your Life* team with a set of conditions for his appearance. At the age of 77, Vola had been tracked down by Diz, who found him working the club Scherezade in Paris where, not content with playing bass, the veteran was doubling on piano and drums. He insisted that the Thames Television fee should cover his three night absence from the bandstand.)

Having recounted a version of the founding of The Hot Club Quintet, Eammon next refers back to Stéphane's first violin and asks how he learned to play it, and Stéphane replies that he 'played with it like it was a toy'. There then follows an emotional reunion with Stéphane's daughter, Evelyne, with kisses for Evelyne and hugs for his grandsons, Gilles and young Stéphane.

The recording took place on 24 January, and Eammon next refers to this early birthday celebration for Stéphane. The context is the introduction of Stéphane Jnr, born unexpectedly 23 years ago at Stéphane's 48th birthday party. (Stéphane was very fond of his grandsons and had a particular soft spot for his young namesake. Ed Baxter later remarked to me on Stéphane's generosity towards the two boys.)

The next guest is Jean Sablon, the first of the great French crooners, two years older than Stéphane and a big star in Paris. Sablon famously cited World War I and the influx of US Army orchestras as a turning point in French popular music. Eammon refers to Stéphane and Jean's early recordings together, suggesting that these took place in 1932, but this seems unlikely. Certainly Stéphane and Django recorded with Sablon in 1934, scoring a success with 'Who's Afraid Of The Big Bad Wolf?'. He tells a funny story of always being invited to Stéphane's house but never quite managing it, until one day he at last phoned to accept the offer only to find that Stéphane had sold the house to buy a violin.

In a technological breakthrough for the 1970s, there follows a live satellite link-up with New York, where George Shearing recounts the tale of how he disturbed Stéphane during the Blitz by reading Braille in the dark, referring to the pub in Lambeth were they met. Then, he offers a tribute to Stéphane: 'You are an international jazz star. Thank you for 40 years of friendship, and may there be many more.'

There next follows a clip from the 1946 film *Stéphane Grappelli And His Quartet*, featuring, appropriately enough, the tune 'Evelyne', with Shearing playing excellent forward-looking piano in his last recording before leaving for American stardom.

Stéphane is delighted to see his next guests, Jack and Audrey Harrison from Devon, who relate the genesis of 'Yellow-House Stomp', a tribute to their country home where Stéphane had convalesced during the war. He and George Shearing supposedly wrote the opus on a restaurant tablecloth.

Next, Douglas Byng makes a surprise appearance. This raffish gent, born in 1893, was the queen of cabaret camp and spent most of his career in drag as a pantomime dame. In the '20s and '30s he was a leading light of the sophisticated international set alongside Noël Coward and famously sang 'Miss Otis Regrets' in drag for Cole Porter.

Cleo Laine and John Dankworth then sing for Stéphane, a tribute pre-recorded in their converted stables at Wavendon, which became a popular music mecca and to which Stéphane was apparently a regular visitor. By this time, the Dankworths were already a significant part of Britain's popular-music scene. Born in 1927, John had come to jazz via the Royal Academy of Music and 'Geraldo's Navy', the affectionate nickname for an apprenticeship to the transatlantic cruise bands. He formed his own band in 1950, then The Dankworth Seven became eight in 1951 with the addition of Cleo Laine (*née* Clementina Dinah Campbell), who hailed from London's Southall and had since gone on to sell out Carnegie Hall. Her live album of that was even nominated for a Grammy.

No doubt Stéphane would have enjoyed the Dankworths' eclectic approach to music, with jazz, Bach, Shakespeare and samba all well represented. In fact, their son Alec would eventually guest with Stéphane in concert as an accomplished bass player. By the 1970s, Cleo was at last receiving due recognition in the United States.

Also regretting the need to pre-record his tribute is Yehudi Menuhin, speaking from Columbus, Ohio. Yehudi remembers his *Parkinson Show* appearance with Stéphane and reveals that he 'always wanted to improvise like that'.

Another violinist then performs off-camera with a spirited attempt at 'Tiger Rag', and this turns out to be Nigel Kennedy, enthusiastic in cloth cap and bow tie, who reminisces about playing with Stéphane at Carnegie Hall. Next, told off by Stéphane for his irreverent dangling of his violin, Nigel adds a tribute to the fiddler who, he says, 'brings a life in his playing which classical music often lacks, the music of the moment'.

An unexpected pre-recorded tribute follows from the great French actress Jean Moreau, who had recently worked with Stéphane on *Les Valseuses*. She tells of accompanying Stéphane to his 1975 Légion d'Honneur ceremony.

The next guest is even more of a surprise, the exuberant Bricktop, who recalls the Paris clubs of the 1930s, announcing offstage, 'Remember, Stéphane? I called you my baby.' With reminders of 'Django de Reinhardt' and his unpredictability, the legendary club owner eventually presents Stéphane with a birthday cake in the shape of a violin, at which Stéphane retorts, 'I can't play that!' As a fitting tribute, Bricktop confides, 'Nobody in the world would have brought me in this kind of weather from New York, but I'm so happy.'

With nothing left to follow that, Eammon presents Stéphane with the big red book and the famous words 'Stéphane Grappelli, this is your life.'

Typically Stéphane was concerned about the audience, and as the cameras stopped recording Ed Baxter remembers that he gave the studio fans a little concert: 'Steph had the boys play – Disley, Phil Bates, John and himself, and Bricktop sang. She said, "We're going to do the 'St Louis Blues'." Pet Clark sang a song. He got everyone there involved in the thing – Jean Sablon singing, Louis Vola playing the bass.'

No doubt this was an emotional day for Stéphane, especially when faced with the notion of retirement. But who in that 1979 audience could have expected that the French wizard had a career before him of another 18 years?

Stéphane still had in his possession the Pierre Hel violin originally lent to him by Michel Warlop in their days together with Grégor et ses Grégoriens. By 1979, Warlop had become a French legend and a tradition had been established of presenting the violin to the protégés of the French Jazz Violin School. Stéphane had already publicly presented it to Jean-Luc Ponty but now it passed on again, this time to Didier Lockwood. The event was celebrated in the French press as Stéphane appeared at Paris's Théâtre de la Ville. In actual fact, the presentation was merely a gesture and Stéphane retained the actual instrument.

Stéphane never missed the opportunity to perform with new young talent, and that didn't change as the septuagenarian's honours arrived. In fact, his new status as 'legend' made it easier, and increasingly he found that the new guard sought him out. During the week that he turned 71, Stéphane spent three days in a studio in Stuttgart with the two guitar stars Larry Coryell and Philip Catherine. The American Coryell he probably knew via Gary Burton and their regular work together, while Anglo-Belgian Catherine had been dubbed 'the young Django' by the great bassist and composer Charlie Mingus and had since gone on to work with Jean-Luc Ponty. Coryell had worked on two of Mingus's albums and was content to let Catherine carry the 'Django' burden.

The guitarists, at 36 and 35, were riding the crest of success on record and at jazz festivals worldwide, their joint albums *Splendid* and *Twin House* both containing Django tributes. All roads seemed to lead to Stéphane, and he clearly enjoyed the association. He was inspired by the guitarists' signature close-harmony riffing and also by their brilliant foil, the greatest of bassists, Niels Pedersen.

On the final release (ironically titled *Young Django*), the repertoire is a mixture of Hot Club Quintet standards and a couple of Coryell-Catherine originals in which Stéphane not only rises to the occasion but immediately becomes the project's focus. Indeed, this later became a familiar pattern.

Stéphane's new international recognition prompted an invite to Carnegie Hall to celebrate Benny Goodman's 70th birthday. This contribution to a concert for one of the swing eras greatest stars would no doubt have meant more to Stéphane than 1,000 guitar tributes, although he would never say that. Ever the pragmatist, he revealed nothing more than 'I make music with my friends and I get paid for it.' However, he would have enjoyed this his first flight on the supersonic airliner Concord, perhaps reflecting on his memories of the Roaring '20s and the Paris celebrations for Charles Lindbergh as he crossed the Atlantic.

In July, Stéphane visited Copenhagen for two dates at Tivoli Hall, where he was accompanied by the best of both worlds, the wonderful piano of Oscar Petersen and the guitar of Joe Pass. The recorded concerts provide an incredible document of Stéphane's versatility. Very few musicians of 71 record two albums in one night.

Joe Pass was, like every jazz guitarist, clearly under the Django spell, and indeed back in 1964 he had dedicated a whole album to the gypsy genius. In this, one of his best albums, he featured four Django originals as well as his own tribute, the title track 'For Django'. Joe was a generation younger than

Stéphane, born in 1929 in New Brunswick, New Jersey, and had always played the electric rather than the acoustic guitar, although he shared with Stéphane a delight in working with Benny Goodman and George Shearing.

Stéphane and Joe also shared a gift for improvised melody, aligned to a composer's understanding of harmony, and the first concert reveals an amazing display of spontaneous counterpoint. Stéphane, Joe and Niels Pedersen all spin their own intricate threads of melody that combine into a rich web, perhaps a salute to New Orleans and the improvised counterpoint of 1910. There are distant echoes of the original Delta-jazz frontline of clarinet, cornet and trombone. The repertoire, too, spans the jazz century, from 'Paper Moon' to the contemporary pop hit 'Time After Time'.

The specific tunes cease to matter as truly these musicians could work magic with 'Three Blind Mice'. Stéphane is clearly happy and his playing has a new freedom, as if his age and a growing sense of jazz having a history, have freed him from the tyranny of fashion. On 'Crazy Rhythm', he demonstrates his effortless speed, something for which Joe was also famous for and something that they both used, but only for musical effect.

Stéphane's violin disciple Ric Sanders offered his own observation on Stéphane's light touch and seemingly effortless technique: 'His bowing leaves little gap, playing very light, not digging in. He floats over the fiddle.'

For 'I Remember April', Joe complements Stéphane's acoustic violin by playing his semi-acoustic guitar without amplification, a tribute to earlier days that would have been appreciated by Stéphane, who responds musically with one of his finest choruses. Pedersen then follows with some astonishing acoustic-bass figures. The three are pre-empting the back-to-basics trend of the 1990s and the audience are audibly delighted.

The second Tivoli concert has become justly famous as the landmark album *Skol*. Oscar Petersen: 'I have to say that Stéphane Grappelli had a very cute way of getting around things. You would ask him, "What shall we play?" and he'd say, "Well, I don't know. What *should* we play?" And we'd name certain tunes to him and he'd say, "Oh, I don't know if I know that tune. How does it go?", and we'd go through the whole thing. And it was only afterwards that we realised that the bottom line was that he really didn't want to play that tune. It was his choice anyway, but he was such a soft man, he wouldn't say, "I don't want to do that." He'd go through the whole thing – "Oh, it's been a long time since I played that, I don't know…", which was wonderful.'

For this set, Oscar Peterson brought on his drummer, Mickey Roker. Drums are, of course, always difficult for an acoustic violinist. Stéphane loved the impetus and colour drums bring to rhythm, but a ride cymbal could too easily crush all colour from his delicate palette and reduce his violin dynamics to *mezzo-forte*. Roker, however, is sensitivity incarnate during this gig and, during a career-best version of 'Nuages', even delicate brushstrokes bow out for Oscars inspired choruses. Peterson remembers 'a pretty hot rhythm section, Mickey Roker and so on. We tried to cool it down, not because of Stéphane but because of the instrument he was playing, because it's different thing when you're in the studio – he's playing into a mic, so they can turn the volume up in the control room – but we had to hear him so that we were able to give him the background that we felt he deserved for what he was playing, so we had to tone our attacks down a little to match him. No matter who you are as a soloist, if you play with somebody, you have to step into the background.'

On this outing, Stéphane clearly relishes the pianist's impressionistic flourishes and comes back with dizzying, time-defying phrases that somehow never lose sight of the melody, finally finishing with a solo cadenza of which Paganini would have been proud. He tips his bow to everything from the art of the Hungarian gypsy to his idol JS Bach and ends with the kind of *bravura* bowing that he'd been hearing a lot of at that time from Yehudi. Oscar and Stéphane both have big ears.

'I think the secret to all that,' muses Peterson, 'the basic bottom line, is that first you listen. Never let what your strong points are overtake that. If you're a hell of a player, that's great, but you're not there to do that at that particular time; you're there to listen and enhance. And that's what I try to do. I learned that from Hank Jones, 'cause I used to sit in the wings when Hank used to play for Ella and I learned an awful lot from him. But he listened intensely.'

The band then proceed to have fun with 'Makin' Whoopee' and 'Skol Blues', but Stéphane's masterpiece is his defining version of Gershwin's 'Someone To Watch Over Me'. Again, it's Oscar's sketched harmony that sets him off, all the while underpinned by Niels Pedersen's bass, which has an inner life of its own. Stéphane's last solo is probably the best starting point for an understanding of his genius; somehow he never loses Gershwin's melodic thread but builds on that an elaborate tower, delicate and fragile, sweet but never saccharine.

Like all great musicians at their best, the band's playing is transcendental, leaving the listener with something that has no fabric beyond the moment at which it touched. Music is the most abstract of arts and the improvising musician the most abstract of all performers, but here, preserved forever on tape, is what

Yehudi meant by magic. Oscar Peterson was also impressed: 'I have to say that, of all the jazz violinists, [Stéphane] had the most romantic sound. He had the best ballad-playing sense of the violin that I know of. Oh yeah, he's a romanticist. I've always felt that, if I was a bachelor romancing a woman, that's the record I'd put on.'

Back in the everyday world of jet flights and early breakfasts, life on the road was starting to take its toll on Stéphane. His health remained astonishingly robust, but for the regular band there was the more subtle issue of personal dynamics. Friendships started to suffer. 'After two years, Diz and I were not getting on and there was talk of changes,' John Etheridge recalls. 'Then I had a call from Michel Chounard in France saying Diz had broken his wrist in a motorcycle accident, [asking] would I organise a deputy? There was a suggestion of working with just one guitar, but at that stage I didn't know enough of the tunes and I relied on Diz. He was a very good musician and knew all the right chords.

'We did do one gig without Diz, in Brighton, which everybody was happy with, but I was still a fusion/jazz-rock player and didn't want the responsibility. So Phil Bates, the bass player, said, "I've just been working with this young boy, Martin Taylor." I went round to the Pizza on the Park and he was playing with Ike Isaacs and I thought, "Stéphane will really like him. He's fine for the job." He played good straight ahead jazz guitar and he was young, so initially he depped whilst Diz was out of it.'

John remembers Martin's debut being delayed slightly: 'The first Martin gig was in Mantes, in France, so I phoned Phil, who was taking Martin, and told him Mantes and he must have misheard. So he and Martin drove across France to Nantes. Meanwhile, Stéphane and I drove to Mantes, the Cinema Normandie, and nobody else showed up. We did a soundcheck, and I suddenly realised what had happened, so we played a half as a duo and then the promoter found a bass player who knew none of Stéphane's stuff and said, "Tell me the key and I'll follow." So I'd shout "'Crazy Rhythm' in F!" and off we would go with the bass player playing random bass lines.'

Later, in the car, Stéphane went mad. 'It was ridiculous,' continued John. 'The promoter said, "Never mind, everybody saw Stéphane Grappelli. They went away happy."'

Martin, however, was devastated. He'd broken off a family holiday to grab the opportunity to play with Stéphane, and there he was in the wrong town, hundreds of miles from anywhere: 'Mantes is near Paris, and we were miles away in the southwest of France with absolutely no chance of making the show. So Phil Bates and I went and had a few beers and I thought, "Well, I almost had a gig with Stéphane Grappelli but I blew it." But we met the next day, at a concert in Deauville, Stéphane was great about it. I think he saw the funny side. He said, "Well, zese tings 'appen, my dear."'

John Etheridge: 'Martin soon settled in and we split the load. Then the message came through that Diz had knocked it on the head and Martin joined permanently.'

Taylor would always remember that first Deauville gig: 'I remember, at the very first concert we played in France together, the fact that Stéphane loved playing for the audience. We played the first set and I can remember, it wasn't like he was being showbiz, it wasn't Las Vegas or anything, but he was, like, "This is the music I play. I love this music and I'm playing it for you." And that really, really struck me.

'I remember playing something in that first set and he said to me, "I really like what you play." But then he said, "Do you know what? If you played…" and he told me something '…and if you build that up that way…that'll be a really nice thing to play. The audience will really like that." At first I still had this kind of jazz-musician thing about not playing to the audience, but then I kind of understood what he meant, because really music is about emotion and conveying emotion.

'The greatest thing I learned from Stéphane was from watching him play and seeing how much he loved to play for an audience. That was the most fantastic thing – he loved playing to the people.'

Typically enigmatic, however, Stéphane remained shy: 'I play often with my eyes shut so I can't see anybody, because I want to escape the people that are in front of me. But at the same time, I like feeling their presence.'

Although still very young, Martin had come a long way from his early doodlings on his father's prized Hofner Jazz guitar. He was now 23 and had enjoyed a thorough apprenticeship doing everything from a stint with Geraldo's Navy on the cruise ships to playing strict-tempo dances with Victor Sylvester, the king of ballroom. He had met Stéphane a few years earlier, in Perthshire, and remembers enjoying the band with Diz and Ike Isaacs as well as being thrilled to see Stéphane with Django's scarf: 'I remember sitting in the dressing room when Stéphane opened his violin case and took out a neatly pressed flowery shirt. Then he took out his violin, wrapped in a red *dilko*, or silk scarf, the type that the older generation of gypsy men always wore. It had violins in the pattern and the music for a Paganini piece in very bright colours… Stéphane treasured that scarf, and when I began touring with him a few years later I would watch him go through the ritual of unwrapping and wrapping his violin in it. I always found it very touching.'

An episode of *The Parkinson Show* captures the early days of the new line-up, introduced as 'Stéphane Grappelli with The John Etheridge Trio'. The recording provides a record of an interesting phenomena, Stéphane as light-entertainment television. Many die-hard jazz enthusiasts have in the past dismissed Stéphane's work as lightweight and perhaps a little cabaret. Indeed, Stéphane came from a music-hall tradition, and although jazz was his passion, he was always ready to provide light entertainment if that's what was required. Many jazzers won't do this, but for Stéphane it wasn't a question of compromise; the tunes were the same, whether the venue was Ronnie Scott's or *The Val Doonican Show*. It was largely a matter of duration and emphasis. For Ronnie's, the band would stretch out and play extended break-it-down solos, while for a variety show they would play a short, three-minute routine and keep it simple.

For Parkinson they played 'Shine', and their performance shows how at first Martin and John stayed with the acoustic-guitar Hot Club sound. Here, John has switched from his Ovation-type modern acoustic guitar to a traditional Martin Dreadnought, while Martin plays an interesting 'cello-type electric jazz guitar, but unplugged. He plays well and Stéphane is visibly impressed. The band play a brand of undemanding swing that works well for television. In concert, 'Shine' would have been adapted to the different kind of audience.

However, the stress of relying on acoustic guitars in frequently difficult live situations encouraged John and Martin to try an experiment, which John later regretted: 'Going over to electric guitars was a mistake. The front of the note, the attack, is so much better on acoustic guitars, but of course we had such problems with sound in those days. We were rehearsing one day with a bass player and we thought, "Why don't we turn up with electric guitars and see what Steph says?" Of course, for us that was much easier. Ed Baxter wasn't happy, but Stéphane was OK – "I like it you are on electric" – and he got himself a little amp.

'But in retrospect, I think that was a mistake. Stéphane didn't like the Hot Club sound. "*Boom-ching, boom-ching* – I hate that." So there was a sort of tension. He encouraged us in his dispassionate way – he never got that close to any of us – and he gave the impression that he quite liked the electrics, but the promoter much preferred the other sound and I got the blame for that.'

With or without electric guitar, Martin was clearly a musician with a future. He was also a fairly good reader (although he denies this), which meant that he would be invited to contribute to the ongoing Menuhin projects. In late 1979, the next of these took Stéphane back to Abbey Road Studios, with Max Harris again handling the arrangements and a wonderful line-up including Laurie Holloway, drummer Ronnie Verrell and the inventive and versatile harpist David Snell. This could easily have resulted in easy-listening *schmaltz*, but Stéphane manages to lift the proceedings with some inventive variations over the lush strings. He was a fiddle player who liked working with strings, and at last he had found a steady income from a major record label that paid a good royalty.

With Yehudi, there was also a genuine and warm friendship, obvious from all the photographs Stéphane kept in his crowded shoeboxes of snaps and memorabilia. In that year, some of the Abbey Road sessions were recorded for *The South Bank Show*, one of Britain Televisions major art showcases, celebrating the duo's success. For Stéphane, it was enough that the sessions were eventually orchestrated by Nelson Riddle: 'The maestro of Frank Sinatra is good enough for me!'

In early 1980, Stéphane was once more playing with Laurie Holloway. 'We used to do things like *Jazz Club* on BBC Radio throughout the '60s, '70s and 80s, whenever he needed a piano player and I was free,' recalls Holloway. 'Before me, Stéphane used to use Alan Clare a lot, a fantastic piano player. Then Stéphane and I did two albums, which I arranged. The music was JS Bach and The Beatles – not a good vehicle to play jazz on. It was a commercial thing.'

Although Stéphane retained his reservations about 'jazz Bach', he was in good hands with Laurie's arrangements. The *Norwegian Wood* album recorded with Holloway and flautist Elena Duran, gave Stéphane the opportunity to experiment with tunes that were already becoming standards: 'Yesterday', 'Eleanor Rigby', 'Here, There And Everywhere' and 'Michelle'. Stéphane brings a classical grace to 'Yesterday', and he and Elena take turns at weaving counterpoint around the familiar melodies. Laurie then gives a Baroque tilt to 'All My Loving' and, although there's not much jazz, the flute and violin are beautifully framed. Laurie even brings a bagpipe-like piano drone to the title track. It's a perfect album for light-entertainment radio.

Asked to do a live gig, Laurie had a surprise introduction to Stéphane's piano playing: 'I remember doing a concert with Steph at Reading, the Hexagon. He'd done the first half with the Hot Club line-up and I was due to come and play piano with him in the second. We were about to go on and he said, "Laurie, I think I'll just play something first," and he went on and played the piano like Art Tatum – absolutely fantastic. It made me feel awful having to follow him on. He was a tremendous piano player.'

For Stéphane, however, Laurie was the perfect pianist: 'My bag was accompanying,' he revealed. 'I never liked being out front. I was on *This Is Your Life* and they all said I was one of the great accompanists. Well, that's what I like doing. I look, listen and I accompany, instead of trying to impress. I try to inspire them to do something different.

'I used to drop out now and then. Some of the best accompanying is silence. If you're too busy all the time, you just get on their nerves, so I just used to tinker along and then just give him eight bars on his own. Well, it picks 'em up a bit – "Whoops! What's going on here?"'

It's notable that the albums released at this time didn't feature the regular trio. It seems that Stéphane was drawing a clear distinction between the recording and performing bands. John Etheridge: 'The album *At The Winery* is on two electric guitars, with Martin Taylor. At the time I was with him, Stéphane wasn't recording with the touring band and was due to record with George Shearing. He said, "I have this album to do at Paul Masson. I'm having difficulties with Shearing. I'll have to do it with you."'

This sad falling-out of George and Stéphane stemmed from Grappelli's story of those early years in London. John: 'Stéphane would say, "He's my pianist! I discovered him." Shearing was very proud.'

Whatever the reason for the split, it provided a good opportunity for the road band to record their developing technique. The live session recorded for *At The Winery* was part of the 'Paul Masson Mountain Winery Vintage Sounds' concert series recorded in Saratoga, California, in September 1980, and the album reflects a lot more than just disaffection with George's keyboard genius. The guitar band now has a sophistication that has moved on from the Hot Club Quintet sound, with both John and Martin contributing inventive and challenging material for Stéphane.

On 'Just You Just Me', Martin displays the solo counterpoint style that will make him rightly famous, his guitar supplying its own walking-bass line to a very inspired intro including subtle use of a foot-operated volume control. Stéphane then responds with violin pyrotechnics and Martin returns with some break-it-down explorations that are a long way from the television lollipops that are becoming so familiar. Together, Martin and Stéphane share intricate unison passages that leave the Californian audience delighted.

At the time that the album was recorded, Stevie Wonder was at the peak of his influence on the contemporary music scene and 'You Are the Sunshine Of My Life' was a current favourite as an improvising launchpad. Wonder's roots in the mainstream pop of Detroit's hit factory Tamla Motown had recently stretched out into what was seen as the jazz territory of complex harmonic patterns beneath an appealingly simple and catchy melody. Both John and Martin contribute their own takes on 'Sunshine', with John sounding the most mainstream, almost evoking Barney Kessel. Stéphane meanwhile sounds as relaxed as ever and clearly states the theme before launching into his melodic arabesques. He listens as hard as ever and echoes his guitarist's ideas while adding gems of his own. During the intros, Jack Sewing provides a solid bass with a rhythmic punch.

Always searching, Stéphane experiments on electric viola for 'Taking A Chance On Love' and 'Willow Weep For me'. The lower register of the instrument obviously interests him, but the real star of 'Taking A Chance...' is John, who performs one of his best ever extended solos. 'Willow...' works best as a viola vehicle, with Stéphane handing over to Jack's bass, playing an illusion of the same octave. The end cadenza is probably Stéphane's most successful recording with the aid of direct current, although the instrument still robs Stéphane of some subtle dynamic shading.

On 'Minor Swing', Stéphane is dazzling, effortlessly bringing invention to a trinket he composed with Django over 40 years earlier. The two guitarists have a ball, swapping electric-guitar phrases, culminating in a carefully-worked-out unison that brings Stéphane back with a cheer-drowned trill. It's another demonstration of just how generously Stéphane gave the spotlight to others. He seems content to let the glory be shared, even if he's left mid-stage for five minutes with nothing to do.

Clearly he had no real sense of his own celebrity, and perhaps occasionally upset others by not acknowledging theirs. 'He never recognised anybody, so you always had to tell him,' recalls John Etheridge. 'We were playing in New York and the dressing room door opened and in came Les Paul. Stéphane's in the corner, taking no notice, and Les goes into one of his stories – "I was in Paris and I tore up a $20 bill and said to a taxi driver, "Find me Django and you can have the other half," and so on. Anyway, we started the gig and Les's amplifier is there onstage, and suddenly, halfway through the gig, he leaps to the stage and starts joining in. Steph carries on bemused and comes over to me and says, "Who is this guy?" So I say, "It's Les Paul, Steph. He's very famous!" He wasn't being snobbish; he just realised he'd done it again, not recognising anybody, so he says, "Come on, baby. One more time!" And then he slings his arm round him and they get their photo taken for *The Village Voice*.'

The gig over, Stéphane quickly reverted to his routine. John again: 'He was so quick, such a fast person. Gig's finished, violin's in the case, *woompf!* Everything economical and quick – done. He didn't like to dwell on things.'

23 Companions For Life

'He had an incredibly engaging personality and everybody felt that. It was incredibly unself-conscious, and that's why it was so engaging, almost like a child.'

– John Etheridge

The 1980s had started badly for entertainment. Stéphane was particularly moved by the loss of innovative storyteller Alfred Hitchcock. According to a friend of his, Stéphane would often sit up in his hotel room, watching his old movies with the rapt innocence of a child: 'He enjoyed a lot of old black-and-white pre-war movies – Humphrey Bogart, Harry Baur. Raimu and Gabin, the classic French stars, they were certainly a favourite.'

At least Hitchcock, the master of suspense, was of a decent age; Peter Sellers, another great original, had been only 55. Sir Billy Butlin, a champion of variety entertainment as well as the 1930s originator of the holiday camp, had had a good innings, but Stéphane was no doubt as shocked as everyone by the premature death from cancer of the film star Steve McQueen. All of these losses occurred within a span of eight months.

Worse news was the cold-blooded shooting of ex-Beatle John Lennon outside his home at the Dakota Building in New York's Manhattan. With the fragility that comes with age, Stéphane must have no doubt wondered at a world that was not perhaps more violent but nevertheless seemed so, with the growing speed of the communications media.

The 1980s also started with a global swing to political conservatism. This was the age of Prime Minister Margaret Thatcher in England, President Ronald Reagan in the USA and President Giscard d'Estaing in France. Although Stéphane himself erred to the political right, this has to be seen in the perspective of French politics, where the left has often been associated with extremism.

As a buffer against life's tragedy and accelerating change, Stéphane sought companionship. Very close personal relationships were rare, perhaps as a result of a very deep-rooted insecurity rooted in loss – he had, after all, lost his mother at the age of four and his father to another wife when only eight. His father passed away in 1939 and Gwendoline Turner tragically in 1940. As long as I knew him, he seemed to keep most people at a polite distance. After so much tragedy and personal pain, intimacy was perhaps too big a risk.

Companionship, though, was important. He always said of Django Reinhardt, 'If I had a friend in my life, it was him.' Their friendship lasted from 1931 to 1953, and from 1952 onwards he had shared his life with Jean Barclay. Then, in 1980, Jean tragically contracted cancer. Her sister Pamela Reid remembers, 'He appeared very little during the year when she was ill. He came over once, I think, with young Stéphane. Never visited in the hospital at all. I think he couldn't bear illness. Jean never complained. When she died, in Epsom, I called to tell him, and we had the funeral in the Catholic church. Stéphane didn't come but Evelyne's husband offered to come, but in the end he didn't. In January 1981, we took the ashes to Ireland, and they are in little graveyard next to the family house. Jean had bought out Stéphane's half of the King's Road lease, and in her will she said she'd like him to stay there as long as he wanted, but he said he didn't want to stay. Stéphane visited the grave during the '80s.' It's the tragedy of those that live to a good age that they suffer the loss of all their friends. Once more, Stéphane was alone.

Ultimately, of course, the star is always alone. People have paid money to see a show and it's their name that draws audiences from their warm fires on cold nights across congested cities in the rain. The celebrity stands alone in the light and delivers. Stéphane occasionally had harsh words for the man who said, 'the show must go on': 'Me, I'm an old trooper so I start alone.'

The loneliness and pressure of life on the road occasionally led to childlike and ultimately harmless outbursts of pique. John Etheridge recalls, 'He used to throw wonderful tantrums. We got used to them, but people who hadn't seen them before were taken aback. I remember Martin and I used to have a laugh over these things. On one particular occasion, in the Montreal Sheraton Hotel, the foyer was packed. Apparently Stéphane went to his room and his room wasn't ready and Abby Hoffer had arrived from New York and forgotten his mail. And this was a big deal. Stéphane used to write 80 postcards every day, so this was the last straw. Martin and I were watching from behind the pillar: "I'm fed up. I've been here with this twerp..." and he does a little war dance like a toddler and leaps up and down. The whole foyer is in shock, mouths open, and you can see the promoter thinking, "He won't play." Martin and I are chortling in the corner. He's completely revved up, and then it gradually subsides and very soon it's all forgotten: "Oh, I'm sorry, Abby, but I was very unhappy about my mail. I need it." It all blows over in about ten minutes, absolutely amazing – dance and rotate at the same time, but completely unmalicious, just like a child's tantrum.'

Stéphane was 73 and still agile and relatively fit when, in 1981, he met Joseph Oldenhove de Guertechin, who would become his manager and his companion for the rest of his life. When he was tired he would call this young man 'Django'. De Guertechin, a Belgian citizen had come to Paris to study. I caught up him in Montmartre, where he still deals with the day-to-day matters of Stéphane's estate: 'I met Stéphane in 1981, completely by chance. I was a student of comic drama and I was renting a room in a friend's apartment. He, Daniel Desvignes, was invited to dinner with Stéphane. He asked me to ring Stéphane to confirm the time. On the telephone, Stéphane, realising I was a friend of Daniel, invited me to join them.

'I know now that it was unusual for Stéphane to invite a stranger, but perhaps it was because he felt I was a friend of a friend. Also I didn't know much about Stéphane. I knew he was a musician and I knew the name, but I didn't know what kind of music. It was only later that I realised he was a very famous musician. At that time, ironically, I wouldn't have recognised his music.

'When I met him for the dinner, he had already forgotten the invitation. It was a misunderstanding. We took flowers to his flat and he had already had dinner. I think Stéphane was just expecting to meet for a drink or something. This was something about Stéphane – when he was at home, away from the show, he would treat many of his friends like family. So he said, "I will go into the fridge, take an egg and I will organise a dinner for you."

At our first meeting, the television was on, and I remember he asked me to sit next to him. He took my hand, and it was like the grandfather I never had. I was only 26 at that time and immediately we had a very intimate contact.

'He was very informal. I have a formal education, and if we have visitors, I will turn off the television. But it's quite nice, in a way – Stéphane would just say, "Come, let's watch the television together, get a tray and enjoy a film together." He would share with visitors that domestic intimacy. The next week, we invited him over to our place and very quickly I became a close friend.

'Before all this, I was a young actor doing stupid things in advertising and small parts in television, having studied theatre in Paris. I had come to drama by chance and I loved it, but I was not yet successful.

I never decided to become Stéphane's personal manager; it was more like fate. In 1981 Stéphane said he would like me to share his apartment in Rue Dunkerque, which he had had since 1968. I was living in a small room in Montmartre's Rue Ramey, and the move benefited us both. Stéphane didn't like to be on his own, so he was pleased to have somebody like me. I realised also that he cared for me very much, and that's how I became part of his life.

'Eventually I would travel with Stéphane to see his agents and make arrangements. I became involved in conversations about the tours and more and more Stéphane considered that I was able to do that for him. Gradually, that evolved into personal management. I had to make the choice: travelling all over the world with a famous musician or continuing the round of castings and all that. I enjoyed what I did, but it was so interesting being with Stéphane. I couldn't do both, so I made the choice.

'Before drama, I had also studied tourism for two years, so I was prepared for travel. Also, I had studied Latin and Greek – good for languages. By coincidence, Stéphane's father was a classical scholar as well.

'Stéphane had many agents and many promoters, some of whom dealt directly with me. It was very flexible. We would try and arrange the travel with a minimum of fuss and allow time to enjoy the places we visited. Sometimes we even went to places purely for enjoyment not for an income. Italy, for instance, was a pleasure destination. I travelled a little with him from '81 onwards and continued my acting. He was always very active and loved to walk. If we went to the opera, he would walk, and I often struggled to keep up with him.'

Stéphane's developing relationship with Joseph came at the right time. His new international fame meant a complicated web of contacts involving theatrical agents worldwide. He was no longer just a jazz artist doing an ad-hoc round of small clubs; he was performing in the world's major venues at sell-out concerts from Sydney to New York and was also recording in the United States, Europe and Japan under major contracts, including the one with EMI. Everywhere he travelled, the local television networks wanted additional dates to add the Grappelli magic to their output.

The stage persona of the now-acknowledged genius had perplexed John Etheridge from the beginning. The guitarist had enjoyed the myth and the magic but remains as mystified by its source as he had been in 1976: 'Martin Taylor and I talked about this a lot. What *was* that magic? People would fall in love with Stéphane Grappelli. Niels Pedersen, Larry Coryell, they all fell under this weird spell that he had. It was very unconscious. We all felt that this was to do with the way he was brought up. For instance, his outbursts re mothers. He would say, "When I hear someone who is rude to their mother, I want to punch them on the nose because I lose my mother when I was three. I know what it is to not have a mother."' Stéphane, meanwhile, felt indebted to Etheridge for his insights into more modern music.

John decided to move on in late 1980 and has since forged a very successful career with his own groups, developing a very individual style that incorporates all the best of a century of jazz guitar.

Back once more in San Francisco in 1981, the indefatigable Stéphane recorded another album for Concord, the label associated with the previous *At The Winery* recordings, this one released under the title *Vintage 1981*. In the UK, Diz Disley was briefly back on guitar, although not for this tour. Instead New Yorker Mike Garri sat in with Jack Sewing and Martin Taylor, providing an economical and understated guitar in a cool West Coast way, very in keeping with the San Franciscan climate.

On Martin Taylor's composition 'Jamie', written for his young son, Stéphane explores the impressionistic landscape presented by the tone colour of the Fender Rhodes piano. This instrument had originated in the same California factories as the Fender guitars and basses by now dominating popular music, but with its soft sustained tone it had found a place in the jazz palette of Miles Davis and his keyboards man, Joe Zawinul. On this session, Stéphane sounds as if he's enjoying this new instrument and exploring its possibilities.

Also new was yet another electric violin, which Stéphane referred to as an alto model or viola, manufactured by Barcus Berry and used on 'I Can't Get Started'. Stéphane clearly loved the amplified fiddle's 'cello-like lower register and draws a lot from it on this track, but ironically his normally faultless intonation wavers. Perhaps he had difficulty in adjusting to the lack of direct aural contact (acoustically the electric fiddle would have made little sound). Then again, it may have been the adjustment to the longer scale length of the viola. Nevertheless, *Vintage 1981* is still a good album.

1981 was also the year in which Stéphane and Matt Glasser published their book *Jazz Violin*. This remarkable volume sets Stéphane's technique in perspective alongside that of his contemporaries, as well as providing an invaluable insight for other players. Matt is himself a fiddler and had worked with Stéphane on *King Of The Gypsies*, and was then playing with a band called Fiddle Fever. Stéphane provides a foreword for the book in which he warns that his isn't a model for others to copy: 'Au contraire, I hope they can find for themselves something new to do.

'I hope this will give young people…some confidence and help them morally – that somebody like me, who never studied the violin, can do it, then maybe they've got a chance themselves.

'For those who are really musicians, there is no problem, they will always find their way; but I'm sure this book will bring them, with the musical transcriptions, considerable help.'

The transcriptions themselves are fascinating. Glasser doesn't just include direct transcriptions of Stéphane's solos, enlightening as they are, but instead takes the imaginative leap of comparing blues improvisations by Jean-Luc Ponty, Sven Asmussen, Eddie South, Joe Venuti, Stuff Smith and Stéphane. He also analyses the trio sessions from Stéphane, Sven and Jean-Luc and duets from Stéphane and Eddie South, even including the prepared variations written for Stéphane's duets with Yehudi Menuhin. These musical examples are bolstered by interviews with Yehudi, Jean-Luc and Stéphane. Grappelli also offers this insight into his mercurial adjustment to the musical company he finds himself in: 'It all depends on the musicians that I'm playing with. If I'm playing with Martial Solal, I won't play in the same style as with Oscar Peterson. The water goes where there is possibility for it to go – music is the same. When I play with people who are playing in Django's style, instinctively I go back to the way I played years ago. And if I was to play with McCoy Tyner, I'm sure that marvellous musician would make me play differently than I do now.'

The McCoy Tyner reference was surely a hint to the future, but that collaboration would wait another nine years before its realisation. However, Stéphane's observation 'water goes where there is a possibility for it to go' is very akin to Zen philosophy. Travel was clearly introducing Stéphane to many new possibilities.

The Solal reference is also very topical. With Martial, he had recently recorded his only ever venture into atonality, 'Et Si l'on Improvsait?', and it clearly wasn't a struggle. The work sat ironically on the track listing for the album *Happy Reunion* next to a rework of 'Stumblin'', the Mitchell's Jazz Kings track that had launched Stéphane into Jazz 57 years earlier. Atonality and New Orleans jazz side by side? Stéphane had no problem with that.

Indeed, this is a crucial point. Stéphane could play anything. What we hear is what he *chooses* to play, and that privilege of genius is fascinating. He preferred the diatonic, the conventional do-re-mi, and liked to play in key, but it was a conscious choice.

The same privilege is evident in another early resident of Montmartre, Pablo Picasso, arguably the greatest artist of the 20th century. From the evidence of his student work Picasso could paint with the technique of Rembrandt at the age of 12, so what he *chose* to paint therefore becomes that much more interesting.

To Matt Glasser, Stéphane made an important point about his choice to explore melodic improvisation: 'I think it's better that, when you start to play, play strictly melody. Everybody should, by politeness to the composer, play what he composed. I got that idea from Benny Goodman when I was 22, 23. I was amazed with his quality, you see, with Gene Krupa, Lionel Hampton. Marvellous. Also Teddy Wilson – he was in fact the favourite pianist of Django. So all these records gave me the idea, because I was in such a hurry to improvise on anything, why not first expose nicely the theme? So if I play the melody first, the audience knows later on what I'm doing; it's based on that melody, but it's absolutely something else. I like to expose the theme, but after I play the theme I like to go somewhere else myself.

'Jazz playing comes naturally. I just put my finger anywhere and be very attentive to what I've got behind me. If the accompaniment is absolutely perfect and I know they are going to play a certain chord in the right moment, then I can launch myself in an arabesque and what you call improvisation, which is in fact improvisation on a theme. You try to find a melodic line. That means you and the composer get very close.'

Away from the platform, Stéphane's taste in fine art was less about choice. Joseph Oldenhove told me about one of Stéphane's slightly reluctant art gallery visits: 'The Museum of Lille had just reopened. He paused in front of a Renoir and enjoyed that. He loved Impressionist art, Monet and Manet. Once we visited Monet's gardens in Giverny when it was quiet, not many people about. He enjoyed that and was also intrigued by the wonderful collection of Japanese prints.'

To Joseph, Stéphane seemed philosophical about artistic taste: 'He wouldn't criticise modern art such as Picasso; he would say, "It's just me. I don't understand it." For instance, he told me that, at an early Paris performance of Bizet's *Carmen*, the audience booed, and now of course it is acclaimed music. It's more a question of period or fashion.'

The reference to Stéphane's slight reluctance to visit the gallery, however, is about choice. Left to his own devices, Grappelli preferred nature: 'In cities, Stéphane would visit the botanical gardens as soon as we could. We also went to museums. I preferred art galleries while he liked the zoo or natural-history museums, also aquariums. He was very, very interested in the natural world. He was so curious, always wanted to learn something new. We would compromise and eventually he would join me at the art gallery.'

The curiosity, the desire for knowledge, fitted well with the sudden surge of global tours. 'That made him very alive and very interested throughout his life,' Joseph continues. 'In a way, that's why he never retired, because he was so pleased to travel, and as he said, to be paid for travelling and to enjoy that, why not go on? He would say, "We live like millionaires without being millionaires." Very good hotels, first-class travel for the long distances. For us, it was an honour that he would go on working. At his age it was good sense – first class because he needed it.

'Also we had suites at the hotel, but Stéphane didn't enjoy that because I was too far away. He preferred connecting rooms so he could call me if he needed anything. He was very practical. He would be happy with smaller rooms.'

Joseph also provides a valuable insight into Stéphane's auto-didactic approach to analysis and understanding: 'Stéphane was very curious. When travelling, if he needed to rest, he would, but if he was OK, he would be off exploring York Minster or Canterbury Cathedral or whatever, always very curious and wanting to learn.

'Stéphane would often look with wonder at very simple things, perhaps a train drawing into a station in the country, or in New York he would be in front of a skyscraper and you could see that he was counting the floors. He would try and comprehend how it was built. At first I thought he was a bit of an idiot, but afterwards I realised that I was the idiot and he could look with innocence and wonder. He would watch a plane take off with that same gaze.

'It was the same in listening to the music that he played. In the recording studio all the musicians would rehearse and Stéphane might have a partition in front of him and would appear to be the one who didn't understand anything. He would ask questions: "Why did you write it that way?" You would think he was the pupil, who had never done that before. He was never ashamed to ask. He was not proud. Then it came to the take and he invariably astonished the other musicians.'

I suggested that this held a valuable clue to Stéphane's understanding of what he played. He was one of the great musical improvisers, and for that you need a complete understanding of what you're playing – not just intellectual understanding but a profoundly felt comprehension of the material as it is, not perhaps as it first appears.

To digress momentarily, music is fascinating in its relationship between device and effect. Changing one note in a chord, the device, can have an enormous emotional effect, and indeed whole songs are based on this principle. George Harrison's 'Something' is a good example. In the phrase 'something in the way she moves', the one-note change on the word 'moves' is a crucial but simple device – everyone hears the dramatic glide from the plain major chord to the Romantic 'move' of the major seventh. Although only one note has changed, that simple device evokes a character. Perhaps this is like Stéphane trying to understand the construction of a skyscraper, mentally taking it apart as a curious child dismantles a watch to see what makes it tick. So much of what we see and hear we take for granted. Stéphane, pursuing the *auto-didacte* education of his youth, had been compelled to build on and retain his child's sense of wonder and endless curiosity. He never seemed to lose that.

Joseph agreed and added, 'He also looked at people in the same way. Everybody who met Stéphane was touched by that.'

So the once-reluctant traveller began to enjoy his new lifestyle, but not the celebrity status, and certainly not at home: 'Stéphane was unrefined and uninhibited, except with strangers. For instance, if a neighbour invited him for a cup of tea with a lot of strangers, he hated that because he was very shy. He didn't like being the celebrity. He didn't consider celebrity as important.'

On the road, however, he would enjoy the treats: 'There were many surprises. Once, after a concert in Belgrade in the former Yugoslavia, he was invited onto a boat for dinner to be greeted by 20 or 30 gypsy violins. He loved that. Also, he had visited Japan on a cruise ship in the late '60s but didn't tour there until the '80s and he loved Japan. He enjoyed the kindness and the welcome of the public. Also the dress.'

Stéphane and I once discussed our separate Japanese experiences and we shared an astonishment at the precision of everything, from trains that ran on time to hectic schedules. Joseph added, 'Everything was so precise. Three months in advance, they want to know the stage layout, the exact distance between the guitar and the violin, an exact plan of the stage and an exact set list. Often at the last minute it all changed. It became very complicated, but in the end I think they even enjoyed the changes.' One member of the Japanese delegation presented Stéphane with a charming geisha doll dressed in silk, and this took pride of place in his Rue Dunkerque sitting room.

The travel meant more opportunities for collecting, but when Joseph met Stéphane collectibles were already a feature of the Rue Dunkerque and Cannes apartments: 'Stéphane had some very good antiques, some good furniture, but he wasn't especially an antique collector. The story is that, when he was in England during the Second World War, he met a lady called Mrs Poulter in Petersham, a friend of Queen Mary, and she had beautiful jade. And I remember Stéphane telling me that, when the Queen was coming to her home, she would hide the jade because otherwise the Queen would say, "Oh, this one is so lovely! I would love to have one like that," and of course she would feel obliged to give it to the Queen.'

Many of Stéphane's musicians remember Stéphane adopting similar tactics when invited to a rich patron's home. However, the core of Stéphane's collection had been built up in his years in England, starting in 1939. 'He had the opportunity to buy many beautiful antiques at that time, and then unfortunately, when he had to move back, he had to get rid of a lot of his beautiful carpets,' recalled Joseph. 'He had a very good eye and instinctive taste. He would spot a piece of wood in the junk box and it would be Louis XIV and maybe nobody realised. Now it's very fashionable, but at one time you could find antiques in a lot of places were people didn't know what they had. Stéphane was able to find pieces like that and to organise them in his apartment in Cannes in a way that was very beautiful, well decorated with a natural taste.

'He was very curious and well read, not especially about antiques but he was well up on history and literature, very *auto-didacte*. He loved English silver. In 1982, in Paris, he was burgled of a lot of Georgian silver and he knew exactly what he had.'

At this stage in Stéphane's life, Ed Baxter was firmly in control of his UK bookings and was more comfortable with the personality: 'At first I was in a wee bit of awe of him, the great Grappelli. "Mr Grappelli", it was, then after a while it was "Steph". Then he was fine, easy. He had no problem. My job was to get him on the platform, make sure the piano was in tune if we had one, that the sound was OK, those kind of things, so that all he had to do was play.'

Ed observed that initially the sound crews, perhaps more used to rock music, where the dynamic is loud and louder, had to adjust to Grappelli's more subtle approach: 'We used to say to the sound guy, "That's it. It's acoustic, it's all set.

Don't touch anything. If he wants to play softer, he'll pull back from the microphone. You don't have to wiggle anything on the sound desk for volume or whatever."'

Stéphane also expected modest creature comforts, particularly 'a comfortable, warm, dressing room,' remembers Ed. 'He always liked warmth, Steph. A good hotel and good food. One of the times he came to Edinburgh with Len Skeat, on the final day we went to the Café Royal in Edinburgh, one of *the* places to have lunch. I paid for the meal and he was tickled pink. He also liked traditional British food – a great guy for steak pie and shepherd's pie. But he liked French cooking as well.

But it was Joseph who often saw to Stéphane's diet at home and on the road: 'As a child, naturally he loved pastries and, as an adult, pasta, probably because of his father. He didn't like Japanese food very much, but he was very open. In New York he loved pastrami, in Morocco cous-cous, but he could eat a hamburger with as much joy when we in the United States. He wasn't a fan of very sophisticated cuisine; he was very open – if a restaurant was good, OK, but if he had to wait an hour between courses, he wouldn't enjoy that. He remained open and free to judge everything on its merit.'

Joseph went on to observe Stéphane's pragmatic approach to his occasional 'hospitality picnics': 'The street urchin of Montmartre would rationalise, "I have food in my dressing room and I will enjoy that much more than waiting an hour in a fancy restaurant for a few oysters, where I have to be interrogated by people I will never see again." It was not avarice; it was just common sense. He also took the bottle of whisky that he had in his dressing room, rationalising, "If I don't take it, the crew will, so why not me?" He wasn't over-concerned about what people thought of that. To him it made sense.'

Ed: 'You took care of these little things for Steph and there were very rarely any problems.'

Like John and Martin, however, Ed observed the occasional outburst: 'He had his tantrums here and there where something was going wrong, but it was invariably something to do with the music. Or if he was sitting on his chair, doing a soundcheck or something, and the microphone was slack and it started to move, he'd get mad at that for a couple of minutes, but that's it.

'Too-strong lights were always a bit of contention. I always used to say. "But Steph, this is a big hall, 2,000 seats. You need them so they can see at the back." "Oh yes, I see what you mean…but if you can make it softer, OK? The lights distract us a bit."

'But any problems we had were always to do with things like that, nothing personal. I never had to worry about him getting his end right. The onus was on me to make everything as nice and comfortable and easy as possible. That was part of the job. I was doing things for him, helping him, and that helped too with our relationship. We never had an argument, really.'

Ed also observed Stéphane's occasional asides and a quiet preparation before a performance: 'The odd time he shared thoughts on people, [he would say], "Oh, I don't like him much. He's a bit chi-chi." I never knew what "chi-chi" meant. Steph knew he was a star in the jazz-music business, but he never flouted it or went round saying, "I'm so-and-so." He wasn't putting that on. He was a bit shy, which seems daft to say about a guy that went on the platform. Steph always liked to go on – *boom!* – so he always warmed up with a tune. He'd play a couple of tunes in the dressing room or maybe, if he was playing a new tune, he'd try out the chords so that, by the time they got on, everything was prepared.'

To me, it's clear that Stéphane was trying to attain a state of relaxation to which many performers aspire. The best playing is often achieved when you're not consciously thinking of the music and, instead, it comes through you. Stéphane clearly attained that state frequently. As Ed notes, 'I remember him saying to the guys once, "When I go, be with me because I can't stop. When I'm into my improvisation, be with me because I don't know where I am. I'm in another world." He used to make some of these tunes sound like a concerto, especially at the end. He used to have the audiences in an absolute whirl, in the palm of his hand. Even after a concert I've heard him say, "You know when I was playing so-and-so? I was thinking about that meal we had," and you think, "How the Devil can you play like that and think about a meal you had in a restaurant?"'

Ed also recalls Stéphane's subtle humour: 'He was good on the platform. He could make a joke. In Edinburgh once, he was introducing the guys: "Diz Disley from London and Martin Taylor from Scotland, and I'm from gay Paree – it's not as gay as it used to be." That's another kind of improvisation.'

In 1982, both Diz and Martin returned briefly to the fold for an American tour. Performing again at the Paul Masson Vineyards in Saratoga, the band were caught on film by Carlos N Broulion and Raymond G Poirier. On the film, the atmosphere is perfect California as a standing-room-only crowd fan themselves in the summer-afternoon heat. Shade is at a premium as the Californians jockey for space beneath colourful sunshades. Stéphane is relaxed in pink trousers and a floral shirt, the band semi-concealed behind colourful flowers and a backdrop of greenery. Everyone is enjoying some fine music-making in a delightful setting, and no doubt some wine has been tasted.

Stéphane is at the top of his form and enjoying the contrasting delights of his two guitarists – Diz sings along happily to his Maccaferri solos on 'Let's Fall In Love' and offers an interesting intro to 'After You've Gone', while Martin is cool and electric, now a seasoned professional with an established solo career. Stéphane jokes with his audience, 'A few weeks ago [*sic*], in 1942 in England with Django Reinhardt, we needed a record so we improvised this little tune, "Swing 42".' The acoustic and electric guitars blend beautifully and Stéphane enjoys himself thoroughly, dancing above them and Jack Sewing's bass. He then goes on to offer the happy Independence Day crowd a fantastically virtuosic 'Honeysuckle Rose' with a very subtle tremolando passage. The master is completely at ease.

Three days later, the same band gathered at San Francisco's Great American Music Hall. The footage from this event shows Stéphane giving the capacity crowd 'Minor Swing' – 'I don't want to remember the date!' – and switching again to the electric viola, which is painted a deep, striking blue. 'It doesn't match my shirt! I give you not *Rhapsody In Blue* but [offstage prompt from Martin Taylor] 'Here, There And Everywhere' by…Lennon…?' Then Martin takes over: 'By Lennon and McCartney. You must learn that!' Then again Stéphane digs in to the low register of the viola, accompanied by Martin's chorus-pedal guitar. Still not wanting to be left behind at the age of 74, Stéphane is still searching for new sounds.

Perhaps prompted by the music-hall setting, Stéphane then gives a very rhapsodic 'Danny Boy' on solo piano, showing he still has complete command of his technique. Then, as a late surprise guest, David Grisman comes on with fellow mandolinist Mike Marshall and another fiddler, Darol Anger. Together with bassist Rob Wasserman, the quintet perform an impromptu 'Sweet Georgia Brown' which soon turns into a fun version of duelling mandolins and duelling fiddles. The crowd gives them all a standing ovation as the sun sinks in a golden crown behind the Bay Bridge.

On returning to Paris, Stéphane next embarked on an important musical relationship with two fellow Frenchmen, guitarist Marc Fosset and bassist Patrice Caratini, who had an established reputation as a duo. Both understood and performed music reflecting Stéphane's roots in the era of the *bals musette*, and Stéphane was particularly taken with Marc's facility as an accompanist: 'He is very sympathetic. For me, it's like working again with Django, not for the virtuosity but the accompaniment.'

Fosset was born in Paris in 1949 and had played the guitar professionally from 1971, including collaborations with Martial Solal, Maurice Vander and the accordionist Marcel Azola.

The two French musicians are soon seen with Stéphane in another video, recorded, as the title attests, *Live In New Orleans*. On this occasion, Martin Taylor remains on electric guitar with Marc taking an acoustic role, though definitely not a back seat; on 'After You've Gone', the left-handed guitarist supplies a sensitive introduction, with Patrice providing some inspired counterpoint. On his solo, Marc plays unusually with a plectrum on a Spanish classical guitar. Together with Patrice's conga patterns on the table of the double bass and Marc's subsequent scat chorus, this is another unusual frame for the classic Grappelli swing, still searching for new pastures.

Being in New Orleans would have been a sort of pilgrimage for Stéphane. He was never overtly sentimental, but he had lived in the jazz century and this city on the Mississippi Delta was the cradle of his art. A snapshot taken at the time shows him in cloth cap and scarf, proudly smiling in the Old French Quarter, a cornet blast away from Preservation Hall.* He must have wondered, as so many have before, about the mysterious roots of jazz.

The ingredients of that gumbo are well documented: the blues, spirituals, ragtime piano and old military brass instruments left over from the Civil War. But what of the Gallic influence in this most French of American cities? Stéphane knew that Jelly-Roll Morton, the self-proclaimed inventor of jazz, had cited French quadrille[†] as an important factor. In Paris, the *quadrilles eccentrique* had become the audacious can-can; in New Orleans, perhaps the cakewalk.

---

*Established in a late-18th-century *porte-cochere* (carriage house) on St Peter Street, in 1961 Preservation Hall became a home for traditional jazz after a varied life as a tavern, shop and artists' studio, and since the 1960s it has become a mecca for the jazz fraternity. Stéphane would have empathised with the words of William Carter, who writes in his masterful book *Preservation Hall*, 'The real secret of New Orleans music comes in the realisation that a man no longer needs to run after it or try to become it, because he already is it. Certainly there is learning to be done in some conventional musical ways. But the essence, formidable to many who lack African roots, is not so much in adding things, tensely filling up every space, forcing, mastering and intending, as in releasing, shedding stiffness, letting go the four-square order, celebrating the accidental and becoming one with the dance. The music creates the player, flowing not from him but through him.'

[†] One of the most popular sets of ballroom dances of the 19th century was *à quadrille de contradanses*. The music of the quadrille was made up of lively rhythmic themes of rigid 8- or 16-bar lengths. Jelly-Roll Morton once told Alan Lomax, 'Many of the earliest tunes in New Orleans was from French origin. I'm telling you, when they started playing this little thing, they would really whoop it up. Everybody got hot and threw their hats away: "C'ette n'aut can-can, paye donc, c'ette n'aut can-can, paye donc."'

Being a practical man, Stéphane would just have listened and played. Here he was at last in the place that inspired his hero Louis Armstrong and his old friend Sidney Bechet, and that would have been enough.

Stéphane was particularly pleased to be at last acknowledged in America, the birthplace of jazz and a place that in 1926 must have seemed no more than a myth. In 1981, he'd been voted Best Violinist in both the critics' and readers' polls of *Down Beat*, the most prestigious jazz journal in the world, and in 1983 he was inducted into the magazine's exclusive Hall of Fame. At 75 years old, he was at last jazz royalty.

24 Sitting Down But Still Dancing

'Now my birthday lasts all year. Wherever I go in the world, it's my birthday. But it's silly to speak of age – there is no age!'

– *Stéphane Grappelli*

For many in the Western democracies, the '80s were years of confusion and suppression. New technologies had brought fear of unemployment and the demise of much traditional industry. The stock market oscillated between boom and bust. Satellite communications continued to shrink the world and the computer age gradually dawned, with the internet emerging from a CIA past towards a dot-com future. The telephone, though still heavy, becomes wireless and fax machines hummed in every office. Royalty and celebrity began to merge in the world of glossy magazines and supermodels commandeered the catwalks. And of course music became increasingly electronic, with the CD revolution bringing lasers to the urban jungle. During this time of disquiet, Stéphane just carried on, happy to make his music wherever that took him.

At home in Paris with Marc Fosset in 1984, the duo recorded an album with just Stéphane's piano providing a change of tone colour, including the track 'Bossa Pour Didier', a tribute to Stéphane's French violin protégé Didier Lockwood.

Stéphane wasn't at home for long, however. 1983 had seen the creation of The Hot Club de France – Holland Foundation, an establishment that had made Stéphane an honorary member, and in February 1984 he gave two concerts in Amsterdam organised by their president, Georg Lankester. In typical fashion, Stéphane replied personally to the Foundation's congratulatory letters.

Later that year, in New York, Stéphane took part in an extraordinary transatlantic 50th-birthday tribute to the great British boxer Henry Cooper after it turned out that the sportsman was a Grappelli fan. Although booked into a week at the Bottom Line club, Stéphane consented to a satellite contribution, live onstage from West Fourth St with Martin Taylor and Marc Fosset, Stéphane played a spontaneous rendition of 'Happy Birthday' before launching into his familiar take on 'Shine'. On the existing BBC video recording,

Stéphane is relaxed, slim and clearly having a good time, finishing with a whispered 'happy birthday' and blowing two kisses to the distant and slightly amazed boxer. Very French!

As the '80s progressed, Stéphane was increasingly courted by the media. He was vaguely amused by this celebrity and didn't mind as long as the fuss was confined to working hours. Ed Baxter remembers the time: 'Say we went to a restaurant. They would like to plonk him down in the middle of a room and he'd always say he'd like to move to a quiet corner. He didn't like to be the centre of attention. That sort of thing was purely for the benefit of the restaurant, the waiters, who would say, "You know who's sitting over there? Stéphane Grappelli!"'

On-duty celebrity, on the other hand, was fine. May 1985 saw Stéphane in the English cathedral city of Canterbury. With his hands in his pockets, scarf jauntily akimbo, the television cameras follow Stéphane on his typical afternoon walkabout, admiring the dreaming gothic towers with a youthful spring in his step in the cathedral gardens, dressed casually like a teenager. Joseph Oldenhove told me, 'He had a common-sense approach to formality. He liked to be able to visit a cathedral in a T-shirt. If it causes offence, then by all means wear a tie, but if it is OK to be comfortable, then be comfortable.

'The visits to cathedrals and stately homes continued, but it wasn't just for architecture; it was for the art within them. For Stéphane, cathedrals, being artistic treasure houses for centuries, meant they were filled with interesting objects.'

For the subsequent televised concert at the Marlene Theatre, Stéphane's band retained Martin Taylor but also included Dutch bassist Jack Sewing and Irish guitarist Louis Stewart, who provided a firm rhythm on acoustic 'cello guitar, with Martin's contrasting electric guitar providing novel intros and dazzling solos. The two guitars complement each other perfectly, allowing Stéphane space to stretch. On 'Let's Fall In Love', he once more demonstrates his great listening facility, picking up and running with ideas from Stewart's acoustic guitar solo.

On 'Don't Get Around Much Any More', after having disappeared into the shadows to let Martin Taylor provide four choruses of very bluesy and inspired improvisation, Stéphane treats the audience to one of his signature virtuoso cadenzas, perhaps the best-preserved example on videotape. In typical fashion, the maestro then reminds the audience of the tune in a simple but elegant restatement, and then he's off. In a free, out-of-tempo style, he initially sticks to the chords, which are then embellished with harmonics, trills, portamentos and double-stops – indeed every trick in the repertoire of a fiddler of 65 years. Then he really takes off, improvising a canon in the style of JS Bach and embellishing this with more harmonics and a *bravura* flourish reminiscent once more of Yehudi Menuhin. The audience responds as expected with a warm ovation.

Fellow fiddler Ric Sanders was amazed when witnessing this display: 'Those late cadenzas are fascinating – bits of Bach, blues, so in the groove, little gems – flat fives and flat ninths, harmonics, all the jazz stuff, and then, on top of that, all the Impressionist stuff, Debussy and so on, all just effortlessly pulled together.'

Earlier, Stéphane had introduced one of his favourite pieces, his 'Gershwin Medley'. This would feature in most of his late concerts and, as here, usually began with the piece that he referred to as 'my lucky number', 'Someone To Watch Over Me'. On this rendition, Stéphane adds a cheeky 'Anybody!?' to his introduction, which gets a laugh but no offers. Martin Taylor's guitar introduction, meanwhile, has bell-like chords swimming in a gentle electric chorus replete with interesting suspensions, bread and butter for Stéphane. Indeed, he would complain if any of his guitarists gave him an uninspiring intro, once remarking to Ed Baxter, 'Did you hear that? What kind of introduction was that? He gives me no inspiration!'

Martin never let him down. Continuing out of tempo in a free and bewildering counterpoint, the two musicians dance around Gershwin with the liberty that only comes of complete understanding. They listen and respond to each other in seemingly effortless variation. As Stéphane once more launches into spine-tingling harmonics, Martin echoes these in arpeggios rich in his own guitar harmonics. Then Stéphane punctuates proceedings with a flourish on open strings, leading to Martin's segue into 'I Got Rhythm'.

This second Gershwin tune is the perfect vehicle for the essence of Grappelli's up-tempo style. Songwriter and Decca record producer Marcel Stellman once called Stéphane 'the epitome of swing' after having just listened to another of the fiddler's takes on the tune, which would became his anthem.

The two-part concert also featured 'Honeysuckle Rose', 'Nuages' and 'Daphne', ending with 'Sweet Georgia Brown', proving that The Hot Club Quintet repertoire and the Reinhardt-Grappelli compositions were still going strong after 50 years. Stéphane was at his physical peak, his musical imagination in full flight. Unbelievably, he was 77.

Meanwhile, *Jazz Hot* magazine celebrated its 50th birthday with a special anniversary edition featuring Stéphane on the cover and an interview, in which he rejoiced, 'I am free. I can do what I want. With the kind of person Django was, you had to wait, but now I'm in a hurry. I don't know if it's age. It's silly to speak of age. There is no age!'

But age has its trials, as Joseph Oldenhove reports: 'In 1985, Stéphane had a very bad illness, a tubercular problem, and many people thought he would not survive.' Stéphane had seemed invincible and consequently the collapse was more of a shock. 'I was very supportive at that time,' Joseph continues, 'and from then on I became much more responsible. I accompanied Stéphane on all the tours. From then on, he needed a lot of organisation from day to day. He had been very good on his feet, and then he became quite frail and he started to play sitting down.'

For many, this setback would have been disastrous, the prelude to retirement, slippers and a graceful step into seclusion. For Stéphane, though, that was all too boring: 'Retire? Why retire?'

Stéphane's playing certainly didn't suffer. The key to this was probably his effortless and largely empirical technique. Kato Havas, a world-renowned violin pedagogue, once commented, 'Stéphane's technique is an example of a perfectly integrated and natural approach to the instrument,' while Ric Sanders noted, 'With many players, often they are quite brilliant but you can see the mechanics of it. When Stéphane played, it was almost like he just smeared over the instrument – there was no sense of a machine, going up and down the instrument. With Stéphane you always felt his fingers should be moving more, there was so much coming out.'

Matt Glasser: 'Very little finger pressure is another Grappelli trademark, just enough to get the job done, no bearing down unnecessarily on notes. This [enabled him] to play at incredibly fast tempos.'

Stéphane himself had told American jazz magazine *Coda*, 'Nothing is difficult when you can do it. The only difficulty at my age is to stand up for long periods.'

Determined and dedicated to his craft, Stéphane was back on the road in a matter of months, his only concession from that point on being to perform sitting down, wherever possible. He was becoming an icon of a lost era, a symbol of swing and also, appropriately, of music hall and its reincarnation as variety.

In 1986, Stéphane was an honoured guest at a very special British Royal Variety Performance. Joseph Oldenhove told me this meant a lot to him: 'Stéphane had a lot of respect for the British royal family, almost as much as if he was British. As Stéphane spent the war in England, the Queen Mother particularly meant a lot to him.'

Indeed, the Queen Mother won the hearts of many of Stéphane's contemporaries on her visits to see the bombed-out citizens of the Blitz in 1940. He once said to me, 'I must look up to her. You must respect your elders.' That year the Queen Mum was 86, Stéphane a mere 78.

That particular Royal Variety Performance – an event by then the high point of Britain's mainstream entertainment calendar – was the 57th. Genuinely started by royal command on 2 July 1912, when even Stéphane was a child, the event was inaugurated when King George V commanded that he be entertained by his favourite music-hall tenor, Harry Lauder, who sang 'Roamin' In The Gloamin'' and the ballerina Anna Paplova, who danced the dying swan from Tchaikovsky's *Swan Lake*. The 1986 show took the theme '50 Years Of Television' and the event took place at the Theatre Royal in London's Drury Lane.

It was appropriate for Stéphane to take part. After all, he had seen the beginnings of television, both at the BBC's Alexander Palace in 1937 and also at Montmartre's Moulin de la Gallette in Paris. He was introduced by the veteran comedian and compere Bob Monkhouse as 'the greatest swing fiddler of your lifetime or mine, ladies and gentleman – the great Stéphane Grappelli.'

The 78-year-old fiddler revelled in this glittering setting. From busking on street corners to performing centre-stage before one of the most revered monarchs in history, his story was becoming a fairytale and he loved it. Once again, he performs his lucky number, playing 'Someone To Watch Over Me' as if it is his life set to music. Here, the street urchin is playing for his adopted Queen and every exquisite phrase has a smile at its core as Stéphane, bursting with pride, gives a career-best performance.

With a brilliant rhythm section comprising Laurie Holloway on piano, Martin Taylor on guitar, Alec Dankworth on bass and Allan Ganley on drums, Stéphane then zips through 'I Got Rhythm' in a breathless show of musicianship, never just showing off but impressing a young Ric Sanders, who gasped, 'His playing was astonishing. I remember thinking, "He's playing better now," and he just seemed to carry on getting better. There were variety-show appearances on the TV billed as "Stéphane Grappelli old-timing it on the violin". I was incensed. I nearly wrote to *The Radio Times*. If there was one thing Stéphane never did it was "old-timed it". If I had to keep one record as a desert-island disc, it would be *Paris Encounter* with Gary Burton – 'Sweet Rain', the Mike

Gibbs composition. He was always moving ahead; it was always modern. And in his harmonies, especially as he got older, you heard the influence of Impressionism, of Debussy.'

Many people were clearly touched that night, not least Stéphane. There's clearly a sense that the organisers almost had to drag him off the stage as a slightly nervous band listen closely to hear if he's going to play one more chorus or wrap it up, and the audience go mad with applause and cheers. It's a fitting tribute.

One of the features of these Royal Shows is the lining-up ceremony backstage where, after the performance, the artists queue like fans to be formally greeted and thanked by the royals. Not all receive the queenly handshake, but Stéphane did and it was surely one of the proudest moments of his life. He pointed out to me the photograph of that moment, which travelled with him for the rest of his life, safely tucked in the lid of his violin case.

The Royal Variety Show is one extreme of Stéphane's venues. Some might see it as too glamorous for jazz, too showbiz, but Stéphane gave his best, with no compromise other than it was *his* show – no solos this time for the band. But then, no doubt the sponsors at the Variety Club Benefit Fund wanted something along the lines of 'The Stéphane Grappelli Show', and that's what he delivered. Ric: 'The other thing Stéphane got right was that he wasn't playing for approval. You would be on shaky ground if you did, like doing an exam every gig. What he did was an act of giving. The energy was flowing from him, out to the audience, and he did that seemingly effortlessly.'

Stéphane's versatility and openness is clearly demonstrated in his other big performance for 1986, this time in Bombay in front of 6,000 enthusiastic Indian fans. Stéphane had recently made one of the strangest albums of his career collaborating with the great virtuoso Dr L Subramaniam, a mutual friend of his and Yehudi Menuhin. Fast approaching 80, Stéphane evidently had as much curiosity and enthusiasm to learn as he had when he'd first begun to experiment with jazz, over half a century earlier.

Frankly, the album has little to offer beyond admiration for Stéphane's boldness, but he was certainly still listening. Much of the disc is dominated by the notion then taking hold that the unifying force in all the world's music is a funky drummer playing four to the bar with a little help from a synthesiser and a bass guitar. However, Stéphane surfaces occasionally and even demonstrates his willingness to bend to those around him, as Ric Sanders observed: 'I suspect Stéphane didn't intellectualise things too much. He was a complete natural, with that connection between thinking what you want to play and playing it, almost like the violin was his voice. I can scat-sing bebop, but I can't play it. For Steph, it was direct. There was nothing in the way of what he was hearing in his head.

'Stéphane was also very generous. He leaned towards the style of the person he was playing with. For instance, with Stuff Smith – a very different sort of player, really behind the beat, digging in and very percussive, more like a horn player – when they did *Stuff And Steff*, Stéphane leaned towards Stuff's style and played more bluesy. Stéphane's technique was far beyond Stuff's, but Stéphane didn't use that as an opportunity to show off; he instead used it as an opportunity to make music.

'Again, with Subramaniam he leans into the style, using a very characteristic downward slide, very Indian – not a parody, not showing off, just genuinely duetting with people by understanding their language and where they are coming from and playing with them with incredible generosity.'

Possibly the most successful track on the Indian fusion album *Conversations* has Stéphane, indeed, exchanging violin conversations with Subramaniam over a bed provided by the aforementioned funky rhythm section. It's still a little reminiscent of a bad Bollywood film soundtrack, but Stéphane deserves to be remembered for his work on the track 'For Valour'. Ironically, on the album's second track, he adopts a gypsy approach to a slow rhapsody. This is probably the most Romany that Stéphane has ever sounded, and the irony of that is compounded by the music's history. Many ethnomusicologists trace the gypsy trail back to India.

From little incidents such as this, it's clear again that one of the keys to understanding the Grappelli genius is that amazing ear. With little formal training, he absorbed music in the best way of all: aurally. He never stopped listening and, consequently, was always learning. 'Essentially jazz is a folk music, and essentially Stéphane was like a folk musician,' observed Ric Sanders. 'Stéphane understood the complexities, but more importantly he understood the simplicity. He understood the folk musician's art. He just took it to unimaginable heights of beauty and eloquence.'

Ric's reference to folk music brings things back to Stéphane's first role model, Louis Armstrong, and his apparently flip but nevertheless profound remark, 'it's all folks music'. In Western society, we've fallen into the habit of regarding folk music as something apart, perhaps even quaint and primitive, possibly due to the tourist-attracting emphasis on national costume and stylised dance troupes. But forget the costume – all music springs from an instinct to communicate in sound. Sometimes that's a shanty or work song that eases toil with rhythm, sometimes it's a lament or blues that plays out emotional pain. When a 'composer' formalises the instinct, refining it in print and orchestration, the music loses something and the musician has to work harder to get back to where we once belonged, as Lennon had it. Stéphane remained a primitive and understood the power of simplicity, but his art took his listeners on an infinitely sophisticated exploration of the possibilities within a popular song. As he said, 'You know what we play is very simple, but it's the way we play it.'

Jazz as a folk art reaches back to spontaneous composition in a way that is beyond many trained musicians, as Yehudi Menuhin readily acknowledged. A trained player can learn the Elgar *Violin Concerto* and give a reading of it and people will accept that, but you can't just read 'Honeysuckle Rose'. For a piece like that to have life in a jazz recital, a performer must know it so well that he can breathe life into every single nuance, every scrap of musical material and give it spirit and share that with an audience. That requires a real musicianship. Yehudi surely knew this, which is why he was so in awe of Stéphane: 'It's as if you could stand next to a volcano and capture its energy coming from deep, deep in the Earth.'

For 'Earth', read 'instinct', the urge to create in sound, to reach others with music. To underestimate good jazz and folk musicians is to misunderstand the origins and nature of music. Yehudi and Nigel Kennedy were worshipping at the source when they courted Stéphane. And all artistic endeavours have a primal source, whether it's the Catalan sculpture and African carvings that inspired Picasso or the Austrian folk tunes that gave life to the symphonies of Joseph Haydn.

While researching Alatri, Stéphane's ancestral home, it was fascinating to discover the local tradition of the *saltarello*, a folk dance played on the medieval *rebec* fiddle and, eventually, part of the Renaissance dance suite. Nothing springs from a vacuum. I don't know if Stéphane heard a saltarello, but somewhere back through the generations his ancestors surely must have. Perhaps the urge and talent for music even exists at a genetic level.

To celebrate his 80th birthday, Stéphane wanted to see the Tower of London, even arriving in London a day early. But instead of enjoying medieval architecture, he found himself whisked away to BBC Television Centre to appear on Britain's biggest chat show at the time, *Wogan*, with its eponymous host, Terry. For the occasion, the brilliant pianist Laurie Holloway provided the only accompaniment. Stéphane was very relaxed in cardigan and the inevitable floral shirt. The informal nature of the appearance suits his temperament, and together with Laurie he turns in a gentle take on 'It's Wonderful'. (Stéphane had literally just arrived from Paris and had not had chance to rehearse with Laurie, but it didn't show.) Presented by Terry with a birthday cake in the form of a violin, Stéphane graciously asked that it be sent to a local children's hospital, 'because they've got some teeth'.

On 26 January 1988, precisely on his 80th birthday, Stéphane celebrated by holding a concert at London's Barbican Centre, selling out this prestigious new venue in the city's commercial heart. BBC Television recorded the concert for broadcast the following June, and the recording reveals Stéphane to be genuinely moved as he tells the audience, 'You know, I'm a little nervous to play for you tonight, but this is the best birthday of my life. Thank you.'

Joining him that night were many friends and colleagues from his world of music, including Yehudi Menuhin and his by then regular guitarists Marc Fosset and Martin Taylor, ably supported by the unusual upright electric bass of Jack Sewing. The band were also augmented for some material by the excellent drummer Allan Ganley.

The most poignant moment was provided by 'Chanson de la Rue' as the veteran fiddler evoked those days, 65 years earlier, when the song of the street provided his daily bread.

In the second half of the concert Laurie Holloway and his wife Marion Montgomery presented their own distinctive style of jazz standards. The birthday boy then duetted with Marion on the classic 'Georgia', the two swapping phrases in a relaxed style leading to an inspired Grappelli solo. Then, with just Laurie, Stéphane performed 'It's Wonderful', providing a rare opportunity for audiences to hear this wonderful pianist given a little space. Stéphane clearly enjoyed the fabulous rhythmic chords and Laurie's brief but engaging solo.

There was also a special tribute to The Hot Club Of France, for which Martin Taylor took up his legendary Maccaferri guitar and Jeff Green provided a third gypsy guitar. Then, on 'Minor Swing' and 'Honeysuckle Rose', Stéphane clearly enjoyed Jeff's bold venture into the spirit of Django, even though Stéphane himself is the only real link to 1934, which was clear in his every chorus.

Yehudi then made a dramatic entrance with an offstage rendition of a Bach Brandenburg concerto before launching into perhaps the duo's most successful live duet. Donning his spectacles, Stéphane joked about having to read music for Jerome Kern's 'Pick Yourself Up' and a Max Harris arrangement of

Gershwin's 'Lady Be Good' before eventually abandoning the manuscript and closing his eyes for some real jazz, but still allowing space for his friend to play some prepared answers.

The concert closed with a jam on 'Sweet Georgia Brown', including Stéphane's clever weaving of some JS Bach into a solo chorus. For the encore reprise, Stéphane, clearly delighted, gently danced to Marion Montgomery's vocal. The power of adrenaline mixed with a little Chivas Regal should never be underestimated!

The concert was presented for television by the distinguished musician and jazz historian Humphrey Lyttelton. As part of the broadcast Humph sat in the dressing room the following day and asked Stéphane about his first UK stage appearance with Yehudi. 'It was great to see that special reception for Yehudi,' replied Grappelli, 'not just for his violin playing, which is marvellous, but also for the good things he does for schools. He is a man of very great importance. We were all astonished at his memory. He plays all that by heart.'

Humph then asked Stéphane about his piano playing.

'I make a better living early on as a pianist, because there was no microphone. For an audience, sitting and listening to jazz music came much later. Then it was always for dancing – jazz meant nothing to them; they just wanted to have a good time. I didn't play piano on the birthday concert because when Laurie Holloway is about, I'm not going to play!'

Asked about his consistency over the years, Stéphane commented: 'You can't change your style. I prefer to stay where I am and to perfect that. I'm sure, if Louis Armstrong were alive, he would always be Louis Armstrong, not copying Dizzy Gillespie. That's what I try to remain myself.'

To Humph's comment on Stéphane's encouragement of young musicians, the violinist replied, 'I play with young musicians because I'm young myself age has nothing to do with it.'

Stéphane closed with a look to the future: 'I want to remain "Fit As A Fiddle"* – somebody sent that tune to me – because without your health you have nothing. Last night was very tiring, but it's a marvellous souvenir.'

Joseph told me about Stéphane's fastidious nature, even after such a demanding performance as the one at the Barbican: 'Even when he was exhausted by the effort of a concert, he would collapse into a chair in his dressing room and clean his violin very carefully, with the same attention that he gave his body. He would check that everything was in order – the Django scarf and all that. Then afterwards there would be a message that so many people wanted autographs. He's really very tired, but still for every person he

*'Fit As A Fiddle', recorded with Grégor et ses Grégoriens, is now available on CD (see 'Discography').

would ask their name, their first name and "how do you like to spell that, with a Y or an I?", very concerned about every detail for everybody.'

Stéphane, the aristocrat of the violin, retained what is perhaps unfairly referred to as 'the common touch': 'In any big hotel, or at the Elysées, Palace he would have the same manner with the person who brings the canapés as the President. His contact with people was respectful in the same way: "You are not anybody; you are someone." I think Stéphane made everybody feel at his best.' If only such manners *were* common!

As Ric Sanders noted, Stéphane definitely valued his audience: 'I saw Stéphane doing a signing after a show, and he had immense warmth. He met my mum and dad and completely charmed them both. She still talks about that one meeting to this day.'

Every city now seemed to want to host a Grappelli birthday, and in April 1988 it was the turn of New York. For his concert at Carnegie Hall, Stéphane became front-page news in New York's *City Guide* and was joined by no less than the great classical cellist Yo Yo Ma and the Julliard String Quartet, while Michel Legrand flew in from Paris and the veteran Toots Thielmans provided a rare jazz harmonica. Stéphane's musical partners seem to grow more eclectic with the decades. Ma shares the love that Stéphane had of Bach, having started work on the 'cello suites at the age of four, while he also shares Stéphane's love of rhythm, the eternal dance. This was Ma's first venture outside the world of classical music, having first met Stéphane at the Blue Note jazz club, the two brought together by musical arranger Roger Kellaway.

Toots Thielmans, meanwhile, born in 1920, is best known for his haunting contribution to the theme to *Midnight Cowboy*, but his jazz credentials include swinging along with Bill Evans and Niels Pedersen.

At the concert, however, Stéphane was firmly top of the bill and, although the tickets had a face price of $30, they were being touted on the street for as much as $1,000.

According to Joseph, Stéphane was stopped on the streets of New York by a pan-handler and Stéphane refused to give him money. Leaving his restaurant, however, he asked for a bag for some food and then took it to the man on the street. Stéphane had a long memory.

June found Stéphane at last in Ireland. *The Sunday Tribune* carried the story of his recent triumphs in Iceland and Dublin. Stéphane's mood was reflective: 'I am a human being. The planes are always late. That dreadful Heathrow!

But in any case, I like to travel, so I am not disturbed too much. More and more, you go someplace and you find some incredible scenery. Reykjavik was a good experience, because it was an experience like being on the Moon. I will never go to the Moon, but now I have seen it... We saw some geysers. I wanted to try the geyser, but I nearly lost my finger – it burned me!' Just like a child, still playing, wondering.

But the child had a purpose in Galway: 'I used to have a lady friend for thirty years. She is dead now. I am so determined to go there.'

With his Irish promoter, Maurice Cassidy, and Joseph Oldenhove, Stéphane at last visited Jean Barclay's grave, near the family summer house that Stéphane had first heard about in 1952, on that lonely lakeside hill that he had never managed to visit in Jean's lifetime. *Je ne regrette rien?*

Stéphane had done some strange gigs in his time, but the Glasgow Garden Festival was surely the oddest. In July 1988, he and Martin Taylor found themselves surrounded by lilies and plastic palms for yet another BBC concert. They obliged with a purely acoustic rendering of 'Honeysuckle Rose' while sitting on a couple of plastic chairs in an abandoned entrance hall. Stéphane was again relaxed and enjoying himself. When asked by the presenter about the date of his birthday, he said, 'You know, I can't remember myself because I do that four times – in Paris, London, New York and somewhere else – and I wish I could do it some more, because that permit me to travel.'

When asked about the simple instrumentation they were using, Stéphane complimented Martin and continued, 'The guitar and the violin, it's the best combination.'

Asked how long they had been together Stéphane replied, 'Ten years. I started with him when he was six months old.'

Then, in response to a question about their rapport, Martin observed, 'It's almost a telepathy. You know what's coming next and manage to follow each other.'

Asked about Django, Martin replied that Reinhardt was the first guitarist he had ever heard, but personally he was now playing very differently. Stéphane interjected, 'You can develop your personal feeling and develop your own ideas. Why play like Django Reinhardt?'

When asked if he would play differently with a different guitarist, Stéphane again refers to listening: 'It all depends on what you hear. You have to be a bit of a chameleon.'

Martin retained fond memories of working so informally with Stéphane and 12 years later responded to my interest by playing the most beautiful rendition of the Reinhardt tune 'Manoir de mes Rêves'.* In London for a business meeting and therefore *sans* guitar, unflustered, he nipped around to Ivor Mairants Guitar Shop and borrowed an antique Kalamazoo guitar of the type made during the 1930s Depression. With inferior woods and cheap components, they were so poorly constructed that the Gibson Guitar Company wouldn't even grace them with their name, but it could have been a Stradivarius for the wonderful sound that Martin produced. 'I used to love sitting there and following Steph,' he remarked. 'You had to follow Stéphane. He was very much his own man. It wasn't like playing with some jazz musicians, where you have a constant interplay; you had to follow Stéphane.' Martin was soon lost in his nostalgic reverie and just played the tune, beautifully. 'It was just lovely playing those tunes with Stéphane and putting those lovely chords underneath what he was doing. I miss that. I miss that a lot.'

*This wonderful and genuinely 'unplugged' version appears on the Music on Earth DVD *Stéphane Grappelli: A Life In The Jazz Century*.

25 Milou En Mai

'We ended up in the studio doing something that was quite similar to what I'd done with Miles Davis.'

– Louis Malle

1989 saw Stéphane engaged in one of his proudest achievements, the music score for the film *Milou en Mai* by Louis Malle, one of the world's greatest film directors. As early as 1956, Malle received the Palme d'Or at Cannes and an Oscar in Hollywood for the documentary *The Silent World*, while in the 1980s he scored feature-film success with *Au Revoir, Les Enfants*. For soundtracks, he had famously used Erik Satie for *Close Up*, Michel Legrand for *Atlantic City* (starring Burt Lancaster) and Miles Davis for *Ascender Pour l'Echafaud*.

More pertinently for Stéphane, the score for Malle's 1974 film *Lacombe Lucien* extensively featured the music of The Hot Club Quintet, of which the director was a fan, remarking, 'Even as I started working on the script of *Milou en Mai*, I could hear Stéphane Grappelli's violin conversing with my characters. When Stéphane watched the first cut of the film, I was overjoyed to see that he felt so much at home with its ironic and tense atmosphere.'

For that first cut, Malle had used guide music, a device employed by many editors and directors to pace a film's early cut. In this instance, he had added existing Grappelli recordings into his rough cut. These were subsequently replaced as Stéphane contributed his original work. 'The rest was a walkover,' remembers the director. 'We worked happily together, each of us quick to take a hint from the other. Stéphane's music, timeless as it is, beautifully underlines the images of *Milou en Mai* but it is also, in itself, another milestone in his distinguished career.'*

Recorded at Les Studios de la Grande Armée in Paris from 13–16 November, for the musicians the sessions were not such a walkover, as Martin Taylor remembered: 'We went over to Paris for a week to record with Jack Sewing, Marc Fosset and an accordion player and pianist. Stéphane being Stéphane

*Copyright CBS/Sony.

couldn't record in the conventional way that they work in the film-soundtrack world, which means working with a click track.'

This convention involves the tight synchronisation of pre-composed segments of music into precisely defined portions of the film. The only real experience that Stéphane had had of this method of working had been on *Two For The Road* with Henry Mancini back in 1966, and he wanted to forget that. For Steph, this would mean wearing headphones dictating a metronome click and then cuing his musicians to start and stop. This of course was anathema to his free spirit and the opposite of every instinct he felt about music. Stéphane, of course, first added music to film in 1922, and that had been live in a silent cinema.

Martin: 'So we had to adopt a way of working which meant receiving directions like, "We need music in this bit here." Louis Malle would come over to the band and say, "We need music from the time the guy puts his bicycle against the wall, walks into the house, goes into the room and looks over there. Then you stop."'

Malle had enjoyed immense success with this method in as early as 1956, for the film *Ascenseur Pour l'Echafaud*, for which Miles Davis had agreed to do the music and, following two viewings, went into the studio with Malle. 'We agreed on the parts where we felt music was needed and we took advantage of the one night he had off from the club,' remembered Malle. 'We rented a sound studio in Paris on the Champs-Elysées and started working, as jazz musicians do, very slowly. We worked from something like 10 or 11 that night until 5 in the morning. In that one night, the whole score was recorded.'

Perhaps Louis thought that Stéphane would be just as quick, and the pressure soon mounted, as Martin recounts in his autobiography *Kiss And Tell**: 'It was a nightmare. Jazz musicians aren't used to playing the same thing over and over again and getting it exactly the same each time – especially Stéphane. It turned into the recording session from hell.

'Malle idolised Stéphane, but you could sense that things were getting a little frayed around the edges because we were taking so long to record some of the scenes. We were booked into the studio for five days and were being paid very well for our time, but there was some sort of friction between Stéphane and Jack Sewing at the time, I don't know what it was about. Every time there was a mistake, Stéphane would turn to Jack like it was his fault, and this was getting on Jack's nerves to say the least. Sometimes Stéphane would have a go at Jack between takes, and this was making matters much worse. Eventually

*Sanctuary Publishing, 2000.

he did it one time too many and Jack, a fiery Dutchman, said "Right, that's it, I'm out of here," put his bass down and walked out of the studio. Stéphane was very upset and, knowing that he'd pushed Jack too far, started crying and saying, "What have I done? We've worked together so long. I didn't mean to upset him. I'm just nervous about this recording." By this time, Louis Malle must have been wondering exactly what he was dealing with.

'I went out, scouring the streets of Paris for Jack, and eventually found him in a nearby bar. I said, "Are you coming back? Because we've got to finish it." But Jack said, "No, no, no. I've had enough." I tried to reason with him, and eventually he did come back, but he refused to speak to Stéphane for the rest of the day.

'We completed that day's recording, but the music still wasn't finished. We were at the end of the allotted time and Louis Malle came up to me and said there was still some more music to record and would I stay on for another two or three days. I was earning quite a lot of money for the recording, but I had such a bad time I said no, even when I was offered lots more. There was nothing that could tempt me to endure any more time in that studio; I just couldn't do it. The atmosphere had turned bad and I wanted to go home.'

Ed Baxter: 'Jack went back to Nice and it was a long time before he spoke to Steph. He did eventually play the odd gig with him here and there. I don't know what Jack thought about Steph! Mind you, Jack had played with Steph for a long time and was a wee bit hard-headed, stubborn, and yet he was good fun and a good bass player. Steph liked him. He could swing.'

Such stories are common in the high-pressure world of professional music-making, and it's a testament to the skill of the artists that the friction almost never shows in the finished music. I've seen many concerts start with flashes of temper and many recording sessions alive with emotional spark, but the paying public sees nothing but smiles and perhaps just occasionally wonders at the depth of emotion in a particular performance.

The missing music and the pressure to complete the film was the probable reason behind Stéphane drawing on his back catalogue for *Milou en Mai*. Some of the themes used were reworkings of material that Stéphane had previously employed as early as 1969. For the 'Riviere', for instance, he drew on 'Arpège', a tune that he had used on *Paris Encounter*, his collaboration with Gary Burton. But many composers are guilty of this plundering of their past; Mozart, Vivaldi and Beethoven, for example, all had morsels tucked away for a rainy day.

Ric Sanders, for one, was pleased to hear 'Arpège' reappear: 'Stéphane was an incredibly gifted composer, which never really figured in his live repertoire but often did on record.

'I'm working on "Arpège" for inclusion in my own repertoire. It's a perfect miniature which displays a wonderful understanding of how to use a violin. Steph's compositions sit on the fiddle – they sit under the fingers with a natural genius in the same way as those of Fritz Kreisler, who also had a fondness for writing miniatures.

'"Arpège" encompasses a wide range of the fiddle. It's a series of arpeggios, based around a major seventh, which is a very relaxing interval. It could sound like an exercise, but in the way Steph structures it, he plays the theme – which glides up and down the violin in arpeggios – then he goes to a central section, a sequence of chords to improvise on, and then he goes back to the main theme to end on and ties it all up. It's just so relaxed and uncontrived. It's far better to negotiate a simple tune and be able to put your heart into it than to play the Bruch *Violin Concerto* badly.'

Louis Malle was certainly happy: 'I love Grappelli and I found it surprising that he had scored only one film before, Bertrand Blier's *Les Valseuses*. It was an excellent score which was hardly noticed – the best compliment you can make about a score. You couldn't say that about a John Williams score!' Even at the scriptwriting stage, he had imagined Stéphane's sound: 'I put a note in the margin: "Milou is Grappelli's violin."'

Malle recalled only one musical disagreement, over the comic inclusion of 'L'Internationale', the famous rally-call of freedom fighters: 'Stéphane was reluctant to do it. He said, "In 1946 we did a recording of 'La Marseillaise' in jazz with Django and we got into a lot of trouble." I said, "You don't have to worry, especially these days; I think people will get the joke," so he agreed.

'Stéphane, greater than ever at 82, was bursting with ideas. We ended up in the studio doing something that was quite similar to what I had done with Miles Davis. It was not a written score but it was all very prepared. But when we got to the studio, then it became an improvisation.'

The 'Valse du Passe' takes the listener right back to the era of the *bals musette* with a nostalgic acoustic guitar and Paris musette accordion. In fact, nostalgia is probably exactly what Malle wanted for the musical mood of the film, particularly in Stéphane's personification of the central character, Milou.

Milou en Mai is set in 1968 against the distant backdrop of the Paris riots and what is seen by the central characters as imminent revolution. Milou himself represents a relic of the old order, ensconced in his country château, faintly eccentric and lost in a world of vintage wines and home-grown honey. As an exact contemporary of Stéphane, Le Quintet du Hot Club de France would have been the music of his misspent youth. So far, so good.

However, the overall score as film music fails, ironically, by being too good. The music stands on its own and too often takes the foreground. The difficulty, as those who have tried composing for cinema know, is to sublimate music to an underscore, to point up the action and illuminate proceedings. In that respect, it's just like lighting – the audience should never end up watching the lighting change. Watching *Milou en Mai*, it's possible to end up consciously listening to the music and forgetting the film. Stéphane, though, had spent his entire life centre-stage, and subliminal pointing of emotion was not his natural forte. For this exact reason, the soundtrack album is a success and the film itself a marvellous little vignette of an era.

Stéphane remained justly proud of his themes for the film and reprised them whenever the opportunity arose. On the soundtrack album, he even included 'Chanson Pour Louis', a solo-violin theme. According to Ed Baxter, as the musicians packed up to leave, 'they were short a couple of minutes, so Stéphane just picked up the violin and improvised for a couple of minutes. Nobody else, just him.' 'Chanson Pour Louis' is a poignant little theme and will return at an important juncture in Stéphane's story.

For Martin Taylor, however, the song had ended, and not purely as a result of these sessions. It was just time to move on: 'I decided to stop touring with Stéphane and concentrate exclusively on my solo career. I'd had ten great years with him, but it was time for a change. The only thing that would make me tour again was if there was another Australian trip, because that would mean that I could see Ike.' Isaacs, a star of one of the first Diz Disley trios and the man who introduced the young Taylor to Stéphane, had recently emigrated to Australia. 'As fate would have it, though, in 1990 Stéphane was offered an Australian tour, so in 1990 we did our last tour together, in Australia and New Zealand. We played Sydney, Adelaide, Perth, Auckland and Wellington and did quite a few television shows along the way. I saw Ike, and it was great to be back. I played my last gig with Stéphane in Auckland. It was sad to go.'

Stéphane would miss Martin's wonderful chords and imaginative solos but, always looking forward, he took the opportunity to return to his love of the piano. Since 1972, when he'd chosen John Coltrane's 'Body And Soul' as one of his desert-island discs, Stéphane had harboured an ambition to work with the man he described then as 'that marvellous pianist McCoy Tyner'. In 1987, through their shared American agent, Abby Hoffer, Stéphane had worked briefly with Tyner's group for a broadcast in Baltimore, Maryland, where they'd both had a good time and had talked of getting together for a record. On the face of it, this seems an unlikely event – left to his own devices, Tyner was never freeform or strictly avant garde, but his muscular explorations were a long way from 'Tea For Two'. However, Tyner had been impressed by Stéphane's youthful attitude: 'Some people couldn't imagine me and Stéphane playing together, but when both of you really love music, you can pair up. Stéphane's a very open-minded person – he adjusts. He has a head full of tunes. He remembered some of the early songs John Coltrane had recorded.'

McCoy Tyner had been born in Philadelphia in 1938, and at the age of 52 he was 30 years younger than Stéphane. However, he earned Stéphane's respect through the music he had absorbed through working with Bud Powell, Elvin Jones, Ron Carter and, especially, his work with Coltrane from the early 1960s. By the 1990s he was an American jazz icon.

On 18 April 1990, Stéphane and McCoy at last got together at New York's BMG Studio B to record the album *One On One*. On hearing the results, the great jazz critic Nat Hentoff was impressed by the duo's instant compatibility: 'What surprised me was how easily and deeply their ways of swinging are so joyously compatible. I expect they both adjusted, much like two distinctive individualists do in marriages that work.'

The common ground, of course, was Coltrane, and the two musicians explored his tunes 'You Say You Care' and 'Mr PC', the latter of which had been written as a tribute to the great bassist Paul Chambers. On this track, Stéphane contributes his own affectionate tribute with imaginative portamento slides and pizzicato plucking, albeit two octaves higher than Chamber's bass.

For Gershwin's 'Summertime', Stéphane first lays the groundwork on the timeless tune, allowing McCoy the space to explore the endless harmonic possibilities open to an innovator such as himself. Stéphane clearly enjoys all the implied rhythm in Tyner's sparse piano and delivers one of his best takes on a tune made more challenging by its familiarity.

It's a shame that the two hadn't got together earlier, for on 'Satin Doll', on which they share a delight in their other common hero, Duke Ellington, Stéphane shows a glimpse of his 1970s peak. Sadly, and for the first time on record, it's evident that Grappelli is 82 and mortal. *One On One* is still a good record but not a great record, and Stéphane would have known that.

On 'How High The Moon', Stéphane still swings like no violinist before or since, but a signature of his immortal sound – that previously unerring pitch – briefly wavers. Fellow violinist Ric Sanders: 'There was a very telling thing that Stéphane says about the early days busking: "I played the 'Meditation' of *Thaïs*, by Massenet" – so self deprecating. "It wasn't very good but it was in tune and I knew that."'

To play so in tune, especially when improvising, is one of the defining qualities that set Stéphane apart from any other fiddler in jazz. As he gently surrendered his technical abilities, however, Ric recognised that something more important remained: 'As well as being this great, natural musician with all that melodic and harmonic gift and the ear to take in all the music he ever heard, he was completely effortless in the way he communicated this music to the audience. He was a great natural communicator. It was so unforced so natural. Perhaps that's part of the nature of genius.'

That genius to communicate continued to sustain Stéphane and inspire audiences for the rest of his life. McCoy Tyner summed up the *One On One* session: 'It was a lot of fun. Music is supposed to make you feel good. That's what music's all about.'

Nat Hentoff agreed: 'Grappelli at 82 is one of the most youthful-sounding improvisers in jazz. I go to hear him not only for his ceaseless melodic ingenuity and buoyant swing but also just to look at him. He takes so much pleasure in making music that the joy of it is reflected in the sunniness of his face and his spirit.'

Remaining in New York, the indefatigable fiddler briefly laid down his violin bow to pursue another long-held ambition. Joseph Oldenhove told me, 'For many years he played "An American In Paris" on the piano at home. He always preferred to play the piano. He found it difficult to play the violin on his own.' Thus was conceived Stéphane's first solo-piano album.

My Other Love is an extraordinary exploit for a man of 82, and indeed a solo record is a challenge that many pianists of 20 would approach with trepidation, yet Stéphane went into RCA Studio C once more with the enthusiasm of a teenager. This wasn't a low-profile vanity recording; the client was Bob Thiele and the record company was the mighty CBS Corporation.

Stéphane contributed 15 titles for the album, three of his own composition and a bold assortment of his lifelong favourites. His performance of 'Three Little Words' evokes the 1930s and The Hot Club Quintet, appearing alongside Ellington's 'Satin Doll', Cole Porter's 'Looking At You', Fats Waller's 'Ain't

Misbehavin'' and Hoagy Carmichael's 'Two Sleepy People', with the spirit of Louis Armstrong gently evoked on 'What A Wonderful World'. Together, all these tunes comprise a soundtrack to Stéphane's life, and listening to this nostalgic little record is to imagine Stéphane viewing his life on a flickering silver screen. Indeed, 'Tea For Two' specifically conjures the 1920s and his boyhood days in the silent cinema.

'Three Little Words' starts with a cinematic flourish, water shimmering on a golden pond, evoking Debussy's 'Ondine' or a sprite dancing in the cloud, reflections on cool water as the curtains gently open onto a love scene. For this piece, Stéphane left New York behind, lost in a reverie of 1923.

When I first heard this record, I could make no sense of it. Stéphane had no pretensions as a professional pianist. When Oscar Peterson, Earl Hines and McCoy Tyner were happy to oblige, why would Stéphane play the piano? After all, he'd given up his ivory-tinkling aspirations in 1932, when he first heard Art Tatum and who wouldn't?

The answer, though, is sheer joy. Stéphane loved the piano, and *My Other Love* celebrates that. Stéphane played the piano at home and, for as long as he was able, for anyone who wanted to listen. The piano wasn't his gimmick; it was his friend. The album bristles with cheek and humour, crying out for the music-hall MC: 'Ladies and gentleman, I give you a nice little turn, a jingle on the ivories, a twinkle in the eye... Let's hear it for Stéphane Grappelli!'

On 11 October 1991, Stéphane received the devastating news of the sudden death of his grandson Stéphane Tanasesco, 'young Stéphane', who had been his favourite. Together they had shared a love of music, the grandfather buying his treasured grandson guitars and other musical instruments. Young Stéphane had showed a flair for stage lighting encouraged by his grandfather, and occasionally they travelled together on the road, the young boy helping with lighting positions and colours. But emotional problems and experiments with recreational drugs had dogged the grandson's short life and he suffered a heart attack at the tragically young age of 35. Stéphane would never recover from the blow.

A mere two weeks later, Stéphane was booked to appear at the Warsaw Jazz Jamboree in Poland, a major event with television coverage and star guests where Stéphane was to be reunited with McCoy Tyner. Once more, Stéphane might have wondered who had said 'the show must go on!' On 25 October, as the television recording shows, the violinist is duly announced and appears smiling for his public. As he finds his seat onstage, however, his face shows the merest glimmer of his true feelings before these are drowned in another smile as the opera-house crowd rises in a standing ovation for a man who had not yet performed a note of music. For this appearance, the self-defined old trouper gives his all, with no sign of his grief except perhaps in the unusual poignancy of his introduction of 'Nuages', 'a tune composed by my late partner'. However, the blues are soon forgotten in a joyous rendition of 'Daphne'.

With McCoy Tyner, he offers two tunes from their recent album, and typically he is better live in this setting than in the New York studio just the previous year. 'I Didn't Know What Time It Was' is particularly heartfelt, Tyner initially providing a subtle outline harmony and then stretching out in his own solos, with Stéphane looking on in delight and coming back with some brilliant improvisations, totally on form. The two then embrace warmly while taking the opportunity to discuss an encore, which turns out to be the bebop anthem 'How High The Moon'. Stéphane revels in Tyner's virtuosity and imagination and returns the compliment in an inspired set of stop choruses. The jazz-starved Warsaw crowd explode with adulation as the two giants take three bows and give them another standing ovation. Stéphane could still turn it on for the crowd.

Since the disbanding of The Gregorians in 1933, Stéphane had left his big-band roots behind, although it's perhaps wrong to call Gregor And The Gregorians a big band; that crazy collective, with its ukulele, banjo and sousaphone, was much more a product of vaudeville. For the increasingly reflective Stéphane, however, another ambition lay unfulfilled.

The French big-band star Claude Bolling had admired Grappelli throughout his career. Claude had conceived 'the Bolling sound', which started with his virtuoso piano before reaching out into arrangements that conjured the glory of Count Basie and Duke Ellington. In December1991, he took the giant step of asking Stéphane to record, and Grappelli was of course delighted.

The classic 17-piece band assembled at the Artistic Palace Studio in Bologne sur Seine. Stéphane must have wondered if this at last was the fulfilment of the promise hinted at back in 1963, when he had first met Duke Ellington. That session with Duke had worked well for Stéphane, although it had really been a rhythm section with violin soloists. The Bolling band were truly big.

It's interesting to compare a photograph of the 1990s ensemble at the studio with an image of Grégor et ses Grégoriens from 1930 aboard the RMS *Alcantara*. In the former, Stéphane is again sitting out in front with his violin, adopting the same jaunty angle as in the latter, although 61 years have broadened his waistline. For the Bolling band, the dinner jackets and bow ties of vaudeville are forgotten; instead it's check shirts and Levi jeans.

The contraption drum kit pictured in the 1990s shot, once a miscellany of percussive gadgets, has formalised into a familiar collection, with big ride cymbals and a small bass drum, the legacy of pioneering big-band drummer Gene Krupa. The sousaphone, meanwhile, has disappeared into the museum, alongside the banjo and megaphone. Only the inventions of Adolphe Sax and the trumpets and trombones remain. Even the violin section has been whittled down to one member. The guitar is now electric and has a jazz history, thanks to Django and Charlie Christian, while the bass has strings and the very latest amplification technology means that it can be a bass viol, not a rock 'n' roll Fender. There's no sign of a canine mascot (which is clearly practical), but it's evident that jazz is now a serious business.

On the resulting album, titled *First Class*, Bolling's arrangements allow Stéphane plenty of air and modern microphones mean it's a fair competition, one violin against 13 brass instruments. On 'De Partout et d'Ailleurs', Stéphane gets to duet successfully with the baritone sax of Jean Eteve and clearly enjoys the sentimental lilt, while 'Crazy Rhythm' is similarly nostalgic but also bold – no violin has ever sat so comfortably with a big band. Stéphane exchanges choruses with a muted trumpet as if that was a regular event. It isn't, though, and without Grappelli it never would have happened.

'Minor Swing' then enjoys one of its strangest outings as it gets the Gene Krupa treatment, echoing with the throbbing tom-toms of 1939 and reminiscent of Chappie Willet's 'Jungle Madness'. Jean-Paul Charlop bravely evokes the spirit of Django on his just-audible acoustic guitar while Stéphane delights with all his tricks, including some cheeky portamento pizzicato.

'Tears' follows next, written with Django over 50 years earlier and always one of Stéphane's favourites. Indeed, Django would have loved this session, perhaps what he had been dreaming of in his letter of 1946, in which he'd asked Stéphane to join him with Ellington. Stéphane is happiest improvising as he does here, floating on a bed of muted brass. Guitarist Jean-Paul has the good sense not to attempt the Reinhardt chorus, wisely leaving it to the imagination.

The most successful track, though, is 'Do You Know What It Is To Miss New Orleans?' Here Stéphane basks in nostalgic memories of his lost friends Sidney Bechet, Louis Armstrong and Billie Holiday, the Bechet role is taken by the soprano sax of Philippe Portejoie. Stéphane had of course seen New Orleans, had obviously heard its soul and, more than any other European musician, he had brought that to Paris. Through Stéphane and his friends, the Seine became a potent tributary of the Mississippi Delta.

The Billy Strayhorn tune 'Lush Life' would have reminded Steph of the man who introduced him to the Duke. On this piece, Bolling catches the Ellington spirit in his sparse piano chords and Stéphane phrases beautifully, evoking his wonderful 1963 performance of 'In A Sentimental Mood'.

Stéphane also enjoys Bolling's JS Bach-style introduction to 'Blue Skies', responding with a lyrical chorus of his own. Indeed, so impressed is Stéphane with the band's bravura ensemble that he inadvertently names the album – in English. As the reverberation of the last *tutti* dies away, he erupts with a spontaneous 'First class, man, first class!' Obviously, the band's sound was so convincingly redolent of New York that Steph forgot which side of the Atlantic he was on.

The album remains true to its title, though, and allowed Stéphane to fulfil another portion of his wish list. Two days later, on 6 December, the Bolling-Grappelli big band gave a live version of their labours to an enthralled audience at the Théâtre Andre Malraux de Rueil Malmaison. In the only onstage photograph of this event, Stéphane is clearly ecstatic.

Steph was 83 and, although mentally very alert, he was becoming increasingly aware of his physical limitations. Typically, though, his considerations were practical. Joseph Oldenhove recalls, 'In the last four or five years, he was very afraid for his violin, in case he fell and damaged it; he had great respect for his violin. He was also very practical – he gave a concert for people with special needs in Avignon. Normally he would risk the walk to his onstage chair, but he said, "Tonight I will enter the stage on my wheelchair, and it's OK – they will understand."'

At home, he was the same: 'If he needed to sleep, he would say so and do that, and he never accepted early morning appointments. In those late years, he had great respect for his metabolism. He respected others' rhythms but he also respected his own. And he also felt it was important to respect your body. As a violinist, it was important to attend to his fingernails, and he did. He wouldn't dream of a manicurist doing that; he was too afraid they would cut his fingers.'

As his dependence increased, Stéphane perhaps involuntarily addressed Joseph in the name of the man he called his best friend: 'When Stéphane was tired, sometimes he would call me Django. Not for my musicianship, though he thought I had a good ear!'

Stéphane Grappelli, Judy Caine and Paul Balmer, 1996
(© Alan Williams)

Lord Lew Grade
(© Alan Williams)

Stéphane Grappelli and Paul Balmer in the music room at the Rue Dunkerque apartment, 1995 (© Judy Caine)

Paul Balmer and Lord
Menuhin, 1996
(© Alan Williams)

Diz Disley and Paul Balmer
at the 100 Club, London,
summer 2001 (© Judy Caine)

Evelyne Tanasesco-Grappelli
and Paul Balmer in Cannes,
May 2002 (© Judy Caine)

Stéphane's first, three-quarter-size violin, Figure 1 in 'Appendix 1: Instruments' (© Paul Balmer)

The Warlop violin by Pierre Hel, Lille, 1924, Figure 2 in 'Appendix 1: Instruments' (courtesy of the Musée de la Musique, © Cité de la Musique; photograph by Jean-Marc Anglès)

Django's Julian Gomez Ramirez guitar of 1932, seen in La Boîte à Matelots band in 1933, Figure 3 in 'Appendix 1: Instruments' (courtesy of the Musée de la Musique, © Cité de la Musique; photograph by Jean-Marc Anglès)

Django's last Selmer Petite Bouche guitar, made in 1940 and presented by Naguine Reinhardt to the Museé de Musique, Paris; seen in Django's last portrait at Samois in 1953; Figure 4 in 'Appendix 1: Instruments' (courtesy of the Musée de la Musique, © Cité de la Musique; photograph by Jean-Marc Anglès)

Django at home in Samois-sur-Seine in 1953 with the 1940 Selmer Petite Bouche, Figure 5 in 'Appendix 1: Instruments' (© Hervé Derrien)

Django's 1940 guitar, with his name carved into the headstock, Figure 6 in 'Appendix 1: Instruments' (courtesy of the Musée de la Musique, © Cité de la Musique; photograph by Jean-Marc Anglès)

★

Stéphane continued to work with much younger musicians and enjoyed performing live with them, encouraging and endorsing their innovation. Philip Catherine, whom he'd joined on the *Young Django* album of 1979, was by now a firmly established musician. Ironically, Catherine had been born in London during the war as, like Stéphane, his Belgian parents had escaped from the Nazi invasion of Europe. He eventually arrived in Brussels with his family at the end of hostilities. By the age of 17, Philip had become a professional guitarist who, like every other young musician of his generation, had fallen under the spell of Miles Davis and his pioneering brand of jazz rock. Catherine had even gone as far as to dedicate his *Guitars* album to the dark prince of cool, and his experimental textures took the guitar into the realms of Miles' keyboard wizard Joe Zawinul. By the 1990s, his musical inclinations were a long way from Stéphane's swing.

In March 1992, at La Salle de Spectacles de Columbes, Stéphane gave two broadcast concerts accompanied by his old friends Marc Fosset and Niels Pedersen, with Catherine on electric and acoustic guitar. On this occasion, the Django legacy was evident with the inclusion of 'Minor Swing,' Stéphane inspired as ever and revelling in the joy of a sparse counterpoint with Pedersen's bass. Once again, Stéphane demonstrates his uncanny ability to listen to his young accomplices, echoing their solos but with no need to compromise his own identity. On Catherine's composition 'Galerie des Princes', Stéphane even finds ways of reflecting the guitarist's use of electronic swell pedals in his own unplugged but innovative harmonics.

On 'Ballade', his own composition, Stéphane is back on great form, completely in control of his signature sweet intonation. Maybe the McCoy Tyner slips were just a bad day, or perhaps the modern stage monitoring enabled Stéphane to hear his friends better. Another possible cause is Stéphane's performer's response to a live audience. Whatever the reason, it's wonderful to hear him sounding timeless again at the age of 84.

Next, 'Blues For Django And Stéphane' presents a rare opportunity to hear Stéphane working with Marc Fosset on electric guitar. Marc takes full advantage of the instrument's strengths, enabling a more adventurous role than that he had often taken with the trio. 'Sweet Chorus', meanwhile, is a real Django-esque opportunity for Catherine, and Stéphane comes back with some startlingly beautiful choruses, including an impromptu cadenza.

Stéphane and Niels clearly enjoy the two younger guitarists' virtuosity on

'Oh Lady Be Good', and Stéphane again comes back with nuggets from their solos before ending with his own well-known take on the Gershwin classic.

The ecstatic French audience demand an encore and are rewarded with Stéphane's lucky number the 'Gershwin Medley', played for the thousandth time but still sounding as fresh as ever. The tempo on 'I Got Rhythm' is adrenaline-driven and probably a little faster than Stéphane might have chosen, but he doesn't falter.

The album recording of this concert was later released under the title *Live In Paris* '92, and it's as alive as anything from 1934 but better, with nearly 60 years of swing behind every beat.

26 Mémoires

'Open your ears, dear friends of all ages, to the living voices of cultures, of civilisations. You can only understand through their audible message. They are the pilgrims who have come to reach our hearts, for it is the heart of the listener that is the holy grail.'

– *Yehudi Menuhin*

The 20th century will be remembered as a period of unprecedented and accelerating change. In 84 years, Stéphane had experienced a transformation from a world of candlelight and horse-drawn traffic to that of space travel and satellite communications. A man who first saw aircraft as constructs of balsa wood and wire had flown the Atlantic by Concorde. His musical world had transformed from the *bals musette* and music hall to a digital global empire. In the 1990s, he felt that he should commit his remarkable story to paper. With the help of Jean-Marc Bramy and, more importantly, his companion Joseph Oldenhove, he began to prepare his memoirs.

These reminiscences were eventually published in Paris as *Mon Violon Pour Tout Baggage* (*With Only My Violin*) in 1992, and Stéphane dedicated them '*à mes parents*'. It's a very touching story, especially 'Souvenirs de Mon Enfance', in which Stéphane relates his early years and the sparse, pitiful memories he has of his mother, walking in the Cimitière de Pantin and in the environs of the Square Montholon. He also included an interview with his daughter, Evelyne, and another with his wartime ally George Shearing before eventually finishing where his career began, referring back to the influence he heard of black-American musicians on the music of Maurice Ravel and Arthur Honegger. In the penultimate paragraph, he refers to his own contribution to the idea of jazz concerts, starting with Django and their unique experiment together with the first 'jazz on strings'. He closes with an affirmation of his continuing pursuit of the music he loves.

To stay involved in that music at a professional level, apparently disregardful of age, Stéphane was in fact working hard to maintain his technique. Joseph

Oldenhove told me, 'For four or five years he played Paganini's "Moto Perpetuo". He enjoyed that for its virtuosity. It was good for his dexterity.' The demanding Paganini piece was one approached with caution even by his classical friends Yehudi Menuhin and Nigel Kennedy. 'Sometimes he would just sit watching the television and playing pizzicato just for finger exercise and to maintain the hard skin on the tips of his fingers,' recalled Joseph. I remember Stéphane doing just this at the Rue Dunkerque flat, sitting watching himself playing 'J'Attendrai' from a terrible bootleg video and gently playing *solfege*, all the time complaining about the video quality: 'It looks like we are playing under the sea!'

This technical exercise, 'the gymnastics of music', was for Stéphane a totally different issue from the art of music-making. Joseph observed, 'I think for Stéphane it was important that he be considered as a complete musician, not a violin player. He liked the old term "chef d'orchestre".' And that is precisely the occupation he listed in his well-worn passport.

However, the chef d'orchestre Français still had unfulfilled ambitions and, as he had hinted in his memoirs, orchestral jazz still held his interest. When in 1992 French television celebrated his birthday with another special concert, the first half featured his small group. The second half, meanwhile, presented an opportunity.

At this time, Michel Legrand had been a major figure in French popular music for four decades, with songs such as 'The Summer Knows' (the theme from the film *Summer Of '42*) and 'What Are You Doing The Rest Of Your Life?' making him an international star, and the winner of three Oscars. He had first met Stéphane in 1954, when the violinist had guested on Legrand's first Columbia album, *The Music Of Cole Porter*. Legrand told me that he was delighted to work with someone he had admired all his life: 'Naturally I had always heard Stéphane play. From the age of three I knew the recordings of The Hot Club de France and was delighted every day by hearing them on the radio. For the Cole Porter record I thought that one of the titles, 'In The Still Of The Night', would be perfect for Stéphane. It was sublime. We only did one take.'

Stéphane had probably known Raymond Legrand, Michel's father, who was a chef d'orchestre himself in the days of variety. Now his son, born in 1932, was helping Stéphane to realise his late ambition. 'We played together in a numerous concerts,' recalled Michel. 'I remember one in particular for television in 1992. I was delighted to accompany him with a large orchestra.'

The television orchestra for the date consisted of a huge string section, including orchestral double basses and concert harp, a full brass section and a rhythm section comprising guitars, bass and drums. In the existing video recording, Legrand himself conducts from the piano while Stéphane seems tiny, seated behind his music in one of his still-outrageous floral shirts. The repertoire, arranged by Legrand, leans towards French tunes that were already internationally well known. Many of the tunes were Michel's own hits, but there was also room for Stéphane's theme from *Milou en Mai* and a new, lush arrangement of 'Nuages'. The jazz element of the arrangements, however, is largely subsumed to what the BBC used to call 'light music', yet the musicians are excellent, and when Stéphane and Michel relish their improvised solos, the music really does take off.

From the evidence of the recordings, Stéphane clearly enjoyed working with Michel, but he was a little inhibited, as Joseph later told me: 'The Michel Legrand arrangements were very good, but Stéphane found it difficult being restricted to the written parts. He preferred being free with the small groups. That birthday concert was extremely well intentioned, but it wasn't his best work.'

In the pursuit of orchestral jazz, Stéphane was also returning to Django, who had shared the violinist's ambition, and I can't listen to the recording of this bold venture with Legrand without wondering what might have happened if the gypsy genius had been present to throw a few electric spanners in the works – the trademark eccentric harmonisation, a discordant flurry, a flash of lightning up the fingerboard? All would have given these nuages a little spark as Stéphane would surely have responded to Django as he always did, with fireworks.

For me, Legrand's arrangement of 'Milou en Mai' captures a tragic moment. In the course of my Grappelli profiles on radio, DVD and this book, I've had the pleasure to listen to hundreds of hours of Stéphane's music. I always knew he was good, but as I listened, my admiration grew, until I became sure that Grappelli was a musical genius. Thankfully, I'm not alone; Ed Baxter who possibly heard Stéphane live more times than anyone else, particularly appreciated his constant invention: 'He was the finest improviser I've ever heard. I don't think that there's anyone that could improvise on their instrument like Grappelli. I include Louis Armstrong, the whole kit and caboodle. I put him tops for that. And actually, it's the improvising that used to get to the people. He could improvise like God knows what, and his improvisations were melodic.

'One of the best comments was from Alistair Clarke at *The Scotsman*. He reviewed a Grappelli concert and he said, "The marvel of Grappelli is that he's a musical Houdini," and I thought, absolutely. He'd go into an improvisation on a tune and somehow or other he'd always get out of it at the end and escape from it. And you didn't know where or when. Everybody would wonder, "How's he going to stop? How's he going to get out of that?" He'd be going along at 100 miles an hour and he always found a way out.'

I hear so many people on radio and TV talking about 'genius'. They refer to footballers and sportsmen, etc, and they so often devalue the term. I once said to Martin Taylor, 'Do you think Grappelli was a genius?' and he said, 'Yes, absolutely.' Martin had listened for 11 years, touring the world and meeting every great performing jazzman on the road. My experience was smaller, essentially limited, but Stéphane had rarely sounded uninspired and never played a wrong note.'

Meanwhile, in substantial arrangements such as Legrand's, Stéphane could only improvise within strictly defined limits, so he is largely reading the music, and on the footage of the event his eyes are struggling behind his powerful glasses.

Then, surrounded by 100 great players in front of a television audience of millions, Stéphane fluffed a note. Most of the audience would have missed it, and the television director let it go, but Stéphane didn't, and he was never really comfortable with that birthday appearance. At the age of 84, his frailty had finally accompanied him to his platform. And yet he rarely complained; if asked how he was, he would limit himself to a breathy 'I'm very tired.'

In May, Stéphane and Michel Legrand enjoyed a rematch, this time in the sound-recording studio. Perhaps because of the potential this accorded to retake and edit, this time the resulting 'Milou en Mai' is flawless, especially when Grappelli is allowed the luxury of improvisation, his indelible trademark. On 'Autumn Leaves' from the same record, Stéphane lends a gentle melancholy to an arrangement that even included a vocal chorus with echoes of Ward Swingle and his jazz Bach of the 1960s. Legrand's sister, Christiane, had in fact been a soloist in Swingle's famous French-based ensemble.

Legrand/Grappelli is an impeccable record of its genre and Stéphane particularly enjoys himself in his improvised cadenzas, pushing and pulling the pulse against a bed of swirling strings. Michel Legrand, meanwhile, felt a common thread with Stéphane: 'Our friendship and closeness was always there. Our love of music was the same and I will never forget Stéphane. He remains part of my life forever.'

★

Also in 1992 Stéphane enjoyed a reunion with another, even older, friend – George Shearing. Just as Eammon Andrews had crept up on Stéphane for television's *This Is Your Life* in 1979, now it was the pianist's turn for the big red book treatment. The programme's new presenter, Michael Aspel, saved Stéphane's appearance until last, describing him as 'a larger-than-life personality'. George seemed genuinely pleased to welcome Stéphane and the fiddler, surprisingly light on his feet, virtually kidnapped George in his rush to escape the rigours of television talking, escorting him to the piano, where the old timers played with John Dankworth and his clarinet.

George launched straight into one of his clever 'homage to Bach' intros and his most popular composition, 'Lullaby Of Birdland'. Although clearly unrehearsed, the resulting jam session has some more wonderful Bach from George as Stéphane and John exchange knowing looks and let the man of the moment have his head. The three friends then toss around phrases with an abandon that seems easy but was, of course, the culmination of a total jazz experience of over 100 years. It's a wonderful television moment that couldn't have been planned – it's funny, entertaining and not without music. Most of all, it's good to see Stéphane and George reconciled, even if only for the cameras.

Since officially parting company with Stéphane, Martin Taylor had remained a friend but, like Shearing, had succeeded in establishing a footing as a jazz artist in his own right. Ironically, he was also becoming famous for his tune 'Frankie And Johnny', the popular theme for a series of television advertising sketches for the Renault Clio that had youths across England enquiring, 'Papa?' 'Nicole?' The music world moves in mysterious ways.

Linn Records had been established in 1982 to supply reference-quality recordings for the world-renowned Linn High Fidelity Company. Together with Martin, they had made *Don't Fret*, *Change Of Heart* and *Artistry*, the latter a solo album which made Number One in the JVC jazz chart. In January 1993, the company brought Stéphane and Martin back together at the French studio Miraval for the album project *Reunion*.

This interesting record reveals how Martin's staggering technique and musical approach to the guitar had continued to develop. Stéphane clearly enjoys Martin's exciting and complex counterpoint, the guitarist supplying his own bass, rhythm and harmony in the absence of the usual trio. As Dave Gelly points out in the record's sleeve notes Martin does all this and yet is able to make it sound remarkably effortless.

For me, however, it's also a very sad record in that Stéphane responds to Martin with fantastic ambition, launching into his solos with the energy of a 20-year-old, with dubious success. His head is full of ideas and his imagination and urge to swing is intact and as brilliant as ever, but where so often in the past he seemed merely to think and then do, now his physical resources lag behind. It's particularly sad for me because, on listening to this record, I realised that I had taken his genius for granted. When it began to fail, I suddenly realised that, as Ric Sanders observed, 'he had always transcended his technique'. He could do anything, and so what he chose to do became that much more interesting.

Meanwhile, the slow track 'Willow Weep For Me' has some fine playing. Stéphane's fingers finally catch up with the great mind and Martin provides world-class blues-tinged guitar. In the cadenza, Stéphane still soars. The two friends are truly united.

Martin duets brilliantly with himself on 'Miravel' and the two are on fine form for 'Jenna', both tunes showing the guitarist's gift for composition. Stéphane's solo on 'Jenna' is so poignant it hurts. A master is clearly drawing on resources that he often felt were spent. 'Some days,' Joseph Oldenhove told me, 'Stéphane didn't want to move, but he did, and when he had his violin, he could still summon that strength.'

Like with *One On One*, the McCoy Tyner recording of 1990, *Reunion* is a good record, but it's clear that, for Stéphane, four days from his 85th birthday, conjuring magic was becoming harder.

For all that, however, the French wizard retained orchestral ambitions and his birthday celebration in England had been scheduled for London's Barbican Hall on 6 February, where the resident London Symphony Orchestra was booked to be conducted by Stéphane's loyal friend Laurie Holloway, who would also provide a 'Stéphane Grappelli Overture'. 'Stéphane was staying in Notting Hill somewhere and we had a meeting with the producers,' remembers Laurie. 'The producers said, "What tune are you going to play?" and he said in his own inimitable way, "Oh, Laurie will take care of that." So I did everything and had a great time. It was just wonderful, firstly to work with Stéphane and secondly to work with Stéphane and the LSO. For the overture, I put a selection of his greatest hits together. I did quite a lot of arranging [for that gig]: the overture, "I Got Rhythm", "Someone To Watch…", "Night And Day", "I've Got You Under My Skin" and "Sweet Georgia Brown".'

On that occasion, Stanley Black also arranged, Marion Montgomery sang and Maurice Murphy contributed a startling trumpet solo. The Grappelli Trio that night consisted of Marc Fosset and bassist Jean-Philippe Viret,* while Allan Ganley provided his usual tasteful drumming. Sadly, orchestral costs prohibited any recording.

Back in Paris, President François Mitterrand saluted Stéphane by awarding him with the Commandre de l'Ordre du Mérite, the second degree of La Légion d'Honneur. It was unusual for an artist to be so decorated and is a testament to the esteem in which Stéphane was held in French society. Steph of course kept a photograph in his by-now-bulging shoeboxes which, due to lack of space in his tiny Paris flat, had been assigned to the cellar storeroom.

April 1993 found the adventurer in Loosdrecht, the Netherlands, to record the album *La Copine* with a band performing under the name Capelino. These young musicians, working in the Hot Club tradition, bravely tackled classics such as Billie Holiday's signature 'Lover Man'. Gifted vocalist Saskia van Essen inspired the octogenarian to some of his best late playing (how could Grappelli ever have dreamed of 'Swing '39' becoming 'Swing '93'?), but on the recording it has to compete with the duet violin of Peter van den Bos and the Django-esque guitars of Jan and Evert Martens, ably supported by the bass of Hans Wisselink and the saxophone of Arjen van El. The gypsy-jazz inspiration that Stéphane and Django took to the Hague in the 1930s had taken a firm root in the rich lowland soil and thrived.

On 9 June, Stéphane's year-long Birthday celebrations continued in American style at New York's Carnegie Hall. On the concert recording, Stéphane sounds as if he's having a fabulous time and, most importantly for Stéphane, the audience share his delight. Stan Martin at radio station WQEW referred to the event as 'one of the greatest and most exciting moments of my life'.

As always, Stéphane drew heavily on the musicians he worked alongside, always listening and responding to them. That June night offered two contrasting inspirations, first in the driving New York swing of Bucky Pizzarelli and Jon Burr. These session veterans gave Stéphane a different take on jazz from that of his European regulars, replacing the laid-back charm of Martin Taylor and Marc Fosset with a distinct New York push. Stéphane obviously loves it.

Pizzarelli is the natural heir to the electric seven-string-guitar sound of George Van Eps, and the rich chordal bed recorded here is exactly the stuff to

---

*Born in San Quentin in 1959, Viret was classically trained at Versailles. He had been taking French work with Stéphane since 1989.

set Stéphane off. Meanwhile, Burr, on bass, is an original member of American violinist Mark O'Connor's Hot Swing and is immediately at home with Stéphane's repertoire, although even that is spiced for this occasion with 'All God's Chillun Got Rhythm' and Johnny Mercer's 'I Thought About You'. Grappelli responds with a renewed vigour for a familiar 'I Got Rhythm', which sounds refreshed, as if he's returning the Gershwin tune home after a long time doing Europe. With his 'big ears' focusing hard, he adds an amazing counterpoint to Bucky's solo on 'Night And Day'. (Even though the number of guitars has been interestingly reduced to one, with the synergy of Jon and Bucky it's never an issue.) Then, on the hoary old 'Limehouse Blues', Grappelli gives truth to his own saying: 'Age? There is no age!'

The second New York inspiration came appropriately from Holland, the motherland of the original Neuw Amsterdames colony. Stéphane had met The Rosenberg Trio at the Montreal Jazz Festival in 1991, a family band featuring Stochelo Rosenberg on lead guitar, Nous'che on rhythm and Nonnie on bass. Together, they remain one of the world's foremost exponents of gypsy jazz.* Stéphane would have no doubt enjoyed their adventurous take on the genre, reaching out into the rich seams of world popular music. On 'No More Blues', they give Antonio Carlos Jobim's fast samba the gypsy-jazz treatment, evoking Stéphane's South American memories of the tango. They also contribute the beautiful Chick Corea tune 'Armandos Rumba', returning to the source and breathing new American life into gypsy jazz.

For a finale, the musicians come together for Stéphane's by now traditional jam on 'Sweet Georgia Brown', a piece that inspired Django-esque solos from the guitarists which clearly take Stéphane back for a few moments to the 1930s. Briefly, he sounds as if he were 26 again and swinging at Le Moulin de Gallette. Writing for the *Village Voice*, Gary Giddins was ecstatic: 'The swing he evokes is as decisive as a pendulum... The music soars over the demarcations charged by the beat...and the foot begins to tap the elbow to twitch... It's a kind of hypnosis...a triumph for the ageless violinist and the particular brand of jazz he has made his own.'

During that same summer, BBC Scotland filmed another happy reunion of Stéphane and Martin Taylor, later broadcast under the title *Meeting Grappelli*. This affectionate and unpretentious programme captures beautifully the special relationship that Stéphane had with his wonderful guitarist. The programme shows Stéphane and Joseph Oldenhove arriving at the little airport near Martin's

---

*The Rosenbergs are wonderful gypsy musicians frequently associated with the Samois Festival and with a growing international reputation. This was their US and Carnegie Hall Premiere. Their playing has a taste and restraint rare in the gypsy-jazz genre.

home at Ayr, in Scotland. Stéphane is clearly weak and, in a sad moment, finds it difficult and painful even to get out of the car. But he does, greeting Martin warmly and smiling for the camera: 'You know me, I'm an old trooper!' Martin is heard in voiceover noting, 'He's 50 years older than me and speaks a foreign language. These things don't matter in music. He has his glass of milk and goes to bed – no disco for Stéphane. I get tired touring, but he is 85.'

Later, Martin is shown arriving at Stéphane's hotel where the old violinist greets him, playing him in on the piano. He plays well, and the two men exchange a joke as the fiddler performs a music-hall routine with a silly hat before the film cuts to them having a relaxed dinner. Stéphane is obviously amused to hear that James, Martin's son, has been busking on the streets, and says that he knows all the good sites: 'Django busked with his brother. We did it together a little, but he liked cash on the table.'

Stéphane touches his nose in a little gesture indicating 'toffee nose' or 'stuck up'. I'd seen him use the expression before when a certain celebrity pianist had taken offence at being called an accompanist.

Himself never too proud to busk, Stéphane then recalls, 'I met Django in La Place Pigalle in 1922, at the Musicians' Union rendezvous, during my silent cinema days.' He's never said that before! Maybe that was when a 12-year-old Django first spotted his future partner, or maybe Stéphane has just had too much wine.

When asked about his musical beginnings, Martin describes hearing Django and Stéphane on his dad's 78s, and then gives a wonderful Django-style guitar demonstration on an acoustic guitar. This is interesting in the light of Stéphane's comment, 'He's not Django Reinhardt but he is Martin Taylor,' and Martin's observation that '[Stéphane] never asks you to play like somebody else. He likes me to play the way I play.' Martin virtually always declines to play in the Django style, but he could if he wanted. It's that thing again about what an artist chooses to play being the most interesting, especially when they clearly have the ability to play so much.

The dinner finishes with a typical scenario of Stéphane relaxing on the road, relating a well-known story of Django having great success fishing with a twig and a pin, much to the annoyance of the serious anglers with all the kit yet who catch nothing in the same river. The diners include the watchful Joseph, always attending to Stéphane's needs. In visiting Scotland and its rolling landscape, Stéphane was fulfilling another ambition, as Joseph told me: 'At the end of his life, he was always asking, "Joseph I would like to have a country house," and I had to explain that, with so much travel Cannes, Paris, so many hotels, I didn't know how we could have a country house as well. I opposed the idea for purely practical reasons.'

Back at Martin's country house, the film next cuts to one of Stéphane's most intimate recorded performances, playing 'Daphne' with his host in a casual, friends-at-home way. Martin asks, 'Who was Daphne?'

Stéphane: 'She was a friend of myself and Django. Daphne de Trafford. I don't know if she was an aristocrat, but she was a marvellous lady. That's why we did that [blows a kiss].'

The pair then play an equally relaxed 'Paper Moon' in which Martin has a little fun with the chords. 'I like to throw Stéphane something and he goes, "What's that?",' Martin remarked, 'and maybe that sparks something and he plays something that he hasn't played before. He gives me one of those impish looks: "What did you do there?"'

Clearly impressed, Stéphane comments on film, 'You can't learn jazz. I remember Louis Armstrong saying, "If you don't get it, you will never get it."'

Next, on an impromptu version of 'Sweet Georgia Brown', Stéphane casually throws in a reference to JS Bach's *Brandenburg Concertos* and Martin comments on Stéphane's unique combination of classical and jazz disciplines: 'Only Stéphane does that. He is unique. Stéphane only has to play one note and you know it's him. That's the sign of a great musician.'

Stéphane remarks on their easy dialogue: 'Improvisation must be like classical, like Bach. The best must be respected. You can't go from one chord to another stupidly; there is a sequence, and that's why we play so well together. You saw us play earlier and it wasn't rehearsed. There is a communion between us.'

Next, 'Willow Weep For Me' completes a fascinating late glimpse into Stéphane's effortless technique. Filmed in close-up, it's a must for violin disciples but a lesson for everybody. Seeing Stéphane so relaxed reminded me of a comment from the great English Bach lutenist Nigel North: 'The difference between Grappelli and classical players is that he makes his music from what he can do, instead of wrapping himself around what somebody's written.'

In turn, Martin seems surprised at Stéphane's constant reinvention: 'He's just got better. How does he do it?'

The film ends with one of Stéphane's improvised cadenzas and his resolute wish: 'I like to play to the end. One day maybe my bow will drop, but I will play music to the end.'

The *Meeting Grappelli* programme, directed by David Peat and Jan Leman, was eventually broadcast in November 1993, but sadly only in Scotland. In his autobiography, *Kiss And Tell*, Martin remarks that the only way for a jazz musician to get on English television is to be filmed having an accident. He was only slightly joking.

In October, Grappelli, his bow never dropping, was Yehudi Menuhin's guest in Brussels for a concert under the name All The World's Violins. By this time, Yehudi had established a foundation in the Belgian capital that was devoted to music education and research, and at the Cirque Royal he gathered all his friends to celebrate. From the Yehudi Menuhin School he brought Corina Belcea and Natsuka Yoshimoto to play the Bartók violin duos, and Stéphane would no doubt have loved the Hungarian's fantastic reinterpretation of his native folklore, with its intricate rhythms. The recording of the event next has noted Indian violinist Dr Subramaniam taking to the same platform to play Carnatic music with tampura and mridangam, a percussion instrument. Stéphane initially had his reservations about raga ('it give me the bleu'), but Subramaniam's stately performance on this occasion avoids any fusion and is more representative of the respected Indian musician than their 1986 collaboration.

Next, the Titi Winterstein Quintet, featuring Lulu, Kiegelo and Rigo Reinhardt, play gypsy music – not the Django Reinhardt brand of Manouche jazz but a traditional strand of Eastern European-sounding fiddle, piano and guitar. Yehudi was fascinated by gypsy fiddle and invited Jean-Pierre Catoul to contribute a 'Tango Tzigane', no doubt evoking in Stéphane memories of his role in the film *King Of The Gypsies*.

Following this success, Stéphane takes the stage to warm applause, accompanied by Marc Fosset and bassist Jean-Philippe Viret. They first play the 'Gershwin Medley', with Marc introducing 'Someone To Watch Over Me' very sensitively on classical guitar, inspiring Stéphane to an equally sensitive and rather stately version of what is obviously one of his favourite tunes. Stéphane's tone is much warmer than that on his recent *Reunion* recording with Martin Taylor and he sounds very assured, even in the breakneck choruses of 'I Got Rhythm', responding to the live audience, giving everything and being received rapturously by a delighted crowd.

Next, for 'Sweet Georgia Brown', he again throws in a bit of JS Bach and even some country hoedown double-stops against Viret's solid bass. This performance demonstrates Stéphane return to form, playing for his friends and all the world's fiddles and audibly having a good time. Later, Yehudi joins him for a classically tinged 'Lady Be Good', complete with *arco* bass and classic guitar. The international audience erupts, as these eternal giants of the fiddle seem unstoppable.

On returning to Paris Stéphane suffered a terrible setback, a 'cerebral vascular accident'. This meant hospitalisation and caused considerable concern for his life. Stéphane, however, surprised everybody by bouncing back, albeit with some worrying limitation of movement in his right hand. A crippling event like this is devastating for any musician, but for a violinist of 86 it looked like the end of a career. But everyone except Joseph Oldenhove reckoned without Grappelli's tenacity. 'After three or four weeks, he was performing again in Israel,' recalls Joseph. 'At first he couldn't play the piano, but after about four months he started again. Fortunately, there was no heart attack. After the vascular problem, his violin technique was inhibited, but he still played well.'

Defiantly unstoppable, by 18 January Stéphane was back in the recording studio, easing back ever so slightly with a guest spot on a new album by The Rosenberg Trio. To help him, they came to Davout Studios in Paris and Stéphane largely confined himself to familiar ground: 'Tears', 'Manoir de mes Rêves', 'Embraceable You' and 'Pent-Up House'. However, from the first notes of 'Pent-Up House', Steph is clearly having a ball – it's like he was 26 again, at the forefront of a revolution with his band of cocky wild young gypsy lads. It's as if the ailing Grappelli is experiencing a kind of spiritual *déjà vu*, some wonderful trigger opening a door into memory, propelling him back to a forgotten moment. The session photographs say it all, depicting a beaming Stéphane surrounded by the three T-shirted, moustached gypsies. Curiously, this album was recorded precisely 60 years since Stéphane first ventured into the studio with Django in January 1934.

The recording benefits from a very open and natural live sound, and the well-recorded Maccaferri-type guitars sound good as the guitarists are inspired by Stéphane, and he in return reaches into the depths of his fiddle for a mournful rendition of 'Tears'. Stochelo Rosenberg, meanwhile, offers his own affectionate solo guitar tribute with 'Stéphanesque', which is in fact more reminiscent of one of Django's improvisations, a mixed bag of arpeggios and flourishes with odd quotes – very virtuosic. Curiously, it lacks structure, just like Django's similar work without Stéphane as a foil. That aside, this is a great comeback album, and Stéphane was moved to remark, 'Of all the gypsy-guitar players and groups I have played with during my lifetime, the Rosenbergs are absolutely the best.'

★

By 24 January 1994, Grappelli was back on the international platform, celebrating his birthday two days early at London's Barbican Centre. Yehudi couldn't be there but sent his good wishes: 'For us all, this great musician, everlastingly benign and genial, transcends time. He also transcends national borders, for in England he embodies the ideal Frenchman and in France the perfect English gentleman. May we celebrate more such happy occasions.'

The concert was conceived and organised by the Decca record producer Marcel Stellman and was designed to raise money for the Ravenswood Foundation, an organisation set up 40 years earlier to provide care for people with learning difficulties. Stéphane, his trio and composer/arranger Stanley Black were donating their services for free. Born in 1913, Black had, like Stéphane, made his name in the 1930s through working with Coleman Hawkins and Louis Armstrong in London. He'd progressed through directing the BBC dance orchestra to being musical director at the Elstree Film Studios and won an Ivor Novello Award for the Cliff Richard musical *Summer Holiday*. He remembered encountering Stéphane last in 1979: 'A rehearsal in Winnipeg with the City Symphony Orchestra was proving to be uncharacteristically hard-going; the strings in particular were fidgety and kept looking at their watches. It was only when the concertmaster leaned over to me and whispered, "Stéphane Grappelli is doing a matinée next door," that light dawned, and it wasn't too long before our rehearsal was cut short and practically all the 75 symphony orchestra players were stampeding across to the theatre next door, where a packed house necessitated our having to stand at the back and along the aisles for the remaining half hour of Grappelli magic.'

In 1994, Marcel Stellman revealed how the Grappelli magic worked well at the box office: 'We sold the whole of the Barbican within less than 24 hours' notice. We had kept 200 special seats in the theatre, which would cost £125 each, black tie, and the guests that came to that show would be invited to dinner afterwards at the Barbican with Stéphane and the musicians. We also had the French Ambassador there. Stéphane said, "In all the concerts I've ever given, the French Ambassador was never there," and I said to him, "Well, I've got news for you – I've invited him and he's coming." He couldn't believe it. [The Ambassador] was sitting with us at the dinner, talking to Stéphane.'

The Barbican guest list also included actor Anthony Quinn, entertainer Tommy Steele and singer Dame Vera Lynn, a British national treasure, who had been looking forward to seeing Stéphane again: 'I first met Stéphane many years ago in France,' she recalled. 'My husband, Harry, actually played with him in the '30s in a nightclub in London. I've always been a mad fan, and apparently he is a fan of mine because I know he carries a photograph of me in his violin case.'

Marcel also arranged a surprise guest: 'We wanted someone else to play with him, and that was Nigel Kennedy, but when I approached Nigel he said, "Would I? My God, yes I would. But the situation is that I can't publicise it, because if my agent finds out that I've got another concert when he's got something booked around the same time, it might prejudice the booking." So he said, "I'll do it on two conditions: if Aston Villa don't play on that Saturday, I'll come; if Aston Villa do play – you know I'm a nut – then I have to go." So we were praying that Aston Villa wouldn't be playing. Fortunately they weren't. But I couldn't advertise [his name], even in the programme. He said, "It mustn't be told; put me down as guest artist," which is what we did.

'We finished up the evening with a big cake that came in the shape of a violin. Stanley Black and the string orchestra were playing together. Stéphane and Nigel played together as if they'd played for years, and I'd almost say that Nigel played as well as Stéphane... Stéphane played one solo with Stanley at the piano. I think they played "Misty".'

Stéphane was keen to see the money go to the children, as Marcel relates: 'We arranged to meet him at the airport with a car and bring him into town. I said, "I'll book you at the Savoy." He said, "You will not! Keep the money for the kids. I'll stay at my usual little place in Bayswater." That's the kind of man he was.'

For Marcel, the concert was a great success, both musically and for the charity: 'We raised £50,000 that evening, after expenses, and that fell beautifully. We made a music room at Ravenswood and called it 'the Stéphane Grappelli, Stanley Black, Nigel Kennedy Music Room'. Nigel and Stanley came to the dedication of the room and played for the kids. Stéphane couldn't come – he was in America – but he sent a letter:

To all my friends of Ravenswood,

I'm so pleased to have been able to contribute and help you in the raising of some money which I hope will bring some more happiness to those children and people who need assistance, and so for their family.

Thank you to all of you for your effort, and very specially to Marcel and Jeannie.*

I wish my very best to the Ravenswood Association and all people working for a better world of friendship and harmony.

Sincerely,

Stéphane Grappelli,

August 1994.

*Marcel Stellman's wife, Jean.

27 Mon Livre

'In later years, Stéphane liked to have breakfast in bed, tea and croissant or brioche on a tray. He would spend much of the morning in bed.'

– Joseph Oldenhove

Stéphane the octogenarian was becoming increasingly philosophical – not intellectually preoccupied but, like many people of advancing years, he was putting his house in order.

After dedicating his memoirs '*à mes parents*', sadly the cemetery that had housed his father's ashes for over 50 years was undergoing alterations, prompting a relocation. Having retrieved the urn, Stéphane wanted to return Ernesto's remains to Italy. In the interim, the ashes remained in a cupboard at his apartment at the Rue Dunkerque. As so many of us do, Stéphane and Joseph resolved the nearness of death and mortality with the escape valve of humour. 'We had a little joke about "the father in the closet",' Joseph remembered.

Together with his companion Joseph, Stéphane had researched his family's background in Alatri and Nettuno. Travelling via Rome, the pair visited the town church, with its many inscriptions pertaining to Stéphane's aristocratic ancestors, and the Grappelli Tower, at the foot of which, in a poignant gesture, he and Joseph redistributed Ernesto's ashes. Stéphane was very taken with the local response to his interest in the town – it was planned that he be presented with the equivalent of the keys to the city by the local mayor.

By the 1990s, Alatri had obtained historical significance thanks to the Roman archaeology found there, which dated back to the second century. This interested Stéphane, as Joseph told me: 'He was well up on history and literature, very *auto-didacte*. He loved to read historical magazines – French history, but also a wider span.'

The combination of history and family was irresistible, and Joseph and Stéphane became fascinated. 'Ernesto's father was the mayor of Nettuno,' Joseph continued. 'It was an important locality, and many of Stéphane's ancestors were well positioned in that society – Italian aristocracy. There is even a 19th-century poet called Grappelli in the Vatican circle. In the 16th, there were many mayors of Alatri or Frosinone who were Grappellis, and the gravestones of some are in the chapel San Benedetto in Frosinone, where you can see the Grappelli coat of arms. The 14th-century Grappelli Tower close to the Grappelli Palace in Alatri, is the birthplace of the mother of one of the popes.' Returning to Paris, Stéphane kept part of his fathers ashes in a small box at the Rue Dunkerque.

In Paris, Stéphane was very pleased to be approached by Jean-Marie Salhani, who, with International Music Publications, proposed to publish a book of his compositions, along with some photographs and a short biography in a series called *Mon Livre*. Stéphane became very proud of this project, and was especially excited at seeing his music so beautifully presented. The book included transcripts of 'Minor Swing' and 'Tears' from the Reinhardt years, but also 'Gary' for Gary Burton and 'Milou en Mai'. The presentation included scores for piano and violin, along with a separate violin part, while Yves Marc Ajchenbaum provided some accompanying biographical text, with much help from Joseph Oldenhove.

In the course of picture research, a minor tragedy was revealed. Hundreds of Stéphane's shoebox photographs had been stored in the cellar of his apartment at the Rue Dunkerque, and it was discovered that a basement flood had soaked some of the boxes. Many priceless shots, including some picturing Stéphane with Django and Louis Armstrong, were irreparably damaged, the prints stuck together in a congealed mess. Luckily, many others escaped with only peripheral damage.

Amongst those to survive intact was the original of the most famous Hot Club Quintet photograph of all, showing the Quintet with Roger Grasset on bass, although every record attributes the face to Louis Vola.* Copies of this photograph had graced Decca's album sleeves for decades, and its reverse side proudly carries the stamp of 'Will Collins and Lew Grade Ltd., Theatrical and Vaudeville Exchange, Cecil House, 41 Charing Cross Rd, London'.

One day, Stéphane handed the picture to me in the Rue Dunkerque flat. It was, of course, just a faded piece of paper, but there is a potency in original artefacts that triggers the imagination, like a window opening on the past, taking you back to the time in which they were taken – in this case, to the world of Bricktop's in 1937. It felt like I was in contact with a different world.

We shared these memories in the Rue Dunkerque apartment in 1995, Stéphane surrounded by his treasures – oriental dolls, miniature silver violins and glorious Romanesque art books. He always sat in the same modest armchair, offering a view of Parisian rooftops and geranium-blossomed windowsills. Just

---

*I admit that I compounded this error by believing Decca when attributing the photograph as picturing Vola on my 2002 DVD *Stéphane Grappelli: A Life In The Jazz Century*. I'm indebted to the many fans who spotted this and corrected me.

below were the streets and courtyards where he had busked for centimes a lifetime ago. We drank English tea from delicate china cups and shared a little quiet, the Paris air occasionally spiced with distant car horns, very French in their stuttered impatience.

Much had changed in my life since I'd first met Stéphane in 1978. When I'd had Stéphane's photograph taken with the young Suzuki violinists, I'd been a BBC sound engineer. As I learned that craft, I also produced records and eventually radio programmes. In the 1990s, I was directing television for Channel 4 and presenting radio programmes for BBC Radio 3. As I learned the art of storytelling, I kept returning to Stéphane's amazing story and constantly reminding others that that adventure had never really been properly told. There were books and there were interviews, but it seemed to me that Stéphane's life in the jazz century needed to be visually illustrated. Together with my producer, Judy Caine, we kept turning up little filmed gems, performances by Stéphane in every kind of musical setting.

In Paris, during the course of visiting Stéphane and attempting to establish the source of a particularly intriguing bootleg video called *Jazz Hot*, Judy and I were directed to a tiny basement in the Rue Lacharrière. It seemed that every guitarist in the world had a copy of this tatty bootleg piece of footage consisting of fuzzy images with distorted sound in two conflicting languages, showing Stéphane in the 1930s with Django Reinhardt and The Hot Club Quintet. At the offices of Lobster Films the vintage-film restorer Serge Bromberg told me how this wonderful find had been discovered on lethal, highly inflammable nitrate film stock, and then treated us to a showing of a beautifully restored version. Then came the blow: we could see the film but couldn't buy it. No definitive owner had been established for the film, and a legal dispute was raging in the French courts. Babik Reinhardt had claimed the film on behalf of his dead father and, until a suitable resolution could be found, the film was effectively a ward of court.

However, Serge had another clip in which he thought we might be interested. Astonishingly, he produced a wonderful clip from the late 1920s of Stéphane with Grégor et ses Grégoriens. This film *was* for sale, so we took our finds back to show Stéphane. Naturally, Steph felt he had as much right to the *Jazz Hot* film as anybody else, but at that time there was no solution, although he enjoyed seeing Grégor again after 67 years: 'You know, he was a very funny man, and it's because of him I return to the fiddle.'

Judy and I were by now making some headway as independent film-makers, having won a gold medal in the New York Film Festival and with the US Film and Video Festival having awarded us for 'creative excellence' for a film called *Africa I Remember*. Indeed, much of our recent work had been in the Gambia, West Africa, recording and filming the music of that region for BBC2 and Radio 3. These programmes received wonderful critical responses, including *The Times*' 'Critics' Choice' and *The Radio Times*' 'Pick Of The Week' but, despite this recognition, we could find no broadcaster prepared to finance a film of Stéphane's story.

In New York, I hounded the commissioning editors of major corporations, while in London I tried the major arts-documentary commissioners – Melvyn Bragg at *The South Bank Show* and *Omnibus* at the BBC. All were polite but declined an interest. I persisted, though, eventually finding some interest in Switzerland via a trip to Amsterdam and the Documentary Film Festival, and the Swiss offered to put up £10,000. However, a film on Stéphane's 77-year career, rich in archive film, would need substantial finance, perhaps £100,000 – small change for Hollywood – where a small film costs $50 million – but a lot for a tiny British independent film company.

With help from the Enterprise Council, I visited Germany and spoke there with a spokesman for ARTE, a Franco-German arts broadcasting company, and again there were many smiles but no money. Of course, all this travel was being financed from our own pockets, and in order to stay in business I directed commercials and promotional films, from the deserts of Yemen to the rain of London's north Acton – life was never dull. I soon became determined to somehow share Stéphane's story with a public I felt sure would enjoy it.

Despite his failing health, Stéphane agreed to visit Japan, and on 1 April 1995, All Fools' Day, he appeared at Tokyo's Suntory Hall to take part in a concert, which was recorded by Tokyo FM and features Stéphane being accompanied once more by Marc Fosset and Jean-Philippe Viret. This film shows little sign of Stéphane's physical problems as he launches into a programme of his favourite 20th-century standards, as swinging as ever, treating the enthusiastic Japanese to a rhapsodic 'How High The Moon?' and 'Fascinating Rhythm'. Viret then gives Stéphane an extended rest, soloing on bass for all of 'I've Got The World On A String', and Stéphane returns afresh with a 'Limehouse Blues' freer and more daring than his 1935 version and truly extraordinary 60 years after his first recording of it.

Marc Fosset, meanwhile, is on good form, his guitar sounding like a richly harmonic electric piano on 'How High The Moon?' and offering up his individual brand of scat singing on 'I Won't Dance'.

Stéphane evidently felt well enough to play the piano for this event and derives a lot of joy from a very big-sounding concert grand, rhapsodising again on 'These Foolish Things' and 'The End Of A Love Affair' before hitting his stride style on Ellington's 'Satin Doll'. Then, back on fiddle, he breaks a long tradition by extending his 'Gershwin Medley' to include 'S'Wonderful', giving Marc the opportunity to explore the verse of 'Someone To Watch Over Me'.

Stéphane then addresses the audience in English, thanking them for their attendance and telling them how 'being in this lovely country, we consider this as a marvellous holiday'. Joseph later expanded on this: 'When I knew him, his whole life was a holiday. He enjoyed life, and he enjoyed travel so much. The Japanese were very welcoming, lots of presents everywhere, maybe some origami in the dressing room – a paper bird, flowers, so many presents, the greetings and bowing so theatrical.'

'The favourite place Stéphane's visited was Sicily, but he wouldn't return there, perhaps in case his dream was destroyed. Stéphane was in Italy in the '50s and he arrived in Taormina, in Sicily, at a small hotel called Naomachi. He had a room with a large terrace and a view over the sea of the volcano, Etna, and a Greek temple. He was so entranced, he stayed three months. He described his feelings as "I'm staying – it's paradise!" But he loved all of the south – the Mediterranean, the sun, Morocco, Tunisia, the French Riviera.' This reminded me of the many postcards Stéphane sent to me, their messages always upbeat and alive: 'On the road to Australia, we stop a few days in Singapore. Thank you for your good wishes, Stéphane and Joseph.'

The Japanese concert went on to be released on a CD appropriately entitled *We Love Stéphane Grappelli*. There are the occasional slipped notes, but at 87 Stéphane's swing still defies gravity.

Wherever Stéphane went in these later years, he seemed to be showered with honours. In 1995, he again topped the prestigious *Down Beat* readers' poll, made their Violinist of the Year on their 60th anniversary as well as topping their critics' poll. Perhaps a little embarrassed by all these gongs, Stéphane kept his awards at the Rue Dunkerque flat, tucked out of sight on a shelf behind a door, including his Lifetime Achievement awards from the National Academy of Recording Arts and Sciences. He was never falsely modest, though – they were probably hidden as much for their rather avant-garde designs as for any other consideration. The Rue Dunkerque had a conservative air and Stéphane was traditional in his artistic tastes.

According to Joseph, he avoided Politics with a capital P: 'Stéphane distanced himself from politics. He tended to the right in French politics, but his art was more socialist. But in France, the left do little for poor people and the right are not much different.

'He sympathised with the left-wing minister of culture, Jack Lang, and they became friends. Jacques Delors was also a great friend. Stéphane also liked Jacques Chirac – he trusted him. Stéphane wasn't really left or right; he was too far from the political spectrum. He sided with individuals rather than parties. He was totally against extremism, particularly French communism, but would be excellent friends with various communist mayors. Even when he was poor, he said, he was not jealous of those who had money.

'He didn't buy a daily newspaper but he loved the satirical newspaper *Canard Enchaine*, political satire with excellent cartoons. The satire was light and fun and it had only six pages, so it was convenient to carry around. De Gaulle famously said that you would learn plenty from the *Canard* that you would never discover on radio or television.'

Since recording with Michel Legrand in 1992, Stéphane had longed for a rematch, and in August of 1995 the opportunity arose. This time, however, Stéphane wanted to work a little differently. Joseph: 'Stéphane especially enjoyed the second Legrand record because, when he made the second one, it was a small ensemble. Michel was also happier because he was inspired by Stéphane's playing in his writing. This also influenced the orchestra to play in a certain spirit.'

'The second record was recorded with just Stéphane and a rhythm section,' confirms Michel. 'On top of this, I later added the orchestra.'

I know Stéphane was pleased because I saw him enjoying the record in the flat, sitting in that favourite chair with his ghetto blaster, toe-tapping in perfect time. The idea of overdubbing strings and woodwind is a good one, and on the song themes Michel decorates Stéphane's line artfully. When he improvises, he largely lets the rhythm support, occasionally adding some deft piano. Consequently there is a stronger link to jazz.

Stéphane took a particular delight in 'La Vie en Rose', a great tune with echoes of both Edith Piaf, who composed the lyric, and Louis Armstrong, who famously recorded it. This time, Legrand dares to add sustained strings and brass stabs to Stéphane's extempore and it works, a tribute to both musicians.

Next, on 'Douce France', Stéphane sounds unbelievably nimble, skimming the rhythm with the unmistakable Grappelli touch still firmly in place, while Legrand sets the violin section a challenge by writing for them in imitation of Steph. It's a nice touch.

In February 1996, I made a small breakthrough with the broadcasters: BBC Radio 2 finally agreed to my idea of a broadcast profile of Stéphane. The commissioning editor, David Vercoe, liked the working title, '80 Years On The Fiddle', so we stuck with it. Although radio budgets don't really stretch to trips to Paris, David found the money to pay for a sound engineer and myself to visit Stéphane in his home. I particularly wanted Stéphane to tell his story at home and in his Quartier, feeling that being in his own territory would help him and perhaps trigger memories. I also felt that, if his health permitted, it would be good to get Stéphane reminiscing on the streets of Montmartre, where his story had begun 88 years earlier.

The BBC were keen to have Marcel Stellman present their programme. As well as organising Stéphane's 86th birthday concert at London's Barbican, Marcel had known Stéphane through meetings at MIDEM,* in Cannes. A further advantage was that Marcel was fluent in French – Stéphane would be helped if he could occasionally confer with an interviewer in his mother tongue. Stéphane had already decided to give his story in English, and his English was good, but there were often moments when he struggled for a specific word. Luckily, Marcel was available and delighted to be involved.

At this point I called a meeting with Stéphane; his personal manager, Joseph and his British agent, Ed Baxter. Stéphane was due in England to perform at the Chichester Music Festival and would be staying at the modest Westland Hotel, a family-run place in Bayswater, London, which Stéphane had enjoyed staying in for over 20 years. Although I didn't know it, events had taken a dramatic turn, as Ed Baxter later recalled: 'At Chichester, he had a heart problem and had to go into the clinic in London for a week. We had to cancel two other concerts. He was at the clinic for a week and a half. Joseph stayed with him at the Westland.'

In April, we all met at the Westland and then adjourned for lunch at a nearby Chinese restaurant at Stéphane's request – he enjoyed Chinese food, but he was clearly very unwell. He had no appetite and declined everything except some lychee fruit as a dessert. Stéphane told me, 'I always have a dessert. It reminds me of when I could have nothing.'

*Established in 1967, MIDEM is an annual international trade show for all music genres.

We were later joined at the restaurant by my friend and bank manager Alan Williams, who had been a great help to me as I struggled to establish Music on Earth Productions, dedicated to the production of in-depth music programming. Alan never accused me of madness, even as I plunged all my savings into the idea. Sitting in that busy restaurant, talking to one of the 20th-century's greatest musicians, I had little time to reflect on the origins of my quest.*

Tucking into a plate of Peking duck, Alan was very at home. He's a keen amateur photographer and has a fantastic collection of celebrity portraits. It was about to expand. Alan had recently retired, and when I suggested he work as a production manager for Music on Earth he was delighted.† During lunch, it was soon clear that Stéphane needed somewhere quiet to rest, so we quickly reconvened to the Westland Hotel, where Joseph took Stéphane up to his room.

We then all gathered in the hotel conference room for an urgent chat and Judy, my producer, explained the position over the BBC radio commitment while I made a proposal to film Stéphane's interviews regardless of all the broadcast rejections. It seemed to me that Stéphane's story needed to be told and we couldn't afford to delay any longer. Ed Baxter and Joseph conferred and then agreed that we could go ahead with no payment to Stéphane other than the small radio fee.

We were all shocked and saddened by Stéphane's frailty and resolved to find a solution to this dilemma. I offered to donate my directing services free of charge and Judy made a similar resolution on production and organisation. Judy has a background in music management and a degree in combined arts, but most of all she is the best organiser I've ever met in my 33 years in the business.

We had lots of resolve and determination but little money. Then, in a bold

---

*In establishing Music on Earth, I'd been inspired by Sir David Attenborough and, specifically, his groundbreaking natural-history series *Life On Earth*. Ironically, David had inspired himself through the programmes he'd commissioned as a BBC controller. Single-handedly, David had established the concept of landmark television with bold series such as *Civilisation* and *The Ascent Of Man*. When I proposed the name Music on Earth, he was typically encouraging and enthusiastic, always replying to my letters and even shocking me occasionally by taking time out of his hectic schedule to telephone and ask how I was getting on. Thinking I'd find it useful, he eventually offered me his record collection, which included a superb anthology of world music that he'd collected on his global travels. The discs are full of surprises, including everything from Neolithic musical stones to the songs of Polynesia. I treasure that rare collection and it's become a rich source of reference as well as a constant delight.

†Alan Williams obviously helped me with financial matters as well as introducing me to a friend, the British record producer Tony Swain. Tony was justly famous for his production work with musicians 'Spandau Ballet' and Alison Moyet. Both Tony and Alan were Grappelli fans and keen to see his story told.

and generous gesture, record producer Tony Swain and Alan Williams offered to fund from their own pockets the cost of a camera crew for the Paris interviews.

Within a month, everything was in place. Together, Judy and I set up a production office in a tiny room in a Montmartre Hotel, scouting for evocative and pertinent locations. Some parts of Paris clearly played a crucial part in Stéphane's story, and although we could afford a video crew for only three days, we worked out logistics to record as much as possible. Judy had endless telephone conversations in French, agreeing the legalities of filming in the French capital, and we recruited a local location fixer, Antoine Ricard, to ensure that there would be no delays.

I sat with Stéphane in his Rue Dunkerque apartment and discussed the interviews. We agreed to film him in his favourite armchair surrounded by his collection of books and photographs. He showed me the tiny, three-quarter-size violin that his father presented to him in 1920, when Stéphane was 12, telling me, 'This is the only thing I have where my father put his hands.' I suggested that he should hold it during part of the interview, connecting us with those times.

Stéphane showed me more of the rare treasures in his boxes of photographs, including a precious image of his mother. As the originals were so valuable I arranged to copy some of them for inclusion in his story.

One of Stéphane's most vivid memories was his first hearing of recorded jazz back in 1923, 'Stumblin'' by Mitchell's Jazz Kings, in a bar near the cinema in which he worked. I was curious to hear this piece of history and wanted to obtain a copy to play to Stéphane. This is one of those ideas that screams to be realized but leaves you wondering where to start. No modern record superstore stacked to the rafters with digital wonders is likely to stock 80rpm shellac recordings.

There is, however, a growing band of enthusiasts dedicated to preserving our recorded legacy, transferring rare old masters to the digital domain, such as John T Davies in Britain. I knew of John's work through his brilliant transfers of Art Tatum and thought that perhaps he would know where to obtain a copy of the Jazz Kings record. When I spoke to him on the telephone, though, he felt that there was little chance of finding a copy in Britain, although he thought a Parisien by the name of Daniel Nevers would be able to help.

Taking my trusty digital recorder, I turned up at Nevers' dubious subterranean cavern in Montparnasse. In this digital submarine, bristling with every technology from Edison to Sony, Daniel had a copy not just of 'Stumblin'' but of every record Mitchell ever made. When I tried to pay him for the transfer, he refused, donating his research and expertise to the Grappelli project, which I took as a good omen. It was also wonderful to meet briefly someone who is currently researching painstakingly and releasing every scrap of recording by Django Reinhardt. So far he has reached 1948, in 16 volumes, filling 32 CDs, including all of Stéphane's work with Django and many rare broadcasts.

Throughout May, Stéphane was suffering badly with a bronchial condition and his voice remained very weak. Despite this, however, he agreed to be filmed at the famous cabaret Le Lapin Agile, which was quite close to his flat. Given his health, this was the nearest thing to my notion of a return to the streets, as evoked by his 'Chanson de la Rue', a favourite in his late repertoire. Stéphane knew the owners of Le Lapin and they were happy to help, even agreeing to open early on Sunday.

The film crew arrived on Saturday 25 May and went to work immediately. The Paris weather was cold for spring, but the team were as enthusiastic as ever. Robert Foster is my favourite cameraman, and together we'd been chased by crocodiles in Africa and threatened by landmines in Yemen, but we'd always got the shot. In our discussions, Robert immediately understood the importance of the project, and I knew that he would bring something special to this portrayal of Stéphane.

Meanwhile, I had acquired the services of Tony Wass, one of the world's greatest sound engineers. Over the years, we've recorded everything from African harps to symphony orchestras – occasionally both at the same time. Tony always delivers; in taking on a responsibility like Steph's story, I needed the confidence that such a professional brought.

As the evening descended, we toured Montmartre and La Pigalle, recording vivid atmospheric images of Stéphane's Quartier: Le Moulin Gallette (once a thriving *bal musette*), Van Gogh's house and La Butte, where Stéphane had busked for coins. In a generous moment, the friendly Parisian café owners entered into the spirit of the story and donated warming cafés au lait and pastries, and we needed the warmth as the light faded and the temperature dropped like a piece of loose masonry.

I was desperate to get one good shot of La Cathédrale de Nôtre Dame with the light reflected in the River Seine. This part of Paris, around St Germain, isn't strictly Stéphane's Quartier, but he'd performed here often enough in the jazz clubs of the nearby Latin Quarter and I wanted a shot evoking Paris that wasn't Eiffel's Tower, so we camped our equipment on the Pont de l'Archevêché and waited. The wind whistled up the river and the evening became colder. The light wasn't yet right – I wanted that warm glow known to cinematographers as 'the golden-hour effect' and insisted that everybody had to wait. It became even colder. Finally, as the sun set, a shimmer gilded on the water and Robert executed an impossible developing shot, creating the precise atmosphere for Stéphane's Paris. Curiously, it's one of the warmest shots of Paris I've ever seen. The crew were by now blue.

The next morning, we gathered early at Stéphane's childhood home on the Rue de Rochechouart. This tiny attic flat, were he had lived with his father, still retains its communal tap on the stairs. When we visited, though, Stéphane's old single room housed students and nobody knew of Ernesto or Stéphane Grappelli. There were no harmoniums or language teachers. Despite the few architectural changes, that memory might have been from another century. In this century, my ex-bank-manager friend Alan was driving the crew bus through crazy Parisian traffic and 'the A team' were giving their all to get the story in the can.

At Stéphane's birthplace, L'Hôpital Laribroisière, we dodged ambulances in the still-active hospital and sought some coffee to warm our bones. Unchanged since 1908, the proud stone archway entrance sports the Tricolore and the familiar revolutionary legend: 'Liberté, Egalité, Fraternité'.

We then moved on to Le Lapin Agile. With its bright-green slatted shutters and cottage chimneys, the tiny cabaret remained alive with Montmartre's history. A gnarled tree framed the façade and the Lapin himself – a cartoon figure with a flamboyant red scarf and a precarious bottle of wine – still danced on the wall.

The weather was still cold but dry. I wanted to create a shot evocative of the scene that Stéphane had related, wandering here as a street urchin in 1917. I'd found a postcard in a local flea market that showed the Lapin in the early part of the 20th century, and it had changed very little. The idea was to mix visually to Stéphane seated outside in 1996, telling us his story.

The Montmartre district of La Butte is now a very popular tourist site, and we had soon attracted an eager group of onlookers, especially when Stéphane arrived with Joseph. I was keen to make sure that Stéphane didn't get too cold, so we quickly took seats outside the Lapin and began to film. Stéphane told me about the nearby Bateau Lavoir and the times when he used to fetch clay for the artists in Montmartre's bohemian heyday – and then, predictably, it rained. I was concerned for Stéphane and wanted him out of the wet, but in a characteristic gesture he first offered his coat to Judy, 'the lady', and then with help slowly ambled inside.

Once within Le Lapin Agile, the present manager, Yves Mathieu, made us feel very at home. The walls oozed with colourful history as we sat beneath the surreal crucifixion and the hocked paintings of the long-gone revellers of 1917. The traditional drink of the Lapin Agile is cherry brandy and they served it for Stéphane in an antique jug in the shape of the lapin – or, as Stéphane described it, 'ze frisky bunny'. He was soon comfortable and regaled me with some more stories (which form the basis of the earlier chapters of this book) and descriptions of the many lively characters that frequented the Lapin.

As the rain turned to a picturesque torrent and the cherry brandy slipped down quietly, it became evident that Stéphane was in the mood to talk and our planned exterior filming was obviously doomed. Joseph suggested that, as Stéphane was in relatively good voice, we should carry on the interview in the warmth at his home. This was, of course, a fine idea, but our interviewer, Marcel Stellman, wasn't due to turn up until Monday. As I had done the research and written the questions, it seemed sensible for us to go ahead with me switching roles from director to interviewer. Stéphane was happy to do this, so we returned to the flat on the Rue Dunkerque.

The flat – Stéphane's working base for over 20 years – was immaculate. Although they were quite small, Stéphane had filled the rooms with his treasures. The atmosphere was one of grandiloquence, the home of an opulent grandparent with heavy, elaborate furniture, gilded frames and drapery and furnishings in subtle floral designs. Small sculptures of martyred saints tussled for space amidst oriental porcelain and marble framed clocks. English 18th-century watercolours graced the plain walls.

Every surface had a careful display of interesting objects – three snuff-boxes and porcelain bowl, a willow patterned plate and a pair of silver candlesticks, a glass cabinet containing 12 miniature violins, a silver tea service and some precious china. Nothing was idly placed. As Joseph later remarked, 'Stéphane had a strong sense of décor and arrangement of ornamentation. He would place an ashtray or a paper knife just so. Even as he got frailer he would trouble to do that when he came into a room. He was good at it! After the maid had dusted, Stéphane would get angry if she didn't put everything back precisely as he had arranged it.'

And then, of course, along came a film crew with flight cases, television lamps, cameras, tripods and microphone booms. Despite our clutter, however, I wanted Stéphane to be comfortable, so we arranged our shots around his armchair. From that vantage point he could see Paris through the window, his many family photographs on an opposite table and, when he became bored, his television on a walnut cabinet.

Stéphane liked to have his conveniences at hand and kept three remote controls on a spindle-legged table for his television, video and music centre – this last within arm's reach so that he could change CDs easily, reading the booklets with the help of an ornate brass magnifying glass, more Agatha Christie than Sherlock Homes. A bottle of Chivas Regal rested on one cabinet and a Japanese doll stood watch over the photographs.

Stéphane's voice was now small and frail and so he summoned the housekeeper with a tiny hand bell. If it was Joseph he wanted, the bell would be counterpoint with a hoarse cry of 'Joseph!', shrill but commanding. However frail, though, he began to speak: 'My father was Italian and my mother French. I'm a bit of the north and a bit of the south…'

For three hours he poured out his stories, the subjects ranging from Isadora Duncan and Debussy to Carnegie Hall and Django. Compared with accepted versions, the stories varied in interesting detail and some were revelations. I realised that Stéphane had few secrets as he gave his epic tale one last time. Some areas were difficult for him and he would decline to talk – he could not talk about his wartime love, Gwendoline Turner, for instance, and indeed couldn't even say her name. If he had a distasteful memory, he would expurgate the memory by denying all knowledge: 'That film? No, no. I don't remember. It's all a long time ago.'

Other memories were more vivid, however: the sound of rain on a gypsy caravan roof or laughter and comic imitation as Joe Venuti filled a sousaphone with flour. The happy memories were, of course, the strongest.

On Monday Stéphane's voice had recovered slightly and Marcel Stellman took the interviewer's chair. As I had hoped, the two men occasionally conferred in French and eventually they both posed by the window for an affectionate photograph. Stéphane soon had to sit – his walking days were over and he clearly missed them.

Much later, Joseph took time out to tell me of the recent past and a more active Stéphane: 'We enjoyed the theatre. His favourites were the musicals, the Broadway shows *Ol' Man River* [actually titled *Showboat*] – we saw that twice. We have a director friend who puts on Chekov and Stéphane appreciated it but didn't love it.'

At home, Stéphane also savoured a good novel: 'He enjoyed a lot of 19th-century writers like Maupassant, Zola, Victor Hugo – these were favourites.

Somerset Maugham in French. He could speak English quite well. Also Verlaine – 'Chanson sous la Pluie', a poem evoking the spirit of the water in a garden. He loved the Impressionism; it linked to his taste in music and art.'

In 1996 the Grappelli office was still open for business and kept Joseph very busy fielding calls from the United States, Japan and Australia (Stéphane was still very much in demand), while the household remained very homely and down to earth. I would ring occasionally to confirm some detail and Stéphane would answer the phone, and almost always he would assume that I was Martin Taylor, although this was because of the voice, not the guitar playing!

Ironically, however, I did play guitar for Stéphane once. It was the last day of the video and radio interviews and my guitar travelled with me, as it always does. Back in my hotel room, I had been grappling with the chromatic delights of Django's 'Nuages', trying to better understand the music of Stéphane's era, and at Stéphane's flat, quite without warning, Alan Williams produced my instrument from the luggage. I suspected a plot as the cameras kept turning and I did my best with a couple of choruses of a melody from which Stéphane often conjured miracles. Joseph proffered Stéphane a violin but, to my eternal gratitude, he declined, saying very kindly, 'Oh no, Joseph. I have not practised today.' I would have liked to have accompanied Stéphane that day, but I know I'd have struggled to give the genius much inspiration. Nevertheless, he seemed to enjoy my rendition of 'Nuages'. He took my hand in thanks afterwards and exclaimed at my slender digits: 'With hands like those, I could play like Paganini!'

As the crew hastily packed their kit, late for a plane, I could only reply with gratitude, insisting that he already did. Then we carefully put his home back together.

At the end of the session, I sat on the landing outside the flat, exhausted but happy. Stéphane's story was in the can – or, as Joseph wonderfully put it, 'The vegetables are all in the tin, comme ça?'

The task of producing the radio programme ahead of me was the most challenging edit of my career. Stéphane was halting and meandering, his voice weak and indistinct. For the television version, I still had to find a buyer and I owed money to everybody. Nevertheless, I was happy that Stéphane's remarkable story could now be told in his own words. I bid Stéphane a warm goodbye and wished him luck in Japan and Australia. I couldn't really believe that this frail gentleman would make such trips, but as he dozed in his armchair there was little doubt his spirit was as strong as ever.

28 C'est La Vie

'Feeling – what can you do without that? Jazz is not study but feeling.
It is a thing of the heart. If you have it, you have it. The rest comes later.'
– *Stéphane Grappelli*

Stéphane Grappelli's musical legacy developed seemingly effortlessly over an extraordinary career and created a body of recorded work that will last as long as there are people moved by music. More than this, he created a living legacy of disciples. Backstage at every concert, musicians from every field of music came to Stéphane for advice and inspiration, as Joseph Oldenhove observed: 'Stéphane encouraged many young violinists, but only if they had something to say or were interesting. He was discriminating. He enjoyed Nigel Kennedy's playing, and also many in France, and had many violinists visit him. Sometimes that was difficult because obviously he couldn't meet all of them. He would receive many in his dressing room, though, and sometimes they would court him just because they knew he was influential and sometimes it was a genuine admiration for his playing.'

Kennedy remained a friend and Stéphane enjoyed being his mentor. From the 1970s through to the 1990s, they often performed together in Australia, the United States and in the UK. In 1996, after many false starts they finally recorded together for the album *Kafka*, for which Nigel wrote 'Melody In The Wind'. By this time, the young protégé was an established virtuoso, guaranteeing full houses in venues ranging from Carnegie Hall to the Royal Festival Hall; his recording of Antonio Vivaldi's *The Four Seasons* was the biggest-selling classical record ever; and the honesty and directness of his playing reached well beyond the normal classical audience.

On returning to England, I caught up with Nigel in a pub near to his home in Malvern, Worcestershire. Nigel is endearingly eccentric and at the time of our meeting wished to be known as 'Dr Kennedy', but has since decided that he prefers 'Kennedy' (like 'Madonna' or 'Prince', perhaps). But what's in a name? I don't really mind what he calls himself; he's just a truly great player.

At the time of our meeting, I'd heard Kennedy play only once, live at the Malvern Theatre for BBC Radio 3. Curiously, I'd been recording the concert but never actually got to meet him – he arrived as the concert began and I just put a microphone in approximately the right place and hoped for the best, so I heard him from the mobile control room in the car park, untroubled by his image, his hair colour and his choice of dress. I don't know if he wore a tuxedo, tails or a clown outfit and I don't care. He played brilliantly and with passion.

As we arranged to meet in person, the choice of venue was his. The management of his local pub were very friendly and I set up for a television interview as agreed, awaiting 'Dr Kennedy' and his recollections of meeting and working with Stéphane Grappelli. I had borrowed some more money and booked 'the A team', arranging enough lighting and sound coverage for a simple interview.

As 'Dr Kennedy', arrived I had a bit of a shock: he had brought his band, comprising Stéphane's guitarist, John Etheridge, and the bassist Rory McFarlane. I was pleased to see them but wasn't really sure how to cope. The virtuoso wanted to demonstrate his appreciation of Stéphane rather than just talk. This meant a musical performance in the pub, *now!*

Robert the cameraman was wondering how to light three people with two lamps and his soundman was equally concerned, having set up one microphone for the planned interview, so I talked to 'Dr Kennedy' and we reached a compromise: we agreed to do the interview covering his meeting with Stéphane and the Menuhin school years and would then reconfigure the set-up to accommodate his demonstration.

After we'd had a fascinating talk, something transpired that taught me an immensely valuable lesson. The crew had been struggling to arrange lighting and sound for the impromptu band and weren't really happy. I, on the other hand, was delighted, if a little bemused – here I was being serenaded for free by one of the world's greatest violinists. Nigel explained: 'I've always wanted to do something on record with Stéphane and it had never materialised. I've always appreciated Stéphane's playing, not just as a jazz player but as a personality who was a musician amongst all musicians of different types. [He had] such a distinct style. And I'd written this song which is a really melodic thing, a really sunny melody.

'I've had other great mentors in my life – I've been with Yehudi, and if we'd got Yehudi to play it, it would have probably have been a bit more like this. One, two, three, four...'

Kennedy then launched into a rendition of 'Melody In The Wind' in a discreet early 20th-century style with plenty of tasteful rubato and portamento and with a broad, classical vibrato.

Pausing for a little confirmation from John Etheridge, he continued, 'If I played it, it would be a bit more like this. Well, actually we do have a correspondence, Stéphane and I playing, swapping the melody. But when I play it, it's a bit in between the two, semi-straight...'

Kennedy then played his melody in a late 20th-century style, not as broad as Yehudi's, with less rubato and with a distinct and beautiful tone that was clearly his own. He abruptly broke off, sharing a laugh with John and Rory: 'But what's so great about Stéphane's playing is that he's got this absolutely original sense of timing, like a great singer, and so he'll be pushing things, stretching them, but it still comes out as absolutely the right melody. I can't really imitate Stéphane, but his timing is a bit more like this...'

He then played and talked at the same time – not easy: 'Comes in really early but finishes late, like he's got such an infinite charm in his playing because he's got that kind of timeless feel.' Kennedy's playing had Stéphane's swooping glissando and a hint of his uncanny sense of time. And I understood – it was the perfect connection to Stéphane's respect for Billie Holiday's timing and Ben Webster's big tone and, yes, it was timeless.

That day, Kennedy taught me that a few notes of music, if well played, could speak volumes, and I should have been more willing to listen. From then on, whenever I interviewed a musician, I asked if they wished to play, and it produced some fascinating results, such as Diz Disley demonstrating the Hot Club Quintet rhythmic style and Martin Taylor showing me how he fitted chords around Stéphane's 'Manoir de mes Rêves'. Great moments, and I'm grateful for the lesson.

Sitting next to Kennedy and hearing his tremendous sound was very humbling – this was a world-class musician who had a huge and very honest respect for Grappelli. He had interrupted the making of his current album to pay tribute to the man who had taught him musical freedom, who had demonstrated that his violin could have a life beyond the classical world in which he'd been tutored.

Listening later to the album recording of 'Melody In The Wind' with Nigel and Stéphane, it's obvious that the French violinist enjoyed working in the studio with his protégé. The first statement of the melody rests with Kennedy, and then Steph gives his own inimitable interpretation, 'pulling and pushing just like a great singer'. The two then enter into a little violin dialogue, just like old friends chatting of good times, and it's charming and very affectionate. The track then develops with a star-studded rhythm section of Pino Palladino and Danny Thompson on basses, Manu Katche and Nano Vasconcelos on percussion, Donovan and Doug Boyle on guitars, Ravi on the West African Kora and Naomi Boole-Masterson on cello. Ironically, this could almost be a gathering of the spirit of the Cambridge Folk Festival of 1973, when Stéphane first faced a teenage audience fearful for his life.

The album on which 'Melody In The Wind' appears, *Kafka*, is a very varied and experimental album. On some tracks, Kennedy explores the potential for the electric violin to produce a Jimi Hendrix sonority while on others he multitracks himself as a string quartet. It's a long way from swing, but Kennedy certainly embodies Stéphane's spirit, the spirit of his oft-quoted 'Why not?'

I soon spoke to Stéphane on the telephone to tell him about meeting 'Nigel', as he always called him. He was pleased at Nigel's success and told me, 'I'm off to Japan again. I'm very tired.' He undoubtedly was, yet it was clear that he still wanted to go.

Jazz has a huge following in Japan. As early as 1963, The New Orleans Preservation Hall Band were touring 94 Japanese venues in 32 cities. In Osaka's Festival Hall, they gave 40 consecutive concerts, all sell-outs. The Japanese seemed to enjoy their brand of authentic jazz, and Stéphane had been a great success here. In 1996, he was set to tour and also scheduled to record a rare CD single, an unlikely outing for Neil Sedaka's 'Laughter In The Rain'. An advertising executive had seized on the tune for a campaign and so 'the late trio' of Marc Fosset and Jean-Philippe Viret found themselves recording a one-minute version, alongside a more conventional take. On both cuts, Stéphane sounds as nimble as a college junior. I needn't have been concerned – as tired as Stéphane was, he could always perform when the red light of the studio beckoned.

While he was in Tokyo, Stéphane befriended another great classical musician, the leader of the Osaka Symphony Orchestra, Iwao Furusawa, who expressed a wish to record with him. Even at this late stage, Stéphane couldn't resist a challenge and suggested that they hire as arranger Max Harris, who had so helped Yehudi in his jazz ambitions. Unbelievably, they set an August date to meet back in Paris.

Stéphane's disciples range across the globe. In the United States, Regina Carter is, like Kennedy, a classically trained fiddler. Now the first lady of Detroit jazz fiddle, she resides in Manhattan and her world is the smoke-free basement jazz clubs of America, where she dances the stage freely with her radio-miked fiddle. When she was at school, she had a road-to-Damascus experience that changed her life: 'I was 16 when I saw Grappelli perform at the Renaissance Center Jazz Series, and everything changed. I said, "Wow! He's got a band behind him. There seems to be a freedom – they can improvise; they don't have to play the same piece the same way over and over." He was having such a good time and I felt really elated. I said that if I could feel this way all the time, that would be it. So that's what jazz meant to me, that feeling.

'Stéphane is like Ray Brown, the bassist: when they play, you can tell the instrument is a part of them. They look so happy and there is a transformation comes over them. Unfortunately, I was too shy to go and talk to him.'

Carter, a Suzuki-trained* violinist, learned from Stéphane that it was possible to swing. Previously, the Suzuki method of training had helped her develop her ear and freed her from the shackles of written manuscript: 'The Suzuki method is great because you learn by ear first and you're not stuck to that piece of paper, so that gives you more freedom. Also, improvisation – my teacher would play, then tap you on the shoulder and you had to pick up where she left off. We also played a lot of Baroque music, which is based in improvised music.

'For jazz, you really need your ear and to be unafraid to improvise. Reading makes you nervous because you don't have that freedom any more; you're constantly thinking about the problems ahead, so it's better to remember the piece. From the likes of Stéphane I learned that it's the spirit of the piece that matters, not the literal notes. Players like Stéphane, who have little formal training, have more freedom.'

As the 21st century begins, Regina is in the vanguard of contemporary jazz, a proud black voice seeking her own identity: 'I want to have my own voice. Of course, because of 'Lady Be Good' on [my] *Rhythms Of The Heart* album, a lot of people make the Grappelli connection – there are some nuances that come out that are Grappelli-esque, and if people say that, it's a compliment.'

Regina also shares Stéphane's love of Ben Webster: 'I had a teacher who said I should listen to a lot of horn players and singers to get the language. There's something about Ben Webster and Paul Gonsalves, the way their tone was so dark and so rich, and the vibrato, the way they would stretch the note. You would think, "They're never going to make it to the next note!" That

---

*Shinichi Suzuki, born in Nagoya, Japan, began teaching very young children music as a mother tongue in the 1930s. There are now millions of his 'Suzuki children' worldwide. Despite achieving great success, however, his methods are still remarkably controversial as they rely heavily on ear training (sound before sign). Stéphane sensibly approved.

really created some tension and release. They're not literal influences – I love Stéphane Grappelli and the others but I don't want to make a record trying to sound like them.'

I mentioned to Regina Stéphane's line about Martin Taylor not being Django, 'but he is Martin Taylor' and her response was justly exasperated at the way in which the music business is always referencing the past: 'The industry is so busy looking for 'the next so-and-so', and it's not like that; you have to find your own voice, and it's good to hear Stéphane recognised that. "Don't try and be me; go further than that!"'

Like Stéphane giving time to go to the Menuhin School, Regina feels that education is the way forward: 'The industry is still nervous about string players in jazz, but the great thing is a lot of colleges and universities and even schools are offering jazz programmes for string players. There are lots of books and CDs so young players can get to know this music. I think that, as long as we keep going into the schools, then it will have a chance.

'Being able to get off that paper is just the key. Sometimes, even in middle school, they are petrified even if I say, "Just improvise on one note." I say, "Tell me a story – you've met one note," but they're so afraid. If they weren't stuck to the paper, and if improvising were introduced at a younger age, it wouldn't be so intimidating.'

Regina is proud of jazz being such a great American art form and is happy to see it enriched by the likes of Grappelli: 'This music was born right here. Stuff Smith came from the big bands and is basically a horn player – a horn with strings, if you will. He and Stéphane are just playing with a different accent.' Like Stéphane, she has experimented with all manner of electric fiddles but keeps coming back to having a simple microphone attached to her fiddle: 'It's the only way to really get the right tone.' She plays a European violin and has an ambition to visit Genoa and play one of Paganini's violins.

Paganini is supposed to have played with the Devil at his elbow, and I think I may have glimpsed Lucifer myself amongst the smoke and strobes at the occasional Fairport Convention concert. Fairport have been the undisputed masters of folk rock for over 30 years, filling clubs and halls across the globe and annually holding one of Britain's largest music festivals at Cropredy. Ric Sanders is the undisputed Prince of the folk-rock fiddle and started out by listening to Stéphane: 'I got *Stéphane Grappelli And Friends* on vinyl with Diz Disley and Marc Hemmler, a magnificent record which contains one of my favourite moments of Stéphane – he does a version of 'Willow Weep For Me'. It's magnificent! He soars. It's like a jazz equivalent of Vaughan Williams's *The Lark Ascending* or the Bruch *Violin Concerto* or the Mendelssohn [second *Violin*] *Concerto* – it just soars. Stéphane did that, but it swung as well.'

'Eventually, I did meet him. I was in Soft Machine with John Etheridge and I hung out at the violin shop in Birmingham. I had worked there, but I was useless – I knew nothing about bows or the actual instruments and still don't. In 1978, John brought Stéphane in and he was just charming. I was completely bowled over.'

Ric was clearly impressed by Stéphane's down-to-earth persona: 'He was a jobbing musician, very pragmatic in his own way. As John said to me, quoting Steph on *The Hilton Years*, 'I put some butter on my spinach.' [Steph said,] 'I'm fine. I've got a gig!' He was happy playing music for people without thinking about it, just "that's why I'm here".'

Ric also enjoyed the life Stéphane breathed into a phrase. 'As Yehudi points out, in relation to Stéphane, the great classical musicians play those concertos and they take flight as if they were improvised. That's why Stéphane is my number one as the musician I aspire to. He was self-taught, non-academic, and I was interested to hear that he studied with the great Alfred Campoli but, like myself, rejected formal tuition as something that was just going to give more problems.'

The Grappelli influence is most pronounced in Ric's lyrical moments. By way of illustration, he played for me 'The Lark In The Clear Air' beautifully, simply and with great communication. He then played 'A Londonderry Air' and 'The Bonny Labouring Boy', achieving a powerful sense of intimacy in his playing. He then remarked, 'Stéphane could play the Festival Hall and leave everybody in the audience feeling that he was playing that tune just for them. That's the gift of a great performer."

I told Ric about Stéphane's lost lover from the Blitz, and for him this struck a thought: 'Though he never talked about Gwendoline, perhaps he shared that loss with us through his fiddle. I don't think you can hide who you actually are when you play – who you are will out. He carried that heartbreak with him through life, the tearing at the heartstrings. What you're getting through his improvising is life experiences.

'They say that time heals all wounds, but I'm not so sure. You learn to live with things. You put them in a compartment and tuck grief away, but it never leaves you. And as a musician, without knowing it, unconsciously he would be drawing on that heartache. Stéphane's playing got better. You don't really get jazz prodigies, do you?'

Ric saw a parallel with his own experience: 'In a way, my audience know me. I get letters from people saying they know I will understand – say, a relationship break-up – because they can hear it in my playing. It's very touching and a great weight of responsibility. I'm sure Steph had similar letters. It's a great privilege.

'This year I will play 250 nights with Fairport Convention and every night I will be playing stuff that has been greatly influenced by Stéphane Grappelli.'

Another British disciple is Mike Piggott, who originally met Stéphane in Cannes when his rock 'n' roll band played next door to Grappelli at the Palm Beach Casino and Steph would drop in for a chat. Mike's style is steeped in the Grappelli legacy, along with that of another great player, Stuff Smith. He especially admires Stéphane's art of concealing art: 'Stéphane is a complete one-off, as all the jazz violinists are, but Stéphane seems to tower above them all. The more you listen, the more you realise how much he has. He understands exactly what he is doing, yet he makes it sound so easy. He was the mould – no one had done it before and no one will ever do it after. You can't copy him; you can only pay homage. And part of what makes him distinctive is that he is always full of life, whether in a ballad or up-tempo number, and he enjoys being stretched musically.' Mike now occasionally plays alongside Martin Taylor and John Etheridge on the international jazz scene and in 1998 released an album called *Blues For Stuff And Steff*.

The mandolin – the fretted relative of the violin – has in the United States become associated with traditional bluegrass music, although virtuoso mandolin player David Grisman, who famously worked with Stéphane on the film *King Of The Gypsies*, prefers the term *dawg music* for his brand of 'newgrass'. He and his band would be equally at home at Nashville's historic Ryman Auditorium or onstage at a rock festival.

'I first heard Stéphane on a recording that one of my bluegrass friends, Eric Thompson, had,' recalls Grisman. 'This was about 1964. I was, of course, amazed, and became a devotee of this style of music from that day on. Stéphane eventually came to San Francisco in 1976 and played the Great American Music Hall, where I had been playing for several years with various groups. I was very excited and of course went to hear the master in person. I went backstage and gave Stéphane the first recording of my quintet, which had just been released.

'Stéphane was one of those rare artists who had everything: great technique, great sound, great ideas, and above all it was all so uniquely *him*. It was exhilarating to stand next to him and hear that, something that I'll always treasure. As far as I'm concerned, he made the most beautiful sound possible on the violin. And such feeling! A sound that was both happy and sad.'

In Seattle, fiddler Michael Gray from the band Pearl Django has gone as far as to devote a whole gypsy-jazz tribute album to Stéphane. Appropriately entitled *Souvenirs*, it doesn't attempt an imitation of Grappelli or The Hot Club Quintet, as Michael says: 'Stéphane Grappelli is such a unique voice. No one can play like him. What most hopefully we are striving to capture is his overarching spirit, the joyful abandon, the gypsy hot, the unabashedly romantic and the supremely elegant.'

I caught Pearl Django's performance at the Django Reinhardt Festival in Samois sur Seine, and they succeeded admirably in evoking the spirit of Grappelli. Stéphane kept photographs in his shoebox of Babik Reinhardt and himself at Samois, which is now an annual event. The festival achieves a wonderful atmosphere, and not just on the main stage. Perhaps the most enjoyable music was created off the island, in the quiet village square, where a Breton folk violinist played his own wonderful and spontaneous interpretations of 'Minor Swing' and 'Swing '39'. Sitting in a streetside bistro under a sunshade, with a café au lait and a croissant, the folk fiddler recreated perfectly the spontaneity that was so much a part of the original Hot Club Quintet, telling me that he never really played Stéphane's music but that, when he played the Celtic music of Brittany, a little dash of Grappelli flavoured the cup.

Sitting in a Pizza Express in London at one of Britain's principal jazz venues, I recently heard Christian Garrick playing with John Etheridge's band and, for a few fantastic moments, I felt transported to Bricktop's in the Paris of 1937. Although he ploughs his own furrow, this young fiddler can catch perfectly the spirit of the crazy young man who first dreamt of 'jazz on strings'. Chris had in fact met Stéphane, in his case backstage at the Dankworths' stables at Wavendon in 1979: 'I did of course go on to expand my knowledge of jazz violin and heard Ponty, Smith, Venuti, Lockwood and Seifert, but for me Stéphane Grappelli tops the lot for expression, swing and style, making him the truest and most durable voice ever in the history of jazz violin and also one of the most important figures among the jazz world as a whole. That's what gets me the most, that his voice goes way outside and above merely the realm of jazz violin, transcending the music in the way Miles, Ellington, Parker and Coltrane also do.

'His playing is always within the violinistic, never forcing his instrument. A true ear player rather than a reader, Grappelli's violin always sounds *felt* rather than *played*, which gives everything that irresistible sense of freedom. It is this way that he of all violinists who have played jazz has uniquely resolved the two in a perfect marriage.'

In Paris, meanwhile, Didier Lockwood and Jean-Luc Ponty are the well-known vanguard of a whole French school of innumerable Grappelli disciples. Lockwood has gone as far as to produce his *Tribute* album, an affectionate *hommage à Grappelli*. On this work, together with guitarist Birelli Legrene and Niels Pedersen,* he explores the Grappelli repertoire, occasionally even sounding like Stéphane with signature portamentos and harmonic arpeggios. In fact, the record leaves you wondering what it is that defines Grappelli because, brave as this album is, it's not Stéphane. You end up defining things by what they aren't – for instance, Stéphane has a greater dynamic, probably as he latterly avoided the temptation to use an amplified fiddle, which, although louder, is also compressed and a little one-dimensional. Stéphane also plays around the beat, never on it, although this gives Lockwood a greater affinity to the blues. Stéphane sounds effortless, whereas on *Tribute* you hear the tremendous effort of the participants. But in a version of 'Nuages', Lockwood sounds wistful – one of the trademark Grappelli qualities that Menuhin observed. Perhaps we should be grateful that, just as there was one Louis Armstrong and one Miles Davis, there will only ever be one Stéphane Grappelli. Didier engages in the sincerest form of flattery and we should applaud that.

While Lockwood has mostly remained within the lyrical Grappelli tradition, Jean-Luc Ponty has taken a different path. As with the extreme rock of Frank Zappa, Jean-Luc explores the violin as Jimi Hendrix did the guitar, as being the beginning of an electronic chain. His is a valid direction, it's just a long way from Louis Armstrong. But then, jazz marches on.

Meanwhile, what Stéphane thought of the work of avant-garde fiddler Leroy Jenkins I sadly never asked. Certainly the Chicago veteran is as far from Grappelli as Roland Kirk was from Ben Webster. It's a healthy musical climate

*Here, Pedersen provides as wonderful a counterpoint as ever, while Birelli Lagrene plays *very* fast!

that has room for such a range. I suspect that Stéphane would have taken the same line as he did with Picasso, respecting the difference.

Wherever you encounter the fiddle, Stéphane has inspired a rich and diverse legacy. Even those who don't like his work respect the craft. Faced with any criticism of an apparent conservatism, he would have shrugged and carried on. Stéphane at 88 was a swing musician – he did what he did, and for millions that was enough. As Kennedy so aptly put it, 'He was the style of music.'

Back in London, my urgent need was to complete the BBC radio programme for its transmission in early 1997 and I felt it important to broaden the scope of Stéphane's story by interviewing some of his longtime friends and associates, deciding that it would be a wasted opportunity not to video the likes of Lew Grade and Yehudi Menuhin. We still had no funding, so Judy arranged a hectic but wonderful day – all we could afford – in which to capture both celebrities, along with the journalist Michael Parkinson. They were all very busy people but nevertheless agreed to give their time free of charge to pay tribute to Grappelli.

We started at Lord Grade's office at seven in the morning. Lew was 90 but still wheeling and dealing his film business. Eight o'clock was his only free appointment, and of course we had to rig cameras, lights and mics before his arrival. When he arrived, he was genial and funny and left us with the portentous, cigar-wielded proclamation, 'There will never be another Stéphane Grappelli.' Nor another Lew Grade; sadly this was one of his last interviews. As an icon of British Entertainment and as an entertainer in his own right, he will be sorely missed.

On that one day in London, the bandwagon rolled on, with 'Alan the Bank', as his Welsh ancestors might call him, bravely steering crew and cast through the heavy London traffic. Our next stop was the headquarters of BAFTA, the British Academy of Film and Television. Michael Parkinson was busy doing some work for BBC Sport but again dashed across town to offer his thoughts on one of his favourite musicians. As a bonus, Michael agreed to do a little trailer for the proposed television programme, which he completed wonderfully in one take and with no preparation. These were the dark days of the mid-'90s when, despite his reputation as the greatest chat-show interviewer on British television, he was without a regular television programme.

Once more the caravan took the road, this time to Yehudi Menuhin's home in Belgravia. As we arrived, Yehudi was in the middle of a yoga session and so we set up our interview in his sitting room, amidst the priceless china and the wonderful antiques. At the appointed time, Yehudi appeared, serene and relaxed from his exercises, unperturbed by the lights cluttering the Persian rugs and the boom dangling near the Gainsborough. Here was a man of the world with a set of priorities, and he was ready to tell us of Grappelli. Again, sadly this was one of Yehudi's last interviews, but he was as alive as any athlete and more astute than most philosophers. Describing Stéphane, he observed, 'He is a phenomenon of human nature, bringing us into another world, which is our world, and yet living it – that is the great poet of improvising. It is the fact that the moment becomes a creative moment. It's a new revelation.'

In July 1996, Stéphane was back again in Paris and I visited his apartment on the Rue Dunkerque to check on some biographical details and to expand the video interviews with more informal chats. Without the cameras and lights to distract him, he gave me some personal insights into his years with Django and Diz, meeting the Queen of England, the President of the USA, Lady Diana and every great jazz musician you can imagine. As he spoke, he doodled with his three-quarter-size violin, now in tune and a constant companion. This was unusual for Stéphane – at home he usually only played the piano – but he told me that he'd had to give up the piano after his latest cerebral attack left him with a loss of movement in his right hand.

I didn't mention my guitar attempts at 'Nuages' from the previous visit, but quite casually and without any apparent effort he played it for me, solo violin, to an audience of one. It's a wonderful memory. Yes, my tape recorder was running, and no, that particular performance will never appear on any completist collection. I knew in that moment that I had Stéphane's trust and returned to England with plans for a radio profile that would reflect that.

The following month, Stéphane met up as arranged with Iwao Furusawa and Max Harris at Acousti Studios in Paris. Iwao is a highly accomplished classical player and a great sight-reader, having played Mahler and Takemitsu with one of the world's highest-profile symphony orchestras. Max told me he wrote for Iwao in a jazz style, which the performer immediately took to: 'He's a very capable player. I don't think I spared him anything, technically, and we were all impressed, particularly Stéphane, who liked the way he interpreted the jazz solos. I think Iwao did very well indeed. He had more of a feeling for jazz than perhaps Menuhin did.'

At this time, Max hadn't seen Stéphane for three years: 'I'd met him at his 80th and 85th birthdays and was quite shocked at the condition he was in. He was in a wheelchair, hard of hearing and wearing his glasses, which he seldom used to do. But in his playing he could still conjure up some magic.'

For these late tracks, Stéphane was again accompanied by Marc Fosset and Jean-Philippe Viret. The magic of the session begins with a nod to the classics in the intro to 'Too Marvellous For Words', which has the two violinists in a Baroque-style duet, soon replaced with the unmistakable Grappelli on a free take on the verse. As Stéphane slides into tempo, Iwao joins him with a written counterpoint, and the pair sound like a couple of friends having fun. They then return to a Baroque duet before Stéphane plays some jazz. A similar pattern is followed for 'These Foolish Things' and 'Our Love Is Here To Stay'. Then there is one last track, fated to be Stéphane's last recording.

Whether a complete album was planned, Max wasn't sure: 'I don't know why they only did four tracks. Possibly just to see how it would be received in Japan. It only seemed to be issued in Japan.'

A recording career that began with some forgotten tangos and 'Fit As A Fiddle' for Grégor et ses Grégoriens ended perhaps appropriately with Herman Hupfeld's classic 'As Time Goes By'.

Grégor had other fiddlers, and they all tried to swing, but the bandleader was the first to hear something special about Stéphane. As Michael Parkinson quoted Louis Armstrong when asked to define jazz, 'If you have to ask, you don't have it. And Stéphane never had to ask.' In 66 years, from 78rpm to digital compact disc, Stéphane witnessed and contributed to the creation of the sound-recording art. His legacy includes 1,145 tracks credited to Grappelly or Grappelli in the BBC Gramophone Library alone.

Max Harris was astonished at Stéphane's still-full diary even in the violinist's late years: 'He was still working hard. We had to fit the session around his schedule. He'd just come from Leipzig, and then he was off somewhere else in Europe. He liked to keep working. It was very enjoyable. I was looking forward to his 90th.' Concert halls have to be booked a year in advance, and at that time Stéphane's 90th birthday concert had already been arranged for 20 January 1998 at the London Barbican with Marc Fosset, Jean-Philippe Viret, Laurie Holloway, Marion Montgomery and hopefully Martin Taylor participating.

Back in England, I compiled Stéphane's first-hand story with the contributions of his friends and a presentation by Marcel Stellman. Editing Stéphane's contribution was, as I'd predicted, the hardest job I'd ever done. Although I'd edited thousands of hours of material for hundreds of programmes, the 88-year-old's story presented a particular challenge. He was unwell and, of his own choice, speaking in his second language. He frequently paused, repeated himself and stuttered, often losing his thread and pursuing some other thought that came into his head.

There were times when I genuinely didn't think I could make the programme. Knowing the special difficulties I would face, I wanted to edit Stéphane's interview digitally, on a computer, enhancing every edit with all the technology available. However, radio budgets are small and digital equipment expensive, so I was told by the BBC to cut the interview with a razorblade and stickytape in the age-old tradition. It seems odd now, but I had no choice, so I got on with it. For a week I surrounded myself with all the technology I could muster, squeezing every iota of intelligibility from Stéphane's fascinating tales, and then spent a day in Birmingham with Tony Wass, the original recording engineer, further enhancing and compiling.

On 4 February 1997, the radio programme *80 Years On The Fiddle* was finally transmitted on BBC Radio 2. To my relief, the public and critics enjoyed Stéphane's remarkable story and it became the lead story on the BBC's 'Pick Of The Week' and 'Critics' Choice' in four National British newspapers, with *The Evening Standard* awarding it 'Pick Of The Night'. I was especially pleased as the primary role of an editor is to be invisible. If you do the job right, no one should notice the cuts, fades and omissions; they should just enjoy the story.

More than all of this, I sent Stéphane a recording of the programme and he enjoyed it, which was also a mighty relief. Given his health, I was constantly in fear of not finishing in time. 'He had a second cerebral vascular accident in early '97,' recalled Joseph. 'The blood doesn't arrive at a part of the brain for a while, and this time it affected his speech as well as a little restriction of his movement. For one month he was very rough and then he could speak again.'

Stéphane's health was by now so poor that there was doubt about his attendance for the presentation by the French President of the highest order of the Légion d'Honneur, 'La Commandeur des Arts et des Lettres'. In the event, he did attend, albeit in a wheelchair. Photographs taken at the event show a very weak Stéphane, visibly thinner and with a clinical dressing on his head.

To the last, though, Stéphane still retained musical ambition as Joseph told me: 'He wanted to record the Bach *Double Concerto* as a sort of last testament. He would play on his own, all four parts. I copied the parts for him but sadly he never had time to complete this ambition. This was his way of making amends for the 1937 *Double Concerto* with Eddie South, which he was never happy with.'

From 10–21 March, the still-determined violinist toured the United Kingdom and then set off again for Australasia, giving his last public concert in Christchurch, New Zealand, before returning via Hong Kong, where he enjoyed a few days off. Returning to Paris, Stéphane suffered another cerebral attack, but recovered and even rehearsed with Marc Fosset, although according to Joseph he was experiencing many further medical problems and eventually agreed to be admitted to a nearby clinic: 'He had difficulty forming his words at the Clinic du Mont Louis. Stéphane had been there many times before and he knew all the doctors. His heart specialist had introduced us to that small place. It was very comfortable and I could stay there with Stéphane. It was almost like home. The nurses would greet him, "Bonjour, Monsieur Grappelli."'

Despite the comfort, however, Stéphane was anxious to be home, and it was agreed that he could return to the Rue Dunkerque on the morning of 1 December 1997. Joseph helped him prepare: 'The last thing I did for him on that last morning was to spend a long hour helping him to wash. It was a small thing, but it was important to him. His teeth, his ears, nails, everything to be ready to leave the hospital, and he was very concerned to be very clean. Some might say he was dressed to see his Lord.

'We were helping Stéphane to dress, and when he left his bed to go to a chair he fell down and he suffered heart failure. It was very quick.

'He was always very curious and wanting to learn, up to the last day of his life, he said, and he loved to repeat this: "*On apprend tous les jours*" – "You learn every day". That made him very alive and very interested throughout his life.'

29 Coda

'And when the time comes...I will go without regret. I leave the regret to my friends.'

— *Stéphane Grappelli, 26 January 1908–1 December 1997*

Stéphane's funeral was arranged for 5 December 1997 at the Église Saint Vincent de Paul. Joseph Oldenhove sent out the invitations, each accompanied by a smiling photograph of Stéphane from happier times. It seemed appropriate for this musician famed for his *joie de vivre* to be remembered with a familiar image of him wearing a wild floral shirt, gently cradling his favourite violin.

Judy Caine and I travelled to Paris by train and arrived at the apartment late on 4 December in order to pay our last respects. Joseph was by now a good friend and we wished to offer our support. The tiny and now familiar home was a flurry of activity, so we conveyed our sincere condolences and left the family to this most private farewell.

As we left the apartment, subdued and reflective, we heard the familiar sound of a Paris musette, which was unusual as the Paris buskers generally frequent the other side of the Boulevard Rochechouart – Stéphane's area is quieter, more residential, with less attraction for passing tourists. On the corner, a young girl had set up her pitch and was playing Edith Piaf's anthem 'Je Ne Regrette Rien', the sound echoing eerily from the tall apartments. As I looked back one last time to the window where we had so often talked, I thought back to Stéphane. I'd asked him about retirement and he'd replied quite casually, 'Oh, I'm happy. I make music with my friends and I get paid for it.'

Then I remembered his last words in my radio interview: 'And when the time comes and it will be the last, I will go without regret. I leave the regret to my friends.' It was a very poignant moment, and I wondered at the presence of this mysterious musician on such a lonely pitch, weaving that nostalgic sound, so French and yet also so Italian. Stéphane had busked this same area over 70 years earlier and the tune 'No Regrets' seemed uncannily appropriate.

The next day, Judy and I appeared at the grand double-towered church a little early for the funeral. Already, a press of paparazzi and television cameras were assembled on the stone steps as the dignitaries of Stéphane's mother nation arrived in their limousines. Inside the church, things were little better. Unbelievably the television cameras, complete with lights and booms, continued to film. There was an undignified crush as the press pushed for soundbites from the many celebrities. It all felt intrusive and undignified.

The politician Jacques Delors, a late friend to Stéphane, was in attendance, and I also noticed Sacha Distel and several other well-known faces, including French film stars and many musicians. There were long speeches in praise of Stéphane and the fitting pomp and ceremony of a stately passing.

Then came a wonderful moment as a solo violin reverberated ethereally from the tall arches, the unmistakable strains of Stéphane's recording of 'Chanson Pour Louis' from *Milou en Mai*, the solo he had dashed off so effortlessly for Louis Malle eight years earlier. Suddenly we were surrounded by the spirit of Stéphane Grappelli. The signature grace, the whimsy, an improvisation but also a towering structure, stately yet with that characteristic syncopation, and all his tricks – a little Bach, some portamento and always a smile at the edge of a phrase. 'You know me, I'm an old trooper. I start alone.'

Leaving the church, the family and Joseph departed to attend a private interment. On the steps, Judy and I exchanged a few words with Babik Reinhardt and then crossed the road, where we sat with Martin Taylor, John Etheridge and Ed Baxter and exchanged fond memories and anecdotes of the extraordinary character we had shared the pleasure of knowing.

Leaving Ed and the musicians, Judy and I walked the church grounds and looked up the narrow expanse of the Rue St Vincent de Paul. There, as Stéphane surely knew, yellow in the winter sunlight, were the grand gates to L'Hôpital Laribroisière, where, 89 years earlier, Stephano Grappelli had been born.

30 The Final Cadence

A Life In The Jazz Century

In England, a hurriedly compiled tribute to Stéphane was broadcast on public television and presented by Yehudi Menuhin. The programme wasn't advertised and so few saw it. Despite that, it was now impossible to pursue a considered broadcast of Stéphane's story. All my careful negotiations to that effect collapsed overnight as network and commissioning editors considered Stéphane's story adequately told. I was extremely saddened never to be able to show Stéphane the programme to which he had contributed so generously.

Back at my home in Ealing, I carried on working, covering jazz festivals on video and completing a major environmental project with a contribution from Sir David Attenborough. The latter was originated on the then new technology of DVD and used the interactive potential of that medium to portray an in-depth study. This prompted an idea.

I was increasingly depressed by three large plastic crates in our store room containing all the videotaped interviews with Stéphane that I had accrued, as well as the other interviews I'd collected in 1996 and masses of notes, audio recordings, books and CDs. This was a valuable archive, but an archive needs to be accessible. I wanted to get Stéphane's story out there, along with some of the fantastic range of performances he'd left littered through the film and television libraries of the world. With Judy's research, I'd discovered filmed or videoed concerts by Stéphane from every decade of the 20th century except the 1910s, including everything from appearances with Grégor in the late '20s to footage of Stéphane with Michel Legrand in the '90s, and of course including the spectacular Hot Club Quintet film of the '30s.

DVD seemed to be the appropriate medium via which to tell Stéphane's story. On the new format, we could include footage of the fiddler relating his story as well as complete musical performances. Many music enthusiasts are increasingly frustrated at the way in which so many television and radio documentarians talk over music, demonstrating a basic misunderstanding of the medium of music, which is created to stand on its own without verbal explanation. The DVD format even offered the potential for an optional soundtrack, completely without commentary.

There was another bonus: the format is potentially very long-lasting. Unlike Stéphane's worn out 78s and fading videotapes, the digital medium is a virtual time capsule, its binary code potentially remaining decipherable for millennia.

New technology is expensive, however, and with no commercial interest in the project we had to find the money ourselves, and so, after some agonising, Judy and I raised the capital by remortgaging our house and launched into the creation of *Stéphane Grappelli: A Life In The Jazz Century*. To keep costs manageable, I became second cameraman, director, editor, writer, researcher, sound mixer, interviewer and presenter, while Judy researched, interviewed, production assisted, sound recorded, worked out the DVD navigation and produced. It was all very enjoyable, if exhausting, and halved the capital outlay.

However, we needed more footage of Stéphane's Paris, preferably without the rain, which had plagued our original shoot. Technology again came to the rescue in the form of new lightweight digital cameras. Judy and I had recently visited Central Asia for the BBC and had trained in the new techniques of storytelling, including satellite uplinks and internet connections.

We travelled to Paris several times, staying in Joseph's Montmartre flat, filming, conducting further research and recording extra interviews with Stéphane's friends and family in Paris and Cannes. Back in England, we located Diz Disley and Beryl Davis (visiting from Hollywood to sing with The Glenn Miller Orchestra) and many more of Stéphane's friends and associates.

In the British Film Institute, we received a surprise, accidentally rediscovering lost footage of Stéphane and George Shearing. I'd been there to review the film *The Flamingo Affair* and complained about the sound quality of the print to the projectionist, who had duly gone in search of a better version and returned with the film *Stéphane Grappelli And His Quartet*, recorded on the same set in 1946. Was this of any interest? he asked.

In Paris, meanwhile, the legal shenanigans surrounding the film *Jazz Hot* were finally resolved and we were able to negotiate the rights to include that. From America, Judy obtained remarkable footage of Stéphane's hero Art Tatum, a set of uncut rushes of material that could be edited to taste. Also from America came footage of Paul Whiteman and his band, which was perfect for evoking Stéphane's early memories of hearing Gershwin's *Rhapsody In Blue* and meeting Bing Crosby And The Rhythm Boys.

Bringing all of this material together, the DVD was at last launched at the

British Academy of Film and Television in February 2002. It was a wonderful occasion, mostly because I could at last share with the public the fruits of seven years of research and production. On the night I had the enormous pleasure of playing 'Nuages' with Martin Taylor, Coleridge Goode and John Etheridge and a band that also included John Goldie and the veteran accordionist Jack Emblow. Together, for that night, we were The Spirit Of Stéphane.

The DVD release was a huge critical success, hailed in America by the magazine *Just Jazz Guitar* as 'a masterpiece' and in Paris by *Jazz Hot* as 'indispensable', while the reviewer in *Fanfare*, America's prestigious critical magazine, referred to it as 'the finest documentary of a musician's life I have ever seen'. The final triumph came in September 2002, when the two discs were nominated for a British Academy Award.

This was all very heartening. I was broke, but that didn't matter; I had believed that Stéphane's story needed to be told, feeling that people would enjoy it and perhaps even be inspired by it. Letters and emails flooded in from all over the world. From that public response, I felt that I had to be doing something right, despite the difficulty of conducting any kind of in-depth storytelling in a world increasingly distracted by ephemera.

At that point, in early 2002, I was commissioned to write this book, which produced a whole new layer of fascinating research. In Paris, Joseph gave me access to Stéphane's complete personal archive, and there was a poignant moment as I reviewed Stéphane's shoebox collection of photographs. There, amongst his photos of European and jazz royalty, nestled amongst snaps of Duke Ellington, Miles Davis and Satchmo, were my two little photographs of Stéphane with the Suzuki children, taken in 1978, the day after we had first met.

Looking through the thousands of photographs, I was reminded of the words of so many of the friends they depicted. Lew Grade, recalling seeing Stéphane in Paris in the '30s, remarked: 'When I heard Stéphane play, it was revelation to me. He was remarkable. I just couldn't believe it. There will never be another Stéphane Grappelli.'

Oscar Peterson, pictured onstage with Stéphane at the Paul Masson Vineyards in California, agreed: 'He was a one-off. I don't know that you'll ever hear or see that again. It's like Duke Ellington – he was so unique and so gifted, and he commanded respect without being brash. He was not a brash man. He respected that kind of attention and love just by the way he played and by the way he carried himself. When talking to him, he spoke so softly he just commanded a kind of attention, and he played the same way.'

That other soft-spoken maestro, Yehudi Menuhin, is seen with Stéphane in a birthday photograph from the 1980s, complete with violin-shaped cake: 'He could use any theme to express any nuance – wistfulness, brilliance, aggression, scorn – with a speed and accuracy that stretched credulity.'

His protégé Nigel Kennedy, at the Barbican in 1994, remembered hearing 'such fluency and such beautiful sound quality, great intonation, something which most classical players would be wishing they might have once in a lifetime'.

Michael Parkinson, seen in many pictures from the 1970s, put Stéphane up there with their mutual hero Louis Armstrong: 'If anybody ever defined jazz, it's Stéphane, because it flowed from him. It wasn't anything you learnt in a manual; it was an instinct... I think there were two things about Stéphane that made him a great musician. The first was an innate musical sensitivity – he had great taste; he was incapable of playing an inelegant phrase. The second thing was this instinctive thing about being able to play jazz – he understood it without actually ever comprehending it, like the best players do. I can think of very few musicians who had the two in such abundance.'

John Etheridge, pictured smiling in a studio portrait from 1978, agreed with Stéphane's jazz credentials: '[He was] unique in the way that jazz musicians are supposedly always unique, in that they are themselves. But really, it's very rare for a musician to be so authentically himself. And the feeling you had when you were playing with him was that he was completely relaxed, unhurried, and the flow of ideas was totally uninhibited, so he was completely himself. That's really what jazz should be about and so rarely is.'

Seen in many photos from the Jazz From Europe tour, even estranged colleagues like Diz Disley – who had sadly fallen out with Stéphane in the 1980s – were, in the last analysis, drawn to praise: 'I've driven him hundreds of thousands of miles in different countries and continents and he'd always have some complaint about something. He was a serial complainer and he was a nuisance to work with, really. It was a drag. But his playing was never anything less than good and very often great. He had a perfect tone, the perfect touch and brilliant ideas, and the combination of all that is a very outstanding and superb musician, and that's why his playing will last. There will be very few in the future that will come up to that standard.'

Stéphane and Martin Taylor, meanwhile, are seen in a happy portrait from the '90s, and Martin particularly admired his curiosity for the new: 'I never ever heard Stéphane say, "Oh, in the good old days..."; Stéphane loved the present, he always moved on, and if he heard a musician playing something that he really liked, [he would ask], "Oh, how do you do that? What is that music you're playing? Maybe we should play together.'"

Which prompts a postscript. On 10 December 2002, Martin Taylor visited Buckingham Palace to be decorated by Her Majesty the Queen with an MBE 'for services to jazz' and I met up with him later for a drink in a Soho club. Although it's rightly inappropriate to quote her exact words, Martin told me that the Queen had spoken affectionately of Stéphane and Martin's long and fruitful musical partnership. Ironically, it was one of Stéphane's dreams to be recognised officially in his adopted home, which I'm told would have happened had he lived a few months longer. He would no doubt have been extremely happy to see Martin, one of his favourite musicians, so deservedly recognised.

I had begun my exploration of Stéphane's story with a great respect for an accomplished musician and a great entertainer. As I listened to his vast legacy of recordings, however, I changed my mind as I slowly realised that this extraordinary man was a quiet genius. And what *is* genius, exactly?

I think that the reason why Stéphane Grappelli made so many people happy has everything to do with that strange alchemy of music. In his inimitable sound, he expressed perfectly the triumph of the human spirit. In his often difficult life, nothing – not the hunger of the Great War, the depravity of the Depression, the personal losses of the Blitz, the early loss of his greatest friend, even the slow demise of the swing music he loved – could crush his *joie de vivre*, and when we hear that, we share that.

Talking of the inspiration he had from Stéphane, Ric Sanders put it like this: 'We live in a world torn apart by every kind of conflict, over race, ethnicity, religion, nationality, politics, and I sometimes wonder, "What am I doing?" If music has a function, it's to lift up the hearts of people.'

Luckily, Stéphane lived in the recorded century and, as long as there is a device that will play the recordings, he will carry on lifting our spirits. In 1996 there were 1,145 separate items featuring him in the BBC Gramophone Library, and that collection is still growing. Stéphane's music is continually being reborn in better and better formats, allowing new generations of listeners to hear his work in novel settings. In 2000 he appeared on the soundtrack of the French movie *Chocolat*, newly evoking the spirit of an era. Even his ebullient image remains current; in 2002 a postage stamp based on a late photo from a concert programme appeared in France.

In another, very physical way, Stéphane will always be present. In the early

21st century, Joseph Oldenhove returned to Alatri, Italy and spread Stéphane's ashes at the foot of the Grappelli Tower, thus Stephano and his father, Ernesto, were reunited. Joseph went further: 'I spread the ashes of Stéphane in many, many places. Most of his ashes are in Paris, the rest in Cannes, London, New York, India and the tower at Alatri. He was international and loved everywhere. I felt I could do whatever was respectful. It was a way Stéphane could still travel, and Stéphane loved to travel.'

> ...spread my ashes to the four winds,
> may their spirit whistle softly in your ear,
> like a violin whisper in the long night...

Selected Discography

Stéphane Grappelly or Grappelli is credited with over 1,145 record releases covering a recording career from 1929–96. There is of course huge duplication of releases from the 78rpm era to the vinyl era and thence to compact disc, and soon there will be 20-bit Dolby 5:1 remixes on DVD-A. I have limited this listing to material relatively easy to obtain commercially in 2003 on conventional CD audio. I have also taken the liberty of offering some recommendations.

Abbreviations used are as follows:

as – alto saxophone
bs – double bass
cel – celeste
clar – clarinet
dr – drums
el vla – electric viola
el pno – electric piano
el bs – electric bass
fl – flute
FR – Fender Rhodes
gtr – guitar
h – harmonica

hp – harp
kb – keyboards
orch – orchestra
perc – percussion
pno – piano
tb – trombone
tpt – trumpet
ts – tenor saxophone
vib – vibraphone
vla – viola
vln – violin

STÉPHANE GRAPPELLI

VIOLIN JAZZ 1927–44 – HOLLYWOOD, CHICAGO, NEW YORK, LONDON, PARIS, BRUSSELS, BERLIN, COPENHAGEN (two-disc set)
Stéphane Grappelli + Hugo Rignold + Joe Venuti + Robert Edward 'Juice' Wilson + Stuff Smith + Ray Nance + Svend Asmussen + Ray Perry + Eddie South + Claude Laurence + Django Reinhardt + Michael Warlop + Emilio Caceres + Paul Nero + Helmut Zacharias + Marshall Sosson

Frémeaux & Associés (FA 052), released 1966. Features recordings from 1927–44 made in London, Paris, New York, Chicago, Copenhagen, Hollywood, Hilversum, Brussels and Berlin.

TRACK LIST
Disc 1
Dinah* / Body And Soul* / Them Their Eyes* / I wonder Where My Baby Is Tonight* / Calling All Eyes / The Wild Cat / My Syncopated Melody Man / Goin' Places / Four String Joe / Running Ragged / Kansas City Kitty / After You've Gone / Onyx Club Spree / Midway / Desert Sand / Skip It / "C" Jam Blues / Moon Mist

Disc 2
My Melancholy Baby / It Don't Mean A Thing If It Ain't Got That Swing / Ring Dem Bells / Smart Alec / Eddie's Blues / Lady Be Good / Fiddleditty / Concerto Pour Deux Violons En Ré Mineur / Minor Swing / Vous Et Moi / Strange Harmony / Harmoniques / Oui / Christmas Swing / Jig In G / Solo Flight / Gut Gelaunt / Humoresque – Old Folks At Home

A fantastic piece of historical research and offers a real perspective on Grappelly.

*Grappelly tracks.

INTÉGRALE DJANGO REINHARDT/COMPLETE DJANGO REINHARDT (Frémeaux & Associés, Paris)
An ongoing series attempting to document the complete works of Django Reinhardt. At the time of going to press there are 16 volumes, each a two-disc sets with a comprehensive 40-page booklet in both English and French, including recording dates, personnel and recording history. Not all include Grappelli.

Vol 1 (1928–34): *Presentation Stomp*
Vol 2 (1934–5): *I Saw Stars*
Vol 3 (1935): *Djangology*
Vol 4 (1935): *Magic Strings*
Vol 5 (1936–7): *Mystery Pacific*

Vol 6 (1937): *Swinging With Django*
Vol 7 (1937–8): *Christmas Swing*
Vol 8 (1938–9): *Swing From Paris*
Vol 9 (1939–40): *HCQ Strut*
Vol 10 (1940): *Nuages*
Vol 11 (1940–2): *Swing '42*
Vol 12 (1943–5): *Manoir de mes Rêves*
Vol 13 (1946–7): *Echoes Of France*
Vol 14 (1947): *Django's Dream*
Vol 15 (1947): *Gipsy With A Song*
Vol 16 (1948): *Festival '48*

Superlatives fail for this exhaustive and impeccably researched collection with comprehensive notes by Daniel Nevers. Worth importing but available in major London retail outlets. Please note: no Grappelly on 1940–5 discs.

THE HAWK TAKES FLIGHT – COLEMAN HAWKINS (1933-39)

Coleman Hawkins (ts) + Django Reinhardt (gtr) + Stéphane Grappelli (pno) + Henry Allen (tpt) + Benny Carter (tpt) + Jack Hylton And His Orchestra.

Conifer (CDHD 230), Conifer Records Ltd, released 1993. Recordings from 1933–9

TRACK LIST

Jamaica Shout / Heartbreak Blues / I Ain't Got Nobody / On The Sunny Side Of The Street / Lullaby / Oh Lady Be Good / After You've Gone / I Wish I Were Twins / Blue Moon / Avalon / What A Difference A Day Made / Stardust / Chicago / Meditation / Something Is Gonna Give Me Away / Honeysuckle Rose / Crazy Rhythm / Out of Nowhere / Sweet Georgia Brown / Devotion / I Know That You Know / Swinging In The Groove / My Melancholy Baby / The Darktown Strutters Ball / Body And Soul /

Grappelly appears on piano. Wonderful records.

M. SWING – STÉPHANE GRAPPELLI

Stéphane Grappelli (vln & pno) + Grégor et ses Grégoriens (orch) + Django Reinhardt (gtr) + Joseph Reinhardt (gtr) + Roger Chaput (gtr) + Louis Vola (bs) + Pierre Ferret (gtr) + Marcel Bianchi (gtr) + Wilson Myers (bs) + Eddie South (vln) + Eugene Vees (gtr) + Larry Adler (h) + Roger Grasset (bs) + Emmanuel Soudieux (bs) + Stanley Andrecos (vln) + Harry Chapman (hp) +Reg Canray (vib) + George Shearing (pno) + Jack Llewellyn (gtr) + Hank Hobson (bs) + Al Philcock (dr + bs) + George Gibbs (bs) + Dave Fullerton (dr) + Coleridge Goode (bs).

211753, Radio France, released 1996. Recordings from 1933–46 made in both Paris and London.

TRACK LIST
Fit As A Fiddle / Confessin / Tiger Rag / Djangology / Swing Guitar / Sweet Chorus / Mystery Pacific / Alabamy Bound / Daphne / I've Found A New Baby / Interpretation – Swing and Improvisation / Minor Swing / Fiddle Blues / Christmas Swing / Stompin' At Decca / I've Got Rhythm / Swing From Paris / Swing 39 / Out Of Nowhere / HCQ Strutt / Stéphane's Tune / Jive Bomber / Echoes of France

A good compilation found in Paris and including 'Fit As A Fiddle' with the Gregorians, the first recording of a real 'Grappelly' solo.

DJANGO REINHARDT SERIES, CHRONOLOGICAL VOL 1
Stéphane Grappelly (vln/pno) + Django Reinhardt (gtr) + Joseph Reinhardt (gtr) + Roger Chaput (gtr) + Louis Vola (bs) + Roger Grasset (bs) + Arthur Briggs (tpt) + Alphonse Cox (tpt) + Pierre Allier (tpt) + Eugène d'Hellemmes (tb) + Pierre Ferret (gtr) + Frank 'Big Boy' Gouldie (tpt/clar/ts) + Sigismund Beck (bs) + Jerry Mengo (dr) + Alix Combelle (clar/ts).
JSP CD 3410, released in 1992. Recordings from 1934-1935.

TRACK LIST
I Saw Stars / I'm Confessin' / Dinah / Tiger Rag / Oh Lady Be Good / I Saw Stars / Lilly Belle May June / Sweet Sue, Just You / I'm Confessin' (alt take) / The Continental / Blue Drag / Swanee River / The Sunshine of Your Smile / Ultrafox / Avalon / Smoke Rings / Clouds / Believe It, Beloved / I've Found A New Baby / St Louis Blues / Crazy Rhythm / The Sheik Of Araby / Chasing Shadows / I've Had My Moments / Some Of These Days / Djangology

Excellent transfers of the earliest Hot Club Quintet material. Not as completist as the Frémeaux set and the recording notes are not as thorough.

DJANGO REINHARDT SERIES – CHRONOLOGICAL VOL 2
Stéphane Grappelly (vln + pno) + Django Reinhardt (gtr) + Roger Chaput (gtr) + Eugene Vees (gtr) + Louis Vola (bs) + Roger Grasset (bs) + Joseph Reinhardt (gtr) + Emmanuel Soudieux (bs).
JSP CD 342, released in 1993. Recordings from 1938–9.

TRACK LIST
Honeysuckle Rose / Sweet Georgia Brown / Night And Day / My Sweet / Souvenirs / Daphne / Black And White / Stompin' At Decca / Tournerai / If I Had You / It Had To Be You / Nocturne / The Flat Foot Floogie / The Lambeth Walk / Why Shouldn't I? / I've Got My Love To Keep Me Warm / Please Be Kind / Louise / Improvisation / Undecided / HCQ Strut / Don't Worry 'Bout Me / The Man I Love / My Sweet (alt take) / I've Got My Love to Keep me Warm (alt take) / Improvisation No 2

Excellent.

DJANGO REINHARDT SERIES – CHRONOLOGICAL VOL 3

Stéphane Grappelly (vln + pno) + Django Reinhardt (gtr) + Joseph Reinhardt (gtr) + Eugene Vees (gtr) + Roger Grasset (bs) + Pierre Ferret (gtr) + Emmanuel Soudieux (bs). JSP CD 343, released in the 1990s. Recordings from the 1938–9 Paris Decca Sessions.

TRACK LIST

Billets Doux / Swing From Paris / Them There Eyes / Three Little Words / Appel Direct / Hungaria / Hungaria (alt take) / Jeepers Creepers / Jeepers Creepers (alt take) / Swing 39 / Japanese Sandman / I Wonder Where My Baby Is Tonight / I Wonder Where My Baby Is Tonight (alt take) / Tea For Two / Tea For Two (alt take) / My Melancholy Baby / Time On My Hands / Twelfth Year / Twelfth Year (alt take) / My Melancholy Baby (alt take) / Japanese Sandman (alt take) / Tea For Two (2nd alt take) / I Wonder Where My Baby Is Tonight (2nd alt take) / Hungaria (2nd alt take)

DJANGO REINHARDT SERIES, CHRONOLOGICAL VOL 4

Stéphane Grappelly (vln + pno) + Django Reinhardt (gtr) + Coleman Hawkins (ts) + Michel Warlop And His Orchestra – Arthur Briggs (tpt) + Noel Chiboust (tpt) + Pierre Allier (tpt) + Guy Paquinet (tb) + Adnre Ekyan (as) + Charles Lisee (as) + Alix Combelle (ts) + Eugène d'Hellemmes (bs) + Maurice Chailloux (dr) + (Joseph Reinhardt (gtr) + Eugène Vees (gtr) + Pierre Ferret (gtr) + Louis Vola (bs) + Tony Rovira (bs) + Lucien Somoens (bs) + Freddy Taylor (vocal). JSP CD 344, released in the 1990s. Recordings from 1935–6.

TRACK LIST

Blue Moon / Avalon / What A Difference A Day Made / Stardust / St. Louis Blues / Limehouse Blues / I Got Rhythm / I've Found A New Baby / It Was So Beautiful / China Boy / Moon Glow / It Don't Mean A Thing / I's A-Muggin / I Can't Give You Anything But Love / Oriental Shuffle / After You've Gone / Are You In The Mood ? / Limehouse Blues / Nagasaki / Swing Guitars / Georgia On My Mind / Shine / In The Still Of The Night / Sweet Chorus

---

DJANGO REINHARDT SERIES, CHRONOLOGICAL VOLUME 5

Stéphane Grappelly (vln) + Django Reinhardt (gtr) + Pierre Ferret (gtr) + Marcel Bianchi (gtr) + Louis Vola (bs) + Garnet Clark And His Hot Club's Four + Bill Coleman (tpt + vocal) + George Johnson (clar) + Garnet Clark (pno) + June Cole (bs). JSP CD 349, released in the 1990s. Recordings from the 1937 HMV sessions and the Garnet Clark recordings of 1935.

TRACK LIST

Exactly Like You / Charleston / You're Driving Me Crazy / Tears / Solitude / Hot Lips / Ain't Misbehavin' / Rose Room / Body And Soul / When Day Is Gone / Runnin' Wild

/ Chicago / Liebestraum No 3 / Miss Annabelle Lee / A Little Love, A Little Kiss / Mystery Pacific / In A Sentimental Mood / The Sheik Of Araby / Improvisation / Parfum / Alabamy Bound / Rosetta / Stardust / The Object Of My Affection

Note: The Django Reinhardt *series is not a strict chronology from Vol 1 to Vol 5, but for ease of reference it has been listed here as JSP released it.*

DJANGO REINHARDT VOLUME 2 – PARIS & LONDON 1937–48 (four-CD set)
Various Hot Club line-ups.
JSPCD904A (Paris 1937)
JSPCD904B (Paris and London 1940–6)
JSPCD904C (Paris 1939–40)
JSPCD904D (Paris 1946–8)
Released in 2000. Recordings from 1937-48.

TRACK LIST
Disc A
St Louis Blues / Bouncin' Around / I've Found A New Baby / Bricktop / Speevey / Minor Swing / Viper's Dream / Swingin' With Django / Paramount Stomp / Bolero / Bolero (alt take) / Mabel / Mabel (alt take) / My Serenade / You Rascal You / Stéphane's Blues / Sugar / Sweet Georgia Brown / Tea For Two

Disc B
Stockholm / Younger Generation / I'll See You In My Dreams / Echoes Of Spain / Out Of nowhere / I Can't Give You Anything But Love / Naguine / Naguine (alt take) / Rhythm Futur / Begin The Beguine / Blues / Coucou / Undecided / Swing '41 / Nuages / Pour Vous / Fantaisie Sur Une Danse Norvegienne / Vendredi / Liebesfreud / Mabel / Petits Mesonges / Les Yeux Noirs / Sweet Sue, Just You

Disc C
Swing De Paris / Oiseaux Des Îles / All Of Me / Festival Swing / Dinette / Crepuscule / Swing 42 / Festival Swing 1942 (Part 2) / Belleville / Lentement Mademoiselle / Douce Ambiance / Manoir Des Mes Rêves / Oui / Cavalerie / Fleur d'Ennui / Blues Clair / Improvisation No 3 (Part 1) / Improvisation No 3 (Part 2) / Coquette / Django's Tiger / Embraceable You / Echoes Of France

Disc D
Swingtime In Springtime / Yours And Mine / On The Sunny Side Of The Street / I Won't Dance / R Vingt Six / How High The Moon / Lover Man / Blue Lou / Blues / What Is This Thing Called Love / Ol' Man River / Si Tu Savais / Eveline / Diminushing / Mike / Lady Be Good / Festival 48 / Fantaisie / Bricktop / Just For Fun / To Each His Own (Symphonie)

SOUVENIRS – DJANGO REINHARDT/STÉPHANE GRAPPELLY WITH THE QUINTET OF THE HOT CLUB OF FRANCE

Stéphane Grappelly (vln / pno) + Django Reinhardt (gtr) + Roger Chaput (gtr) + Eugene Vees (gtr) + Louis Vola (bs) + Jack Llewellyn (gtr) + Allan Hodgkiss (gtr) + Coleridge Goode (bs) + Joseph Reinhardt (gtr) + Roger Grasset (bs) + Emmanuel Soudieux (bs) + Beryl Davis (vocal).

Limelight 820 591-2, released in 1988. Recordings from 1938–46.

TRACK LIST

Honeysuckle Rose / Night And Day / Sweet Georgia Brown / Souvenirs / My Sweet / Liza (All The Clouds'll Roll Away) / Stomping At Decca / Love's Melody / Daphne / Lambeth Walk / Nuages / HCQ Strut / The Man I Love / Improvisation No 2 / Undecided / Please Be Kind / Nocturne / I've Got My Love To Keep Me Warm / Louise / Don't Worry 'Bout Me

A good introduction to the classic Decca years with Django.

GRAPPELLI STORY – HISTORIC RECORDINGS 1938–1992

Django Reinhardt (gtr) + Roger Chaput (gtr) + Eugene Vees (gtr) + Louis Vola (bs) + Arthur Young And Hatchet's Swingtette + Stanley Andrews (vln) + Harry Chapman (hp) + Reg Conroy (vib) + George Shearing (pno) + Jack Llewellyn (gtr) + Hank Hobson (bs) + Al Philcock (dr) + Eugene Pini (vln) + Dennis Moonan (vla) + Syd Jacobson (gtr) + George Gibbs (bs) + Dave Fullerton (dr / vocal) + Roy March (vib) + Yorke de Sousa (pno) Joe Deniz (gtr) + Joe Nussbaum (bs) Dave Wilmins (gtr) + Beryl Davis (vocal) + Allan Hodgkiss (gtr) + Coleridge Goode (bs) + Michel Hausser (vib) + Maurice Vander (pno) + Rene Duchaussoir (gtr) + Benoit Quersin (bs) + Jean-Louis Viale (dr) + Pierre Michelot (bs) + Jean-Baptiste 'Mac Kac' Reilles (dr) + Raymond Fol (pno) + Alan Levitt (dr) + Pierre Cavalli (gtr) + Leo Petit (gtr) + Guy Pedersen (bs) + Daniel Humair (dr) + Marc Hammeler (pno) + Diz Disley (gtr) + Lennie Bush (bs) + John Spooner (dr) + Eberhard Weber (bs) + Kenny Clare (dr) + Ike Isaacs (gtr) + Isla Eckinger (Bs) + Andrew Simpkins (bs) + Rusty Jones (dr) + Philip Catherine (gtr) + Larry Coryell (gtr) + Niels-Henning Orsted Pedersen (bs) + Michel Legrand (pno).

515 807 2, Polygram/Verve (two discs), released 1993. Recordings from 1938–92 made in both England and France.

TRACK LIST

DISC 1

Stompin' At Decca / My Sweet / It Had To Be You / Nocturne / Alexander's Ragtime Band / Blue Ribbon Rag / Oh Lady, Be Good / Stéphane's Tune / Tiger Rag / Stéphane's Blues / Jive Bomber / Body And Soul / Liza (All The Clouds Roll Away) / The Folks Who Live On The Hill / Weep No More, My Lady / Nuages / The Nearness

Of You / S'Wonderful / Fascinating Rhythm / Just One Of Those Things / The Lady Is A Tramp / I Want To Be Happy / Dans La Vie / It's Only A Paper Moon / A Flower Is A Lovesome Thing

DISC 2
Minor Swing / Daphne / Makin' Whoopee / Pent-Up House / Django / Darling, Je Vous Aime Beaucoup / Willow Weep For Me / How High The Moon / More / Lonely Street / Time After Time / Misty / Shine / Lover Man (Oh, Where Can You Be ?) / I'm Coming Virginia / La Chanson Des Rues / Sweet Chorus / Mon Homme

A useful compilation including some rare '40s and '50s material.

DJANGOLOGY '49 – DJANGO REINHARDT
A selection of radio acetates recorded by Django Reinhardt and The Quintette Of The Hot Club of France with Stéphane Grappelli. Stéphane Grappelli (vln) + Django Reinhardt (gtr) + Gianni Safred (pno) + Carlo Recori (bs) + Aurelio de Carolis (dr).
BMG Music/RCA/Bluebird (ND90448), released 1990. Recorded in Rome, Italy, during January and February 1949.

TRACK LIST
The World Is Waiting For The Sunrise / Hallelujah / I'll Never Be The Same / Honeysuckle Rose / All The Things You Are / Djangology / Daphne / Beyond The Sea / Lover Man / Marie Minor Swing / Où Es-Tu, Mon Amour? / Swing 42 / I Surrender, Dear / After You've Gone / I Got Rhythm / I Saw Stars / Heavy Artillery / It's Only A Paper Moon / Bricktop

The dream was over, but fascinating anyway.

JAZZ MASTERS 11 – STÉPHANE GRAPPELLI
Stéphane Grappelli (vln) + Niels Pedersen (bs) + Alex Riel (dr) + Diz Disley (gtr) + Ike Isaacs (gtr) + Isla Eckinger (bs) + George Shearing (pno) + Andrew Simpkins (bs) + Rusty Jones (dr) + Michel Legrand And His Orchestra + Marc-Michel Lebevillon (bs) + Andre Ceddarelli (dr) + Marc Hemmeler (pno) + Eberhard Weber (bs) + Kenny Clare (dr) + Philip Catherine (gtr) + Larry Coryell (gtr) + Niels Pedersen (bs) + Marc Fosset (gtr).
Verve (516 758-2), released in 1993. Recordings from 1966–92.

TRACK LIST
Pennies From Heaven / Solitude / Ain't Misbehavin' / Star Eyes / Insensiblement / The Folks Who Live On The Hill / Nuages / Manoir De Mes Rêves / Daphne / Are You

In The Mood? / Tears / Djangology / Shine / A Nightingale Sang In Berkeley Square / Someone To Watch Over Me / I Got Rhythm

A fine compilation.

LIMEHOUSE BLUES – STÉPHANE GRAPPELLI AND BARNEY KESSEL
Stéphane Grappelli (vln) + Barney Kessel (gtr) + Nini Rosso (gtr) + Michel Gaudry (bs) + Jean-Louis Viale (d).
Black Lion (BLCD760158). Recorded at Studio Davout, Paris, 23–4 June 1969.

TRACK LIST
It Don't Mean A Thing If It Ain't Got That Swing / Out Of Nowhere / Tea For Two / Limehouse Blues / Copa Cola / Honeysuckle Rose / I Got Rhythm / Blues for Georges / Barniana / Perdido

All the Black Lion recordings can be recommended.

STÉPHANE GRAPPELLI MEETS BARNEY KESSEL
Stéphane Grappelli (vln) + Barney Kessel (gtr) + Nino Rosso (gtr) + Michel Gaudry (bs) + Jean-Louis Viale (d).
Black Lion (CD 877647-2). A release of DA Music. Recorded at Studio Davout, Paris, 23–4 June 1969

TRACK LIST
I Remember Django / Honeysuckle Rose / I Can't Get Started / What A Difference A Day Made / More Than You Know / Et Maintenant / I Found A New Baby / It's Only A Paper Moon / How High The Moon / Willow Weep For Me / Little Star / Undecided

---

VENUPELLI BLUES – STÉPHANE GRAPPELLI AND JOE VENUTI
Stéphane Grappelli (vln) + Joe Venuti (vln) + George Wein (pno) + Barney Kessel (gtr) + Larry Ridley (bs) + Don Lamond (d).
Le Jazz (CD 18). Recorded Paris, 22 October 1969

TRACK LIST
I Can't Give You Anything But Love / My One And Only Love / After You've Gone / Undecided / Venupelli Blues / Tea For Two / I'll Never Be The Same

A piece of history as the two giants finally record together. Best when Stéphane plays the piano.

PARIS ENCOUNTER – GARY BURTON AND STÉPHANE GRAPPELLI
Stéphane Grappelli (vln) + Gary Burton (vib) + Steve Swallow (el bs) + Bill Goodwin (dr).
Label M (495738). Recorded Paris, 4 November 1969

TRACK LIST
Daphne / Blue In Green / Falling Grace / Here's That Rainy Day / Coquette / Sweet Rain / The Night Has A Thousand Eyes / Arpège / Eiderdown

A good album with Stéphane demonstrating he could hold his own with the young lions.

I HEAR MUSIC – STÉPHANE GRAPPELLI
Stéphane Grappelli (vln/pno) + Marc Hemmeler (pno/organ) + Jack Sewing (bs) + Kenny Clarke (dr/pno).
RCA Victor Gold Series (74321796242). Recorded in Paris, 13 December 1970.

TRACK LIST
Tea For Two / Danny Boy / Let's Fall In Love / Coltrane / Dear Ben / I Hear Music / Dany / Smoke Gets In Your Eyes / Body And Soul / Gary / Flower For Kenny

---

PAUL SIMON – PAUL SIMON
Warner Brothers 7599-25588-2. Recorded 1971.

TRACK LIST
Mother and Child Reunion / Duncan / Everything Put Together Falls Apart / Run Than Body Down / Armistice Day Me And Julio Down By The Schoolyard / Peace Like A River / Papa Hobo / Hobo's Blues / Paranoia Blues / Congratulations

On this, Paul Simon's first solo album Stéphane plays on one track, 'Hobo's Blues' which is credited jointly as being composed by 'Simon/Grappelli'. An interesting album.

MENUHIN & GRAPPELLI PLAY...GERSHWIN, BERLIN, KERN, PORTER, ROGERS & HART AND OTHERS
Stéphane Grappelli (vln) + Yehudi Menuhin (vln) + Alan Clare Trio + John Etheridge (gtr) + Pierre Michelot (bs) + Ronnie Verrell (dr) + Martin Taylor (gtr) + Laurie Holloway (kb / pno / harp) + Alan Ganley (dr) + David Snell (hp) + Derek Price (perc) + Ray Swinfield (fl) + Eddie Trip (bs) + Lennie Bush (bs) + Marc Fosset (gtr) + Jack Sewing (bs) + Brian Lemmon (pno) + Max Harris/Nelson Riddle (arrangements/conducting).

EMI Classics (7243 5 73380 2 8, two-disc set). Released in 1999. Recordings from 1972, 1973, 1975, 1977, 1979, 1981 and 1983. Mostly recorded in Studio 1 at Abbey Road, London, except the 1977 recordings, which were made at EMI Bovema Studios, Heemstede, Holland.

TRACK LIST

DISC 1

Fascinatin' Rhythm / Soon / Summertime / Nice Work If You Can Get It / Embraceable You / Liza / A Foggy Day / S'Wonderful / The Man I Love / I Got Rhythm / He Loves And She Loves / They Can't Take That Away From Me / They All Laughed / Funny Face / Our Love Is Here To Stay / Lady Be Good / These Foolish Things / Laura / April in Paris / Autumn Leaves / Autumn in New York

DISC 2

Cheek To Cheek / Isn't This A Lovely Day? / Change Partners / Top Hat, White Tie And Tails / I've Got My Love To Keep Me Warm / Heat Wave / The Way You Look Tonight / Pick Yourself Up / A Fine Romance / All The Things You Are / Why Do I Love You / I Get A Kick Out Of You / Night And Day / Looking At You / Just One Of Those Things / My Funny Valentine / Thou Swell / The Lady Is A Tramp / Blue Room / Jealousy / Skylark

---

MENUHIN AND GRAPPELLI PLAY 'JEALOUSY' AND OTHER GREAT STANDARDS

Stéphane Grappelli (vln) + Yehudi Menuhin (vln) + Alan Clare Trio + John Etheridge (gtr) + Jan Blok (gtr) + Pierre Michelot (bs) + Ronnie Verrell (dr) + Martin Taylor (gtr) + Laurie Holloway (kb) + Alan Ganley (dr) + David Snell (hp) + Derek Price (perc) + Ray Swinfield (fl) + Niels Pedersen (bs) + Lennie Bush (bs) + Marc Fosset (gtr) + Jack Sewing (bs) + Brian Lemmon (pno) + Max Harris/Nelson Riddle (arrangements/conducting).

EMI Records (CDM 7 69220 2). Released in 1988. Recordings from 1972, 1973, 1977, 1979, 1981 and 1983. Mostly recorded in Studio 1 at Abbey Road, London, except the 1977 recordings, which were made at EMI Bovema Studios, Heemstede, Holland

TRACK LIST

Jealousy / Tea For Two / Limehouse Blues / These Foolish Things / The Continental / A Nightingale Sang In Berkeley Square / Sweet Sue / Skylark / Laura / Sweet Georgia Brown / I'll Remember April / April In Paris / The things We Did Last Summer / September In The Rain / Autumn Leaves / Autumn In New York / Button Up Your Overcoat

---

MENUHIN AND GRAPPELLI PLAY GERSHWIN

Stéphane Grappelli (vln) + Yehudi Menuhin (vln) + Alan Clare (pno) + Max Harris (pno) + Lennie Bush (bs) + Ike Isaacs (gtr) + Denny Wright (gtr) + Ronnie Verrell (dr) +

Pierre Michelot (bs) + Laurie Holloway (pno / harpsichord) + Martin Taylor (gtr) + Alan Ganley (dr) + David Snell (hp) + Eddie Trip (bs) + Derek Price (perc) + Ray Swinfield (fl) + Alan Clare Trio + Max Harris/Nelson Riddle (arrangements/conducting).

EMI Records (CDM 7 69218 2). Released in 1988. Recordings from 1972, 1973, 1975, 1977 and 1981. Mostly recorded in Studio 1 at Abbey Road, London, except the 1977 recordings which were made at EMI Bovema Studios, Heemstede, Holland.

TRACK LIST

Fascinating Rhythm / Soon / Summertime / Nice Work If You Can Get It / Embraceable You / Liza / A Foggy Day / S'Wonderful / The Man I Love / I Got Rhythm / He Loves And She Loves / They Can't Take That Away / They All Laughed / Funny Face / Love Is Here To Stay / Lady Be Good

---

JAZZ IN PARIS VOLUME 1 – OSCAR PETERSON AND STÉPHANE GRAPPELLI QUARTET

Stéphane Grappelli (vln) + Oscar Peterson (pno) + Niels Henning Orsted-Pedersen (bs) + Kenny Clarke (dr).

Gitanes Jazz Productions (013 028-2), Universal Music. Recorded 22–3 February 1973

TRACK LIST

Them There Eyes / Flamingo / Makin Whoopee / Looking At You / Walkin' My Baby Back Home / My One And Only Love / Thou Swell

For me, some of Stéphane's best mature work was done alongside Oscar Peterson, and although the recording quality varies, both these discs and *Skol* contain music to enjoy.

STARDUST – STÉPHANE GRAPPELLI

Stéphane Grappelli (vln) + Alan Clare (pno & cel).

Black Lion, a release of Da Music (Germany, CD 877630-2). Recorded at Anvil Studios, Denham, England, 19 March 1973.

TRACK LIST

Stardust (take 1) / The Nearness Of You (take 7) / Tournesol (take 6) / Greensleeves (take 10) / You Go To My Head / Nature Boy / Can't Help Loving That Man O' Mine We'll Be Together Again / The Talk Of The Town / Amanda / I Saw Stars / Greensleeves (take 17) / Tournesol (take 8) / The Nearness Of You (take 8) / Stardust (take 2)

Alan Clare was Stéphane's favourite pianist. He said it was 'like having Debussy behind you'.

JUST ONE OF THOSE THINGS – STÉPHANE GRAPPELLI
Stéphane Grappelli (vln) + Marc Hemmeler (pno) + Jack Sewing (bs) + Daniel Humair (d).
Black Lion (BLCD 760180). Recorded live at the Montreux Jazz Festival, Switzerland, 4 July 1973.

TRACK LIST
Just One Of Those Things / Misty / More / All God's Chillun Got Rhythm / Que Restent-Ils De Nos Amours ? / Don't Get Around Much Anymore / Them There Eyes / Honeysuckle Rose

---

PARISIAN THOROUGHFARE – STÉPHANE GRAPPELLI
Stéphane Grappelli (vln) + Roland Hanna (pno + el pno) + Jiri Mraz (bs) + Mel Lewis (dr).
Black Lion Records (BLCD760132). Recorded at Chappell Studios, London, 5/7 September 1973.

TRACK LIST
Love For Sale / Perugia / Two Cute / Fascinating Rhythm / Shangri-La / Nice Work If You Can Get It / Star Eyes / Parisian Thoroughfare / Improvisation On Prelude In E Minor / Wave / Hallelujah

This is Stéphane at his peak 1970s form.

STÉPHANE GRAPPELLI LIVE IN LONDON
Stéphane Grappelli (vln) + Diz Disley (gtr) + Denny Wright (gtr) + Len Skeat (bs).
Black Lion (BLCD 760139). Recorded live at the Queen Elizabeth Hall, London, 5 November 1973.

TRACK LIST
This Can't Be Love / I Can't Believe That You're In Love With Me / Flamingo / Them There Eyes / Satin Doll / Manoir de mes Rêves / Daphne / Tea For Two Honeysuckle Rose / Misty / After You've Gone / Nuages / Sweet Georgia Brown / S'Wonderful / Summertime / But Not For Me / I Got Rhythm

A fine record of the first comeback band.

STÉPHANE GRAPPELLI MEETS EARL HINES
Stéphane Grappelli (vln) + Earl Hines (pno).
Black Lion (BLCD 760168). Recorded at Chappell Studios, London, 4 July 1974.

TRACK LIST
Fine And Dandy / Over The Rainbow / Manhattan / Moonlight In Vermont / Memories of You / There Will Never Be Another You / I Can't Get Started / You Took Advantage Of Me / Sometimes I'm Happy

A good album.

STÉPHANE GRAPPELLI/YOUNG DJANGO
Stéphane Grappelli (vln & pno) + Philip Catherine (gtr) + Larry Coryell (gtr) + Niels Henning Orsted-Pedersen (bs).

MPS Records (815 672-2). Recorded at Tonstudio Zuckerfabrik, Stuttgart, Germany, 19–21 January 1979.

TRACK LIST
Djangology / Sweet Chorus / Minor Swing / Are You In The Mood? / Gallerie St Hubert / Tears / Swing Guitars / Oriental Shuffle / Blues For Django And Stéphane

---

SKOL
Oscar Peterson (pno) + Stéphane Grappelli (vln) + Joe Pass (gtr) + Mickey Roker (dr) + Niels Henning Orsted-Pedersen (bs) in Scandinavia.

Fantasy, Inc (OJC20 496-2). Recorded live at the Tivoli Concert Hall, Copenhagen, 6 July 1979.

TRACK LIST
Nuages / How About You / Someone To Watch Over Me / Makin' Whoopee / That's All / Skol Blues

Excellent.

TIVOLI GARDENS – COPENHAGEN, DENMARK
Stéphane Grappelli (vln) + Joe Pass (gtr) + Niels Henning Orsted-Pedersen (bs).

Fantasy, Inc (OJCCD 441-2). Recorded at the Tivoli Concert Hall, Copenhagen, 6 July 1979.

TRACK LIST
It's Only A Paper Moon / Time After Time / Let's Fall In Love / Crazy Rhythm / How Deep is the Ocean / I'll Remember April / I Can't Get Started / I Get A Kick Out Of You

Stéphane enjoyed Joe Pass's approach to harmony and he was clearly inspired.

VINTAGE GRAPPELLI – STÉPHANE GRAPPELLI (two albums on CD: *At The Winery* and *Vintage 1981*)

Stéphane Grappelli (vln) + John Etheridge (gtr) + Martin Taylor (gtr) + Jack Sewing (bs) + Mike Gari (gtr).

Concord Jazz (CCD2-4977-2, two-CD set). Released in 2001. *At The Winery* recorded live at the Paul Masson Mountain Winery, California, September 1980. *Vintage 1981* recorded in the Coast Recorders Studio, San Francisco, July 1981.

TRACK LIST

DISC 1 – *AT THE WINERY*

You Are The Sunshine Of My Life / Love For Sale / Angel's Camp / Willow Weep For Me / Chicago / Taking A Chance On Love / Minor Swing / Let's Fall In Love / Just You, Just Me

DISC 2 – *VINTAGE 1981*

Blue Moon / It's Only A Paper Moon / Jamie / I'm Coming Virginia / I Can't Get Started / Do You Know What It Means to Miss New Orleans? / But Not For Me / If I Had You / Isn't She Lovely / Swing 42 / Honeysuckle Rose

Very relaxed, mature Grappelli, like a good wine.

NORWEGIAN WOOD

Stéphane Grappelli (vln) + Elena Duran (fl) + Laurie Holloway (pno/arrangements).

RCA (RCA LP 6007). Not reissued on CD and at the time of going to press deleted. Recorded at CBS Studios, 1981

TRACK LIST

Yesterday / All My Loving / Eleanor Rigby / Norwegian Wood / Can't Buy Me Love / Here, There And Everywhere / Michelle / Hey Jude / The Long And Winding Road / Hard Day's Night

For light music, I prefer these to the Menuhin material. Laurie's arrangements are superb.

CONVERSATIONS

Stéphane Grappelli (vln/pno) + L Subramaniam (vln/vla/violectra/tambura/surmandal/perc) + Frank Bennett (perc) + Anthony Hindson (gtr) + Handel Manuel (pno) + Mark Massey (pno) + Frank Morgan (as) + Manoochehr Sadeghi (santoor) + Joe Sample (keyboards) + Gorge Strunz (gtr) + Niles Steiner (steinerphone) + Ron Wagner (dr) + Jerry Watts (bs)

Milestone (MCD 9130 2). Recorded May 1984 at Culver Street Studio, California.

TRACK LIST
Don't Leave Me / Memories / Caprice No 5 (Paganini) / Conversation Walking In A Dream / Illusion / Tribute To Mani / French Resolution

Stéphane plays violin on most tracks but plays solo piano on 'Tribute To Mani'. Not a wholly successful fusion.

PIANO: MY OTHER LOVE – STÉPHANE GRAPPELLI
    Stéphane Grappelli (pno)
    CBS (MK46257). Recorded at RCA Studio C, New York, 1990.

TRACK LIST
Three Little Words / Time After Time / Satin Doll / A Cottage For Sale / Ain't Misbehavin' / You Better Go Now / What A Wonderful World Looking At You / Two Sleepy People / Was That The Human Thing To Do / Jacqueline / Tea For Two / A Foggy Day (In London Town) / Stéphane's Blues For Abby / Ballade

Stéphane plays 'the soundtrack to his life' on his 'real' instrument, the piano!

ONE ON ONE – STÉPHANE GRAPPELLI AND McCOY TYNER
    Stéphane Grappelli (vln) + McCoy Tyner (pno).
    Milestone (MCD-9181-2). Recorded at BMG Studio B, New York, 18 April 1990.

TRACK LIST
How High The Moon / St Louis Blues / I Want To Talk About You / Mr PC / Summertime / Satin Doll / I Didn't Know What Time It Was / You Say You Care / Yours Is My Heart Alone / I Got Rhythm

Stéphane enjoyed the challenge and they find some common ground.

FIRST CLASS – THE CLAUDE BOLLING BIG BAND AND STÉPHANE GRAPPELLI
    Stéphane Grappelli + Claude Bolling Big Band.
    Frémeaux Associés (FA 451). Recorded at Studio Artistic Palace, Boulogne-Billancourt, France, 3–4 December 1991.

TRACK LIST
Stéphane / De Partout et d'Ailleurs / Minor Swing / Tears / Just One Of Those Things / Blue Skies / Cute / Do You Know What It Means To Miss New Orleans / Crazy

Rhythm / Lush Life / Moon Glow / Nice Work If You Can Get It / Moon Mist / Lady Be Good

Stéphane enjoyed the big-band setting, and although it's very late in his career, he plays well.

LIVE IN PARIS 1992 – STÉPHANE GRAPPELLI
Stéphane Grappelli (vln) + Philip Catherine (gtr) + Marc Fosset (gtr) + Niels Henning Orsted Pedersen (bs).
Dreyfus Jazz (FDM 37006-2). Recorded live at La Salle des Spectacles de Colombes, France, 27–8 March 1992.

TRACK LIST
Minor Swing / Galerie des Princes / Ballade / Tears / Blues for Django And Stéphane / Stella By Starlight / Sweet Chorus / Oh, Lady, Be Good ! / Some To Watch Over Me /I Got Rhythm

---

MICHEL LEGRAND/STÉPHANE GRAPPELLI
Stéphane Grappelli (vln) + Michel Legrand (pno/arrangements/direction) + Orchestra + Marc-Michel Lebevillon (el bs) + Andre Ceccarelli (dr).
Verve (517 028-2). Recorded in Paris, May 25–7 1992.

TRACK LIST
Parlez-Moi d'Amour / C'est Si Bon / Les Feuilles Mortes / Theme From Summer Of 42 / Revoir Paris / Mon Legionnaire / The Good Life / Clopin-Clopant / Mon Homme / What Are You Doing The Rest Of Your Life? / Insensiblement / Les Parapluies de Cherbourg / Milou En Mai / Irma La Douce / Nuages

Stéphane was less happy with this album than with the rematch in 1995.

REUNION – STÉPHANE GRAPPELLI AND MARTIN TAYLOR
Stéphane Grappelli (vln) + Martin Taylor (gtr).
Linn Records (AKD 022). Recorded Studio Miraval, France, 21–2 January 1993.

TRACK LIST
Jive At Five / Willow Weep For Me / Drop Me Off At Harlem / Miraval / Jenna / Reunion / Emily / Hotel Splendid / La Dame du Lac / I Thought About You / It's Only A Paper Moon

ALL THE WORLD'S VIOLINS – YEHUDI MENUHIN LIVE
    Yehudi Menuhin (vln) + Stéphane Grappelli (vln) + L Subramaniam (vln) + Titi Winterstein Quintet + Trio Avodah + Roman and Larissa Grinkiv (bandoura & vocals) + Jean-Pierre Catoul (vln) + Corina Belcea (vln) + Natsuko Yoshimoto (vln) + Kalamakar Rao (mridangam) + Probhu Sen (tampura) + Gwenael Micault (bandoneon) + Marc Fosset (gtr) + Jean-Pierre Viret (bs).
    IMA Records (IMA-002). Recorded live at the Cirque Royal, Brussels, 21 Oct 1993.

TRACK LIST
Duos For Two Violins (Béla Bartók) – The Yehudi Menuhin School: 'Arabian Song' / 'Rumanian Whirling Dance' / 'Transylvanian Dance'. Carnatic Music From India – Dr L Subramaniam: 'Kriti/Raga Mohanan'. Traditional Gypsy Music – The Titi Winterstein Quintet: 'Fur Dich' / 'Fulli Tschal'. Urkrainian Bandoura (Roman And Larissa Grinkiv): 'Vesnianka' / 'Tehoriti Voli Pasu Ya' / 'Garbuz Bili Katchaestia'. Trio Avodah: 'Avodah'. Jean-Pierre Catoul: 'Tango Tzigane'. Stéphane Grappelli: 'Someone To Watch Over Me' / 'I Got Rhythm' / 'Sweet Georgia Brown'. Yehudi Menuhin And Stéphane Grappelli: 'Lady Be Good'.

An interesting and eclectic mix for violin enthusiasts.

CARAVAN – THE ROSENBERG TRIO
    Stochelo Rosenberg (gtr) + Nous'che Rosenberg (gtr) + Nonnie Rosenberg (bs) + Stéphane Grappelli (vln) + Jan Akkerman (gtr) + Frits Landesbergen (vib).
    Polydor (523 030-2). Recorded 18 January 1994 at Davout Studios, Paris.

TRACK LIST
Viajeiro / Mélodie au Crépuscule / Pent-Up House / La Promenade / Embraceable You / Tears / The Zebra / Chez Moi Stéphanesque / Caravan / I Surrender Dear / Donna Lee / Night And Day / Manoir de mes Rêves / Batida Diferente / Manha de Carnaval

Stéphane declared the Rosenbergs his favourite gypsy-jazz group.

WE LOVE STÉPHANE GRAPPELLI – STÉPHANE GRAPPELLI TRIO
    Stéphane Grappelli (vln) + Marc Fosset (gtr) + Jean-Philippe Viret (bs).
    Mannenberg Records (CAC 0023). Recorded at Suntory Hall, Tokyo, 1 April 1995.

TRACK LIST
How High The Moon / Fascinating Rhythm / All God's Chillun' Got Rhythm / I've Got The World On A String / Limehouse Blues / I Won't Dance / Medley – These Foolish Things / The End Of A Love Affair / Satin Doll / Medley – S'Wonderful / Someone To Watch Over Me / I Got Rhythm / Medley – A Nightingale Sang In

Berkeley Square / The Lady Is A Tramp / Sweet Georgia Brown / Medley – I'll Never Be The Same / Oh Lady Be Good

---

DOUCE FRANCE – MICHEL LEGRAND/STÉPHANE GRAPPELLI

Stéphane Grappelli (vln) + Michel Legrand (pno/arrangements/direction) + Orchestra + Marc-Michel Lebevillon (el bs) + Umberto Pagnini (dr).

Verve (529 850-2). Recorded at Studios Guillaume Tell, Suresnes-Paris, 28–9 August and 2–3 October 1995.

TRACK LIST

Le Temps des Cerises / La Marche de Menilmontant / Je Tire ma Reverence / Couches Dans le Foin / Vous Qui Passez Sans me Voir / Sous Les Ponts de Paris / Sous Le Ciel de Paris / La Vie En Rose / Douce France / Boum! / La Chanson des Rues / Que Reste-t-il de nos Amours? / Et Maintenant / J'ai Deux Amours

Stéphane was pleased with this and played it at home.

AS TIME GOES BY – STÉPHANE GRAPPELLI AND IWAO FURUSAWA

Stéphane Grappelli (vln) + Iwao Furusawa (vln) + Marc Fosset (gtr) + Jean-Philippe Viret (bs) + Max Harris (arrangement).

Epic/Sony Records (ESCK 8036). Recorded at Acousti Studios, Paris, August 1996.

TRACK LIST

Two Marvellous For Words / These Foolish Things / Our Love Is Here To Stay / As Time Goes By

Poignant as a last recording but not his greatest work.

HAPPY REUNION - STÉPHANE GRAPPELLI MARTIAL SOLAL

Stéphane Grappelli (vln) + Martial Solal (pno).

Universal (Owl 013 430-2). Recorded 17 February 1980, Studio Acousti, Paris.

TRACK LIST

Shine / Valsitude / Sing For Your Supper / God Bless The Child / Nuages / Parisian Thoroughfare / Grandeur et Cadence / Stumblin' / Et si l'on improvisait?

The last two tracks of this excellent album demonstrate the range of Stéphane's musical genius. 'Stumblin'' is the melody that started him on his jazz career in 1923, heard then on the Pathé brothers' jukebox as played by Mitchell's Jazz Kings – Stéphane revisits his 'ragged time' roots 57 years later. 'Improvisait' is an abstract atonal soundscape – Picasso in music. For me, an interesting aspect of musical genius is what those 'who could play anything', in fact, then chose to play.

BACKGROUND AND INFLUENCES

1850-1899 – LES CHANSONS DE CES ANNÉES LA...
A single disc containing songs from the latter part of the 19th century digitally remastered from original cylinders and 78rpm discs. Artists performing include Aristide Bruant, Yvette Guilbert, Vanni Marcoux, Yvonne Printemps, Fortin, M Mailoire, Fred Gouin, Théodore Botrel, Felix Mayol, Stello, Esther Lekain, Lyx Gauty, Georges Elval, Polaire, Ferdinand Gabin Père and Berthe Sylva.
Forlane (19161). Released 1999.

ACCORDEON – MUSETTE/SWING/PARIS 1913–1941
A two-disc reissue set of classics of the musette direct from their creative source by the composers and performers of the day.
Discothèque des Halles (DH002CD). Released 1999 – recordings from 1913-1941.

No Grappelli, but this paints the musical world he grew up in. Many Italians, some Reinhardt and other future Hot Club players.

DIXIELAND AND THE ORIGINS OF JAZZ
25 phonographic memories from 1918–39 compiled from early and, in many cases, historic recordings.
Déjà Vu (DVRECD 20). Released 1989. Recordings from 1918–39.

TRACK LIST
Tiger Rag / Look At 'Em Doing It now / Copenhagen / Careless Love / She's Crying For Me / That's No Bargain / Way Down Yonder In New Orleans / I'm More Than Satisfied / Royal Garden Blues / Nobody's Sweetheart / Coquette / I Found A New Baby There'll Be Some Changes Made / Shake Your Can / Moanin' Low / Strut Miss Lizzie / Georgia On My Mind / Georgia Grind / After You've Gone / Spider Crawl / The Eel / When The Saints Go Marchin' In / All The Jazz Ball / Relaxin' At The Touro

Fantastic perspective on early jazz recordings with good notes.

MISTINGUETT
Two-CD set, 40 tracks of the best of her music-hall work from 1920–42.
EMI Music France (856 000 2). Released 1997. Recordings from 1920–42.
Stéphane's first attempt at music was 'The Java Of Mistinguett' – on the piano !

JAZZ CITY – PARIS (JAZZ GREATS)
Part of the Marshall Cavendish *Jazz Greats* 1998 series of magazines with CDs. A CD containing some of the best sides cut in Paris by visiting musicians, starting with Mitchell's Jazz Kings' 'Everybody Step' in 1922 through to Stéphane Grappelli's own recording of 'Tea For Two' in 1947.

Number 54 in Marshall Cavendish Series. CD not available separately. Released in 1998. Recordings from 1922–46.

Fascinating background, including some Grégor material.

LOUIS ARMSTRONG HOT FIVES AND SEVENS
Remastered four-CD set. All four discs remastered by John RT Davis.
JSP Records (JSPCDLOUISBOX100). Released in 1999. Recordings from 1925–9.

The most decisive influence on Grappelli. Wonderful transfers.

WILD CATS – JOE VENUTI AND EDDIE LANG.
ASV Living Era (CD AJA 5386). Released 2001. Recordings from 1926–33.

TRACK LIST
Stringing The Blues / Bugle Call Rag / Doin' Things / Goin' Places / Kickin' The Cat / Beatin' The Dog / A Mug Of Ale / Four String Joe / Dinah / The Wild Dog / The Man From The Shouth / Wild Cat Running Ragged / I've Found A Brand New Baby / Little Girl / I'll Never Be The Same / To To Blues / Raggin' The Scale / Hey Young Fella! / Jig Saw Puzzle Blues / Pink Elephants / Beale Street Blues / After You've Gone / Someday, Sweetheart / Farewell Blues

---

JOSEPHINE BAKER
Two-CD set of transfers from original 78 test pressings and metal plates. Accompanied by many unidentified musicians along with Jacob's Jazz + Fray and Braggiotti (piano duet) + Melodic – Jazz Du Casino De Paris (conducted by Edmond Mahieux) + her own orchestra + Trio with Jacques Pills and Georges Tabet + Le Jazz Du Poste-Parisien (directed by Al Romans) + Comedian Harmonists and Erwin Bootz (pno) + The Lecuona Cuban Boys.

Elysèe/Sandstone Music (D233072-2). Released in 1991. Recordings from 1926–36, Paris.

TRACK LIST
DISC 1
Who / That Certain Feeling / Dinah / Sleepy Time Gal / I Wonder Where My Baby Is Tonight? / Bam Bam Bamy Shore / I Want To Yodel / You're The Only One For Me / Feeling Kind Of Blue / I Love My Baby / I Found A New Baby / Skeedle Um / Always

/ Pretty Little Baby / Where'd You Get Those Eyes? / After I Say I'm Sorry / Then I'll Be Happy / Bye Bye Blackbird / Lonesome Lovesick Blues / I Love Dancing / Breezing Along With The Breeze / Hello Bluebird / Blue Skies / He's The Last Word / I'm Leaving For Alabamy

DISC 2

La Petite Tonkinoise / Suppose! / Pretty Little Baby / J'Ai Deux Amours / Voulez-Vous De La Canne A Sucre ? / Dis-Moi Josephine? / Pardon Si Je T'Importune / Aux Iles Hawaii / Love Is A Dreamer / King For A Day / My Fate Is In Your Hands / Confessin' / You're Driving Me Crazy / You're The One I Care For / Madiana / Mon Rêve C'etait Vous / Je J'etais Blanche / Sans Amour / Les Mots D'Amour / Ram Pam Pam / C'est Lui / Haiti / Rêves / Sous Le Ciel D'Afrique / La Conga Blicoti

La Revue Nègre fuelled Paris jazz with a bang. Fantastic background to Stéphane's story. No Grappelli.

BLUE GUITARS VOLUMES 1 & 2 – EDDIE LANG AND LONNIE JOHNSON
Two-CD set featuring Eddie Lang (gtr) + Arthur Schutt (pno) + Lonnie Johnson (gtr) + Frank Signorelli (pno) + Louis Armstrong (tpt) + Jack Teagarden (tb) + Happy Caldwell (ts) + Joe Sullivan (pno) + Kaiser Marshall (dr) + JC Higginbotham (tb) + Albert Nicholas (clar/as) + Charlie Holmes (clar/as) + Teddy Hill (ts) + Luis Russell (pno) + Eddie Condon (banjo) + Lonnie Johnson (gtr) + George 'Pops' Foster (bs) + Paul Barbarin (dr).
BGO Records (BGOCD327). Released in 1997. Recordings from 1927–9, New York and Memphis

---

TRACK LIST
DISC 1
Hot Fingers / Eddie's Twister / Playing With The Strings / Have To Change Keys To Play These Blues / A Little Love, A Little Kiss / Stompin' 'Em Along Slow / Midnight Call Blues / Knockin' A Jug / Blue Room Blues / Add A Little Wiggle / Away Down In The Alley Blues / Blue Guitars / Rainbow Dreams / Blues in G / Deep Minor Rhythm / Mahogany Hall Blues Stomp

DISC 2
I'll Never Be The Same / April Kisses / Prelude In C Sharp Minor / The Melody Man's Dream / Perfect / Church Street Sobbin' Blues / There'll Be Some Changes Made / Jeannine (I Dream of Lilac Time) / Two-Tone Stomp / Guitar Blues / Bull Frog Man / A Handful Of Riffs / Work Ox Blues / The Risin' Sun / Jet-Black Blues / Blue-Blood Blues
Django probably heard some of this wonderful material.

THE BIG BAND RECORDINGS 1930–1932 – LOUIS ARMSTRONG
   Remastered two-CD set, both discs remastered by John RT Davis.
   JSP Records (JSPCD3401). Released 2000. Recordings from 1930–2.

Track 2 on disc 1 of this set is 'I Can't Believe That You're In Love With Me', which Stéphane chose as one of his BBC Radio 4's Desert Island Discs. This is where Stéphane drew much of his inspiration. Glorious music.

---

50 ANS DE GRANDS ORCHESTRES DE MUSIC HALL
   Six-CD set. EPM Musique (1980542). Released in 2001. 120 tracks of original recordings.

TRACK LIST
DISC 1
Tracks 1–8: Ray Ventura et ses Collégiens (Tout Va Très Bien Madame)
Comme Tout Le Monde / Ca Vaut Mieux Que D'Attrapper La Scarlatine / Les Trois Mandarins / Le Refrain Des Chevaux de Bois / Qu'Est Ce Qu'on Attend / Tiens Tiens Tiens / Cans Mon Coeur); Tracks 9–16: Fred Adison; Tracks 17-20: Jo Bouillon

DISC 2
Tracks 1–8: Jacques Helian et son Orchestre; Tracks 9–16: Raymond Legrand; Tracks 17–20: Alix Combelle (Elle Et Lui / Ca S'Fait Pas / Ce Qu'il Faut Demontrer / Oui)

DISC 3
Tracks 1–10: Xavier Cugat Orchestra; Tracks 11–20: The Lecuona Cuban Boys

DISC 4
Tracks 1–3: Jack Hylton (September In The Rain / There's A Small Hotel / Sing My Heart); Tracks 4–6: Harry Roy; Tracks 7–8: Lew Stone; Tracks 9–11: Billy Cotton; Tracks 12–14: Ambrose; Tracks 15–17: Carroll Gibbons; Tracks 18–20: Geraldo (You'll Never Know / How Sweet You Are / Summertime)

DISC 5
Tracks 1–10: Mantovani And His Orchestra; Tracks 11–20: Barnabas Von Geczy

DISC 6
Tracks 1–4: Le Grand Orchestre Bohemien; Tracks 5–8 Marek Weber; Tracks 9–12: Dajos Bela; Tracks 13–16: Albert Locatelli; Tracks 17–20: Georges Boulanger

These discs conjure up the world that Stéphane encountered with Grégor and at The London Palladium, but there's no Grappelli and sadly no useful discographical notes.

ART TATUM/BEN WEBSTER
Art Tatum (pno) + Ben Webster (ts) + Red Callender (bs) + Bill Douglass (d).
Pablo (CD 2310 737). Recorded 11 September 1956, Los Angeles, California.

TRACK LIST
Gone With The Wind / All The Things You Are / Have You Met Miss Jones? / My
One And Only Love / Night And Day / My Ideal / Where Or When
One of Stéphane's Desert Island Discs. Fantastic.

THE VERY BEST OF JOHN COLTRANE
John Coltrane (ts/sop sax) + Tommy Flanagan (pno) + Paul Chambers (bs) + Art
Taylor (dr) + Wynton Kelly (pno) + Jimmy Cobb (dr) + McCoy Tyner (pno) + Steve
Davis (bs) + Elvin Jones (dr).
Rhino/Atlantic Jazz Gallery (8122-79778-2). Released 2000. Recordings from
1959–64.

TRACK LIST
Giant Steps / Cousin Mary / Naima / Like Sonny / My Shining Hour / My Favourite
Things / Central Park West / Summertime / Mr Syms / Equinox / Body And Soul

Another of Stéphane's Desert Island Discs.

MENUHIN MEETS SHANKAR
Yehudi Menuhin (vln) + Alla Rakha (tabla) + Ravi Shankar (sitar) + Kamala
Chakravarti (tamboura) + Nodu Mullick (tampura).
HMV Classics (HMV 5 73470 2). Released 1988. Recordings from 1966–8.

TRACK LIST
Prabhati / Raga Puriya Kalyan / Swara-Kakali / Raga Piloo / Raga Ananda Bhairava

Interesting and quite successful fusion. Yehudi was extremely sincere in these
adventures. No Grappelli.

PARIS MUSETTE
Three volumes of single CDs from Label La Lichère – Frémeaux et Associés. As
with all Frémeaux releases, a thorough and informed set of discs about Paris musette.
Vol 1: CD LLL 137. Recorded 23–8 April and 5–6 June 1990 at Sun Studio, Paris.
Vol 2: CD LLL 207. Recorded 3/5/15/16 March and 18/20/21/22 April 1993 at
Studio Acousti, Paris.
Vol 3: CD LLL 217. Recorded between Jan '93 and March '94 at Studio Acousti, Paris.

Excellent background. No Grappelli.

THE LEGACY

BLUES FOR STUFF AND STEPH – THE MIKE PIGGOTT QUARTET
Mike Piggott (vln) + Brian Dee (pno) + John Rees-Jones (bs) + Dave Trigwell (dr).
DOZ Records (DOZ001). Recorded 12 October/2nd November 1988 at DOZ Studio, Kent, UK.

TRACK LIST
September In The Rain / Skip It / This Can't Be Love / Nuages / My Little Suede Shoes / Only Time Will Tell / I Can't Believe You're In Love With Me / Waltz For Sachma / Timme's Blues / Autumn Leaves / Vous Et Moi

A good example of the Grappelli legacy in the UK.

DJANGO MEETS THE DUKE – IAN CRUICKSHANK'S GYPSY JAZZ
Iain Cruickshank (gtr) + Alan Barnes (as) + Jez Cook (gtr) + Andy Crowdy (bs) + Johnny Van Derrik (vln) and 'Pearl Django'.
Fret Records (FJCD 109). Recorded live in concert, April 1995, and at David Lange Studios, Tacoma, Washington, USA, May 1997.

TRACK LIST
Ultrafox / Billets Doux / Tears / Djangologie / Nocturne Lotus Blossom / Caravan / Django Meets The Duke / Fleche D'Or / In A Sentimental Mood / Vous Et Moi

---

KAFKA
Nigel Kennedy (vln/vla/cello/pno/mandolin/space sax/harp) + Stéphane Grappelli (vln) + Pino Palladino (bs) + Manu Katche (dr) + Bill Dillon (gtr) + Paul Inder (gtr) + Nana Vasconcelos (perc) + Paul Bruce (bs) + Darren Abraham (dr) + Doug Boyle (gtr) + Simon Clark (Hammond organ) + David Bottrill (rhythm programming) + David Heath (bass fl/piccolo) + Ravi (kora) + David Roscarrick-Wholey (vocal) + Donovan (gtr) + Naomi Boole-Masterson (cello) + Danny Thompson (bs) + Rupert Brown (dr) + Brixie Smith (vocal) + Stephen Duffy (Vocal) + Caroline Dale (cello) + Philip Dukes (vla) + John Etheridge (gtr) + Rory McFarland (bs) + Jane Siberry (vocal) + Simon Heath (tpt) + Rachel Fletcher (oboe) + Keith Bragg (fl) + Jonathan Rees (vln) + Caleb Clarke (vocal) + Caroline Lavelle (vocal).
EMI Records (7243 8 52212 2 4). Recorded 1996 at Rockfield Studios, Monmouth, UK, with additional recordings at Malvern and Air Lyndhurst.

TRACK LIST
Autumn Regrets / I Believe In God / Transfigured Night / Melody In The Wind / From Adam To Eve / Fallen Forest / Innig / Soleil Levant Sur La Seine / New Road / Solitude / Breathing Stone

Stéphane's only official recording with Kennedy. He is only on 'Melody In The Wind'.

SOUVENIRS: STÉPHANE GRAPPELLI REMEMBERED – MICHAEL GRAY/ PEARL DJANGO

Neil Andersson (gtr) + Rick Leppanen (bs) + Michael Gray (vln) + Dudley Hill (gtr) + Shelly D Park (gtr) + guests: John Bishop (dr) + Doug Miller (bs) + Marc Seales (pno) + Will Dowd (dr) + David Lange (accordion) + Paul Sawyer (gtr).

Modern Hot Records (Modern Hot 004). Recorded 1999 at David Lange Studios, Edgewood, Washington, USA.

TRACK LIST
Minor Swing / Souvenirs De Villengen / Pent-Up House / Splendor In Feathers / Saskia / In My Solitude / I'll Remember April / It's Only A Paper Moon / Sweet Lorraine / Tears

The Grappelli Legacy in the USA.

MOTOR CITY MOMENTS – REGINA CARTER

Regina Carter (vln) + Werna 'Vana' Gierig (pno) + Darryl Hall (bs) + Alvester Garnett (dr) + Mayra Casales (perc) + Marcus Belgrave (tpt + flugelhorn) + James Carter (bs clar/ts) + Barry Harris (pno) + Russell Malone (gtr) + Lewis Nash (dr).

Verve (543 927-2). Recorded 19–21/25 April 2000 at Avatar Studios, New York.

TRACK LIST
Don't Git Sassy / Don't Mess With Mr T / For Someone I Love / Forever February / Higher Ground / Love Theme From *Spartacus* / Prey Loot / Fukai Aijo / Chattanooga Choo-Choo / Up South

Another aspect of the Grappelli legacy in the USA.

TRIBUTE TO STEPHANE GRAPPELLI – DIDIER LOCKWOOD

Didier Lockwood (vln) + Bireli Lagrene (gtr) + Niels Pedersen (bs).
Dreyfus Records (36611). Recorded 2000.

TRACK LIST
Les Valseuses / I Got Rhythm / Nuages / Barbizon Blues / All The Things You Are /

My One And Only Love / The Kid / Someday My Prince Will Come / Minor Swing / Misty / Pent-Up House / Tears / In A Sentimental Mood / Beautiful Love

---

SOLEDAD

Manu Comté (accordion) + Nicolas Stevens (vln) + Alexander Gurning (pno) + Patrick de Schuyter (gtr) + Philippe Cormann (bs).

Virgin Classics (7243 5 45503 2 4). Recorded February 2001 at Acousting Recording Service Studio, Brussels.

TRACK LIST

Milonga del Angel / Michelangelo 70 / Escualo / Tango Pour Claude / Tango / Habanera Ballet-Tango / Tango I / Tango II / Libertango / Nuestro Tiempo / De Part Et D'Autre Fascinating Tango

No Grappelli, but plenty of authentic tango.

RIC SANDERS GROUP IN LINCOLN CATHEDRAL

Two-CD set featuring Ric Sanders (vln) + Vo Fletcher (gtr) + Michael Gregory (dr/perc). Special guest appearance by Rick Wakeman (pno).

Heliopause Records (HPVP 101 CD). Recorded September 2001 at Lincoln Cathedral.

TRACK LIST

DISC 1

A Lifetime's Love / Little Wing / Tune For The Land Of Snows / Crystal Silence / Life Itself / Threedom / In A Silent Way – It's About That Time / Remembrance Day / The Rose Hip / Calico Skies

DISC 2 (BINAURAL SECTION)

Little Wing / Life Itself / Threedom / Remembrance Day / It's About That Time / DTS Warning

DTS SECTION

Life Itself / Tune For The Land Of Snows

MPEG VIDEO

In A Silent Way / It's About That Time

The Grappelli Legacy in the UK. Ric boldly takes the violin where previously only cherubs dared to tread. Great use of natural acoustics. Stéphane would have enjoyed this.

Videography

DVDs AND VIDEOTAPES

STÉPHANE GRAPPELLI: A LIFE IN THE JAZZ CENTURY
DVD – PROFILE WITH CONCERT FOOTAGE (2002)
Music on Earth Productions, written and directed by Paul Balmer.
Licensed to and distributed by Decca Music Group Ltd.
Catalogue number: MoE001.
BAFTA-nominated two-disc set. Contains all known film footage of Django Reinhardt.
'The finest documentary of a musician's life I have ever seen' (Martin Kossins, *Fanfare*)
'Immaculately profiles Paris's greatest gift to jazz' (Fred Dellar, *Mojo*)
'Indispensable' (Yves Sportis, *Jazz Hot*)

STÉPHANE GRAPPELLI LIVE IN SAN FRANCISCO
DVD – CONCERT FOOTAGE (1982)
Idem Home Video Productions
Produced and directed by Carlos N Broullon and Raymond G Poirier.
Catalogue number: IDVD 1033.
Recorded live in 1982 at the Paul Masson Vineyards, Saratoga, on 4 July and at the
Great American Music Hall, San Francisco, on 7 July.

STÉPHANE GRAPPELLI AT THE WARSAW JAZZ JAMBOREE
DVD – CONCERT FOOTAGE (1991)
TDK/EuroArts
Produced by Robert W Schachner/Lyra Productions, America, Inc.
Features Stéphane performing with Marc Fosset and Jean-Philippe Viret. Poor audio quality.

KING OF THE GYPSIES
VIDEOTAPE FILM (1978)
Paramount release directed by Frank Pierson in which Stéphane plays a gypsy fiddler.
Available on NTSC format only.

SOME ARCHIVE TV/FILM PERFORMANCES

ALL FEATURING ON THE DVD *STÉPHANE GRAPPELLI: A LIFE IN THE JAZZ CENTURY*
FILM (1928): Grégor et ses Grégoriens
Lobster Films (Paris) (complete)

FILM (1937): Hot Club Quintet at the Hague, Netherlands, with Django Reinhardt
(Complete)

FILM (1938): *Le Jazz Hot*, with Django Reinhardt and The Hot Club Quintet.
Lobster Films (Paris) (complete)

FILM (1946): *Stéphane Grappelli And His Quintet*
British Film Institute (complete)

FILM (1948): *The Flamingo Affair*, with George Shearing
British Film Institute (excerpt)

TV (1969): Playing 'Tangerine' with Teddy Wilson at Ronnie Scott's
BBC Television (UK) (complete)

TV (1971): *The Michael Parkinson Show*, with Yehudi Menuhin
BBC Television (UK) (complete)

TV (1978): Playing 'Lady Be Good' in *Coming Along Nicely*
BBC Television (UK) (excerpt)

TV (1985): Playing 'Night And Day' at the Canterbury Festival*
BBC Television (UK) (excerpt)

TV (1985): Playing 'Nuages' and 'How High The Moon' at the Canterbury Festival*
BBC Television (UK) (complete)

TV (1986): Playing 'Someone To Watch Over Me'/'I Got Rhythm' on *The Royal
Variety Show*
BBC Television (UK) (complete)

TV (1988): Playing 'Chanson de la Rue' at his 80th-birthday celebrations from the
Barbican Hall, London*
BBC Television (UK) (complete)

TV (1979): *This Is Your Life*
Fremantle Media (UK) (excerpt)

TV (1996): Playing 'Milou en Mai' with The Michel Legrand Orchestra*
INA (France).

Not on *Stéphane Grappelli: A Life In The Jazz Century*

TV (1989): *Stéphane Grappelli: Live In New Orleans*
An Interprom production, Performance Channel (UK)
(NB: In 2001 this was also released as a Region 1 DVD by Image Entertainment)

TV (1991): *The Django Legacy*, directed by John Jeremy (no footage of Grappelli)
Channel 4 (UK)

TV (1993): *Latcho Drom*, an award-winning documentary tracing the history of itinerant Romany people and celebrating their music, directed by Tony Gatlif (no footage of Grappelli)
Film Four

Bibliography

AUFFRAY, MARIE-FRANCE: *Montmartre: La Mémoire de tes Chemins* (*Memories Of Your Heritage*) (Hervas 2001, ISBN 2-84334-017-9)

BACON, TONY and DAY, PAUL: *The Fender Book: A Complete History Of Fender Guitars* (Backbeat Books 1999, ISBN 1-871547-65-2)

BACON, TONY; COOPER, COLIN; VAN EIK, JAAP; FOWLES, PAUL; JEFFREY, BRIAN; JOHNSTON, RICHARD; MIKLAUCIC, TIM; MORRISH, JOHN; REBELLIUS, HEINZ; RICHARDSON, DR BERNARD; SPARKS, DR PAUL; WADE, GRAHAM; and ZERN, BROOK: *The Classical Guitar: A Complete History* (Balafon Books 1997, ISBN 1-871547-46-6, limited edition)

BARCLAY, JEAN: *The Brave Never Die* (Imperial War Museum, London, 1993)

BEATLES, THE: *The Beatles Anthology* (Cassell & Co 2000, ISBN 0-304-35605-0)

BRENDON, PIERS: *The Dark Valley: A Panorama Of The 1930s* (Pimlico 2000, ISBN 0-7126-6714-8)

BRICKTOP with HASKINS, JAMES: *Bricktop* (Welcome Rain 2000, ISBN 1-56649-114-2)

BURTON, HUMPHREY: *Menuhin* (Faber & Faber 2000, ISBN 0-571-19311-0)

CARTER, WILLIAM: *Preservation Hall: Music From The Heart* (Cassell 1999, ISBN 0-304-70517-9)

CHINERY, SCOTT with BACON, TONY: *The Chinery Collection: 150 Years Of American Guitars* (Balafon Books 1996, ISBN 1-871547-40-7, limited edition)

CLARKE, DONALD (editor): *The Penguin Encyclopaedia Of Popular Music* (Penguin 1998, ISBN 0-14-051370-1, second edition)

COOK, RICHARD and MORTON, BRIAN: *The Penguin Guide To Jazz On CD, LP And Cassette* (Penguin 1994, ISBN 14-017949-6)

CRUICKSHANK, IAN: *Django's Gypsies: The Mystique Of Django Reinhardt And His People* (Ashley Mark Publishing 1994, ISBN 0-872639-06-2)

CRUICKSHANK, IAN: *The A-Z Of Django* (Fret Publishing 2002)

CRUICKSHANK, IAN: *The Guitar Style Of Django Reinhardt And The Gypsies* (Wise Publications 1982, ISBN 0-7119-1853-8)

DAWES, RICHARD (editor): *The Violin Book* (Balafon Books/Outline Press Ltd 1999, ISBN 1-871547-70-9, limited edition)

DELAUNAY, CHARLES: *Django Reinhardt* (Ashley Mark Publishing 1981, ISBN 0-9506224-6-X)

FOSTER, MO: *Seventeen Watts – The First 20 Years Of British Rock Guitar, The Musicians And Their Stories* (Sanctuary Publishing Ltd 1997, ISBN 1-86074-169-X

FRASER, ANGUS: *The Peoples Of Europe: The Gypsies* (Blackwell, ISBN 0-631-19605-6)

FRENCH, PHILIP (editor): *Malle On Malle* (Faber & Faber 1966, ISBN 0-571-17880-4)

GLASSER, MATT and GRAPPELLI, STÉPHANE: *Jazz Violin* (Oak Publications 1981, ISBN 0-8256-0194-0)

GOODE, COLERIDGE and COTTERRELL, ROGER: *Bass Lines: A Life In Jazz* (Northway Publications 2002, ISBN 0-9537040-2-5)

GRADE, LEW: *Still Dancing: My Story* (Collins 1987, ISBN 0-00-217780-3)

GRIFFIN, PETER: *Less Than A Treason: Hemingway In Paris* (Oxford University Press 1990, ISBN 0-19-505332-X)

GROETSCHEL, YVES and LE HALLÉ, GUY: *Village Montmartre: Clignancourt* (Village Communication 1995, second edition, French only)

HORRICKS, RAYMOND: *Stéphane Grappelli* (Midas Books 1983, UK, ISBN 0-85936-235-3; Hippocrene Books Inc 1983, USA, ISBN 0-88254-727-5; out of print at time of writing)

KENNEDY, MICHAEL: *The Concise Oxford Dictionary Of Music* (Oxford University Press 1991, ISBN 0-19-311320-1)

KURTH, PETER: *Isadora: The Sensational Life Of Isadora Duncan* (Little, Brown & Company 2001, ISBN 0-316-85435-2)

LANGLEY, GRAHAM (editor): *Music Master: Jazz And Blues Catalogue* (Retail Entertainment Data Publishing Ltd 1994, second edition, ISBN 0-904520-82-X)

LARKIN, COLIN: *The Encyclopaedia Of Popular Music* (Macmillan, ISBN 0-333-32556-7)

LEACH, MARIA (editor): *The Standard Dictionary Of Folklore, Mythology And Legend* (Funk & Wagnalls)

LOMAX, ALAN: *Mister Jelly Roll* (Virgin 1991, ISBN 0-86369-318-0)

MANN, CAROL: *Paris: Artistic Life In The '20s And '30s* (Laurence King Publishing 1996, ISBN 1-85669-084-9)

MEEKER, DAVID: *Jazz In The Movies* (Talisman Books Ltd 1981, ISBN 0-905983-40-8, out of print at the time of writing)

MENUHIN, YEHUDI: *Unfinished Journey* (Macdonald & Jane's Publishers Ltd 1977, ISBN 0-354-04146-0)

MERCER, DERRIK (editor): *20th Century Day By Day* (Dorling Kindersley 2000, ISBN 0-7513-2162-1)

NICHOLLS, GEOFF: *The Drum Book: A History Of The Rock Drum Kit* (Balafon Books 1997, ISBN 1-871-547-25-3)

NICHOLSON, STUART: *A Portrait Of Duke Ellington: Reminiscing In Tempo* (Pan Books 2000, ISBN 0-330-36732-3)

OLDENHOVE, JOSEPH and BRAMY, JEAN-MARC: *Stéphane Grappelli: Mon Violon Pour Tout Baggage – Mémoires* (Calmann-Lévy 1992, ISBN 2-7021-1855-0, French only)

ORWELL, GEORGE: *Down And Out In Paris And London* (Penguin 1940, ISBN 0-14-028256-4)

PANASSIÉ, HUGHES: *Douze Années de Jazz* (Corréa 1947, French only, out of print in January 2003)

PEPPERCORN, LISA: *The Illustrated Lives Of The Great Composers: Villa-Lobos* (Omnibus Press 1989, ISBN 0-7119-1689-6)

PETERSON, OSCAR and PALMER, RICHARD (editor and consultant): *A Jazz Odyssey: The Life Of Oscar Peterson* (Continuum 2002, ISBN 0-8264-5807-6)

PINKSTERBOER, HUGO: *The Cymbal Book* (Hal Leonard Publishing Corporation 1992, ISBN 0-7935-1920-9)

RÉVÉSZ, G: *The Psychology Of A Musical Prodigy* (Routledge, ISBN 0-415-20970-6)

ROSE, JONATHAN: *The Intellectual Life Of The British Working Classes* (Yale University Press 2001, ISBN 0-300-08886-8)

SADIE, STANLEY (editor): *The Grove Dictionary Of Music And Musicians* (Macmillan 2001, second edition)

SADIE, STANLEY (editor): *The New Grove Dictionary Of Jazz* (second edition)

SALHANI, JEAN-MARIE (editor): *Stéphane Grappelli: Mon Livre* (*My Book*) (Mon Livre Collection 1996, ISBN 2-911567-01-3, in both French and English)

SAYAG, ALAIN and LIONEL-MARIE, ANNICK (editors): *Brassaï – No Ordinary Eye* (Hayward Gallery Publishing 2001, ISBN 1-85332-215-6)

SEGURET, CHRISTIAN: *The World Of Guitars* (Greenwich Editions 1999, ISBN 0-86288-282-6)

SMITH, GEOFFREY: *Stéphane Grappelli: A Biography* (Pavilion Books 1987, ISBN 1-85145-01202, out of print at time of writing)

SUZUKI, SHINICHI: *Nurtured By Love: The Classic Approach To Talent Education* (Exposition Press Inc 1983, second edition, ISBN 0-682-49910-2)

TAYLOR, MARTIN with MEAD, DAVID: *Kiss And Tell: Autobiography Of A Travelling Musician* (Sanctuary Publishing Ltd 2000, ISBN 1-86074-315-3)

WEINREB, BEN and HIBBERT, CHRISTOPHER (editors): *The London Encyclopaedia* (Macmillan 1983, ISBN 0-333-325567)

WERTENBAKER, LAEL: *The World Of Picasso, 1881* (Time-Life Books 1967, written before Picasso's death and currently out of print)

WOOD, EAN: *The Josephine Baker Story* (Sanctuary Publishing Ltd 2002, ISBN 1-86074-394-3)

ZIEGLER, PHILIP: *London At War, 1939–1945* (Sinclair-Stevenson 1995, ISBN 1-85619-384-5)

Appendix 1: Instruments

Stéphane's first violin, a three-quarter size instrument (see photographs – Figure 1) was still in his possession at the end of his life, in 1997. He had owned it for over 77 years. It's a modest, student instrument bought via one of Ernesto Grappelli's Italian friends and unsurprisingly shows considerable wear and tear. Stéphane treasured it as a precious link to his father, who had arranged its purchase in 1920, when Stéphane was aged only 12. Stéphane lost the instrument during the Second World War but they were reunited in 1947.

Stéphane's first full-sized instrument was purchased for him by the bandleader Grégor Krekorian, who was the first to recognise clearly Stéphane's talent. He actually bought him a Tua, handmade in Nice, although the current whereabouts of this instrument are unknown.

From 1981 Joseph Oldenhove was the only person allowed to handle Stéphane's instruments. He offered these thoughts.

Violins

'First of all, Stéphane respected his instrument very much. He cleaned the surface of it after each concert very carefully with a silk handkerchief and would let nobody touch it other than myself or a violin-maker. I remember how shocked he was if somebody didn't care for an instrument or left it in a car on its own. Once a musician left his instrument on the floor and, distracted, walked on it. For Stéphane, that was the equivalent of somebody carelessly hurting a child. For him, an instrument was a little bit like a child, and he was very concerned not to damage it.

'At the end of his life, he preferred to enter the stage with a wheelchair so that, if he collapsed, he wouldn't damage the violin. When he played the piano in the middle of his show, we always organised a small carpet on the piano to rest the violin on in order that the varnish wouldn't be affected by the vibration of the piano.

'Stéphane used a violin case from Hills, the British violin-maker, or similar

– a little bit heavy but very strong and very protective for the instrument – and regularly he would visit different violin-makers to make sure everything was OK with his violin or his bow. He was closest to Etienne Vatelot in Paris but also used to visit Andrew Hill in England or Jacques Français in New York, and they were like family to us. He almost never travelled with two violins but with two bows and, of course, with a set of strings.

'In his violin case he had a comb, a small mirror, a bottle opener, a tuning fork and a large *foulard* in which to envelope the instrument. Also in the case he had a few pictures of people he cherished and pictures of different meetings he was proud of – for instance the one with the Queen Mother and the one with Lady Diana and with Jacques Delors.

'Stéphane used mainly at the end of his life an 18th-century violin made in Milano by Giovanni Battista Guadagnini, from Piacenza, with workshops in Milan and Turin. That was a precious and beautiful instrument, *circa* 1750. Stéphane had previously owned instruments by Cappa or Gagliano, but since the 1980s he mainly played the Guadagnini. On holidays he would take with him a less valuable violin, attributed to Thomas Eberlé, while for bows he played a Eugene Sartory or a Benoit Rolland. I remember that, when Stéphane was playing in the Club Saint-Germain, he played on a violin by Carlo Tononi, but then he changed that for the Eberlé, which worked better when amplified by a microphone.

'Stéphane was very often approached by a Californian friend of his, John Berry, an electric-violin maker. Stéphane received many different violins by 'Barcus Berry' in several colours: blue, red, white, black. These he used for one or two tunes during his concerts at the end of the '70s and beginning of the '80s, but he finally preferred so much the sound of old violins that he stopped playing electric at the end of the '80s.

'For microphones, he preferred a stand microphone in front of him. Many proposals were made to fix a mini microphone on the bridge of his violin but Stéphane was not happy with that and was afraid it might damage his violin.'

Pianos
'At concerts Stéphane always asked that the piano was tuned. He preferred a soft action; he played very soft. Very often he got to play a Steinway or a Yamaha. At home he played a piano made in Paris by Gaveau. He was very pleased with it. That piano was very stable and almost never needed to be tuned. Stéphane used to say that Vladimir Horowitz, another great admirer of Art Tatum, liked a soft piano action.

'Stéphane would never accept a glass of whisky or water on top of the piano because it could damage it, so he used a little table set to put his glass on. Stéphane was very discreet about his instruments – he knew only too well how valuable they were and thought that the best way was to be careful and discreet with them.

'In Finland a lady violinist gave him a Stradivarius to play for one night and Stéphane remarked that, for him, it was "too much like driving a Rolls-Royce". He didn't feel comfortable. But he enjoyed good violins.'

THE PARIS MUSEUM EXHIBITS

Several interesting instruments pertaining to Stéphane Grappelli and The Hot Club Quintet Of Paris are kept in the central museum of music in Paris. The violin known as 'the Warlop', for instance (see photographs), is now in storage along with three guitars pertaining to the Quintet. These will hopefully be displayed in 2003/4 as part of a new salon dedicated to 20th-century music.

The Warlop violin (shown in Figure 2 – see photographs) is by Pierre Hel of Lille and is dated 1924 (catalogue number E995.25.1) and was presented to Stéphane's friend Michel Warlop as a prize at the Paris Conservatoire. Stéphane began playing it in 1929, when Grégor Krekorian encouraged him to return to playing the instrument. Having no full-sized instrument of his own, Michel lent Grappelly the Pierre Hel. Subsequently the instrument has taken on an iconic position in French jazz, being ceremoniously passed from player to player as a symbol of the Grappelli/Warlop tradition. In fact, Stéphane always retained the instrument until he gave it to the museum. The instrument is identified in use by Grappelli as late as 1963, when it was used on the Duke Ellington sessions. (A small double crack behind the upper f-hole serves as provenance for the instrument's use, as seen in the session photos.)

DJANGO'S GUITARS

Also kept at the Paris museum are three interesting guitars, two of which are by Selmer Maccaferri.

Mario Maccaferri (1900–93) was born in Italy and from the age of 11 apprenticed to an instrument-maker named Luigi Mozzani. Maccaferri's classical-guitar studies took place at the Sienna Conservatoire from 1916–19. He took to full-time guitar design and manufacture following a swimming accident which curtailed his playing career, eventually moving in 1929 to London, where he taught guitar and also manufactured an instrument for the London branch of Selmers.

Selmer were seeking a design for a guitar loud enough to be heard in the new jazz ensembles and the company were impressed by Maccaferri's ideas for an extra soundbox within the guitar to improve the resonance and projection. In 1932 they sent Maccaferri to France, where he oversaw the manufacture of 100 of these new and distinctive guitars at Mantes la Ville, outside Paris. The Paris Museum now has one of these type, under the Selmer reference number 19430 from 1933 (E994.21.3). There is no provenance for Django using this particular instrument, however, and in fact this particular one is intended for Hawaiian-style playing. Django did play a similar instrument with a D-shaped soundhole and cutaway body from 1933 until 1934 (he is seen with one in photographs as late as 1938, but this probably belonged to one of his 'cousins').

In 1933, Maccaferri fell out with Selmer and left the company. From 1934, the instrument was modified – the neck was extended and the soundhole was reduced to a more conventional size. The Paris collection includes a 1940 example of this 'Petite Bouche' model, presented by Naguine Reinhardt (19457, E.964.5.1 – see Figure 4). The provenance of this guitar is further enhanced by a photograph of Django at Samois-sur-Seine in 1953 (Figure 5) holding an instrument with similar identifying marks and soundboard damage (caused by Django's adoption of a clamped-on electric pickup). The headpiece of the instrument is carved with the legend 'Django Reinhardt' (Figure 6) and the guitar has been restrung – it originally had silk and steel strings with coloured bobbles indicating gauge, as seen in library photographs in the museum's collection. (These photographs have been reverse-printed, giving the illusion of a left-handed guitar!)

Approximately 500 of this latter type of instrument were manufactured by Selmer in Paris. Between 1932 and 1952, they made a total of less than 1,000 guitars of varying types, including four-string tenor guitars. Many photographic advertisements for Selmer in *Jazz Hot* magazine between 1934 and 1939 show Django playing the early D-hole-type Maccaferri guitar.

(NB: The guitarist Les Paul also has a similar Selmer guitar presented to him by Naguine following Django's death. This has undergone extensive restoration by the American luthier John Monteleone.)

The third guitar in the Paris collection is one made for 'M Ferret' by Julian Gomez Ramirez in 1932 (ref 19383, E994.12.1, Figure 3). Django is seen playing this unusual instrument in a photograph taken at La Boîte à Matelots in 1933 with Pierre Ferret. Born in Madrid, Ramirez studied with the famous Ramirez family of guitar makers but is not directly related to that family. He set up a workshop in the 1920s at 38 Rue Rodier, Anvers, Montmartre.

These museum instruments can currently be viewed electronically via the museum's intranet facility and on 35mm transparencies. The Musée de la Musique in Paris is part of the wonderful Cité de la Musique complex at 221 Avenue Jean Jaurès, 75019, Paris.

The last word on musical instruments must come from Stéphane via Joseph Oldenhove: 'I can still hear Stéphane saying, "Joseph, fais gaffe à mon petit bout de bois – c'est mon gagne pain!" ("Joseph, pay attention to that piece of wood – that's my bread-winner!")'

Appendix 2: Glossary Of Musical Terms

Arpeggio (It)/*Arpège* (Fr, from '*arpe*' [harp]): A spread chord – ie the notes are heard one after the other from the bottom upwards, or sometimes from the top downwards, as on the harp.

Cadenza (It.): A flourish (properly, improvised) inserted into the final cadence of any section of a vocal aria or solo-instrument movement.

Coda (It.): 'Tail'. Originally a section of a movement added at the end to clinch matters rather than to develop the music further. However, from the 18th century onwards, composers occasionally gave codas integral formal significance, and they became at times a second development section within the work, sometimes containing new material. Later composers increased and extended this tendency.

Colla voce (It): 'With the voice'. Direction to the accompanist to follow closely the singer's fluctuations of tempo, etc.

Counterpoint: The ability, unique to music, to say two things at once comprehensibly. The term derives from the expression *punctus contra punctum* (ie 'point against point' or 'note against note'). A single part or voice added to another is called 'a counterpoint'.

Double-stop: Term used in connection with stringed instruments to indicate stopping and playing on two strings simultaneously to produce a two-part effect.

Glissando (bastard It): From the French *glisser*, 'to slide'. On bowed instruments, it refers to the act of passing all or part of the way from one note to another on the same string by sliding the finger along the string gradually, altering the pitch till the final desired note is reached.

Harmonics: On stringed instruments the open string is the *fundamental* note. Harmonics are *overtones* at fixed higher intervals above the fundamental. They are obtained by setting the string to vibrate in fractions of its length.

Obbligato (It): 'Indispensable'. Adjective attached to the name of an instrument where the instrument's part is obligatory and special or unusual in effect.

Pentatonic (from Grk *pente* ['five']): As in blues, a 'gapped' or five-note scale.

Pizzicato (It): 'Pinched'. A direction determining that notes on a stringed instrument are to be produced by plucking the string, not bowing it.

Polyrhythm: Several different rhythms performed simultaneously.

Portamento (It.): 'Carrying'. With the violin or a bowed instrument, the carrying of the sound from note to note smoothly without any break.

Rasguedo: Rapid strumming of the guitar strings in the manner of flamenco.

Spiccato (It): 'Separated'. In playing a bowed instrument, a form of staccato bowing in which the bow is allowed to bounce on the string.

Staccato (It): 'Detached'. Method of playing a note so that it is detached from its successor by being held for less than its full value.

Stop chorus: A chorus where the accompanying musicians play only the first chord/note of each phrase then stop, leaving the soloist to improvise on the tune alone.

Tremolando (It): 'Trembling'. In playing a bowed instrument, the rapid reiteration of a note or chord by back-and-forth strokes of the bow. Also the very rapid alternation between two notes.

Trill: Ornament comprising rapid alteration of main note and note above or below.

Thanks to The Concise Oxford Dictionary Of Music, *on which many of the above definitions have been based.*

Index

Note: The abbreviations SG and DR have been used to indicate Stéphane Grappelli and Django Reinhardt.